The
Anglo-Irish Novel
and the Big House

Sanford Sternlicht, *Series Editor*

Bellegrove, County Laois
Copyright © 1997 Bonnell Robinson

The Anglo-Irish Novel and the Big House

Vera Kreilkamp

Syracuse University Press

Permission to reprint or modify material from the following sources is gratefully acknowledged: "The Persistent Pattern: Molly Keane's Recent Big House Fiction." *The Massachusetts Review* 28, no. 3 (1987): 453–60; "Social and Sexual Politics in the Big House: Edith Somerville and Molly Keane." *Éire-Ireland* 23, no. 2 (1988): 74–87; "Reinventing a Form: The Big House in Aidan Higgins' *Langrishe Go Down*." *The Canadian Journal of Irish Studies* 11, no. 2 (1985): 27–38. Reprinted in *Ancestral Voices: The Big House in Anglo-Irish Literature,* edited by Otto Rauchbaurer. 207–20. Dublin: Lilliput, 1980.

Library of Congress Cataloging-in-Publication Data

Kreilkamp, Vera.
The Anglo-Irish novel and the big house / Vera Kreilkamp. —1st
ed.
p.   cm.
Includes bibliographical references (p.) and index.
ISBN 0-8156-2752-1 (cloth : alk. paper)
1. English fiction—Irish authors—History and criticism.
2. Country homes in literature.   3. Literature and society—Ireland—
History.   4. Upper class in literature.   5. Landowners in
literature.   8. Gentry in literature.   I. Title.
PR8807.C68K74   1998
823.009'355—dc21   97-40324

Manufactured in the United States of America

To Tom Kreilkamp and Adele Dalsimer

Vera Kreilkamp is the Josephine Abercrombie Professor of Writing at Pine Manor College and coeditor of *Éire-Ireland: An Interdisciplinary Journal of Irish Studies.*

Contents

Acknowledgments

I owe thanks to many people for their encouragement and advice. My interest and subsequent research in Irish literature was initiated and sustained by an enduring friendship and academic collaboration with Adele Dalsimer, who introduced me to Ireland and insisted that I had something to say about its culture. Her readings of the manuscript through its various stages provided invaluable support. Early encouragement for this project came as well from Shaun O'Connell and from my dissertation advisor, Morris Dickstein, both of whom read and advised me on versions of this study. My recent discussions with Angela Bourke and Philip O'Leary have encouraged me see my project on the Big House in the context of a larger Irish culture. The fierce attention of Louise Glück to the language and logic of the manuscript provided me with invaluable help in the final stage of my work.

At Pine Manor College former colleagues Fred Cabot and Burnham Carter read and helped clarify my thinking about several early chapters and former President Rosemary Ashby generously supported my work by granting me released time for research. The college's Lindsey Professorship and a summer grant from the National Endowment for the Humanities provided additional support for work on the manuscript.

In Ireland, excursions with Sean and Mary White to the ruins of Tyrone House and with Marie Heaney to the remnants of Bowen's Court—as well as visits with Luke Dodd at Strokestown Park House—reaffirmed the complexities of ascendancy decline I was learning from the novels. At home, the intellectual curiosity of my sons Ivan and Jake about my topic, and in Ivan's case, a shared professional interest in nineteenth-century fiction, has been sustaining. The support of my husband Tom—my best but gentlest critic—made the completion of this project possible.

The
Anglo-Irish Novel
and the Big House

Fiction and History

Each revival of interest in conservative cultural forms reminds us that social and political revolutions seldom embody permanent breaks with the past. What is discarded recurs, stirring submerged needs and common longings—suggesting both the incompleteness of revolutionary narratives and an enduring fascination with hierarchical social and aesthetic formulations. Monarchist sentiments reemerge in a newly liberated eastern Europe; city dwellers decorate their condominiums with gentry country house furnishings sold by Ralph Lauren; record-breaking crowds of middle-class Americans visited the *Treasure Houses of Britain* exhibition at the National Gallery in Washington. In literary studies, however, such signs of middle-class recidivist tendencies are opposed by a vigilant left, which is increasingly dominated by cultural materialists in England and by new historicists in America. A suspicion of *any* goodwill toward the colonial record encourages postcolonial critics to ferret out the implicit patriarchal and condescending nuances in all imperial discourse.[1] Critics turn with increased vigilance against the (seemingly) enlightened voice of an imperial society as masking—in its more sympathetic or reformist programs—a particularly suspect and dangerous form of pressure toward colonial hegemony.

The persistence of fiction about Anglo-Irish gentry life has elicited predictable responses; some have emerged from a nostalgic pleasure in the survival of older forms, others from a steadfast hostility to reactionary tendencies assumed to be implicit in the recent "re-

1. Marjorie Sabin (1991) analyzes how British opposition to the ritual of suttee (widow burning) is particularly unsettling to postcolonial critics. Her essay is a refreshing reminder of the awkward positions in which modern totalizing critics of colonialism sometimes place themselves.

nascence" (Kelly 1987, 231) of the Big House novel. An article in *The Bulletin of the Irish Georgian Society,* for example, evokes a nostalgic reader in search of symbols of continuity. It suggests that as the Big House died as a social actuality, it was reborn in Irish literature, "transfigured as a symbol of order and culture." For that critic, "in a world of disorder, lost faith and world chaos, the house has become a symbol of unity, a stage setting for an image of cohesion" (Kennedy 1989, 27). Alternatively, a major nationalist critic in Ireland, reading Big House texts as though they emerge from a virtually identical framework of nostalgia, condemns the whole sub-genre as reactionary. "The reemergence of the Big House novel, with all its implicit assumptions, demonstrated the comparative poverty of the Irish novelistic tradition" (Deane 1985, 32).

Both of those responses misread a complex and ambivalent form that is, generally, neither elegiac nor nostalgic. Novels in which the gentry life of the Protestant ascendancy appears as setting, subject, symbol, or motif represent an enduring tradition in Irish fiction, albeit a tradition that undergoes major shifts and refocusings between its emergence in the late eighteenth century and its most recent appearances.[2] In view of the current postcolonial discourse in cultural criticism, Anglo-Irish novels are of particular interest as responses to ideological crisis. In their interactions with extraliterary texts—the houses to which they allude, the families that they evoke, the historical resonances of place names and political events—they demand an awareness of political perspective that has long dominated the field of Irish studies but only recently reentered a wider critical discourse.

Although the plots and characters of these novels about a declin-

2. My use of the term "tradition" is less honorific than F. R. Leavis's (*The Great Tradition,* 1964). Moreover, the Big House tradition that I examine has little in common with Yeats's valorization of an Anglo-Irish tradition. I rely on the *Oxford English Dictionary*'s loosest definition of tradition—"a long established and customary method of procedure"—rather than the definition that emphasizes the "handing down" of tradition from one author to another. Whereas Leavis, for example, sees George Eliot as profoundly influenced by Jane Austen's novels, I do not emphasize a similar role for literary influence among the Big House novelists I consider. Undoubtedly, Irish writers read *Castle Rackrent* (Lever was a particular admirer of Edgeworth's fiction), but the major sources of the tradition I examine in this study are as much political, economic, and social as they are exclusively literary. W. J. McCormack's discussion of the social and cultural dynamics by which a tradition is created (1985, 332–67) helped clarify my own use of the term.

ing gentry society are generally invented, behind the fictional narrative lies another account that intrudes on and conditions our reading of the fiction. That second narrative is, of course, a historical one: our extratextual impressions of the role the Anglo-Irish gentry class played outside the world of the fiction. The relationship between the two narratives—the invented story of the novel and the story we call history—is central to this study, complicating the critical task and obviating the possibility of conducting a straightforwardly formalist reading of Big House novels. It may be, as attacks on political criticism assert, that art lifts the documentary into the symbolic (e.g., Vendler 1990, 25), but the weight of the documentary remains intrusive and powerful for the reader of Irish fiction.[3] This study assumes that the successes or failures of Big House novels lie not simply in a writer's talent for fictional narration, but also in the complexity of her confrontations with the political and historical matter she chooses as subject and setting.

The realistic Irish novel has long been a problematic genre for critics, invariably compared with the masterpieces of English and European fiction. Attempts to account for Ireland's missing integrative nineteenth-century novel—its *Middlemarch* or *War and Peace*—focus on the special conditions of life in a colonized territory. Because di-

---

3. Among historians, the novel, in contrast to other genres, has long enjoyed a privileged role. Not surprisingly, Big House novels have drawn the attention of Irish cultural historians. Oliver MacDonagh, for example, describes the realistic nineteenth-century novel as "ample, discursive, domestic and generally, if quite innocently, sociological in content." He turns, perhaps too hesitatingly, to the Big House novel as a metier—"as close, perhaps, as it is possible to get in literature to that of the historian"—that yields, if in a fragmentary and subjective form, central insights for a recovery of the Irish past (1970, 3). In his social and cultural history of modern Ireland, Terence Brown uses analyses of Big House literature to evoke the situation of a Protestant minority culture in an emerging Catholic sectarian state (1981, 110–13; 119–20). Tom Dunne, editor of *The Writer as Witness: Literature as Historical Evidence*, notes an earlier "symbiotic relationship between history and fiction" (1987, 3) and advocates a greater role for cultural studies that call attention to the historical dimensions of literary sources. Emphasizing the similarity in method between the historian and literary artist, Hayden White insists on the fictive basis of all narrative and describes the act of writing history as choosing a metaphor to order the world (1978, 47). The refusal of literary critics like Stephen Greenblatt or Louis Montrose to separate literary text from social text, or literature itself from history, supports my emphasis, in Montrose's terms, on the "historicity of texts" and "the textuality of history" (1986, 8).

visions between nineteenth-century gentry landowners, tenants, and shopkeepers were based on religion, national origin, and language, not simply on economic class, the dubious impulse to find a "representative" literary voice in any society is particularly doomed in Ireland. The movement of Ireland's locus of economic and political power to London after the Act of Union in 1801 meant that not only ruling-class landlords but also authors and readers were drawn to the metropolitan center rather than to the colonized periphery.

Many causes have been cited for Ireland's failure, until Joyce's modernist reformulation of the novel, to produce great novels in the European or English tradition: its lack of a stable middle class, of a politically secure environment, of a single language or "transforming medium" for literary production (Lloyd 1993, 129), and of the "material base" or economic substructure that is the foundation of culture (Eagleton 1995, 145). Nineteenth-century Ireland was, then, in David Lloyd's apt phrase, an "anomalous state" (1993), experiencing a "crisis of representation" that subverts the narrative of social reconciliation—the ur-plot of the classic European or English novel. Declan Kiberd asserts that, whereas the English novel describes a "land of stable gradations of made lives," Irish writers depict an unstable society of "lives in the making" (1988, 40). According to yet another critic, Irish novelists create something closer in form to the "cryptic fictions of American puritanism," to allegorical American romance narratives, than to English fiction that depicts the individual's integration into a stable social and moral community (McCormack 1988, xl). Because Anglo-Irish fiction emerges from a history of conquest and occupation, to study the genre of the Big House novel is to trace the gradual evolution of a literary symbol set against the political history of class and sectarian conflict, rather than conciliation.[4] The endurance of the genre in contemporary fiction suggests the persistence of Irish historical memory.

Publishing her Irish novels in the early nineteenth century, as Jane

4. Thomas Flanagan's analysis of Irish fiction points out that, unlike English writers, the nineteenth-century Irish novelist was preoccupied with national self-definition, with writing not only Irish novels but novels about Ireland. "That a novel should take as its theme the shape and feel of the culture itself was an assumption that ran counter to the English novel, because it ran counter to English life. Fielding and Richardson and Jane Austen wrote English novels, to be sure, but not novels 'about England.' Only a culture that felt urgently and consciously a need for definition could have produced the novels of Maria Edgeworth" (1959, 101).

Austen was beginning to write in rural England, Maria Edgeworth did not take the political stability of her society for granted. Although Austen's fiction describes the jockeying for position of a newly moneyed mercantile class within the less fluid but still changing patterns of the agrarian gentry world, Austen assumed that the political structure she lived in was permanent. Maria Edgeworth could not make the same assumption. In 1798, with the rebellion of the United Irishmen, the French invasion of Ireland, and the near lynching of her father as a French spy, the colonial system that Edgeworth and her family represented and sought to reform seemed on the verge of collapse. Living amidst an escalating hostility toward landlords, Edgeworth wrote in 1796, "All that I crave for my own part is that if I am to have my throat cut, it may not be by a man with his face blacked with charcoal" (1895, 44). To write a novel set in Ireland was to write about a culture in crisis; thus, the subject of Edgeworth's Irish fiction was shaped by her responses to questions of national identity.

This responsiveness to issues of national identity that distinguishes the nineteenth-century Irish novel from its British counterpart continues in much twentieth-century fiction. The Irish writer's readiness to write national allegory, when grafted onto the tradition of the social novel, produces an idiosyncratic literary form—a form alien to the English novel's embodiment of a seemingly organic solidity of British social institutions.[5] Thus Irish novelists find themselves in trouble when they too randomly impose English forms on their fiction, as when Edith Somerville (in *Mount Music*) or Charles Kickham (in *Knocknagow*) conclude novels of political or sectarian tension with traditional marriage plots. As Terry Eagleton puts it, "Irish history is too palpably ruptured, turbulent and discontinuous for the tropes of a sedate English evolutionism to take hold, and the latent triumphalism of such metaphors is flagrantly inappropriate to it" (1995, 7).

The fate of actual Big Houses in the twentieth century reflects the working out of such rupture and turbulence in Irish history. During the struggle for independence from 1919 to 1921 and the subse-

5. Jennifer Johnston's reluctance to call herself a Big House novelist, in spite of her use of many conventions of that tradition in her work, suggests a contemporary uneasiness with the political categories of Irish fiction that I discuss in this study. Johnston prefers to see herself as a novelist in the less marginalized canonical tradition of Jane Austen or E. M. Forster (Johnston 1984a).

quent civil war, nearly two hundred Irish country houses were destroyed as the symbols of a colonizing force, sometimes without consideration for the politics of their owners. Some Big Houses associated with Anglo-Irish literature survived as tourist attractions (the Gore-Booths' Lissadell), as convents or nursing homes (Maria Edgeworth's Edgeworthstown House), or through purchase by new, often foreign, owners who took on the burdens of preservation (Aidan Higgins's Springfield House or Edward Martyn's Tulira Castle). A few, like the Knight of Glin's castle, remained in private hands, but were generally rented out or turned into country hotels. Still other houses withstood the years of political crisis only to fall victim to the inability of their owners to maintain them or to the neglect (benign or not so benign) of a new nation ambivalent about its colonial heritage. Thus, Lady Gregory's Coole Park, the eighteenth-century Big House that served as the center of the Irish Literary Revival, was torn down in 1941, reputedly for the price of its stone. In 1961, a few years after Elizabeth Bowen found herself unable to meet the costs of maintaining Bowen's Court, the house was demolished by a new owner who was more interested in acquiring fertile farm land than in preserving a historic mansion. Yeats's premonition about the fate of Coole Park represents his fears for a Big House that he had virtually transformed into a mythologized ideal—and into a center for nostalgic pilgrimages by countless literary tourists.[6]

Defining the Form

Big House novels represent a major tradition in Irish fiction. Set on isolated country estates, they dramatize the tensions between several social groups: the landed proprietors of a Protestant ascendancy gentry; a growing, usually Catholic, middle class; and the mass of indigenous, rural Catholic tenantry. In the course of two centuries, these novels reveal recurring themes and conventions, most notably the setting of a beleaguered and decaying country house collapsing under the forces of Anglo-Irish improvidence and the rising nation-

6. Here traveller, scholar, poet take your stand
   When all these rooms and passages are gone,
   When nettle wave upon a shapeless mound
   And saplings root among the broken stone, (Yeats 1956, 238)

alism of the Irish society outside the walls of the demesne. For the Anglo-Irish novelist, the gentry house becomes the most compelling symbol of ascendancy survival: on occasion the assertive economic, political, and social power center of rural life, but more often the shabby object of derision and contempt.

The very expression used in Ireland to describe the homes of the Anglo-Irish gentry is revealing.[7] The fictional homes in the following chapters indicate how "Big House" (or "castle") is a far from exact description, given that the same term may refer either to shabby gentry farms or to far grander edifices. Maria Edgeworth's description of Ballinahinch Castle, part of Richard Martin's 200,000-acre estate in Connemara, as a "dilapidated mansion with nothing of a castle about it," surrounded with cow house, pigsty, and dunghill (1950, 44), suggests the characteristic slippage between gentry home and peasant hovel that occurs in many of the novels I will consider here.

The Big House was most often constructed of native limestone in alien architectural forms by the representatives of a colonial power.[8] It was built on land usually expropriated by men and women who considered themselves Irish, but who were caught between two countries and two identities, separated from their tenants not only by class, but by religion, language, and national origin as well. Roy F. Foster reminds us of the insecurity, not just the triumphalism, that lies behind the architectural stamp of ascendancy culture on the Irish landscape. "The Ascendancy built in order to convince themselves not only that they had arrived, but that they would remain. In-

7. W. J. McCormack argues that the term "Big House" does not enter into cultural discourse with any frequency until the late nineteenth century, when Anglo-Irish dominance was ending. Noting the increasing role of the Big House in literature written during the Home Rule movement and the establishment of the Irish Free State, he suggests that the term emerges into critical language as an elegiac trope—or alternately as a sign of the incomplete success of revolution (1992, 49–50). Although McCormack is correct in calling attention to the clustering of Big House literature in the early twentieth century, my study will argue against any emphasis on a persistent elegiac quality of Big House fiction as a necessary consequence of such a chronology.

8. The architectural history of the Irish country house is recorded in Mark Bence-Jones's *Burke's Guide to Country Houses: Ireland* (1978, vol. 1). Many houses began as Norman strongholds and thus incorporated an earlier tower house into their domestic additions over time. Toward the end of the sixteenth century semifortified "castles" appeared, to be replaced in the eighteenth century by architectural styles reflecting English fashions: the broadly spreading Palladian structure and the more familiar three-story Georgian block.

security and the England-complex remained with them to the end" (1989, 194). To the native Irish, gentry houses were simply Big Houses, not, as in England, great houses. And, as one commentator suggests, "scale may not be confused with moral grandeur" (McCormack 1981, xx).

In comparison to the rural mansions of England, typical Anglo-Irish gentry homes, and certainly most of those houses depicted in the fiction, are modest in size. The smells of the farmyard penetrating Big House walls in several novels suggest not only social decline and physical decay, but also the marginal status of so many country gentry families. Although great estates like Castletown, Powerscourt, and Russborough—mansions with sweeping wings, colonnades, and elaborate façades—did arise in Ireland, the typical Big House was built, as Elizabeth Bowen notes, to house a family, its dependents, and a modest number of guests. "They have few annexes, they do not ramble; they are nearly always compactly square" (1986, 26). In *Classic Irish Houses of the Middle Size*, Maurice Craig points out that the term "Big House" indicates more about the position of landlord than it does about the actual size of the residence (1976, 3). Bowen's analysis of the expression suggests that the height of these Georgian stone blocks in a country of peasant hovels, as well as the historical resonances of colonial oppression they evoke, creates a special inflection of "hostility" or "irony" when the term is used (1986, 26).[9] In describing the Big Houses of his youth, Thomas Henn, another former resident of an ascendancy estate, emphasizes their isolation from the main thoroughfares of Ireland. "The avenue that leads off the main road will be long, winding, perhaps as much as a mile" (1976, 208). Such distances between the gentry home and the village, even when significantly shorter than in Henn's recollections,

9. Eric Partridge's *A Dictionary of Slang and Unconventional English* (1973) reports that since 1925 the term "Big House" has become a general expression for large and threatening institutions, particularly prisons and mental hospitals. Donald Fanger, a Russian scholar at Harvard University, reports that during the Soviet period the term was used colloquially to refer to the secret police headquarters in Moscow and Leningrad. The negative connotations of the term clearly transcend its Irish setting. When I told an American friend that I was writing a study of Big House novels, he inquired whether there were enough works about Sing Sing prison to justify my study.

suggest both the social isolation and defensive self-sufficiency of Anglo-Irish life and the spatial barriers that the Big House had erected against Catholic Ireland by the early twentieth century.

Despite the total eclipse of Anglo-Irish ascendancy, the Big House novel is far from a moribund literary form in modern Ireland. Emerging into prominence as a literary response to colonial life in 1800 with Maria Edgeworth's *Castle Rackrent* and persisting into the twentieth century with the contemporary novels of Aidan Higgins, Molly Keane, William Trevor and Jennifer Johnston, the genre has remained a recognizable, even thriving, source of Irish fiction since independence from England in 1921.[10] Perhaps because these novels have long been associated with the ideologies of a reactionary colonial society unable to adapt to a rapidly changing country, the form received little sustained critical attention until the 1990s. Although most surveys of Irish literature mention the Big House novel, and several studies discuss it in at least a few paragraphs,[11] the continuing thematic relationships between major novels in this tradition have not been explored.

Changing attitudes in Irish society, however, have been more hospitable to Anglo-Irish fiction about the Big House. The nation's concern with the ongoing conflict in the north and its growing commitment to membership in the European community have undermined the domination of a nationalist historiography. Revised historical assessments of the Big House during the nineteenth-century Famine, for example, foreground the landlords' substantial economic losses rather than the brutal land clearances of more than a half million persons that were carried out during and after the Famine (Donnelly 1995, 156). Revisionist historians have rehabilitated the Anglo-Irish landlord and have undermined an older nationalist interpretation of official responses to the Famine as a genocidal plot carried

10. See, for example, Aidan Higgins's *Langrishe, Go Down* 1966; John Banville's *Birchwood* 1973, *The Newton Letter* 1982; Jennifer Johnston's *The Captains and Kings* 1972, *The Gates* 1973, *How Many Miles to Babylon* 1974, *Fool's Sanctuary* 1987, and *The Invisible Worm* 1991; Molly Keane's *Good Behaviour* 1982, *Time After Time* 1983, *Loving and Giving* 1988; William Trevor's *Fools of Fortune* 1983 and *The Silence in the Garden* 1988; Barbara Fitzgerald's *Footprint on Water* 1983.

11. Cronin (1980, 17–18); Rafroidi (1975, 12–14); Madden-Simpson (1987); Kelly (1987); Donnelly (1975).

out by landlords working hand-in-glove with imperial forces.[12] Such revisionist interpretations of the Anglo-Irish landowning class, coupled with the persistent nostalgia for a lost grandeur that characterizes modern consumer societies, transforms the nationalist's alien colonizer into a complex Chekhovian figure—Ireland's new dispossessed. Two collections of essays on the Big House theme—(Genet 1991; Rauchbauer 1992)—suggest a growing interest in the fiction of the newly elegized landlords. Even more pointedly, in 1994 Julian Moynahan published *Anglo Irish: The Literary Imagination of a Hyphenated Culture*, a book-length study emerging from a revisionist view of the Anglo-Irish. Moynahan privileges administrative structure over economic and social realities when he assumes that after Ireland's union with England in 1801, the Anglo-Irish are best viewed as fully Irish rather than as an imperial presence (3–6).

By virtue of its declared subject matter, my study necessarily participates in the undermining of a nationalist criticism that has minimized the importance of Big House novels in the canon of Irish writing. But in urging a reassessment of a literary genre, I do not align myself with that revised interpretation of Anglo-Irish society underway in current historiography. The novels explored here—usually written from within an ascendancy or postascendancy society—do not make much of a case for the Big House. With the exception of a few (but not all) texts by Elizabeth Bowen, Jennifer Johnston, and William Trevor, the novelists dramatize a gentry class propelling itself into oblivion through greed, careless improvidence, and historical myopia—common failings of colonists who will not or cannot apprehend their exploitative role. Although my discussions of individual works will reveal several novelists (Lever, Somerville and Ross, and Trevor) who approach the trauma of Irish famine through the philanthropic martyrdom of self-sacrificing wives and daughters of

12. See, for example, Roy Foster's *Modern Ireland* (1989); L.M. Cullen's *An Economic History of Ireland Since 1660* (1987); Barbara Lewis Solow's *The Land Question and the Irish Economy, 1870–1903* (1971); W. E. Vaughan's *Landlords and Tenants in Ireland, 1848–1904* (1984). In "Immoral Economy: Interpreting Erskine Nichol's 'The Tenant'" (Whelan 1996a), even an economic historian with serious reservations about revisionism repositions the Irish landlord as a victim of hostile British public opinion and legislation during the Famine. See chapter 7 on the fiction of William Trevor and Jennifer Johnston for a fuller discussion of the effect on literature of historical revisionism.

the Big House, such idealizations of neo-feudal tenant–landlord relationships remain the exception rather than the rule.

For all the arrogance of any colonial enterprise, Anglo-Irish novelists made surprisingly modest claims for themselves. Unlike the great innovators of the Literary Revival—Yeats and Standish O'Grady come most immediately to mind—the major novelists writing in the same period did not seek to appropriate new territory or to reconstitute an alliance with an imagined peasantry as their power slipped away. Unlike Yeats, they failed to transform the material wealth of a colonial class (particularly its houses) into a trope of spiritual ascendancy. Instead, they wrote with an increasing awareness of Anglo-Ireland's isolation and homelessness, of an unraveling culture that existed, finally, without purpose or power. Thus the Big House novelists of the late nineteenth and early twentieth centuries were unwilling to enter into the great imaginative transformations through which the revivalists repossessed and redefined the notion of Irish identity. They were not, as Declan Kiberd so aptly puts it, "inventing Ireland" by reimaging the colonial territory as the new center rather than the imperial periphery (1996, *passim*). Instead of appropriating the heroic and nonsectarian aristocratic Celtic tradition, an appropriation which was controlled nevertheless by assumptions of Anglo-Ireland's spiritual ascendancy, the novelists focused on the narrow lives they saw on their decaying estates. Neither revivalists nor revolutionaries, they confronted a social reality—the breakdown of their imagined community of loyal tenants and their failure to achieve hegemony—and turned often to irony or self-parody when depicting their culture. Their literary creations failed to provide them with the comforting assertions of cultural dominance that the revivalists were able to assume through redefinitions of themselves as modern inheritors (through literary appropriation) of an aristocratic ur-Celtism. Collectively, the Big House novelists arrived at self-judgments that were strikingly similar to the judgment of them by a leading Marxist critic: "The real test of hegemony is whether a ruling class is able to impose its spiritual authority on its underlings, lend them moral and political leadership and persuade them of its own vision of the world. And on all these counts, when the record is taken as a whole, the Anglo-Irish must be reckoned an egregious failure" (Eagleton 1995, 30).

For nationalist critics from Daniel Corkery to Seamus Deane, the Protestant ascendancy world that the Big House genre purports to represent is merely a creation of the Literary Revival. As I have already suggested, however, the Anglo-Irish novelists do not share with Yeats an idealized and mythologized vision of their own culture. The tradition I am describing suggests common anxieties, insecurities, and on occasion, feelings of shame and guilt—similar ways of looking at society by members of a beleaguered and superannuated class. Maturin's and Le Fanu's allegorized Gothic versions of the Big House novel represent the most flamboyant versions of such guilt. Alternately exalting and castigating the creations of Yeats and the Literary Revival, Irish criticism has left little space for the modest claims of a divergent yet persistent Anglo-Irish literary form.[13] By the 1980s, Seamus Deane (1985, 28–38) and Declan Kiberd (1982) had demythologized the Literary Revival and repositioned the claims of an Irish literature unfiltered by the nostalgia of a disenfranchised colonial class. But the neglect and persistent misreading of a strand of Anglo-Irish fiction that, in fact, makes few claims for the ascendancy needs to be addressed.[14]

To some extent, of course, Anglo-Irish country house novels inevitably create a discomfort that emerges largely from extratextual sources. The ideology of the colonial landlord—and of many of the novelists—is remote not only from the history of Irish nationalism, but from modern notions of egalitarianism as well. Social change in these novels is perceived not as organic process but as threatening disruption ushering in an order inimical to perceived notions of civilized behavior. Thus, the literary texts themselves are for the most part ambivalent about change, anchored in traditional assumptions

13. The Big House novel has long had an uneasy reputation in twentieth-century Ireland; critical responses to the form are as ambivalent as the narrative stances of the novels themselves. In 1931, within a decade of the establishment of the Irish Free State, Daniel Corkery attacked the tradition as part of an alien "colonial literature" of "spiritual exiles" who were writing to explain Ireland to English audiences (1966, 7–9).

14. The critical neglect of Anglo-Irish literature in the Big House tradition has been noted by Roy Foster in his review of *The Field Day Anthology of Irish Writing*. While discussing the attack on the anthology for excluding women writers, Foster notes that Molly Keane's absence from and Elizabeth Bowen's and Somerville and Ross's underrepresentation in the collection may have more to do with their accents than with their gender (Foster 1992, 6).

about class, and anxious about the tide threatening to engulf Anglo-Ireland. (The titles of two twentieth-century novels are revealing: M. J. Farrell's [Molly Keane's] *The Rising Tide,* and Barbara Fitzgerald's *We Are Besieged.*) The following chapters will reveal that authorial ambivalence toward both Catholic and Protestant Ireland is a striking characteristic of these novels; in some cases, however, ambivalence can lead to aesthetic incoherence, as when fictional narratives seem to be at odds with the historical narratives lying behind them. The happy endings imposed on some texts—the survival of the Big House or the rebuilding of it in a revolutionary Ireland in Somerville's *Mount Music,* Farrell's *Two Days in Aragon,* Fitzgerald's *We Are Besieged,* for example—belie historical probability and sentimentalize the novels they conclude.

In view of the historical record, the central ideologies lying behind Big House society—the ideologies of a colonial state and of the anti-egalitarian great house—were limited, exclusionary, and doomed. But as Eagleton reminds us, some ideologies are less flawed than others (1978, 69); some do a better job of accounting for and interpreting the available historical facts. Were the Big House novelists simply prisoners of their societies' systems of belief, their novels would betray the limitations of any popular artifact that reflects but seldom explores or transcends its ideological sources. The special responsibility of significant eighteenth- and nineteenth-century realistic fiction—its commitment to a degree of mimetic accuracy or circumstantial realism—suggests that a novel that is locked into a limiting ideology will fail to persuade us of the adequacy of its vision of human needs and possibilities as they are revealed by the historical record. For better or for worse, we judge novels that deal with social and political change through hindsight. We read them with privileged information unavailable to the authors. Most readers would, therefore, disagree with Marilyn Butler's choice of *Ennui* or *Ormond* over *Castle Rackrent* as Maria Edgeworth's most successful Irish novel, because *Castle Rackrent* engages itself with a vision of history that persuades us of its predictive power. Although we need not demand that a novelist write from any particular ideology, we do ask that significant art grasp the historical forces that act on individuals. Thus, Eagleton suggests, paraphrasing Lukacs, that even "overtly reactionary" art can be "socially progressive in the sense that whatever the author's conscious political allegiance . . . , it realizes the vital 'world-

historical' forces of an epoch which make for change and growth"
(1976, 29).

Although the Big House novel is part of the literature of colonialism, it is about and by a group of colonizers whose identity is far
more ambiguous and fluid, for example, than the British raj in India.
As he is presented in the historical and literary record, the nineteenth-century British sahib felt less conflict about his identity as an
Englishman than did his Anglo-Irish counterpart. He was in India to
forge an empire and to govern a primitive and childlike (and therefore untrustworthy) people. His essential Englishness remained uncom-
promised even when he spent most of his life on the subcontinent.
He expected, in retirement, to return to the certainties and rational-
ities of English life, either enriched and educated by his imperial du-
ties or embittered by his loss of status, but in either case reaffirmed
in his identity as an Englishman.

The experience of Ireland, England's only metropolitan colony, is
not parallel. The geographical proximity between the two countries,
the centuries and many layers of English colonization, the (often unacknowledged or repudiated) racial similarities between the English
and Irish, the early assimilation of a wave of Norman or Old English
conquerors into the native Irish population—all of these variables
suggest that the experiences of the Anglo-Irish ruling caste in Ireland were different from those of other English colonial societies.[15]
The assumptions of superiority by one group over another, which en-
abled the imperial system to function in all its bigotry and brutality,
were certainly present among Anglo-Irish colonials, but other competing assumptions about nationality and identity complicated their
experience. Unlike the British sahib, who was retired to England at
the age of fifty-five to ensure that the Indians saw a white man only in
his prime (Kiernan 1969, 55), the Anglo-Irish colonizer settled permanently in Ireland. His shifting sense of identity as both Irish settler
and as British subject produced an ambivalent literary tradition, particularly as Anglo-Ireland moved toward a painfully schizophrenic relationship with England after the mid-nineteenth-century Famine.
Moreover, the religious fluidity among landowning Catholics, some

15. Frederic Jameson's Field Day pamphlet *Modernism and Imperialism* (1988) lo-
cates a major source of modernism in this very difference: Because Ireland differs
from other colonies, in that it exists simultaneously as a Third World and First World
social formulation, it produced the central modernist text, *Ulysses*.

of whom turned apostate to save their property under the eighteenth-century penal laws, suggests a history of complex sectarian ties between some landlords and tenants.

Big House novels are worth examining because they are neither irrelevant artifacts of a declining society, nor, for the most part, nostalgic evocations of a lost ascendancy Eden. In Georg Lukacs' terms, all of the works examined here, from Edgeworth's to Keane's, are historical in their focus. They are written with a sense of how the individuality of character derives from the historical peculiarity of an age and with an awareness of human existence as always historically conditioned (1963, 24). Place and time in these novels represent not simply neutral backdrops or settings for human behavior, but, as Lukacs suggests, problematic and specific worlds in which the struggle between different classes becomes, to a large extent, the central focus of the narrative action. Although Big House novels are not technically historical novels, according to the criteria of some critics,[16] they emerge from and dramatize—most often on a private rather than on a public level—the major political conflict in Irish history.

The nineteenth- and twentieth-century Anglo-Irish novels considered here all emerge from ideologies, from systems of belief and representations of experience that have served to define and account for history in particular ways and that for Eagleton signify "the way in which men live out their roles in class society" (1976, 16). The degree to which the novelists accept or modify those ideologies shapes their use of the central image of the Anglo-Irish Big House. As literary artifacts, creations of a particular historical locale and circumstance, the novels are the products of a colonial society and are

16. In *Great Hatred, Little Room* (1983) James Cahalan defines the Irish historical novel as a form that deals with periods of political crisis in modern Ireland prior to the author's experience, that concerns itself with a public political focus, and that depicts at least one real historical personage (xiii). In *The English Historical Novel* (1971) Avrom Fleishman also insists on the presence of a real historical personage (3–4). None of the novels examined in this study fulfill all these criteria. McCormack's analysis of what it means to call *Castle Rackrent* a historical novel is far subtler in its insistence on including the experience of the reader. "*Castle Rackrent* is a historical novel, but its historical aspect does not lie inert in its temporal setting. As with all such fiction, its historical dimension is the dynamic relationship between that setting and the historical moment of that composition; and beyond that, it involves also that relationship in interaction with a historically defined readership" (1985, 99).

related in their assumptions and ideologies to other colonial literatures. They are, therefore, novels about dispossessors. But another
competing ideology lies behind the genre: that of the English country house poems. This second ideology provides an idealized ethos of
the hierarchical world of the rural estate in order to legitimize a new
and threatening agrarian capitalism. Those two ideologies—one emphasizing the alienation of the colonizer from the colonized, the
other positing a conservative feudal ideal of social cohesiveness—exist in constant tension in the Big House novel. Between those polari-
ties of separation and cohesion, the Anglo-Irish novelist maps out a
world.

The Myths of Feudalism

A central task of cultural criticism—to discover what has been excluded from a text and to show how culture masks unpalatable structures of exploitation and oppression—lies at the center of much
recent work on Irish literature. Edward Said's call for a historically
grounded criticism that affirms the connections between texts and
"politics, societies and events" (1983, 5) is answered, in part, by Irish
interpreters like Seamus Deane (1985, 23–37), Declan Kiberd (1982,
28–37), and W. J. McCormack (1985, Ch. 2 passim). These critics explore the idealization of the Anglo-Irish Big House and the eighteenth-century Protestant ascendancy as a mythologizing of history.
In their eyes, Yeats's recreation of Irish history allowed him to transcend the conditions and contradictions that perturbed and violated
the Literary Revival's vision of an ideal Ireland as a premodern and
organic community. In their contemplations of the past, the revivalists turned to a body of Celtic folklore rather than to the oppression
and exploitation of Ireland's colonial history. Instead of writing
about the Catholic middle class, many revivalists peopled their worlds
with a more distant and idealized Celtic peasantry, and, in Yeats's
case, with the hard-riding country gentlemen who made up the gentry world.

The colonist's desire to create a historical mythology that implicitly perpetuates systems of division is not unique to Ireland. In India,
for example, the post-Mutiny response to the growing politicization
of the Bengali middle classes led to the Anglo-Indian idealization of

the Punjab peasant as representing the "real" India. Concomitantly, the city-bred Bengali, particularly if he was European-educated and thus politically suspect, was regarded as an effete anomaly (the hated Babu of Anglo-Indian tradition) and negatively contrasted with the sturdy and conservative peasant (Wurgaft 1983, 13). When viewed in the context of a larger colonial experience, Yeats's need to reject the growing Catholic middle class and its "greasy till" from his brand of nationalism becomes more than an aesthetic elitism. The retreat to the imagery of eighteenth-century ascendancy Ireland suggests the poet's anxious longing to retain imagined versions of colonial social structures—his vision of a coherent community—in a new nation. In creating a mythos of history—in Fredric Jameson's words, a "strategy of containment"—Yeats shuts out significant levels of truth about exploitation and conflict that make up Irish history. (Yeats's early acknowledgement in "The Fisherman" that the ideal character he writes for is "a man who does not exist" suggests the complex layers of awareness that underlie his myth making.)

Yeats's recreation of Irish history is related to a long tradition of neo-feudal mythologizing. Behind the historical tenant–landlord relationship in both Ireland and England lies a literary formulation of an ideal feudal community of hierarchical reciprocity, a lost Eden in which loyal vassals serve their beneficent lords in exchange for economic security and stability. One nineteenth-century Irish version of this Edenic community was nostalgia for the native chief and the clan loyalties that he evoked. This tribal community occasionally appeared in Anglo-Irish novels, written for English consumption, that depicted the precarious survival of old Irish chieftains. In *The Wild Irish Girl* (1806), Lady Morgan exploited an early nineteenth-century interest in romantic primitivism to create a best-seller about the indigenous and (relatively) unconquered nobility of Ireland. As subsequent chapters will indicate, more ambivalent evocations of a world of archaic tribal loyalties appeared in nineteenth-century Big House novels by Edgeworth and Lever.

The neo-feudal ideals of gentry life appears in earlier English literature as well, specifically in seventeenth-century country house poetry. In *Happy Rural Seat* (1972), Richard Gill demonstrates that such ideals are still evident in a group of twentieth-century novels envisioning the great house as a symbol of community and rootedness.

Ben Jonson's "To Penshurst" expresses the aristocratic justification of hierarchy and celebrates an idealized vision of reciprocity between lord and tenant. An examination of the sources for country house poetry suggests how the Anglo-Irish novelists simultaneously embrace and dismantle the pieties of that idealized feudal trope. The English country house genre is grounded in the symbol of a great estate that concretely embodies a notion of social reciprocity between man and nature and landlord and tenant. The poems celebrate a harmonious world in which a hierarchical society defends itself against the threat of social change through the reaffirmation of traditional values. These poems—from Jonson's "To Penshurst" through Marvell's "Upon Appleton House"—are panegyrics to a fast-disappearing rural society that was purportedly based on the transfer of land through inheritance rather than capital. They support the values of a rooted traditional world organized around the lord's wise stewardship of his estate and its bounty. Recurring values in English country house poetry are an ethos of service by both hospitable lord and loyal tenant and a bountiful yet unostentatious use of nature's wealth. In their numerous references to architecture the poems attack grand edifices that are constructed for show, or as one critic suggests, buildings in which functionalism has been sacrificed to stateliness (Hibbard 1956, 161). Houses are praised if they are places in which to live and to form organic social relations; they are not praised if they exist merely to feed the vanity of their owners. "Thou art not, Penshurst, built to envious show, / Of touch or marble, nor canst boast a row / Of polish'd pillars, or roof of gold." To some extent, the estate represents—in the tradition of Horace—the possibility of a retreat from the trials of urban life and creation of a "manageable little power structure" (Kenny 1984, 26).

Edmund Burke's use of great house imagery in *Reflections on the Revolution in France* suggests how deeply imbedded the country house ethos was in the politics of conservatism by the late eighteenth century. As Burke catalogues the horrors he saw in France, he turns repeatedly to the image of the collapsing great house as a metaphor for loss and ruin. "It is with infinite caution that any man ought to venture upon pulling down an edifice, which has answered in any tolerable degree for ages the common purposes of society" (1968, 152). Similarly, the failure to construct upon the foundations of past buildings serves as a metaphor for political disorder in France: "You might have repaired those walls; you might have built on those old foundations. Your constitution was suspended before it was perfected" (121–22). Burke's equation of political stability with the architectural image of the great house and the castle replicates the longing for an older rooted order that the seventeenth-century country house poems express so powerfully.

Raymond Williams's analysis of the country house poems of England insists, however, that we read such literature not merely as the texts that lie before us, but as products of a particular social, political, and economic world. For Williams, behind the idealized descriptions of rural mansions in the country house poems lies a world of labor, exploitation, theft, and dispossession that is excluded from the texts of the poems. Seemingly written to celebrate a rooted traditional world, the poems mythologize estates acquired through capital, not inheritance: "for the majority of men it was the substitution of one form of domination for another; the mystified feudal order replaced by a mystified agrarian capitalist order" (1973, 39). Williams's search for the social and economic subtext of the poems becomes a model of the kind of criticism that attempts to look beyond literary tropes (the idealized vision of the feudal community of lord and tenant, for example) and to explore instead the historical forces that generate the creation of such forms.

The subtext of history that Williams searches for in seventeenth-century English country house poems is far less buried in Anglo-Irish fiction. Although a similar longing for rootedness exists in both literary forms, the narrative ambivalence of the Big House novels reflects the special complications of Irish history. Among contemporary Irish commentators, even the existence of an ascendancy culture is disputed. Critics such as Deane (1985, 30) and McCormack (1985, 8–9) point out the problematic nature of the term "aristocracy" when it is used to refer to ascendancy landowners. Both critics argue that the Protestant ascendancy was historically a predominantly bourgeois rather than aristocratic social formation. "The Anglo-Irish were held in contempt by the Irish-speaking masses as people of no blood, without lineage, with nothing to recommend them other than the success of their Hanoverian cause over that of the Jacobites" (Deane 1985, 32). Even Elizabeth Bowen, a powerful spokeswoman for the purportedly aristocratic ideals of her own Anglo-Irish class, admits the dubious origins of her Cromwellian ancestors, whom she describes as late-seventeenth-century "squatters" without an idea of social life to integrate them. "They had as yet no position. To the Catholic gentry, to the workers left on their land, they were still anathema—they could buy service, they could not buy good regard. They were confronted everywhere by cryptic faces or disparaging smiles. The vanished old order still held the country people in a thrall of feeling" (1979, 87).

Whereas the proto-capitalist sources of land acquisition and exploitation are masked by the seventeenth-century country house poets of England as they celebrate and idealize a passing (or past) order, the savage colonial expropriations lying behind the Big Houses of Irish fiction are far less easily disguised by neofeudal mythologizing. For the conquered Irish, the Big House evoked memories of dispossession, exploitation, and injustice—and, simultaneously, of a remote and glamorous power, of inaccessible social position and wealth. Despite the success of the Anglo-Irish conquerors in establishing themselves as rulers, the claims of an older, uprooted native Irish aristocracy existed as the constant discordant threat, the subterranean and derisive response to the pretensions of parvenu Anglo-Ireland. In Big House fiction, loyal feudal retainers produce sons who dispossess the landlord (Edgeworth), vote against his candidate in local elections (Lever), or threaten his daughter as she hunts (Somerville). The insecurity of ascendancy society before the native Irish expresses itself just as frequently in sexual anxiety about—or fascination with—misalliance (Lever, Somerville, Bowen, and Keane) as in an idealization of a loyal peasantry. The persistent anxiety about the loss of the Big House—through fire, decay, or financial insolvency—provokes moral judgments of the landlord class far more often than idealization and nostalgia. Thus, the urge to mythologize the past is undercut by the ironic self-scrutiny that the Anglo-Irish novelists direct at their own culture.

Conventions of the Big House Novel

Although the recurring formal conventions of Big House novels suggest the role of literary influence in the tradition, the strongest continuities among these writers emerge from their responses to political, economic, and social conditions in Irish life. The conventions of these novels arise from a growing comprehension of the breakdown of the systems of domination that had supported Anglo-Ireland and from the failure of the ascendancy to achieve hegemony. Central to the Big House tradition is a deeply ironic and, for the most part, unsentimental vision of gentry life as the ascendancy world moves towards collapse.

Big House novels reveal a preoccupation with a dying landlord class that is the thematic center of Maria Edgeworth's seminal novel, *Castle Rackrent.* Like *Castle Rackrent,* these works combine domestic realism with a mythologizing sense of Irish social history. By imposing the circumstantial realism of the novel form onto the neo-feudal myths that helped sustain Anglo-Irish gentry life, Big House novelists create the special irony of the literary tradition. Several twentieth-century works by Somerville, Keane, and Banville incorporate the satiric view of a dying class that controls Edgeworth's masterpiece. Although authors differ in their emphases, recurring patterns emerge in the tradition.

1. The significance of the decaying house as the archetypal image of a declining social class dominates, for example, not only *Castle Rackrent,* but many subsequent Anglo-Irish novels as well: *Uncle Silas, The Big House of Inver, The Last September, Langrishe, Go Down, Birchwood, The Captains and Kings, We Are Besieged, Time After Time,* and *The Silence in the Garden.*

An anecdotal story about Sheridan Le Fanu's recurring nightmare suggests the haunting power of that symbol in the collective psyche of nineteenth-century Anglo-Ireland. According to critic Nelson Browne, Le Fanu dreamed of "a mansion so ruinous and tottering that it looked as if it might at any moment fall upon and bury the helpless dreamer" (1951, 30). Although undoubtedly indebted to the gothic tradition and to early romanticism, the image of the ruined house carries a far heavier political charge in Ireland than it does in England. As a result of the War of Independence and Civil War of the early twentieth century, when hundreds of Big Houses became targets for "outrages" and raids, scenes of great destructive conflagration dominate novels by Somerville, Bowen, Keane, Fitzgerald, and Trevor. Nostalgia about such destruction exists in Big House fiction, but it is in surprisingly short supply.

A sense of place is central to the Big House novel, but settings—country, region, estate, demesne, or house—exist more often as the troubled sites of negotiation, anxiety, alienation, and loss than as landscapes evoking home and community. Seamus Heaney's description of Yeats's relationship to his tower, Thoor Ballylee, evokes the struggle of an Anglo-Irish poet to *make* a tradition. Heaney suggests that Yeats's act of possession and imaginative transformation of a picturesque relic into a triumphant imaginative symbol—the poet's re-creation of a Norman castle into a "place of writing"—is essentially an imperial act of assertion (1989, 22).

But for the ascendancy novelist, the imperial place—the castle, the mansion, the Big House—declines into a shabby edifice that is perceived with relentless irony. Yeats's "possession" of his Norman tower shapes some of his greatest poems, but his aesthetic has little in common with the strategies of Big House fiction. In the opening line of *The Big House of Inver,* Edith Somerville evokes the arrogance of the ascendancy's place, an arrogance expressed through its architectural assault on the land. "The Big House of Inver stood high on the central ridge of the promontory of Ross Inver, and faced unflinching the western ocean" (1978, 7). Yet in the course of the novel the reader witnesses the slow undermining of such pride as Inver House is neglected, filled with tawdry Victorian furniture laboriously gathered by an illegitimate descendant of the Big House family, and finally destroyed by its drunkenly improvident owner. In depicting Yeats's identity with his imperial tower, Heaney notes how the poet appropriates the language of royal builders; he orders "great"—that is, castle-like—beds, chairs, tables, and ceiling for Thoor Ballylee (1989, 23). My discussion of *The Big House of Inver* will indicate how that novel, on the other hand, through its focus on the "great" house in decline, subverts such imperial notions of place and architecture. Elizabeth Bowen's *The Last September* similarly stresses the dissonance between the imperial house and its setting: "The house seemed to be pressing down low in apprehension, hiding its face. . . . It seemed to gather its trees close in fright and amazement at the wide light lovely unloving country, the unwilling bosom whereon it was set" (1942a, 66). Shame, apprehension, and a premonition of final destruction—not proud imperial appropriation—is written into that evocation of the Big House's spatial occupation of an alien land.

2. An account of the decaying family line, of genealogical breakdown and collapse, accompanies the depiction of the decline of the house. Thus, as in Poe's "Fall of the House of Usher," Big House nov-

els symbolically merge the decaying family with its residence. Such a fusion of house and family line appears in *Castle Rackrent* but is particularly evident in the gothic strand of the Big House form (Maturin and Le Fanu) that is exploited by Banville's contemporary *Birchwood.* In many of the novels, beginning with *Castle Rackrent,* ascendancy families fail to produce heirs, and legitimate lines of succession are threatened. When children do appear, they usually remain trapped, festering within the walls of the Big House; they are often sexually dysfunctional, often victimized by their powerful mothers.

In late nineteenth- and early twentieth-century fiction, the role of women in the Big House becomes increasingly dominant. As patriarchal colonial landlords become marginalized by the decline of their social, economic, and political power, Big House wives begin to dominate the novels. Particularly in fiction by women—Somerville, Bowen, Keane, Fitzgerald, and Johnston—ruthless gentry chatelaines mimic the roles abdicated by defeated and increasingly impotent landlords. Without an adequate social and political arena for their ambitions, however, these women prey not on a dwindling tenant or servant class, but on their own children. Thus with the decline of imperialism, the colonizers turn the habits of a moribund political system inward and savagely attack their young.

3. A major figure in many Big House novels is the deracinated or alienated landlord whose irresponsibility is experienced by his tenants as the loss of order, security, and permanence in their lives. Nineteenth-century rescue fantasies, centering on the return of the absentee landlord and the dramatic expulsion of the evil agent, are dominant narrative themes. Such themes appear not only in the work of an Anglo-Irish novelist like Edgeworth but also in the fiction of Irish writers like Carleton or Kickham, who view the Big House from outside the walls of the demesne. Recurrent narratives about miraculous returns and reformations of the landlord effectively deflect attention from the systemic injustice of the colonial land tenure system. Whereas Edgeworth's novels about absentees focus on the possibility of the moral education of the absentee, subsequent novelists describe increasingly isolated and powerless landlords. In twentieth-century novels the source of alienation is no longer absenteeism or irresponsibility but political and social irrelevance.

4. Through devious economic manipulations and the power of cash, the figure of an outsider, usually a Catholic land agent or rising

professional man, usurps control of the Big House from its heirs. A central theme in the nineteenth-century Big House novel is the threat of these outsiders to the snobbish social insularity and economic stability of Anglo-Ireland. Marriage between the ascendancy class and an aspiring Catholic (or in *The Big House of Inver,* a middle-class Protestant) is viewed with alarm; generally, Catholics are acceptable only when they adhere to the roles set up by traditional landlord–tenant relationships, when they remain the loyal and picturesque "house niggers" of colonial society. Beginning with Lever's mid-nineteenth-century novels, we see how the rising Catholic middle class allies itself with nationalist ideology; thus from the perspective of the Big House novel, the middle class is a threateningly destabilizing force rather than the integrative social bond it is in English fiction.[17] In nineteenth- and early twentieth-century novels, the outsider elicits sexual anxieties in an ascendancy class contemplating its growing social and economic impotence. Later in the twentieth century, when the Big House is an economic liability rather than a prize, the outsider's depredations are almost exclusively psychological rather than economic.

Castle Rackrent, which depicts the breakdown of order and the collapse of systems of reciprocity, establishes several patterns in future Anglo-Irish novels. Instead of celebrating social and economic stability, Irish Big House fiction records the absence of any security; instead of depicting the country house as the symbol of organic community, the novels reveal the increasingly isolated and alien worlds of the Big House and the cabin; rather than existing in the timeless world of a mythic Eden (or in Jane Austen's small villages, isolated from contemporary political upheaval), the country estates in Irish fiction are usually depicted in periods of acute historic crisis for Anglo-Irish society. Novels examined in this study are set in the decades, for example, preceding and following union with Britain (Edgeworth and Maturin), during and following Catholic emancipation (Lever and Le Fanu), during the late nineteenth- or early twentieth-century periods of land agitation (Somerville), in the midst of the

17. David Lloyd observes that, whereas in England the landowning yeoman farmer is the "presiding spirit" over English political integrative spirit, the Irish situation is strikingly different. In Ireland, because of a colonial system of land distribution, the formation of a nonlanded middle class produced the greatest social, political, and economic instability (1993, 139).

twentieth-century War of Independence (Bowen, Keane, and Trevor), and in the contemporary world of economic and social impotence for Big House proprietors (Higgins, Keane, and Johnston).

In the nineteenth century, Maria Edgeworth and Charles Lever relegate the formulations of an idealized relationship between land-lords and tenants—the powerful myth of feudalism—to the mouths of characters who are destined to be discarded by history. Thus, in *Castle Rackrent* the family retainer Thady Quirk, who loses his very identity with the fall of the Rackrents, is the spokesman for an out-dated feudal fealty. Charles Lever's young heroine, Mary Martin, who advocates an idealized neo-feudal stewardship of the family estate, is isolated and abandoned by the end of *The Martins of Cro' Martin.* Later Big House novelists, writing in the twentieth century, continue to emphasize the growing irrelevance of a landlord class to the course of Irish history. Edith Somerville describes how the re-actionary politics, the inertia, or the moral failures of Anglo-Irish landlords encourage the depredations of a predatory Protestant mid-dle-class agent or Catholic professional man. Contemporary novelists go farther, indicating that which their nineteenth-century predeces-sors barely implied: that the ever-receding ideal of the cultivated Big House at the center of an organic community is based on false inter-pretations of the past. The ideal of a harmonious and morally ascen-dant ruling class, suggests Keane in *Good Behaviour* and *Time After Time,* rests on carefully constructed patterns of delusion, on willful misinterpretations of the past in order to construct self-protecting il-lusions of stability. John Banville's contemporary parodies of the Big House literary form carefully depict the process by which such illu-sions are created.

Establishing the Form
Maria Edgeworth's Irish Fiction

Maria Edgeworth wrote her Irish novels with an ideological anxiety that expressed itself in contradictions and discontinuities rather than in any explicit questioning of the colonial system that framed and sustained her world. Although Edgeworth was a conservative social thinker, committed to her father's plans to reform estate management in Ireland in order to buttress and preserve a colonial system, her Irish fiction reveals a series of ambivalences that undermines its own didactic thrust. The narrative of past injustice—brutal conquests, expulsions of Catholic owners from their land, and a century of penal laws—is never a concern of Edgeworth's writing and is absent from the discourse about Ireland that was produced at Edgeworthstown House by Richard Lovell Edgeworth.[1] In significant moments as a novelist, however, Maria Edgeworth acknowledges the power and subversive appeal of a disorderly and intractable native Irish culture that she and her father sought to reform and transform into a model colonial community.

Castle Rackrent, a seminal novel of the Big House tradition published

1. In spite of his youthful support of the ideals of the French Revolution, his early opposition to the Act of Union, and his lifelong belief in Catholic emancipation, Richard Lovell Edgeworth, in his *Third Report of the Commissioners of the Board of Education in Ireland,* asserted that any harping on the past in such a way as to "inculcate democracy, and a foolish hankering after undefined liberty" was particularly dangerous in Ireland. In his educational plan, readings that encourage "piety, and morality, and industry" are admitted, but "everything that leads to restlessness and adventure should be carefully avoided." Instead, attention should be turned to "sober realities" (Edgeworth 1821, 258), by which he presumably meant the reality of the Act of Union and the necessity of building a solid economic basis for rural Irish life.

in 1800, demonstrates in its text, preface, notes, and postscript how truths about colonial relations in Ireland were simultaneously revealed and evaded by Anglo-Ireland's first major novelist. My interest in *Castle Rackrent* lies not only in its subversive narrative of colonial misrule, but also in the strategies Edgeworth used to mute the significance of the historical process that she depicted: the beginning of a slowly accelerating decline of an economic, political, and social system of domination. The tension between evasion and revelation—between what is included or foregrounded and, conversely, excluded from or overshadowed in the text—that is so striking in *Castle Rackrent* disturbs virtually every subsequent Big House novel. In Edgeworth's later Irish novels, a didactic emphasis on the moral development of the landlord into a rational estate manager dominates contrapuntal and competing themes of, for example, her vision of an "undisciplined" but attractive generosity of the native culture or the power of the "primitive" Irish scene to restore the absentee.

Although the last three of her four Irish novels conclude with expectations of well-run estates managed by reformed young landlords, Edgeworth is celebrated by most critics and readers for her creation of the carnival of disorder that exists at Castle Rackrent rather than for the didactic schemes in the works that she wrote between 1809 and 1817: *Ennui, The Absentee,* and *Ormond.*[2] Reading Edgeworth in the context of subsequent Big House fiction privileges certain motifs in her Irish novels: the absentee or improvident landlord, the neglected and decaying house, the trajectory of family decline, and the upstart Catholic retainer. Many of those motifs are repeated and reworked by succeeding writers. Each implies a crisis in identity for the hybrid Anglo-Irish landowner, the colonizer in danger of going native who exists without a wholly satisfactory national identity, and

2. Marilyn Butler's view of *Castle Rackrent* is a striking exception to the general critical assessment. Butler's belief that *Castle Rackrent* is the "least historical" of Edgeworth's novels leads her to a highly idiosyncratic judgment of it. "There is no sense of the impending future in it—no clash between the Rackrents' values and those of the people replacing them" (1972, 357). Butler asserts that the "anxiety" the Edgeworths felt about the reception of the novel demonstrates how "the tale as a whole is at odds with itself and at odds with Maria" (360). Her own critical appraisal reflects the Edgeworth's discomfort with *Castle Rackrent*; thus Butler finds the later didactic novels—*Ennui* and *Ormond*—more successful than Maria's early masterpiece. The sociological detail in the the middle section of *Ennui* causes Butler to praise that novel as "perhaps the best of Maria's Irish tales except *Ormond*" (365).

whose relationship to a native culture is poised between fear and desire. Edgeworth's Irish novels record the lives of a group of anomalous landowners who situate themselves uneasily between the demands of colonial "civilization" and the temptations of native "primitivism," between their competing attachments to both imperial English and Irish social forms, between culture and nature.[3]

Her fiction is overtly controlled by beliefs about how men and women are to order their lives in a civilized world. Those convictions emerge from English Enlightenment ideals and reassert familiar precepts about self-control, social hierarchy, and service; about the necessity of disciplining the untutored emotional response and serving the greater good of the community rather than the self. But in Edgeworth's Irish fiction her controlling didacticism is in various ways undermined and shifted off-center by her response to the new country she found herself in as a girl of fifteen. Although she writes, inevitably, from the perspective of the outsider gazing in at a native culture, attempting to preserve and strengthen a colonial system, her resentment of English condescension toward Ireland and her ambivalent responses to the strange "otherness" of her adopted country suggest a higher degree of irresolution than the controlling didactic patterns of the later Irish novels indicate. Although the disordered Big House in Edgeworth's fiction is ostensibly a proper site for a program of moral reformation, her certainty about the feasibility of such a program is, on occasion, less than convincing. Even in *Ormond*, her last and most successfully executed didactic novel about the Irish landlord, her confident relegation of her young hero to a life of rational estate management (on the Edgeworthstown model) is qualified by his choice for his future home of the Black Islands, an isolated, feudal setting. That site of primitive regression, which rep-

3. In *Orientalism* (1979), Edward Said argues that the dominant culture's portrayal of the colonized serves both to legitimize the colonizer's positional superiority and to express his covert identification with the native culture "as a sort of surrogate and even underground self" (3). More recently, Peter Stallybrass and Allon White, examining the relationship between high and low levels of discourse, suggest how, in depictions of slum dwellers, servants, and colonized people, "the low-Other is despised and denied at the level of political organization and social being whilst it is instrumentally constitutive of the shared imaginary repertoires of the dominant culture" (1986, 5–6). The Anglo-Irish colonizer, neither firmly English nor Irish, provides a unique opportunity to examine such conflict between fear and desire.

resents the object of desire for the purportedly reformed and anglicized young hero, suggests a yearning for a way of life that has, supposedly, been undermined by much of Ormond's moral education.

Maria Edgeworth's family holdings in Ireland predated the Williamite victory of 1690 that ushered in the penal laws and large groups of new landowners; as "old" Elizabethan landlords, the Edgeworth social position within the increasingly parvenu ascendancy class was impeccable. But even a cursory reading of Edgeworth history reveals a familiar tale of ebbing family fortunes and a typical Anglo-Irish ascendancy use of Irish holdings solely as a source of revenue. The Edgeworths of the seventeenth and early eighteenth centuries were absentees, soldiers, and courtiers, not landlords. Thus, the focus of their lives was London or Dublin rather than the family estate in County Longford. Lavish hospitality and extravagant spending by John Edgeworth did not save him from the wrath of his Catholic tenantry in 1641, when his home was burned and his family barely spared. Later Edgeworths, recklessly extravagant, took to mortgaging the estate and gambling away their wealth (Butler 1972, 14–16).

In her biography of Maria Edgeworth, Marilyn Butler insists that the "well-documented" ancestral tales available to her subject provided the models for the characters in *Castle Rackrent.* Butler interprets *Castle Rackrent* as a novel heavily dependent on Edgeworth family history and, thus, on the history of eighteenth-century Anglo-Irish moral bankruptcy. She takes Maria Edgeworth's preface—written shortly before the publication of *Castle Rackrent* in England and probably several years after the novel was conceived in 1793—at face value.[4] The preface positions the novel in the era of eighteenth-century misrule and disorder preceding Richard Lovell Edgeworth's resettlement in Ireland in 1782. By associating the Rackrents with Henry Fielding's roistering Squire Western (and, thus, with a novel of comic satire published one-half century before her own), Maria Edgeworth clearly wished to avoid any suggestion that she was de-

4. Butler's chronology suggests that the first part of *Castle Rackrent* was written between 1793 and 1796 and that Condy's story was added in 1796 (Butler 1972, 354–55). George Watson, editor of the Oxford University Press edition of *Castle Rackrent,* assumes that the preface was added late in 1799, because of its final reference to the union of Great Britain and Ireland as a foregone conclusion (Watson 1980, 119). In *Ascendancy and Tradition,* however, W. J. McCormack reminds us of the "incompleteness of our knowledge of the timetable of composition" (1985, 99).

picting her real subject, the social and economic world she and her father inhabited and envisioned for the future. By authorial fiat, thus, Edgeworth repositioned the novel she had begun composing several years earlier to prevent a misreading of the text at a time of major change for Ireland.[5] The disorder that *Castle Rackrent* presents as Irish gentry life is anxiously interpreted as retrospective narrative.

> The Editor hopes his readers will observe, that these are 'tales of other times;' that the manners depicted in the following pages are not those of the present age: the race of the Rackrents has long since been extinct in Ireland, and the drunken Sir Patrick, the litigious Sir Murtagh, the fighting Sir Kit, and the slovenly Sir Condy, are characters which could no more be met with at present in Ireland than Squire Western or Parson Trulliber in England. There is a time when individuals can bear to be rallied for their past follies and absurdities, after they have acquired new habits and a new consciousness. Nations as well as individuals lose attachment to their identity, and the present generation is amused rather than offended by the ridicule that is thrown upon their ancestors. (1980, 4–5)

In *Ennui* and *The Absentee,* novels about absenteeism emerging from the didactic realism that dominates Edgeworth's later Irish writing, the serious deficiencies of the landlord class are amenable to reform. Similarly, in *Ormond* the undisciplined young hero learns to educate his passions. But in her first work about Ireland, in which her protagonists are presented through the consciousness of a gullible victim of colonial feudalism, Edgeworth relentlessly exposes the landlord as greedy, indolent, philandering, drunken, and irresponsible—as, in short, unreformable. Yet, any contemporary relevance of her portrayal of the Rackrents is anxiously denied. As Vivian Mercier suggests, Maria Edgeworth was never again able to master the subtle satire and irony of *Castle Rackrent* in her later works as she came to feel more implicated in the conditions of postunion Ireland (Mercier 1969, 197).

5. Edgeworth's seeming optimism regarding the future of postunion Ireland, which George Watson (1980, x) and Marilyn Butler (1972, 355) see as encouraging her to relegate the Rackrents and their kind to the past, is skillfully undermined by John Cronin's careful analysis of the "blatantly self-contradictory" arguments in the preface and postscript (1980, 29). Cronin finds evidence of anxious contradiction and irony, not confidence about Ireland's future, in *Castle Rackrent.*

The relationship between the narrative of history and the narrative of fiction that is so pertinent to colonial and postcolonial Irish literature has become the grounds for a compelling attack on *Castle Rackrent*. To what extent does the author's ideological perspective—her identity with ascendancy assumptions about class and power—control the historical detail presented in her text? Furthermore, to what extent does the purported accuracy or inaccuracy of such historical detail determine the success or failure of her novel? A recent controversy surrounding *Castle Rackrent* reflects critical problems that emerge as we read other colonial novels—works that are obviously historically conditioned, but not necessarily historically "correct" in the same way to all readers. Edgeworth's mistaken assumption in the preface, for example, that postunion Ireland would easily shed its identity as a nation elicits predictably critical modern commentary.

Maurice Colgan explores *Castle Rackrent* primarily as historical document and finds it evasive, remarkably deficient in its depiction of Irish sectarian history. Colgan argues that Edgeworth's historical evasions leave the reader of *Castle Rackrent* "dissatisfied" and prevent the book from achieving real greatness (1987, 57). Many of his specific complaints—that as the formerly Catholic O'Shaughlins the Rackrents cannot own land, or that as a Catholic, Jason would be inadmissible as a lawyer under the penal laws—are dissolved if we consider the waning power of the penal laws by the late eighteenth century and assume that in changing their name the Rackrents also changed their religion.[6] But Colgan's underlying criticism of Edgeworth's historical evasiveness is inarguable. The novel is written from within the Big House by an author who devoted much of her life to reforming and, thus, shoring up the colonial system of land tenure.

The subversive view of gentry culture in *Castle Rackrent* emerges not simply from a pattern of references to the historical conditions Maria Edgeworth experiences and recorded as the daughter of Edgeworthstown House but also from her transformation of sociological detail into a symbolic narrative of decline. Were we to judge *Castle Rackrent* solely by the accuracy and completeness of its sociological and historical data, were its meaning to emerge wholly from the ac-

6. See Cronin (1980, 32–33); Flanagan (1959, 70); and McCormack (1985, 118–19) for the arguments against Colgan's assertions.

cumulation of such detail, Colgan's criticism would carry considerable weight. But, although we may well wish that Edgeworth were clearer, for example, about the sectarian history of the Rackrent family, our judgment of the novel surely rests on its grasp of a social movement: the decline and fall of one class and the accompanying rise of another. By presenting and judging the Rackrents through the transparently unreliable narrative voice of their devoted servant Thady, whose own son destroys them (with some unwitting complicity on the part of his father), Edgeworth creates a complex narrative of social mobility that becomes the ur-text for a tradition of subsequent Big House novels.

Simultaneously oppressors and victims, the Rackrents are not—as Edgeworth would have them in her preface—just the remnants of a long-past breed; they are also predecessors of a long line of landowners in future colonial and postcolonial novels. As McCormack reminds us, the historical dimension of *Castle Rackrent* "does not lie inert in its temporal setting" (1985, 99). However diligently we attempt to arrive at an understanding of a novel's readership and moment of composition, we read all fiction both within and outside of that moment, registering its predictive power as well as its depiction of a historical setting.

Edgeworth's interpretation of Irish history is fraught with the anxieties and evasions that represent the burden of the double-edged identity that was constructed by the Anglo-Irish ascendancy. Although she never challenges ascendancy claims to the Big House, she questions the landlord's wisdom, decency, and capacity to retain his legitimate rights. *Ennui* and *The Absentee* are controlled by a sustained moral exhortation directed at her class that is absent from the earlier novel. The portraits of improvident landlords in *Castle Rackrent*, in fact, call into question the possibility of the reform (through Richard Edgeworth's Enlightenment ideals of rational estate planning) that the later novels advocate. By giving the Rackrents an Irish rather than an Anglo-Saxon or Anglo-Norman ancestry, as well as by presenting her tale as past history in the preface and full title of the novel,[7] Edgeworth attempts to dissociate her subversive criticism of land tenure practices and Irish landlordism from the contemporary

7. *Castle Rackrent: An Hibernian Tale Taken From Facts, and From the Manners of the Irish Squires Before the Year 1782.*

ascendancy world. Such strategies are particularly crucial for her at a time when she and her father anticipated benefits to Ireland from the approaching union with England. Writing from within a colonial class, Edgeworth does not acknowledge the radical discontent that was to threaten her family in 1798, a discontent preceded by a series of isolated attacks on landed property throughout the late eighteenth century.[8] When she does briefly describe the uprising in *Ennui,* she fearfully refers to the spirit of rebellion as a "disease" or "epidemic infection" (1992, 245) that contaminates the peasants and is quelled when the influence of "men of property, and birth, and education, and character, once more prevailed" (248).

A careful reading of *Castle Rackrent* reveals the strategy whereby a colonial writer shapes her intransigent material into subversive fiction and then packages it for the English audience she wishes, for Ireland's sake, to conciliate. What Colgan calls her historical evasions are not, as he implies, the mark of a deficient novelist, but rather the means by which an artist thoroughly entrenched in her society's ideologies defends herself against the all too revealing world she nevertheless uncovers in her literary masterpiece. Without the savagery that Swift directed against the Anglo-Irish in "A Modest Proposal," *Castle Rackrent* performs the moral function of all great satire. For all of Edgeworth's qualifications about the meaning of her work, for all of her inability to know it as the product of a contemporary and future ideological crisis, her novel exposes the hypocrises, improvidences, and trajectory of ascendancy decline with an authority she was never again to achieve. In her most interesting moments as a writer, moments that often operate at cross-purposes to the didactic themes in the later Irish fiction, Edgeworth begins to reach beyond her own world and to acknowledge the subversive appeal of another.

8. Marilyn Butler reports threatening disturbances in the countryside surrounding Edgeworthstown beginning in the late 1780s (1972, 114), and Edgeworth's *Memoirs* clearly indicate an awareness of the tensions in rural Ireland before the 1798 United Irishman uprising. Richard Lovell Edgeworth nevertheless notes that prior to 1794 his "neighbourhood continued tolerably quiet" (1821, 2:84). Even as late as a June 20, 1798, letter, two months before her father was nearly lynched as a French spy, Maria describes the county as "quiet" in spite of reports of "dreadful disturbances" elsewhere in Ireland (1895, 1:55). Maria's failure to mention political unrest in *Castle Rackrent*—presumably begun in 1793—is less significant than Colgan implies.

Writing without any inclination to transcend the conservative colonial ideology of her class, in *Castle Rackrent,* nevertheless, she establishes the central pattern of exposure that is to dominate the Big House genre.[9]

Castle Rackrent: The House, the Landlord, His Retainer, and His Antagonist

Domestic Order in the House

For the modern reader, the status of the particular class that Edgeworth presents in *Castle Rackrent* warrants clarification. As readers, we need to know exactly how the object and symbol of decline—the Big House itself—operates in the novel and why it is not an image of a tragic national loss, as a romantically inclined critic such as Thomas Flanagan asserts.[10] Edgeworth's care in describing the debased gentry life of the Rackrents denies us any nostalgic regrets for the fall of the great. Although the name of the Rackrents' home suggests some grandeur to the twentieth-century tourist, virtually every Irish county house built before the middle of the seventeenth century was a castle of some sort—usually a simple fortified tower with an attached domestic wing, or in later forms a semifortified domestic building (Bence-Jones 1978, xviii). The larger and grander country homes, those monuments to Irish classicism or Palladianism which were introduced toward the end of the 1720s by the Irish architect Sir Edward Lovett Pearce (Bence-Jones 1978, xix) and which have become part

9. Edgeworth's achievement can be compared to Rudyard Kipling's more than a century later in *Kim.* To read either author through a narrowly anti-imperial lens is to miss their subtle ideological subversions. In *Ennui* Edgeworth envisions Ireland's major rebellion before twentieth-century independence as a "disease." Similarly, Kipling never questions the need for British domination of India and in *Kim* presents a defining event of Indian nationalism—the 1857 Mutiny—through the disapproving recollections of a native soldier loyal to the raj. Nevertheless, the two novelists, in spite of their assumptions about colonial or imperial rule, convey the subversive pleasures and power of an indigenous native culture that challenges the British imperial systems they themselves embrace.

10. "*Castle Rackrent* was to be the brilliant requiem of the Protestant Nation, for Maria Edgeworh had seen its history as the life of a family which rose from obscurity, fought bravely, lost meanly, and at last perished in squalor and pride" (Flanagan 1959, 23).

of the tourist's image of the Irish Big House, have little to do with the "castle" that Edgeworth describes in her novel.

Castle Rackrent suggests the social and economic complexities lying behind Anglo-Irish fiction. If we posit the well-managed estate of the English country house tradition as an ideal and the Irish hovel as the object of fear, then the Anglo-Irish Big House is situated—in actuality if not in intention—somewhere between the two. In its solidity and size—big even in its typically modest forms—it represents the authority of the dominant culture. Ordinarily isolated from the sprawling collection of huts and cabins constituting the tenant village, its demesne protects it from contamination by the alien countryside. Its gates, long avenue, lodges, and gardens proclaim its exclusiveness, wealth, and hauteur. But, as depicted in much of Irish fiction, the actual Big House is memorable more for its filth and decay than for its elegance. Like the peasant hovel, albeit at a vastly different economic scale, it bespeaks poverty and decline, not wealth and prosperity. The crumbling walls, leaky roofs, and overgrown drives and gardens of the Big House suggest, like the ramshackle one-room tenant cabins, a culture of improvidence or despair. The drunken brawls within the gentry mansion, most vividly evoked by Edgeworth or by Somerville and Ross, mimic the worst excesses of a wild and savage native culture as envisioned by the colonial overlords. The "Irishness" of the house—its energy, excesses, emotional receptivity, and hospitality—identifies it with a society that exists in an adversarial relationship to the colonial system.

Maria Edgeworth spent much of her life attempting to stem the tide of what she and her father understood to be the threat of domestic political disarray. In her account of her family's return to Ireland in 1782, the disorder of the country is signaled by the condition of the house to which Richard Lovell Edgeworth brought his third wife and numerous children. In her additions to her father's memoirs, written after his death in 1817, Maria Edgeworth foregrounds domestic details of home improvement in her account of the well-governed life. The Irish house must be put in order, purged of its native shiftlessness; the state of the house and the state of the nation are related.

Things and persons are so much improved in Ireland of latter days, that only those, who can remember how they were some thirty of forty years ago, can conceive the variety of domestic grievance, which, in those times, assailed the master of a family, immediately upon his arrival at his Irish home. Wherever he turned his eyes, in or out of his house, damp, dilapidation, waste appeared. Painting, glazing, roofing, fencing, finishing—all were wanting. (Edgeworth 1821, 2:7)

The task of the good landlord is clear: before attempting to reform his tenants, he must reform his own domestic life. Maria Edgeworth reports that her father insisted that he could not pursue his principal objects until he set an example of "neatness and order, or of propriety and proportion in his own mode of living." He "began, where all improvements should begin, at home" (2:8). As the chapter progresses she describes the dangers facing all Irish landlords, which her father prudently avoids. The most seductive temptation is to overbuild, especially for a landlord facing as unprepossessingly designed a structure as Edgeworthstown House, where all the rooms are "small and gloomy, with dark wainscots, heavy cornices, little windows, corner chimneys" (2:9). Maria Edgeworth disapprovingly describes the superb mansions built by travelled gentlemen, the construction of which led to forced sales or lives "in debt, danger, and subterfuge the rest of their days, nominally possessors of a palace, but really in dread of a jail" (2:9). Equally wrongheaded are those landowners who hope to avoid such financial disasters and live, like the Rackrents, "in wretched houses out of repair, with locks of doors out of order, the pulleys of the windows without a sash-line; in short, without what we are accustomed to consider as the common comforts and decencies of life" (2:9). Others, unable to maintain a "safe middle course," plan a palace but live a permanently provisional life in their stables or coach house—"leaving the rest to fate, and to their sons"(2:9). Not unexpectedly, Richard Edgeworth avoided all such errors; through hard work and steady, slow improvement he transformed the unprepossessing Edgeworthstown House into "a comfortable residence for a large family" (2:10). His description of his domestic ideal resembles a middle-class family retreat rather than the grand country houses or the peasant hovels that the Edgeworths condemn.

The *Memoirs* suggest the Edgeworths' understanding of the temptations facing the Big House landlord. He must negotiate a path between the danger of overreaching his resources and an equally culpable resignation to sloth and squalor. For Edgeworth, her father's commitment to slow and steady hard work—he started landscaping his estate the day after he arrived—rather than to infinitely postponed grandiose plans lies at the heart of his exemplary life in Ireland. She ends her summary of her father's attitude toward domestic improvement by paraphrasing from an unnamed "celebrated" authority who "would ask no better test for judging of the understanding of his fellow-creatures, than the houses they build, and the improvements they make"(2:10). Significantly, in a later chapter describing national progress in postunion Ireland, she alludes to the domestic advances in the lives of the lower classes: "increasing attempts toward order and neatness in their dwellings, apparel, and mode of living, became in this part of Ireland, everywhere visible"(2: 206).

From the little direct evidence that Edgeworth offers her readers, Castle Rackrent is a modest edifice indeed, failing utterly to achieve the level of domestic comfort that she presents as a standard of moral judgment for household and nation in the *Memoirs*. Castle Rackrent is, therefore, a symbol of the disordered nation, of a gentry world that is slipping into decline and displaying that dangerous improvidence that is, for the Edgeworths, a mark of how Irish habits infect the ruling class. Its demesne consists of desolate peat bogs and too recently planted trees (Edgeworth 1980, 27). When one proprietor and his new bride approach the castle by the back road, they must walk rather than ride, for the back way is too narrow for a carriage. The scale of the castle is often far from grand: the door to the smelly kitchen is so low that the feathers on the bride's hat are broken as she enters. When she complains of the odors, her husband assures her, certainly with some characteristic understatement, that "it's only three steps across the kitchen" (47).

Instances of grander aspirations do exist. Although the first Rackrent proprietor accommodates his guests in a converted chicken house, later Rackrents possess a barrack room, which Edgeworth wryly tells us in her glossary was the customary accommodation for large numbers of occasional visitors in "gentlemen's houses in Ireland" (108). Moreover, the cultural aspirations of the last Rackrent bride, who has "fine taste for building and furniture, and playhouses"(48), mandate that the barrack room be turned into a theater. Overbuilding, the temptation resisted by Richard Edgeworth, is a constant danger for the ramshackle Rackrents, who add on and renovate rather than repair their leaking roof. Rooms in Castle Rackrent are sometimes described in the modest terminology of the ordinary home rather than in language suggesting the aristocratic castle. Thus, Thady speaks of the "parlour" rather than drawing room where Condy Rackrent takes leave of his wife; Lady Rackrent, on the other hand, orders the servants to call the leaking and shabby "long passage" between the two master bedchambers the "gallery," a word which evokes the architecture of a legitimate great house (65). In the course of the novel, the Rackrents' aspirations for social status increase—the last heir squanders all his money running for Parliament—but their financial circumstances and the condition of their house decline.

In *Classic Irish Houses of the Middle Size,* Maurice Craig reminds us that the Big House in Ireland is often modest in scale (1976, 112). Brian de Breffny and Rosemary Ffolliott observe in *The Houses of Ireland* that many smaller eighteenth-century houses designed to resemble gentlemen's residences were constructed around essential farm buildings and given "grandiloquent names which were not necessarily a measure of their grandeur" (1984, 84). Such evidence from architectural historians supports W. C. McCormack's careful analysis of the protean architectural imagery of the novel as implying "less than a guarantee of castle-like scale in Castle Rackrent" (1985, 115), and as suggesting instead the power of bourgeois social dynamics in ascendancy literature. In Edgeworth's novel, the pretenses of castle living are reduced to a declining gentry farm life, collapsing further into peasant squalor. Village and Big House flow into each other, and the interdependency of two worlds is geographically inscribed by an uneasy proximity. Unlike the typical Anglo-Irish Big House in later fiction, Castle Rackrent is not isolated from the local village; its door opens onto the village streets and at one point attracts an angry mob incensed that the last Rackrent has been dispossessed by his agent (Edgeworth 1980, 79).

Just as the domestic setting mirrors the state of the nation for Edgeworth, the private behavior of men and women provides the crucial means of judging them. In the preface of *Castle Rackrent,* Edgeworth defends her concentration on domestic settings, asserting that people reveal themselves best in the "privacy of domestic life" rather than in their public roles (2). "It is from their careless conversations, their half finished sentences, that we may hope with the greatest probability of success to discover their real characters"

(1). Edgeworth's careful distinction between public "history" and private "anecdote" serves as the best possible introduction to a literary tradition that, for two centuries, has straddled that slippery arena between domestic and historical fiction, or, even, between fiction and history itself. The public implications of *Castle Rackrent*—its covert indictment of a ruling class—are achieved not through elaborations upon historical events and characters, as in the classic historical novel, but through exploration of the private lives of ordinary men and women. Thus, the diurnal life of the house and its inhabitants remains the focus of a fictional tradition that demands interpretation within the larger context of nation and empire.

Thady and Jason: Servant and Usurper

For Maria Edgeworth, the decaying house and the neglected land speak to the Big House landlord's failure. The inadequate landlord is the dominating theme of *Castle Rackrent* and the didactic center of two of her subsequent Big House novels, *Ennui* and *The Absentee.* In *Castle Rackrent,* the image of the neglected estate becomes a central topos, exposing moral decay and social exploitation. The literary complexity of the point of view of the novel, in which the unreliable narrator ironically reveals the offenses he himself cannot register, should not obscure the detailed, near documentary condemnation of exploitative land-tenure practices implicit in the authorial voice behind Thady Quirk's. *Castle Rackrent* consists of Thady's descriptions of four Rackrent landlords, beginning with his memories of stories told to him about the semimythical Sir Patrick and ending with an account of the lonely death of the last Rackrent. In fewer than one hundred pages, Thady's admiring voice invokes those very qualities in the Rackrents—improvidence, dishonesty, sloth, drunkenness, and greed—that the author (and the reader) condemns. With a Swiftian economy, Edgeworth thus manages to expose almost every possible abuse of the landlord class and to write what Vivian Mercier has called "the best satire on the Protestant Irish after Swift" (1969, 186). In the long tradition of the Big House novel, only Molly Keane, in *Good Behaviour,* so successfully exploits the ironies of the unreliable narrator—the duped victim of Big House life.

In her characterization of Thady and his son Jason in *Castle Rackrent,* Edgeworth sees beyond the decline of her own class to the transformation of a whole nation. Her depiction of Thady as a character caught between a feudal loyalty to the Big House and the demands of his own class suggests the complexity of her grasp of his narrative possibilities. Early in the novel Thady proudly watches his clever son Jason's machinations: first to become a low-paying tenant of profitable Rackrent land, and then, with evident duplicity, to arrange the dismissal of the family land agent in order to take the position for himself. Similarly, as Thady describes the different methods by which the Rackrents plunder their tenants, he never condemns his masters. Instead, he notes how well the fruits of Lady Murtagh Rackrent's greed—or successful transformation of old feudal practices into a form of brutal colonial exploitation—feed the whole household (including himself). When, at the end of the saga of family decline, Thady turns against Jason and allies himself firmly with his dying master, his progression from proud father of a duplicitous son to loyal retainer has not been without moments of real ambiguity. We have seen Thady, for example, inadvertently betray Condy when he introduces "my poor master's greatest of enemies" (1980, 58) to his son, thereby setting in place the partnership that will deprive Condy of all his property.

Much critical attention has focused on Thady's syntactical confusion, his tendency to lapse into the characteristic trope of the Irish bull ("a self-contradictory proposition . . . an expression containing a manifest contradiction in terms involving a ludicrous inconsistency unperceived by the speaker [*Oxford English Dictionary*, 1971]). While Cóilín Owens argues for the intentionality of such tropes (1987a, 72), Joanne Altieri is surely more accurate in reading Thady's speech as a "mirror of the novel's world, its refusal to see causality, to make choices, to think" (1987, 98). Through the manifest contradictions implicit in the Irish bull, Edgeworth suggests Thady's inability to differentiate and to judge. Of Sir Murtagh's lawsuits, Thady proudly claims, "[O]ut of forty-nine suits which he had, he never lost one but seventeen" (1980, 15). Of Condy's parliamentary career, Thady reports indignantly, "He . . . was very ill used by the government about a place that was promised and never given, after his supporting them against his conscience very honorably, and being greatly abused for it" (61).

The twists and turns of Thady's behavior and speech do not suggest that he is a master of irony and a calculating opportunist, as some critics insist (Owens 1987a, 71; Newcomer 1967, 144–45). Although Thady is morally confused and torn between his social role as loyal servant and his personal role as father of an ambitious son, he is never the "shrewd," "unsentimental" calculator that Newcomer describes; he resembles neither Dickens's Uriah Heep nor Melville's Babo in *Benito Cereno*. Thady has, rather, a deeply impaired sense of identity and is torn by his loyalties to conflicting worlds. His fate at the end of the novel, when he firmly repudiates his son's avarice but is left with nothing except a dead and ruined master and an ill-attended funeral, suggests Edgeworth's understanding of the heavy costs of colonialism. As in the American antebellum South, where the house servant identified himself with an alien class and denied the claims of his own race, Thady exists finally with no identity of his own. A victim of his sentimental entrapment in a system of oppression, he, not his drunken and self-destructive masters, becomes the most significant casualty of the Rackrents' failures. Thady is, as John Cronin so aptly describes him, a "magnificently realized slave, a terrifying vision of the results of colonial misrule" (1980, 36).

Jason Quirk, the Rackrents' sly adversary, is the representative peasant turned middle class, the usurper of the estate and the inheritor of ascendency power and property. Although for Marilyn Butler, Jason represents only the abuses of the past—"the parasite of the old system, not the herald of the new" (1972, 357)—he anticipates future Big House adversaries in nineteenth- and early twentieth-century fiction. The characterization of the successful usurper in this and many later Big House novels suggests Anglo-Ireland's uneasy understanding of its own growing powerlessness. In the novels of Lever and Somerville, for example, we witness a similar transfer of power from the Big House to the growing middle class. By the end of *Castle Rackrent,* Jason, after managing to buy up all the Rackrent debts and mortgages, owns the Big House and all of its land—even the cramped lodge to which Condy retires to die. In the character of Jason, Edgeworth suggests the human costs of personal advancement but avoids succumbing to the sentimentality of any simple condemnation of his self-serving ambitions. Although Thady condemns his own son, Edgeworth's ironic narrative stance allows the reader an ambivalent response: Jason's small-minded and efficient manipulations are always seen in the context of the large, sloppy generosities of a doomed class.

The portrayal of Jason, the upstart peasant lawyer, is not original with Edgeworth. As the cold, efficient outsider or protocapitalist whose ruthless efficiency will sweep away the untidy and improvident structures of a dying feudalism, Jason's figure appears in earlier English literature as an agent of rural change. He still exists, in fact, as the speculative developer/despoiler of the rural countryside who buys up land cheaply from "old families" in need of cash. Raymond Williams (1973, 49) points out that in the sixteenth and seventeenth centuries, as estates in rural England were lost by earlier owners through the workings of agrarian capitalism, the transformation of the land came to be identified with the coming of "an outsider," often a lawyer.[11]

In discussing the evolving division and redistribution of land in rural England, Williams warns against an easy confidence in the innocence of the "traditional" landlord. He reminds us of our "deep and persistent" illusion that the familiar and "traditional" patterns of acquisition are any less ruthless than new ones. "Whenever we encounter their proceedings in detail, the landlords, old and new, seem adequately described in the words of a modern agricultural historian: 'a pitiless crew' " (1973, 50). In the Anglo-Irish novel, the usurper generally comes from within rural society. He appears, most often, in the guise of a peasant turned agent or lawyer who persistently threatens the estate that was, in all likelihood, itself ruthlessly acquired. The Rackrents' implied denial of religious and national identity in order to gain their land undermines their claims for fullest sympathy as they are themselves dispossessed. To Maria Edgeworth's credit, her portrayal of Jason as the acquisitive agent of the Rackrents' destruction is always mediated by her devastating critique of the family's improvidence and irresponsibility. The elegiac note of English country house poetry is quite missing from *Castle Rackrent*, except as it is heard through the poignant but unreliable voice of Thady Quirk.

The threatening ascent of a commercial ethos over defunct neo-feudal social patterns is acknowledged in the portrayal of Jason, the

11. We see those changes daily: the fair land
   That were the client's, are the lawyer's now;
   And those rich manors there of goodman Taylor's
   Had once more wood upon them, than the yard
   By which they were measured out for the last purchase.
   (Jonson, "The Devil is an Ass," quoted in Williams 1973, 50)

hard-headed emerging middle-class professional who turns against his old playmate Condy Rackrent. Jason's mental agility is revealed and his victory over his future employer foreshadowed when Thady tells us that in the village grammar school Jason helped the grateful Condy with his school learning. On occasion, Jason anticipates William Faulkner's Snopes clan, leaders of the emerging social class in Yoknapatawpha County. The outrages of the Snopes in Faulkner's fictional landscape become their means of reconstructing the social order in their own image; Jason, too, is creating a new world for himself. His mental acuity and success in plotting his own ascendancy is a familiar theme in the subsequent literature of class fluidity, not only in Ireland, but in nineteenth- and twentieth-century European and American fiction and drama.[12]

The "natural" feelings that Thady finds so lacking in Jason and so alive in the villagers who live on Rackrent land are perceived, however, with Edgeworth's characteristic ambivalence. In one of the key scenes of the novel, Jason pressures Condy to sign his last possessions over. "Crying like a child" and accused by his son of being "old and doting," Thady turns for comfort to some neighboring children playing at marbles: ". . . seeing me in great trouble, [they] left their play and gathered about me to know what ailed me; and I told them all, for it was a great relief to me to speak to those poor childer, that seemed to have some natural feelings left in them: and when they were made sensible that Sir Condy was going to leave Castle Rackrent for good and all, they set up a whillalu that could be heard to the farthest end of the street" (1980, 78).

The comfort and reassurance that Thady receives from the village children takes the form of their "great anger against my son Jason, and terror at the notion of his coming to be landlord over them" (79). Yet, the mob of villagers expressing their indignation is easily appeased by Condy, who reassures them that he and Jason are still good friends and sends them some whiskey to drink. "That was the last time his honor's health was ever drunk at Castle Rackrent" (80). Thady's understated description of Condy's funeral suggests the lim-

12. Chekhov's *The Cherry Orchard*, published in 1904, and Shaw's *Heartbreak House*, published in 1917, echo the shifting sociology of class that *Castle Rackrent* depicts. In *The Little Foxes*, which appeared in 1939, Lillian Hellman explores the same theme of social climbing and social decline that is so central to Faulkner's vision of the American South and to that of the Anglo-Irish novelists.

itations of "natural" feelings, for, unlike his ancestor Sir Patrick, Condy is buried with few mourners; "he had a very poor funeral, after all" (96). The loyal feudal peasants do not flock to honor their ruined master. Like Judy M'Quirk, the peasant girl whom Condy almost married, they do not follow the misfortunes of a dying order.

The Rackrents

In *Castle Rackrent,* Maria Edgeworth articulates a moral indictment of the landlord class that controls most subsequent Big House novels and permits their authors to avoid confronting the systemic failures of Irish colonialism. *Castle Rackrent* insists that power and position are lost from within, from internal rot, not through the stresses of political change or historical inevitability. History, alone, is never to blame for personal loss. The Rackrents lose their land and their position as well as their family line because of slovenly irresponsibility, arrogant assumptions about their own entitlement, and an inability to see beyond their own hedonism and greed. Above all, they allow themselves to be corrupted and coopted by their failure to maintain domestic standards.[13]

But Edgeworth's indictment is mediated by Thady's admiring voice. The house servant's pride in the royal lineage of his masters is undercut by his simultaneous revelation that only by disavowing that ancient line, by changing the family name from O'Shaughlin to Rackrent (and, by implication, by changing the family religion from Catholicism to Protestantism), did the landlord retain his property. Thus, in this seminal Big House novel we are presented with a denial of Irish identity undertaken to secure possession of the land.

Sir Patrick Rackrent, the first of the four generations chronicled in the novel, exists in the gullible underling's mythic memory as the personification of abundance, the archetypal hospitable Irish land-

---

13. Although Edgeworth's novel insists that the breakdown of individual responsibility causes the decline of the Big House, the tension between human failure and the seeming fatedness of history remains operative throughout the Big House tradition. In Aidan Higgins's *Langrishe, Go Down* the German outsider who preys on the Big House asks with puzzlement: "Why fail? I don't understand it. You have seventy-four acres of land, ten of that in tillage. You had a herd of cattle once, a supply of eggs, pullets, a vegetable garden, a fruit garden, an orchard. You did not live riotously; so why had it to fail?" (1966, 189)

lord. That his body is seized for debt at his lavish funeral matters
less to Thady than that his life fulfilled a grand vision of Irish hospitality: "On coming into the estate, he gave the finest entertain-
ment ever was heard of in the country—not a man could stand
after supper but Sir Patrick himself, who could sit out the best man
in Ireland, let alone the three kingdoms itself. He had his house,
from one year's end to another, as full of company as ever it could
hold, and fuller"(9). This Irish version of the landlord whose hospitality becomes (in Thady's eyes) a sign of his beneficence simultaneously recalls and debunks the myth of feudal plenitude praised
by the English country house poets. Thady's remarks about the
condition of Castle Rackrent after Sir Patrick's death reveal the
costs of such excess and introduce a central motif of the Big House
genre: the progressive stripping down of the house and the slow
disintegration of its already dubious authority. "The cellars were
never filled after his death—and no open house, or any thing as it
used to be—the tenants even were sent away without their whiskey—
I was ashamed myself, and knew not what to say for the honor of
the family"(12).

The next owner of Castle Rackrent indulges in quite another
abuse—less congenial to Thady's feudal notions of stewardship and
even more transparently criticized by the authorial presence behind
the narrator. Sir Murtagh Rackrent reverses the lavish hospitality of
his predecessor and institutes a régime of exploitation that bleeds his
oppressed tenants. With the help of his deplorable wife, "of the family of Skinflints," he undermines the feudal bond between tenant
and landlord. Sir Murtagh and his wife perfect the exploitative agrarian capitalism (disguised in the trappings of a colonial version of feudalism) whereby the Irish landlord exercised arbitrary power over
his tenants. In the guise of a Lady Bountiful, Lady Murtagh exacts
every possible item of labor and goods from her tenants: "However,
my lady was very charitable in her own way. She had a charity school
for poor children, where they were taught to read and write gratis,
and where they were kept well to spinning gratis for my lady in return; for she had always heaps of duty yarn from the tenants, and got
all her household linen out of the estate from first to last . . ." (13).

Thady's descriptions of Lady Murtagh's policies reveal how she
manages to feed her household without expense, relying instead on
feudal "gifts" from her tenants: ". . . duty fowls, and duty turkies, and

duty geese, came as fast as we could eat 'em, for my lady kept a sharp look out" (14). As the landlord grows rich on his tenants' labor, Thady tellingly identifies himself not with the plundered peasants of his own class, but with the gentry household that benefits from the greed of colonial agrarian exploitation. Sir Murtagh's contributions to the bleeding of the tenants include demanding rents on the exact day they are due ("making English tenants of them, every soul"); discouraging the repair of fences so that he can impound stray animals; and calling in his *herriot,* the payment of the tenant's best animal upon the tenant's death. The duty fowl or tribute exacted by Lady Murtagh is more than matched by her husband's abuse of the feudal tradition of duty work, which bound tenants to furnish their landlords with labor and horses for several days a year. By forcing them to use their labor to pay his rents, he prevents them from improving their own holdings.[14]

Like most Rackrents, the childless Sir Murtagh dies suddenly. His widow, a woman with "Scotch blood in her veins" (13), leaves none of her personal wealth in the estate after her husband's death, but instead flees Castle Rackrent with her personal fortune intact. Thady poignantly expresses his own loss and sense of abandonment, but also reiterates the theme of the depleted house: "So the house was quite bare, I had nobody to talk to, and if it had not been for my pipe and tobacco should, I verily believe, have broken my heart for poor Sir Murtagh"(19).

The career of Sir Kit, the next proprietor of Castle Rackrent, ushers in the specter of the absentee landlord that dominates Edgeworth's next two Irish novels. Kit's dissolute career in Bath exemplifies the dangers of absenteeism for Irish tenants. Kit leaves his newly inherited estate after a brief spree of lavish spending that harkens back to

14. Maria Edgeworth's detailed knowledge of the abuses to which the Big House landlord subjected his tenants was based on personal experience. In her contribution to her father's memoirs she describes the appalling conditions Richard Edgeworth found on his estate and the measures he took to remedy them. Edgeworth resolved to collect his rents himself and thus ended the tyranny of the oppressive land agent. Subdivisions were forbidden to protect the land from dangerous overpopulation. The kind of unspoken blackmail the Murtagh Rackrents engaged in was abolished. "He never made any oppressive claims of *duty fowl—of duty work, of man or of beast.* In the old leases made in his father's time, such had been inserted; but he never claimed or would he accept of them, though such were at that time common. He was, I believe, one of the first to abolish them" (1821, 2:15). Through such measures Edgeworth sought to reform and thus to preserve a colonial system of land distribution.

Sir Patrick's days. "A fine life we should have led had he stayed amongst us, God bless him!—he valued a guinea as little as any man—money to him was no more than dirt" (20).

Once Sir Kit is gone, his land is turned over to the worst scourge of the tenant in Irish fiction: the agent or middle man who does the beloved landlord's dirty work for him. The tenants are "fettered" to provide Sir Kit with the money he needs for his life in Bath. Leases are offered to the highest bidder, old tenants turned out, improvements ignored, yet Thady absolves Kit of any blame. "But I laid it all to the fault of the agent; for, says I, what can Sir Kit do with so much cash, and he a single man? but still it went" (21). Kit's solution for his desperate financial state (even his agent resigns in despair) is to marry a rich Jewish heiress, but after harrowing her to sell her diamonds and locking her up for seven years, he dies in a duel. This much abused Lady Rackrent escapes with her jewels and her income, leaving Castle Rackrent in the hands of the new agent, Jason Quirk, Thady's grasping son who oversees the final collapse of the estate.

The darker second half of *Castle Rackrent* concerns Sir Condy, who is for Thady the most sympathetic of the four masters depicted in the novel. Sir Condy's slovenly failure as a landlord and his subsequent loss of the estate are linked by unreliable Thady to his generosity, and even to a kind of Yeatsian exaltation of "the wasteful virtues" that Maria Edgeworth and her father so vigorously opposed as landlords. Thady affirms that Condy is ". . . an easy-hearted man that could disoblige nobody, God Bless him" (44). Like his predecessors, however, Condy marries unwisely, oversees his lands irresponsibly, and dies childless. With his death, in fact, the whole pretense of an aristocratic emphasis on a genealogy of the the Big House collapses; of the four landlords presented in the novel, only Sir Patrick produces an heir.

With his lowly origins, Condy Rackrent differs from his predecessors. Thady tells us that Condy is from a "remote branch" (38) of the family and that he spent his childhood "barefooted and headed, running through the street of O'Shaughlin's town, and playing at pitch and toss, ball, marbles, and what not, with the boys of the town, amongst whom my son Jason was a great favorite with him" (38–39). That Condy seriously considers marriage to Thady's niece, Judy M'Quirk, suggests the last Rackrent's affinity for the peasant class and the apparent genealogical breakdown of the family. His decision to marry a landowner's daughter instead is determined by a drunken toss of a coin, while he proudly disclaims mercantile matrimonial aspirations. Condy's inheritance of the Rackrent estate marks significant genealogical decline in a family purportedly related to the kings of Ireland, and a decline, certainly, from the aristocratic pretenses of the colonial class they have joined. Unable to produce their own children, the Rackrents are forced to turn to remote and plebeian relatives. This theme of the declining patriarchal line is taken up in virtually every later Big House novel, particularly successfully in Edith Somerville's *The Big House of Inver,* in which the decay of a neofeudal family is again accompanied by the rising power of a bourgeois, capitalist line.

Under Condy's disastrous stewardship, Castle Rackrent rapidly deteriorates. Condy and his bride can no longer drive up to the house, for the great piers have tumbled across the front approach. His wife's meager monetary contribution to the estate is spent in turning the barrack room into a theater, but there is no money for candles or turf to light and heat the house. In order to raise cash, Condy signs away the house and land to Jason for next to nothing; he then squanders money on electioneering, and as a member of Parliament maintains an expensive residence in Dublin. Thady's reaction to the departure of the family for Dublin prefigures the final loss of the house and stirs up Chekhovian visions of the old family retainer Fiers, in *The Cherry Orchard,* who is left to die on the abandoned estate. "I was very lonely when the whole family was gone. . . . There was then a great silence in Castle Rackrent, and I went moping from room to room, hearing the doors clap for want of right locks, and the wind through the broken windows that the glazier never would come to mend, and the rain coming through the roof and best ceiling all over the house, for want of the slater whose bill was not paid . . ." (61).

The novel begins with the old servant narrating the tale of his own fall—he is "poor Thady" by the end of the novel—as he witnesses the Rackrents' decline. Thady loses virtually everything he values, not only his beloved masters and his identity as a Rackrent retainer, but his paternal bond to his son as well. He finds nothing to celebrate in his son's victories over the Rackrents, for with Jason's rise comes human loss: "Now I could not bear to hear Jason giving out after this manner against the family, and twenty people standing on the street. Ever since he had lived at the Lodge of his own he looked down,

howsomever, upon poor old Thady, and was grown quite a great gentleman, and had none of his relations near him—no wonder he was
no kinder to Sir Condy than to his own kith and kin"(62).

Again and again, Thady is shocked by his son's tough-mindedness
toward his supposed betters. He objects to Jason's "short and cruel"
riding of the exhausted Condy over his unpaid bills and can finally
control his sorrow no longer: "Oh Jason! Jason! how will you stand to
this in the face of the country, and all who know you, (says I), and
what will people tink and say, when they see you living here in Castle
Rackrent, and the lawful owner turned out of the seat of his ancestors, without a cabin to put his head into, or so much as a potato to
eat?" (77).

By choosing a peasant retainer as her narrator, Edgeworth foregrounds a particular failure of the Big House proprietor who oper-
ated through waning feudal systems. The victims of the Rackrent
inadequacies are made articulate in Thady's voice, a voice that represents more than two hundred years of service. The Rackrents bleed
and betray those who love them most; their weaknesses and inability
to fulfill their responsibilities bring to power the Jasons of the world,
who usher in a new, cold, bourgeois order of efficiency and self-interest. Although Thady begins his tale by telling us that he washes his
hands of his son's doings and will die "true and loyal to the Rackrent
family" (8), he is left with nothing but his memories. The last of the
Rackrents dies dispossessed and, but for Thady, friendless and un-
mourned. Even Thady's niece, Judy M'Quirk, the peasant girl whom
Condy once considered marrying, abandons her old admirer when
she hears that he has lost his estate: "Better luck, any how Thady,
(says she) than to be like some folk following the fortunes of them
that have none left" (92).

Judy's remark reveals that she, unlike the three Rackrent wives,
has escaped the mythologies of power, wealth, and romantic love that
presumably enticed Lady Murtagh, Jessica, and Isabella into their disastrous marriages. In following the fortunes of Jason rather than
Condy, Judy proclaims the death of sentiment in matters of love and
flaunts those categories of behavior and belief (loyalty, subservience,
and submission) that entrapped her uncle, honest Thady, into the
Rackrent ruin. Yet as Anne Weekes points out (1990, passim), the
critically ignored domestic subplot of the novel—the story of
the Rackrent marriages—provides an unexplored source of Edge-

worth's subversive criticism of patriarchal dominance, both in household and in colony. The Rackrent wives, for all their mistakes in choosing husbands, resist becoming docile helpmates or willing victims. Lady Murtagh's insistence on collecting her traditional dues from the tenants drives her husband into a fatal apoplectic fit that releases her (and her money) from his control. Jessica stubbornly refuses to sell her diamond cross and share her wealth with her abusive husband Kit. Isabella, if damaged and scarred by the marital aftermath of her romantic elopement with Condy, manages to escape from his final ruin with the loss of only a small personal inheritance. Although the Rackrent holdings are swallowed up by her husband's improvidence, her family fortune is intact. Moreover, each of these Rackrent wives—harassed, abused, or seduced by attempted male dominance—fails to produce the heir that is contractually her marital obligation and that will ensure the continuation of the Big House line.

The reversal of the traditional marriage plot in *Castle Rackrent* anticipates several twentieth-century Big House novels. Later Anglo-Irish novelists like Somerville and Ross, Molly Keane, or Jennifer Johnston focus on the relationship between waning patriarchal power on the gentry estate and the strategies whereby Big House women, often becoming tyrannical matriarchs themselves, wrest power from improvident or impotent landlords. In twentieth-century fiction by Irish writers looking into the Big House from beyond the walls of the demesne, landlords are, on occasion, portrayed not simply as political and social failures, but as sexually dysfunctional males.[15]

In *Castle Rackrent*, Maria Edgeworth establishes the central characteristics of a literary tradition that survives today. The decaying house, that archetypal image of social decline evoking the irresponsible landlord, reappears in subsequent Big House novels, most recently in works by Aidan Higgins, Jennifer Johnston, John Banville, and Molly Keane. In several of the novels that follow Edgeworth's seminal work—Lever's *The Martins of Cro' Martin* or Edith Somerville's *Mount Music* and *The Big House of Inver*—the antagonist of the

15. See, for example, Padraic Colum's *Castle Conquest* (1923); Sean O'Faolain's "Midsummer Night Madness," published originally in 1932; Liam O'Flaherty's *Famine*, published in 1937, and *Land* (1946); Julia O'Faolain's *No Country For Young Men* (1980).

Big House is, like Jason Quirk, an aspiring land agent or emerging professional who slowly and inexorably displaces the hereditary proprietor. In more recent fiction, in which the Big House has lost its economic and political ascendancy, antagonists make psychological rather than economic assaults on Anglo-Ireland. Edgeworth's portrayal of the retainers in *Castle Rackrent* suggests the ineffectuality of sentiment in preserving outmoded social and economic structures that are presided over by inadequate landlords.

The most accurate commentary on Edgeworth's prescient vision of the doomed colonial system, which she and her father devoted their lives to reforming, emerges not from a literary critic but from the parodic recasting of her themes by the contemporary novelist John Banville. In *Birchwood,* Banville sums up the effect of the landlord's domestic decline on his tenantry: "The first unmended fence will mean the first snigger behind your back outside the chapel yard, an overrun garden will bring them grinning to the gate, and a roof left in visible disrepair will see them poaching your land in daylight"(1984a, 50). Although the forms of an economically or politically moribund feudal relationship seem to retain a genuine emotional content in Thady Quirk and in later characters in several Big House novels, Maria Edgeworth anticipates the course of social history in describing Condy Rackrent's funeral: the Big House is not saved by the sentiment of a loyal tenantry. Thus, in spite of Edgeworth's assertion that her work describes the forgotten practices of a bygone age, *Castle Rackrent* exists in literary history as the first of a series of novels to depict the decline of Edgeworth's own class and the rise of another.

The Landlord in Edgeworth's Later Irish Fiction

The occupants of the Big House in Maria Edgeworth's novels may be of old Irish stock, as in *Castle Rackrent* and *Ennui,* or of Anglo-Irish lineage, as in *The Absentee.* In all of Edgeworth's novels about Irish landlords, those who own the land are deracinated—alienated from or at odds with the proper role of the landlord. In Edgeworth's conservative ideology, the landlord–tenant relationship, which forms the moral basis for Ireland's land tenure system, is disturbed; she attributes such disturbance neither to an active national political movement against the Protestant ascendancy (that was to figure later for her with Daniel O'Connell's campaign for Catholic emancipation) nor to any inherent injustice of a colonial system.

For Edgeworth, only the landlord's personal irresponsibility can account for the social breakdown that she depicts. Such personal failures created far-reaching moral as well as practical costs for Ireland. By identifying the unreformable landlords in *Castle Rackrent,* as well as the more promising protagonist in *Ennui,* as men of Irish rather than of English origin, Edgeworth explicitly attempts to avoid any wide-ranging critique of the colonial system. She thus works carefully to evade the larger historical forces that determined the world she describes. Society will be improved by the correct moral choices of individual men, not by changing political and economic systems that would involve a redistribution of land. Yet, in spite of her efforts in the preface and postscript to deny many of the subversive implications of her novel, Edgeworth wrote *Castle Rackrent* with a grasp of historical inevitability and a perception of class movements that she was never again to achieve. Jason's role in particular suggests so much of the coming class antagonism and struggle that her editorial attempts to set the tale in the past fails utterly to control its predictive powers.

Edgeworth's preoccupation with the costs of absenteeism in two of her Irish novels after *Castle Rackrent* was influenced by a knowledge of her own family history, as well as by her observations in County Longford. Her father's experiences when he returned to Edgeworth House from England, as well as his situation in a county where virtually all large landlords were nonresident (Butler 1972, 115), undoubtedly lie behind her choice of the theme in *The Absentee* and *Ennui.* Absentee owners regarded their estates as a source of capital, not community, and delegated all responsibility to an agent whose success was measured by his ability to produce the most income with the least drain on the owner's profit. Long-term estate improvements and the quality of the tenants' lives were subordinated to the cash demands of the absentee's London or Dublin life. Thus, nineteenth-century Irish fiction is filled with accounts of villainous agents who rackrent tenants, neglect good husbandry, and subdivide the land to increase profits.

In attacking absentee landlords, Edgeworth joins a tradition of writers who observe, with various degrees of indignation, the misuse of Ireland by nonresident landowners. To Jonathan Swift, writing a century earlier, Anglo-Irish absentees (the "Mongril Breed") were rapacious parasites: "But all turn Leasers to that Mongril Breed / who from thee sprung, yet on thy Vitals feed; / Who to yon rav'nous Isle thy Treasures bear, / And waste in Luxury thy Harvests there" (1967, 389). Arthur Young, writing in the second half of the eighteenth century, reports that the landlord's great distance from his tenants isolated him from all complaints, all miseries, and the possibility of remedying evils (1892, 2:116–17). In the nineteenth century, novelists as different as Lady Morgan, Lever, Carleton, and Kickham return again and again to that central theme, most often, like Edgeworth, seizing upon the return of the good landlord and the displacement of the rackrenting agent as the solution to social ills.[16] For all of these writers, as for Edgeworth, the complaint is against the perceived misuse of a colonial system, never against the system itself. The attack on absenteeism even becomes a covert means of defending colonialism; implicit in the attack is the assumption that the resident colonial landlord can become an enlightened estate manager who will bring prosperity to his tenants if he will only return to his true home.

As Carole Fabricant observes, absenteeism is the strongest possible indictment of the mythos of community that lies behind English country house literature.

> The absentee system possesses a very special relevance to the country house ideal—or rather, to the destruction of this ideal. Traditional country house existence presupposes an intimate bond between the estate owner and the soil. Rooted in a vision of warmth, closeness, and community, it assumes a physical propinquity (indeed, actual and continuing physical contact) between the landowner and his ancestral property. . . .
> In contrast, the system of absentee landlordism, as the name itself would suggest, was founded upon *absence*, not presence; upon *distance*, not propinquity. Under this system the relationship between men and their territorial possessions was above all a mediated one; it was characterized by a bureaucratic remoteness and impersonality inimical to

16. See, for example, Lady Morgan's *The Wild Irish Girl*, published in 1806; William Carleton's *Valentine M'Clutchy: The Irish Agent*, published in 1845; Lever's *The Martins of Cro' Martin* (1856); Kickham's *Knocknagow*, published in 1879.

the country house code of hospitality and direct participation in all aspects of domestic economy. (1982, 106)

The widespread use of the absentee landlord as a character in nineteenth-century Irish novels indicates the complex ways by which historical situations are exploited in fiction, not only to register specific contemporary economic abuses, but also, and more obliquely, to mask deeper social pathologies. In Edgeworth's and Lever's fiction, absenteeism becomes an emblem for the landlord's estrangement from his land, for his fractured relationship with his tenant.[17] Thus, in *Ennui* and *The Absentee*, for example, absenteeism becomes a thematic means of studying the landlord's deracination. But already in *Castle Rackrent*, when Kit returns from his dissipations abroad looking like a "skeleton" of himself, Edgeworth succinctly delivers her judgment about the effects on the landlord of abandoning his responsibilities in the homeland. In *Ennui* and *The Absentee*, she explores the costs to the landlord's social position and psyche of willful denial of Irish identity. In these didactic novels, the point of view shifts from that of the loyal retainer, who inadvertently reveals the failures of his landlord, to that of the landlord himself, in the process of discovering his own deracination.

In her later Irish novels, which move in focus from decline and loss to regeneration and reeducation, Edgeworth's moral didacticism marks an aesthetic retreat from the achievement of *Castle Rackrent*. Both *The Absentee* and *Ennui* are filled with long, diagramatically organized sections that contrast corrupt with moral agents and con-

17. Despite the literary popularity of the theme, in *An Economic History of Ireland since 1660,* Cullen notes that absenteeism decreased in the eighteenth century; as a proportion of total rents, rent to absentees fell from one-quarter or one-sixth in the 1720s to one-eighth in the 1770s. Cullen argues that "absentee landlords have been given too much significance in the story of rural Ireland" (1987, 83). His statistics suggest, however, that the literary focus on absenteeism may well represent, not only an effective narrative metaphor for conveying the failures of land policy, but also another strategy for avoiding a more sweeping critique of the colonial land tenure system. Cullen's revisionist historical narrative, when juxtaposed with the literary narrative, suggests how different sorts of texts are needed to gain access to the lived experience of the past. The sustained critique of absenteeism recorded in novels by both Anglo-Irish and native Irish authors emphasizes how the perception of history by those living through it remains a powerful revelatory discourse even when set against seemingly more ascendant facts.

tain implicit exhortations to Irish landlords to oversee their estates by importing rational English agrarian policies. But inherent in these later novels—particularly in *Ennui*—is Edgeworth's ambivalent attitude toward Ireland and her uneasy affection for precisely those traits that she would eliminate. Her ambivalence—or ideological slippage—manifests itself, for example, in the contradictions between her overt belief in the modernization and rationalization of estate management and her covert affection for an older, less rationalized way of life. Her ambivalence appears again in the complicated plot devices she invents to establish the Irish identity of good landlords. Whereas in *Castle Rackrent* the native Irish genealogy of the improvident squires frees her to criticize the landowners' behavior, the Irish ties of her later landlords confer a moral legitimacy on their positions. In *The Absentee,* for example, her Anglo-Irish landlord with a recently acquired union title achieves reconciliation with Ireland— his true home—only when he takes up his responsibilities there and marries a woman whose name, Grace Nugent, suggests her relationship to the Catholic Norman-Irish Jacobite line that his own family has dispossessed.[18] As the following brief plot summary demonstrates, *Ennui* employs even more complicated stratagems to give the seemingly Anglo-Irish landlord the legitimacy conferred by a native Irish identity.

Ennui is a long, rambling tale of an absentee ascendancy landlord, Lord Glenthorn, who leads a purposeless and dissipated life in England. Returning to his Big House in Ireland, he begins to confront his responsibilities; in spite of the difficulties he encounters, he learns to distinguish between effective stewardship and his former neglect of his land. In the novel's melodramatic and largely unassimilated stock ending, he discovers that he is not the genuine Lord Glenthorn, but a changeling, the son of his nurse, who substituted him for the true heir. A nobleman in character if not in blood, he relinquishes his position to the real earl (who has been raised as an Irish peasant) and pursues a career in law. Without the benefit of wealth and position, the former Lord Glenthorn achieves prominence in his new profession. Subsequently—through a highly contrived plot device—he marries a woman who inherits his former

---

18. See McCormack for a full discussion of the implications of Grace Nugent's name (1985, 144–47).

estates after the real Lord Glenthorn begs to relinquish his unwelcome title and position. Thus, most improbably, an Irish peasant, the genealogically false but morally and socially fit heir, is restored to the Big House. Nurture, not nature, determines true nobility.

On occasion, the much maligned *Ennui* provides a rudimentary psychological study of an absentee landlord who is so out of touch with his Irish roots and the real purpose of his life—stewardship of his vast Irish domain—that he is physically impaired by a near suicidal ennui. Although Marilyn Butler praises *Ennui* as one of the best of Edgeworth's Irish tales, inaugurating a new style of social realism, critical readings of the novel have generally been negative.[19] Although *Ennui* is undoubtedly overly didactic and rambling, it suggests a connection between the protagonist's disease and his identity as a man uprooted from his Irish origins. Moreover, the novel's early attention to the healing power of a disorderly and unsocialized country reveals how Edgeworth's ambivalent acknowledgement of the primitive appeal of Irish landscape and society[20] undermines her overt emphasis on the landlord's moral education (according to enlightened English standards).

Ennui begins in England, where we observe the effects of deracination on the fabulously rich Lord Glenthorn. His illness, which is Edgeworth's judgment on his failure of stewardship, is spelled out in rudimentary psychological terms. Glenthorn's ennui is a neurotic "disease" that manifests itself in his "utter abhorrence" of and "incapacity" for voluntary exertion: gaming, gluttony, epicurism, sensual indulgence, and marriage to an heiress all fail to appease Glenthorn, whose personality combines the characteristics of the late nineteenth-century decadent and the twentieth-century depressive.

Only when he meets Ellinor, his old Irish nurse (later revealed to be his real mother), who comes to seek him out in England, does he

19. Harden, for example, suggests that Edgeworth's depictions of Glenthorn represent a "didactic attack upon the sins of boredom and laziness" that is poorly balanced by her literary descriptions of Ireland (1971, 148). Flanagan suggests that much of the novel "is not fiction at all, but an exposition of Lovell Edgeworth's theories of politics, economics, social arrangements, education and morality . . ." (1959, 83).

20. A similar, if less ambivalent, view of the Big House as a retreat from modern decadence appears in Elizabeth Bowen's twentieth-century portrayal of Mount Morris, the Irish estate in *The Heat of the Day* (see chapter 6 of this study).

begin to feel the first stirrings of his eventual cure. Ellinor's appearance on his English estate leads to a nearly fatal accident when Lord Glenthorn's horse shies at the old Irish woman in her red great cloak. Glenthorn's fall, his subsequent illness, and his near death result in a temporary spiritual renewal, which unleashes a new source of vitality. Although he is knocked senseless and almost brought to death by Ellinor's arrival, his eyes are opened to the treachery of his English servants and to his wife's infidelity. Ellinor speaks to him as no one has ever spoken to him before; her unpolished sincerity and awkward want of propriety delight him.

> When she sat up with me at nights, she talked on eternally; for she assured me there was nothing like talking, as she had found, to put one *asy asleep.* I listened or not, just as I like; *any way* she was *contint.* She was inexhaustible in her anecdotes of my ancestors, all tending to the honour and glory of the family; she had also an excellent memory for all the insults or traditions of insults which the Glenthorns had received for many ages back, even to the times of the old kings of Ireland; long and long before they stooped to be *lorded;* when their "names, which it was a pity and murder, and moreover a burning shame, to change, was O'Shaughnesee." (1992, 160)

Ellinor reveals that the Glenthorns (like the Rackrents) are of old Irish stock and can trace their heritage to the Gaelic kings of Ireland. As she nurses the seemingly dying Lord Glenthorn, she gathers symbolic resonances. Ellinor is the strange Irish hag on the English estate of a powerful landowner, but she also evokes the *Shan Van Vocht,* the traditional female personification of Irish sovereignty. In her talks with Glenthorn she suggests that he has lost power and position by deserting his native land and his true home. She tells him that in Ireland he would be no mere landlord, but a feudal lord with possession of vast territories and with tenants who were his vassals. "I was only a lord, as she said, in England; but I could be all as one as a king in Ireland" (160).

The issues of power and powerlessness loom large in Edgeworth's fiction about landlords. Kit Rackrent returns from England looking like a man near death, a skeleton of himself. In *The Absentee,* the Irish landlord and his wife are the laughingstock of London society: Lord Clonbrony surrounds himself with his social inferiors in order to simulate a sense of self-respect, while his wife humiliates herself and her son in her fruitless search for acceptance from the fashionable London society that mocks her efforts to disguise her Irish roots. In *Ennui,* Lord Glenthorn suffers from a debilitating psychic illness while he resides on his vast estates in England. The fabulously rich young man agonizes in the grip of his ennui and depression. Immediately after Ellinor tells him of his feudal powers in Ireland, he loses his young wife (his potency?) to his unscrupulous English steward. Edgeworth's description of the physical and psychic costs of deracination suggest her sense of the unacknowledged power of Irish identity for the absentee landlord.

For Edgeworth, the Big House in Ireland embodies a different pattern of meaning from that of the English country estate. Like Marilyn Butler, who emphasizes Edgeworth's neoclassical aesthetic authorities (1972, 67), Norman Jeffares argues that her classical attitudes toward landscape generally lead her to stress its "practical" and "utilitarian" qualities rather than its emotional resonances (1975, 17). However, in her Irish novels, Edgeworth writes with more affinity for late eighteenth-century Irish antiquarianism and a gothic romanticism than Jeffares or Butler acknowledge. In *Ennui,* the descriptions of Lord Glenthorn's two properties—Sherwood Park in England and Glenthorn Castle in the west of Ireland—reveal the power of an Irish identity for the landlord. Sherwood Park, in its tasteful merger of nature and art, recalls Jane Austen's Pemberley, the great house in *Pride and Prejudice* that is the embodiment of an easy coexistence between social man and the natural world. Yet the very tastefulness of Sherwood Park, the cultivation of nature expressed by the estate and its demesne, becomes an attack on absenteeism, for Lord Glenthorn's ennui is only intensified by the perfection of his English holdings. The formality of the park and the artistic expression it evokes (a traditional ode) plunges its owner into a deeper ennui.

> Sherwood Park, my English country seat, had but one fault, it was completely finished. The house was magnificent, and in the modern taste; the furniture fashionably elegant, and in all, the gloss of novelty. Not a single novelty omitted; not a fault could be found by the most fastidious critic. My park, my grounds displayed all the beauties of nature and of art, judiciously combined. Majestic woods waving their dark foliage, overhanging—But I will spare my reader the description, for I remember falling asleep myself whilst a poet was reading to me an ode on the beauties of Sherwood Park. (1992, 145)

The savage splendor of Glenthorn Castle, his Irish holding, which he first sees as it emerges from behind a promontory of rock, suggests a more primitive set of values, a substitution of the romantic vision for the neoclassical. "It seemed to rise from the sea, abrupt and insulated, in all the gloomy grandeur of ancient times, with turret and battlements, and a huge gateway, the pointed arch of which receded in perspective between the projecting towers" (177).

Glenthorn's arrival at his castle underscores the medieval setting of Ireland. "These people seemed 'born for my use': the officious precipitation with which they ran to and fro; the style in which they addressed me; some crying 'Long Live the Earl of Glenthorn!' some blessing for me for coming to reign over them: all together gave more the idea of vassals than of tenants, and carried my imagination centuries back to feudal times" (178). The gothic description of the Big House, a vast, gloomy castle hovering against the western coast with "an air of savage wildness" (179), suggests a deep and repressed source of power in the Irish landscape—this in spite of Butler's assertion that neither Maria nor her father held "any brief for primitivism" (1972, 59). Upon arriving at his ancestral home, Glenthorn muses about his literary response to his ancient estate: ". . . if I had not been too much fatigued to think of anything, I should certainly have thought of Mrs. Radcliffe" (Edgeworth 1992, 179). Yet the insomnia that plagued his civilized life disappears, and in Ireland he falls into a profound and restorative sleep. Like the Black Islands in *Ormond*—a primitive western setting that exists as the regressive site of childhood romance—Glenthorn Castle emerges as an object of desire in *Ennui.*

But gothic romance is accompanied by chaotic disorder for the landlord. In Ireland, in a scene modeled on Richard Edgeworth's experiences upon returning to his estate in Ireland, Glenthorn is overwhelmed by crowds of petitioners begging for favors. He discovers that he is no longer a man with a will of his own or with time at his disposal; he ends the day exhausted but exhilarated by the enormous power he seems to wield. Suddenly involved in the day-to-day operation of his vast holdings—and expressing a true Edgeworthian utility—he finds himself, "a man who had never looked into an account," jealously settling the affairs of his estate with his agent "without a yawn of boredom" (183).

Edgeworth's critique of Irish peasant society as slovenly, and in need of the training that she and her father advocated, significantly mediates the covert symbolic implications of her gothic evocation of Glenthorn Castle. Nevertheless, her juxtaposition of the descriptions of the English and Irish country houses foregrounds not the cultivated taste of Sherwood Park, but rather its effeteness, overrefinement, and tedium. Moreover, in her vision of the anachronistic survival of a neo-feudal fealty of vassal to lord, she comes close to dramatizing the lost ideal of a feudal community that underlies the Big House tradition, an ideal that she subverts so powerfully in *Castle Rackrent.* Glenthorn's servants in England, insistent on their rights and privileges, are the product of a society beginning to deal in contracts and capital exchange. In Ireland he encounters another kind of domestic: feudal retainers rather than hired servants. Although his Irish tenants and domestics can be manipulative and childlike, and after the troubles of 1798 a few engage in conspiracy against the Big House, they are always depicted as being personally involved with the ancient Glenthorn line. Unlike an English servant at Sherwood Park who refuses to comply with a request unless it is written into his contract, the Irish servants at Glenthorn Castle respond to a master rather than to an employer.[21]

An unacknowledged contrast between Irish romantic primitivism and English effeteness—as embodied in the descriptions of Glenthorn's two estates—lies covertly beneath Edgeworth's themes of moral education. The Big House in Ireland is the scene, not of decadence (a sin of civilized England), but of a potential disorder, of a dissoluteness arising as the anxious colonist envisions the intermingling two cultures. The apparent disorder of Irish society becomes, for example, an invigorating stimulus for the jaded, deracinated hero of *Ennui*—primarily because it creates an opportunity for self-exertion, but also because it reveals a more vigorous life that lacks the social restraints and refinements of cultivated England. One of the more interesting questions inherent in any literary study of the

21. In *The Martins of Cro' Martin,* written forty-seven years after *Ennui,* when Charles Lever describes the worship of a young Big House mistress by tenants on an isolated estate in the west of Ireland, the Big House novel again dramatizes the lost feudal bond to the "chief" rather than to the Anglo-Irish landlord (Lever 1895, 2:309). Still later, writing memoir rather than fiction in the early twentieth century, Violet Martin envisions the nineteenth-century tenants on her family estate as satisfied with a patriarchal "Master" who rules them through intimacy and affection (Somerville and Ross 1918, 4). Such longing re-creations of idealized feudal relationships suggest the ways in which Big House novelists occasionally do seek to appropriate a vision of an ancient (i.e., precolonial) legitimacy.

Big House lies in the connection between disorder and energizing vitality—both of which are represented in *Ennui* by the native Irish scene and society. But if Ireland invigorates the overcivilized and decadent Englishman in Edgeworth's novel, its transgressive energies also threaten the "civilized values" of England and can lead to corruption, ruin, and decay. Writing more than a century after the publication of *Ennui*, Edith Somerville, in *The Big House of Inver*, turns again to the disorderly commingling of native and Big House cultures in Ireland.

In *Ennui*, as in all of Edgeworth's Irish fiction after *Castle Rackrent*, any appeals to the transgressive elements in the native culture—to the irrational or the disorderly—are contradicted and undone by the larger didactic framework of the novel. Glenthorn's confrontation with Ireland brings him only temporary relief from his ennui; he is again overcome by boredom and depression once he has quelled the domestic uprising following the 1798 Rising. In another attempt to overcome his depression, he embarks on a tour of Ireland's major scenic sites, the Giant's Causeway and the lakes of Killarney. In these scenes, for which Edgeworth used a travel book to describe tourist sites she herself had never visited, she mocks the notion that magnificent scenery will cure the vacuity of an uninformed or undisciplined mind. At the Giant's Causeway, Glenthrorn is seized with a fit of yawning; at Killarney he wishes himself quietly asleep in his castle until he is revived by the savage novelty of a brutal stag hunt: "The sublime and the beautiful had no charms for me: novelty was the only power, that could waken me from my lethargy" (252).

The strange or exotic charge of Irish culture for the English sensibility is underscored in Edgeworth's Irish fiction most frequently for its comic potential. In *The Absentee*, Colambre steps out of his ship onto his "mother earth" and finds himself "surrounded and attacked by a swarm of beggars and harpies, with strange figures and stranger tones" (1988, 80). In *Ennui*, Glenthorn travels into a bedlam world where passengers are expected to ride in a coach "in a most deplorable and crazy state; the body mounted up to a prodigious height, on unbending springs, nodding forward, one door swinging open, three blinds up, because they could not be let down, the perch tied in two places, the iron of the wheel half off, wooden pegs for linch pins, and ropes for harness" (1992, 171).

Her sense of Ireland as the "other place," the savage and disorderly land that resists the civilizing forces of English reason and good sense, allows Edgeworth to develop her didactic ideology of colonial rule. In *Ennui* that didacticism expresses itself in a plot illustrating the moral education of the landlord; Glenthorn must curb his undisciplined desire to express seemingly unlimited feudal powers through easy gestures of largess, which reward lazy supplicating tenants at the expense of the industrious. After many errors of judgment, he begins to follow the advice of his austere Scotch agent, Mr. M'Leod, and to apply Edgeworthian principles of responsible estate management to his holdings. The domestic arrangements of M'Leod's estate impress him with "such an air of neatness and comfort, order and activity" that he thinks himself in England again. "How could all this be brought about in Ireland!"(215) The sight of M'Leod's woodbine-covered cottages and neat gardens (and an interdenominational school modeled on the one in Edgeworthstown) inspires Glenthorn to praise a "Paradise amid the wild" (215).

Ennui's insistent didacticism in the service of a rationalized colonial system of estate planning deflects attention from the novel's evocation of the phantasmagoric world of Ireland. With its emphasis on the decaying family house and the dissipations of generation after generation of a family line, *Castle Rackrent* can be seen as a type of gothic fiction. But even in the later novels, written after union and thus more consciously concerned to persuade the English reading public of the Irish landlord's moral improvement, Edgeworth still uses gothic motifs to express her ambivalent recognition of the subversive power inherent in disorder and eccentricity. Julian Moynahan's observations seem particularly relevant to *Ennui,* in which Edgeworth's occasional use of the gothic mode undermines her moral thesis. "Gothic literature often carries a heavy political or metapolitical charge. The Gothic seems to flourish in disrupted societies, to give a voice to the powerless and unenfranchised, and even at times to *subvert or contradict the overt best intentions of the author*" (1982, 44; emphasis mine).

In *Ennui,* the most memorable reminder of Ireland's resistance to alien civilizing forces occurs when Glenthorn attempts to build his foster mother a slate-roofed English cottage to replace her smoke-filled peasant hovel. To his chagrin, the house decays rapidly, partly because of the inability of the Irish workmen to construct it properly, but also because of Ellinor's domestic disorder and her desire for a smoky turf-thatched home. Glenthorn reacts with rage to Ellinor's dissatisfaction with his gift; he reproaches her as "a savage, an Irish-woman, and an ungrateful fool" (1992, 200)—presumably synonymous terms for him. Her response, however, shames him into compliance with her wish to live in a thatched Irish hut rather than an English cottage. " 'Savage I am, for anything I know; and *fool* I am, that's certain; but ungrateful I am not,' said she, bursting into tears. She went home and took to her bed; and the next thing I heard from her son was, 'that she was *lying in the rheumatism,* which had kept her awake many a long night, before she would come to complain to my honour of the house' " (200).

Glenthorn's capitulation to Ellinor is accompanied by recognition that his own standards of comfort are inappropriate for an Irish countrywoman. Behind his newly awakened sense of cultural differences lies a certainty of the higher values of his own standards and a perception of Ellinor's habits as simply the product of her insufficiently advanced civilization. Certainly, he cannot recognize that the dung heap in front of her home and her smoke-filled thatched hut where animals and humans cohabit are more rational responses to the conditions of her life than is his gift of a slated-roofed English cottage.[22] As a student of the austere M'Leod, he resolves to control his benevolent but irrational impulses to transform the Irish. "In the impatience of my zeal for improvement, I expected to do the work of two hundred years in a few months . . . " (200). The didactic point of the scene is clear: The "civilizing" of the native Irish will proceed slowly, and the wise Big House landlord must adapt to the native's developmental pace or risk failure. The emotional dynamics of the scene between Ellinor and Glenthorn, however, suggest something quite different. Above all, Glenthorn is shamed by his anger toward Ellinor. In spite of the scene's didactic framework, which insists on the validity of English values of order and tidiness, Edgeworth valorizes the affect of Ellinor's life, even as she is depicted as disorderly

22. Glenthorn's urge to reform Irish sloth and inefficiency ominously anticipates a similar reading of those traits thirty-three years later by the British government during the Famine. Economic historian Kevin Whelan points out, for example, that in rural Ireland "the dung heap beside the door was not, as casual observers all too frequently asserted, a symbol of indolent slatternliness, but of persevering industry" (1996b, 12). According to Whelan, British opinion about Ireland during the Famine expressed "the utopian ideal of the *tabula rasa*—a clean Irish slate on which the new English values could be legibly inscribed, deleting the chaotic scrawl which the Irish has scribbled all over their dishevelled landscape" (57).

and slovenly. When Glenthorn hears that Ellinor lies suffering from rheumatism that she contracted in the uncongenial cottage he built for her, he accepts his mistake and is reconciled to her. "I let her take her own way, and thatch the house, and have as much smoke as she pleased, and she recovered" (200). The reader's response to Glenthorn's moral education, in which he learns to sympathize with the needs of an Irish countrywoman and to feel ashamed of his own anger, diminishes the effect of his priggish colonial superiority.[23]

The characterization of Ellinor as a loving peasant woman tragically estranged from her own son, who has been raised as an aristocratic landlord, is, as Marilyn Butler recognizes, one of Edgeworth's major achievements in the novel. "Ellinor is something rare and perhaps new in literature, a peasant character who is treated with respect"(Butler 1972, 371). Uneducated and—in legal English terms— amoral in her insistence that Glenthorn keep his title after she reveals that he is her son, Ellinor is nevertheless presented without any condescension—and with significant complexity. Unlike Thady, who never comprehends the implications of what he tells, Ellinor understands only too well the barrier she has created between herself and her son. When Glenthorn insists, against her remonstrances, on renouncing his title after he learns the truth of his parentage, she simply wills herself to die, rather than live with the burden of estrangement from her son.

For all her faith in the power of benevolent English standards of stewardship, Edgeworth cannot quite manage to end *Ennui* with the fully satisfying vision of Glenthorn Castle ruled by an improved landlord whose genealogical deficiencies are more than balanced by the moral superiorities of his reformed character. The ending of *Ennui*, in which Lord Glenthorn discovers that he is not a real earl, but a changeling, allows Edgeworth to return with renewed didacticism to

23. In *Their Fathers' Daughters*, Beth Kowalski-Wallace emphasizes Edgeworth's depiction of the maternal body through images of dirt, disorder, and farmyard beasts. In this reading Ellinor emerges as the representative Irish mother whose appeal must be rejected by her new style colonial son. "In summary, she is at once the displaced image of Lord Glenthorn's repressed corporeality and his own 'nature.' At the same time, she is the embodiment of Ireland, the representation of what he must learn to subordinate and control through the careful practices of new-style patriarchy" (1991, 164). By foregrounding Ellinor's comic but dangerous bestiality this reading supports Edgeworth's overt didactic theme in *Ennui*, but it allows the character significantly less dignity than I find in her.

her father's emphasis on nurture over nature. The blacksmith's praise of his foster brother's selflessness in renouncing his position touches the heart of Edgeworth's belief in moral education: "Any man, you see, may be made a lord; but a gentleman, a man must make himself" (1992, 290). The former Lord Glenthorn, upon learning that his mother had exchanged him for the genuine heir, abdicates his title and wealth and undergoes a period of moral growth in relative (middle-class) poverty. Finally, he becomes the model hero— just, benevolent, self-educated, and hard-working—and marries an heiress who will conveniently (and improbably) restore his property to him. In theory, his new tenure as landlord should represent the perfect assimilation of Edgeworth's ideal English character traits into an Irish setting.

But Ellinor's treatment of her English cottage foreshadows the final destruction of the Big House at the hands of the family of Christy O'Donoghoe, the authentic Lord Glenthorn who was raised as Ellinor's son. Glenthorn Castle is destroyed when a disorderly peasant culture is corrupted by the wealth of the Big House. Christy's wife, emboldened by Rackrenty pretensions of being related to the old kings of Ireland, squanders and wastes her new wealth. M'Leod reports on the "melancholy and disgusting . . . scene of waste, riot, and intemperance" (309) occurring at the castle under the new stewardship of the O'Donoghoe family. Christy cannot contain his wife and son, who prodigally riot and deplete the resources of the estate. Finally, the Big House is consumed by flames ignited by "peasant" behavior: Christy's son drunkenly falls asleep with a lit candle in an antique mansion filled, not with the mud of the peasant hovel, but with old wood and draperies. Having lost his wastrel son in the conflagration, the real Lord Glenthorn (Christy O'Donoghoe) relinquishes his title and retreats in despair to his blacksmith forge. Nurture prevails over nature.

More than a century after Edgeworth wrote *Ennui*, scores of Irish Big Houses were destroyed by fires lit by hostile Irishmen. Edgeworth's occasional depictions of the power of the native culture—capable, for example, of wrecking an English-style cottage and torching a feudal Big House—account for some of the anxious fictional contrivances and evasions with which she attempts to legitimize her campaign for enlightened resident landlords. As Maurice Colgan suggests, her efforts in *Ennui* to suggest that the "good" landlord can be from Irish peasant stock so long as he displays the proper English virtues simply obscures the realities of colonial policy in eighteenth-century Ireland (1982, 37).

In some of her most interesting moments as a writer, however, often unassimilated moments that work against the didacticism of her position as a spokesman for enlightened English systems of land tenure and for the effect of nurture (in the form of rational self-help) over nature, Edgeworth imaginatively acknowledges the subversive power and moral economy of the culture she plans to reform. But any acknowledgment of such power is carefully masked. As *Ennui* ends, the former Lord Glenthorn, reformed into the model estate owner through his own efforts and the inheritance of his new wife, plans to rebuild his Big House and, presumably, usher in a period of responsible and benevolent landlordism. However, this peasant who was raised as an earl does manage to shed his real name—the uncomfortably Irish O'Donoghoe—and take on the more acceptable Anglo-Norman name, Delamere, of his new wife. If Irish origins can be reformed and refined out of social and moral conduct, then all reminders of them had best be destroyed. Edgeworth does not tell us in what architectural style the new Big House will be built, but we can conjecture that the savage splendor and "gloomy grandeur . . . with turret and battlements" of the old feudal castle will be replaced by a more practical and efficient structure in the mode of her father's utilitarian ideals.

The plot of Edgeworth's last Irish novel traces the moral development of a future Irish landlord and reveals her most successful mastery of a didactic and schematic narrative; however, the conclusion of that work reveals her continuing ambivalence about Ireland. *Ormond* posits various directions for a young man, each embodied in a mode of life represented by a different Big House. Three establishments are presided over by distinctive landlords, each of whom is judged by his domestic life and by his governance of his dependents. Ormond's uncle and guardian, Sir Ulick O'Shane, an apostate Catholic, is a politically shrewd jobber and courtier who holds a Parliamentary seat and a peerage. As a landlord, he favors and protects his own tenants and winks at their crimes so long as they pay his rent. Irascible, good-natured, and calculating, Sir Ulick fills the ironically named Castle Hermitage with the society he needs in order to advance politically—and with the heavy drinking, marital friction, and extravagance that result from such socializing. His fall from wealth brings down a bank and plunges others into poverty; at his sparsely attended funeral, his servants—hired help rather than feudal retainers—wear only the conventional face of grief.

In his laxity as a landlord and his easy disinclination to live by moral codes, Ulick is significantly different from his cousin Corny O'Shane, who rules his isolated "kingdom" and Big House on the Black Islands as a Gaelic chieftain, isolated from Ulick's Anglo-Irish politics. But, although he lives without Sir Ulick's persistent calculus of self-interest, Corny, too, embodies the wasteful virtues; thus, he welcomes young Ormond to Black Island with a "six-oared boat, streamers flying, and piper playing . . . ," a twelve-gun salute, and a horse decked with ribbons (44–45). In Corny's house, a magnificent drawing room with painted ceilings and a marble chimneypiece is alternately used as a granary, barn, storage room, and hospital; meals are served with "profusion and carelessness" (46); and his crowds of retainers are treated with more kindness and openness than are those at Versailles. "King" Corny is a feudal figure, uncalculating and excessive—an anachronistic, heavy-drinking chieftain whose charms seduce the young Ormond before he begins to use his reason.

Corny operates in the novel as a child's dream hero, "the most warm-hearted man on earth" (44). His towering rages, arcane knowledge of herbal medicine, and skill with boats, guns, and fishing tackle—as well as his more eccentric ability to make a violin, cobble a pair of shoes, or knit a stocking—make him a "personage" for young admirers. Only when he becomes a man does Ormond begin to recognize the price of Corny's stubborn isolation from the modern world and to question the wisdom of his choices. Having "seen and compared Corny's violin with other violins, and having discovered that so much better could be had for money" (58), Ormond moves from the world of romance to the world of Edgeworthian utility in his changing attitudes toward his former hero. Nevertheless, Corny's firm adherence to codes of honor and loyal generosity bring him a feudal devotion. The death of this natural aristocrat draws crowds to his wake; his funeral mass is attended by thirteen priests; and his burial is accompanied by the cries of a concourse of mourners.

The third landlord in *Ormond,* the bloodless and tubercular young Herbert Annaly, exists as an ideal figure, probably inspired by Richard Lovell Edgeworth, who was dying as his daughter wrote the novel. Sir Ulick's good-natured and irascible dishonesty is in striking contrast with the rational estate governance of the English-educated Annaly, whose seaside land adjoining Sir Ulick's is populated by reformed tenants. Whereas Urlick's tenants are an "idle, profligate, desperate set of people" (274) who hang out false lights to encourage the shipwrecks they live off and who lie shamelessly to Ormond about their thievery, Annaly encourages his tenants to build a lighthouse and become law-abiding citizens. Valuing "justice more than generosity" (276), Annaly teaches the young Ormond that a landlord must administer his estate "neither by threats, punishments, abuse, nor tyranny; nor yet . . . by promises nor bribery favour and protection, like Sir Ulick" (275). Annaly's private funeral lacks all display and is praised for its absence of "vain pageantry" (306). "No pomp of funeral was, indeed, necessary for such a person. The great may need it; the good need it not" (306). With such a remark, the narrator foregrounds Annaly's resistance to the Irish world of emotional excess—and to a society that honors its dead with a public display of mourning. Annaly's moral superiority is thus equated with his distance, even in death, from native Irish custom.[24]

Ormond's inevitable choice of Annaly as his mentor marks the culmination of the hero's moral development and indicates his acceptance of responsible stewardship. However, Edgeworth undermines the apparent symmetry of Ormond's choice (Annaly over Ulick or Corny) as well as her own didactic theme by having her young hero purchase Corny's Black Islands as the site of his future home. Ormond's choice of the Black Islands is dictated by senti-

---

24. The differences between Annaly's and Corny's funerals become even more significant when we recall Edgeworth's remarks about traditional Irish rituals. Edgeworth specifically criticizes the Irish wake and funeral in her long glossary notes in *Castle Rackrent*. She emphasizes the degeneration of early customs and ceremonies into occasions of "profligacy and drunkenness." "To attend a neighbor's funeral is a cheap proof of humanity" (1980, 102). The old Irish wakes, according to Edgeworth, have been perverted into "orgies of unholy joy" (113). Her inclusion of her father's directions about his own funeral in the *Memoirs* further suggests the Edgeworths' resistance to Irish "excess." Richard Lovell Edgeworth desired to "be buried in as private a manner, and at as little expense as possible." "I have always endeavoured to discountenance the desire, which the people of this country have for expensive funerals. I would have neither velvet, nor plate, nor gilding employed in making my coffin, which I would have carried to the grave, without a hearse, by my own laborers." His daughter reports: "His orders were obeyed." She tells us that at his funeral there was "the most respectful and profound silence" (1821, 2:251).

ment, not reason: "For the Black Islands he had a fondness; they were associated with all the tender recollections of his generous benefactor." As "King" Corny's successor, Ormond plans to bring civilization to the islanders, who worship him as their former ruler's "lawful representative . . . and actually offered up prayers for his coming again to reign over them" (399). But the possibility of modern and utilitarian estate management, governed by Annaly's principles of justice rather than Corny's impetuous generousity, seems remote indeed from such a setting. Corny's kingdom—evoked by images of medieval pageantry, feudal bonding, and childhood romance—operates in much of the novel as a regressive world of the past, to be cherished but abandoned by the adult hero.

Thus, *Ormond* ends in contradiction—with a vision of the future bound up with the past: of a feudal Big House in the Black Islands governed by a reformed Edgeworthian landlord. The novel's conclusion embodies the ambivalence and indeterminacy that complicate Maria Edgeworth's relationship with Ireland. Whereas in the preface and postscript of her first Irish novel, she tells us that she has created an old feudal family—the Rackrent/O'Shaughlins—to embody the past corruptions she and her father sought to eradicate, *Ormond* ends with the future Edgeworthian landlord retreating back, as it were, into the primitive world of Patrick Rackrent and his retainers. For all of her didactic commitment to a new, enlightened colonialism presided over by reformed landlords in the English mode, Maria Edgeworth's Big House fiction, like that of so many of her successors, is haunted by the ungovernable world outside the walls of the demesne.

Social Dissonance in
Charles Lever's Novels

Wise stewardship of the Big House is the moral touchstone of Maria Edgeworth's Irish novels. The decaying house signals the improvidence of the landlord; the abandoned estate suggests the absentee's loss of identity. The tension between fear and longing in Edgeworth's Irish fiction—between her depiction of a regressive nation and her covert sympathy for its disorders—culminates in silence. Edgeworth could continue to write novels about Ireland only so long as she could assume the permanence of a world in which her father's program of estate reform would be carried out by the Anglo-Irish ascendancy. With the beginning of organized Catholic opposition to Protestant domination of Ireland, her vision of a humane and enlightened ruling class governing its tenants with benevolent firmness became untenable as the didactic goal of her fiction. The election of 1832, in which Edgeworthstown tenants voted against the Big House candidate, was a source of sorrow and disillusionment to her. Puzzled and alienated by the new Ireland ushered in by Daniel O'Connell's Catholic emancipation movement, Edgeworth ceased writing fiction about a country she now regarded as distorted and feverish, driven by passions she could no longer bear to contemplate. On Febuary 14, 1834, she wrote to Michael Pakenham Edgeworth: "It is impossible to draw Ireland as she now is in a book of fiction—realities are too strong, party passions too violent to bear to see, or care to look at their faces in the looking-glass. The people would only break the glass, and curse the fool who held the mirror up to nature—distorted nature, in a fever. We are in too perilous a case to laugh, humour would be out of season, worse than bad taste" (quoted in Butler 1972, 452).

Edgeworth's admiring disciple, Charles Lever, however, chose the turbulent political climate of O'Connell's Ireland as the center of a major Big House novel, *The Martins of Cro' Martin*. In essence, his novelistic subject in that work is the very social dissonance that Edgeworth sought—particularly after *Castle Rackrent*—to mask or ignore. A novelist from the Protestant middle class, Lever was fascinated by the ways in which social change emerged from political realignments and pressures. With a father who was a prosperous English-born builder/architect married to a descendant of a Cromwellian planter family, Lever was raised not within the world of the landed ascendancy but among prosperous Dublin Protestant merchant and professional families. As a young man he studied and practiced medicine and then turned to journalism and finally to novel writing as a profession. In 1845, attacked by Tories and Nationalists alike, Lever began a self-imposed exile. He left Ireland to escape the political factionalism in which he found himself embroiled, both as editor of the *Dublin University Review* and as author of popular novels of military life. Once abroad, Lever turned with greater and greater seriousness to the urgent political and social problems of Ireland.[1]

1. Lever occupies an uneasy position in the world of Irish letters; although he was once viewed as a rival of Dickens, his novels are now unread and out of print. His early comic fiction—for example, *The Confessions of Harry Lorrequer*, published in 1837; *Charles O'Malley, The Irish Dragoon*, published in 1841; and *Jack Hinton*, published in 1843—established his reputation as a light-hearted recorder of Anglo-Irish military high life. His later works, written after he left Ireland for a life of self-imposed exile, were largely ignored by his critics, who gave little evidence of having read them. Lever was attacked, on the evidence of his early novels, by a long list of distinguished critics: by Carleton for "bearing false witness against his country" (1843, 826); by Duffy for basing his characters on other literary texts rather than on reality (1843, 554); by Yeats (1979, 25–26) and by E. A. Boyd (1922, 73) for using the Irish for comic relief; and by Corkery (1966, 10) for writing colonial literature. Although conceding that in *The Martins of Cro' Martin* the novelist "seems to be fumbling toward a subject which might engage his feelings," in *The Irish Novelists* Flanagan calls Lever's novels "travesties" and excludes them from his seminal study of nineteenth-century Irish fiction (1959, 46). Even a less-hostile critic such as Gwynn dismisses Lever's significant later works as having value only because of his sympathy for a doomed and picturesque landlord class (1936, 79). For the most part Lever has been passed over as a serious novelist; unlike several lesser figures, his work was omitted from the Garland reprint series of nineteenth-century Irish fiction.

Signs of a critical reappraisal are evident, however, in a series of articles in which critics turn to his middle and later Irish novels for their somber depictions of the political and social complexities of nineteenth-century Ireland (Meredith 1977; Jeffares

An acute political observer of changes destroying traditional patterns of rural life, Lever wrote without Maria Edgeworth's earlier optimism about the survival of the landowning class. The novels he published after he left Ireland openly confront anxieties and contradictions implicit in Edgeworth's earlier Irish fiction, anxieties which are overpowered by her didactic emphasis on the landlord's reform. In spite of his roots in middle-class Protestant Dublin society, Lever's deepest loyalties lay with the conservative pieties of a feudal land tenure system that Edgeworth satirized in *Castle Rackrent* and celebrated only obliquely, in moments that contradicted her dominant didactic themes. Even in a relatively early novel like *The O'Donoghue* (1845), middle-class Lever portrayed the remnants of a doomed, improvident, and backward-looking Gaelic order with significant sympathy. The novel depicts an older society as it is being engulfed by a new cash-driven world of rationalized land tenure—a flawed version of the new enlightened colonialism that Maria Edgeworth and her father sought for Ireland. But Lever's political conservatism is seriously undermined, and by his last novel, *Lord Kilgobben*, virtually dislodged by his understanding of those historical forces that will bring progress and change.

Lever was torn between impulses that led him to write longingly of a feudal dispensation between landlord and tenant and his acute po-

---

1975a; Rix 1982). Norman Jeffares, especially, claims Lever as a major novelist who, as he wrote his thirty-three novels, moved "toward a detached impartiality" in his portrayal of Irish political life, a detachment that culminates, for Jeffares, in his last and greatest novel, *Lord Kilgobbin* (Jeffares 1975a, 48). But the debate over Lever continues. Flanagan's chapter on nineteenth-century Irish literature in *A New History of Ireland* offers a reappraisal of Lever as a "genuine novelist of Victorian Ireland," who produced "the least provincial of nineteenth-century Irish novels" (1989, 493–94). In *Ascendancy and Tradition,* McCormack argues that the picaresque English heroes in Lever's early fiction demonstrate the failure of union between two countries rather than patronizing ascendancy attitudes toward Ireland (1985, 200). Christopher Morash provides a thoughtful historical analysis of Lever's critical fate. He suggests that the novelist's gloomy depiction of post-Famine Ireland threatened English readers, particularly because Lever focused "on one of the visible pillars of the social order in both England and Ireland—the country house" (Morash 1992, 63). However, in a recent collection of essays on the Big House theme, Lever is once again summarily dismissed by a critic who relies on superannuated critical generalities. "Following Maria Edgeworth, Charles Lever and Samuel Lover gave a somewhat inferior picture of the Big House since they rarely resisted the temptation of stage-Irishness in their characterization" (Fehlmann 1991, 16).

litical sense of change and disorder in a country where he saw feudal pieties exploited and abused by the colonial system. His shifting attitudes toward his subject matter are often as compelling as the stories he tells. Buffeted between conflicting impulses—one leading back into an imagined past, the other resolutely forward-looking—he was unable to suggest any solutions for the disordered social system depicted in his fiction. Writing about Ireland from self-exile in Europe between 1845 and 1872, Lever created a body of work that, for all the ponderousness of his Victorian plots, conveys the despair, irresolution, and social dislocation so familiar to a modern sensibility.

The range of Lever's oeuvre and the ambivalence of his tone support Frederic Jameson's argument that the Irish colonial experience constituted an exceptional situation, one in which incommensurable realities—the world of the colonizer and the colonized, the lord and the bondsman, the metropolitan center and the colony— overlapped and created a distinctive sensibility that culminated, for Jameson, in the central modernist text, Joyce's *Ulysses* (1988, 19–20). Lever's recurring subject was a colony of the imperial center, but a colony whose otherness was disconcertingly like *and* different from England. His novels are written, like Edgeworth's postunion Irish fiction, with a growing sense of Ireland's role beyond its island borders. Thus, the range of experience in his fiction is sweeping—embracing both provincial Ireland and cosmopolitan Europe. The settings incorporate what we would now term both First and Third World conditions: splendid great houses, crumbling castles, and peasant hovels; bailiffs and agents; young men educated at Trinity, Cambridge, or Oxford; poverty-stricken peasants; emerging middle-class merchants; politicians at Dublin Castle; chieftains in decaying castles; rebels in the mountains; and absentee landowners in Paris. These political novels, firmly placed in the complex imperial world of nineteenth-century Ireland and Europe, begin to explore themes of dislocation, social breakdown, and alienation with a particularity and historical range that emerges later in English fiction. Lever anticipates Victorian and early modern preoccupations with the dissonances between a society's interpretive ideological frameworks (in his case, the ideology of colonialism) and the lives of the men and women who populate that society. In his fiction, an imperial system no longer functions coherently (in *Lord Kilgobbin,* a viceroy is chosen for his post only because he knows nothing about Ireland), while memories of a precolonial feudal bond between landlord and tenant are fast eroding.

Relatively early in his career as a novelist, Lever launched a powerful critique of the Enlightenment program of patriarchal moral and economic "improvement" that was central to Edgeworth's last three Irish novels. In *The O'Donoghue,* a well-intentioned London banker, a returning absentee landlord, attempts to reform and rehabilitate the lives of the impoverished tenants on an estate he has purchased in Ireland. Unlike Edgeworth's Lord Glenthorn, a depressed and self-indulgent decadent who must himself be reformed, Lever's Sir Marmaduke Travers is generous, kindhearted, and benevolent, filled with the optimistic energy of the nineteenth-century British capitalist. Although he is convinced that his program of anglicizing the habits of his tenantry will cure the ills of Ireland, his failures emerge from deep cultural misunderstandings, which Lever viewed far more pessimistically than did Edgeworth. For Lever, Sir Marmaduke cannot simply be reformed and reeducated; his miscomprehension suggests those willful misreadings of national character that propel all colonial policy. Misunderstanding the needs and motives of his tenants, Sir Marmaduke eliminates thatched roofs in favor of slate (like Edgeworth's Glenthorn), imports English pigs that demand better food than the tenants are themselves accustomed to eating, and encourages farmers, who would rather raise cattle, to keep bees. In his ignorance of custom, he divides the mountainside into separate fields in order to prevent his tenants' cattle from straying; but in so doing, he undermines their traditional sharing of pasture land and creates dissension. Marmaduke's "reforms" disrupt a traditional pre-Famine moral economy, in which land use was regulated not by "abstract rights" but by a communally determined distribution system based on environmental factors and kinship, as much as on lease obligation (Whelan 1995, 25). As Marmaduke's bailiff suggests, the new landlord is undermining and destroying a culture, dispossessing an already dispossessed tenantry of its traditional social patterns. "When they had the mountain among them, they fed on what they could get . . . and they didn't mind if one had more nor another, nor where they went, *for the place was their own;* but now that it is all marked out and divided, begorra, if a beast is got trespassing, out come some one with a stick and wallops him back again" (1897, 159–60; emphasis mine).

By exposing both Sir Marmaduke's failures as a colonial landlord and Anglo-Irish incompetence in Dublin Castle, Lever suggests the growing dissonance between imperial assumptions and the reality of Ireland's nineteenth-century rural moral economy. Sir Marmaduke's inability to comprehend cultural differences between two nations is framed by an Edgeworthian assumption about the superiority of the more "advanced" English systems and habits. But Lever also underscores the ease by which the thwarted English landlord ascribes savagery and barbarism to a subject people who recognize—and therefore intelligently exploit—the landlord's ignorance and wrongheadedness. For Lever, Sir Marmaduke's failures imply the failure of all attempts to graft the customs and habits of one country onto another. "Every moment disclosed some case where, in his honest efforts to improve the condition of the people, from ignorance of their habits, from total unconsciousness of the social difference of two nations essentially unlike, he discovered the failure of his plans, and unhesitatingly ascribed to the prejudices of the peasantry what with more justice might have been charged against his own unskillfulness" (160).

The characterization of Sir Marmaduke Travers as a generous and well-meaning, if inept, colonial landlord complicates the novel's judgment of English imperial efforts but nevertheless suggests Lever's distance from Edgeworth's optimism about importing English habits to Ireland. Although in his 1872 preface to *The O'Donoghue* Lever maintains that his creation of Sir Marmaduke was provoked by an English tourist's "crude notions . . . for the betterment of Ireland" (1897, xvi), the actual character is far from mere caricature. Unlike the stock English tourists who populate Maria Edgeworth's *Ennui* and *The Absentee* (for example, the comic Lord Craiglethrope in *Ennui* who understands nothing and believes everything about Ireland), Lever's English landlord is disarmingly like Richard Lovell Edgeworth himself. Filled with the highest Enlightenment aspirations, like Richard Edgeworth, Sir Marmaduke is "impatient until he had reached the country, and commenced the great scheme of regeneration and civilization, by which Ireland and her people were to be placed among the most favored nations" (1897, 17).[2] After he

2. Sir Richard Edgeworth, too, came to Ireland with idealistic goals. In 1782, the year of his permanent settlement in Edgeworthtown, he wrote the following: "I returned to Ireland, with a firm determination to dedicate the remainder of my life to

contemplates "Irish indolence and superstition; Irish bigotry and intolerance; the indifference to comfort; the indisposition to exertion;
the recklessness of the present; the improvidence of the future," in
short, the traditional English catalog of indictment against the Celt,
Sir Marmaduke's response is gloriously provincial. "Why should these
things be, when they were not so in Norfolk nor in Yorkshire?" (17)

For all their desire to do good, however, the Travers are finally no
Edgeworths; they are neither permanent settlers nor seriously engaged reformers. They move in and out of Ireland at whim, deserting
the country when the 1798 rebellion makes Irish residence undesir-
able. With the marriage of Sir Marmaduke's daughter and Herbert
O'Donoghue, the younger son of the declining Irish chieftain family
Sir Marmaduke has dispossessed, Lever suggests the complex cultural costs of anglicizing and "reforming" young Irishmen—costs
that are never fully acknowledged in Edgeworth's didactic novels, in
which absentees return to their Irish estates and become good landlords. The younger O'Donoghue's successes at Trinity, conversion to
Protestantism, and marriage into the Traver family transform him
into an admirable exile who abandons Ireland for a successful career
as a colonial judge in India. (Accustomed to a life of social and political ascendancy, the Anglo-Irish made excellent soldiers and colonial
administrators in other British possessions like India—in colonies
that were, for Lever, presumably more amenable to rational control
than was Ireland.) In *The O'Donoghue,* Herbert's service to empire
represents a version of Edgeworth's reformed Irish landlords (Glenthorn, Colambre, or Ormond) who seek to bring the Edgeworthian
program of reform to the "primitive" inhabitants of western Ireland—rather than to the dark-skinned natives of a more distant imperial colony.

Writing three decades after Edgeworth wrote her last Irish novel,
Lever questions the benefits of grafting rationalized English systems
on Irish life. In *The O'Donoghue,* and even more powerfully in his final
novel, *Lord Kilgobbin,* his analysis of cultural differences between
Saxon and Celtic cultures leads him to a deepening pessimism about
the colonial society he depicts—rather than to an ideologically driven set of solutions for Ireland. Unlike Edgeworth before him or

---

the improvement of my estate, and to the education of my children, and further, with
the sincere hope of contributing to the melioration of the inhabitants of the country
from which I draw my subsistence" (1821, 2:7).

Matthew Arnold after him, Lever finds himself unable to support a hierarchy of cultural traits in which, for example, English order, control, and discipline are privileged over passion and disorder.[3] The Irish O'Donoghues—selfish, improvident, hospitable, passionate, and self-destructively tied to hatred of their Saxon overlords—are not romanticized, but neither are they condemned as were the Rackrents. Moreover, the older O'Donoghue brother, Mark, who rashly joins the United Irishmen and finally flees his country, is a sympathetic, brooding hero who wins the hand of his cousin Kate, herself the most admirable character in the novel. Whereas in Edgeworth's preface to *Castle Rackrent,* the Rackrents represent the well-lost past, in Lever's darker vision of postunion "reform" the fall of the similarly improvident O'Donoghue house suggests cultural loss and national decline.

In Lever's final novel, *Lord Kilgobbin,* the attempts of an aging Gaelic Big House landlord to describe a foreign English society undermine the very categories of traditional colonial discourse. The ancient Lord Kilgobbin, now simply Mr. Kearney, speaks of a young Englishman who seeks the hand of his niece:

> I neither approve nor disapprove of him. I don't well know whether I have any right to do either,—I mean so far as to influence her choice. He belongs to a sort of men I know as little about as I do of the Choctaw Indians. They have lives and notions and ways all unlike ours. The world is so civil to them that it prepares everything to their taste. If they want to shoot, the birds are cooped up in a corner, and only let fly when they're ready. When they fish, the salmon are kept prepared to be caught; and if they make love, the young lady is just as ready to rise to the fly, and as willing to be bagged as either. Thank God, my darling, with all our barbarism, we have not come to that in Ireland. (1899, 364)

Kearney's remarks insist that a colonized people's resistance to order and system should not be read as simple barbaric opposition to

3. Arnold's *On the Study of Celtic Literature,* published in 1867, posits so-called Celtic qualities such as emotion, sentiment, love of beauty, charm, spirituality, and sexuality in contrast to the Anglo-Saxon qualities of steadiness, hardiness, and political effectiveness. See chapter 3, "An Essentially Feminine Race," in *Writing Ireland* (Cairns and Richard 1988) for a discussion of the political implications of Arnold's categories.

the rewards of civilization—as the colonizers would have it—but rather as an acute judgement of "civilization" itself from outside narrow cultural boundaries. Mr. Kearney of Kilgobbin, the representative of an old chieftain culture that is labeled primitive by the colonial overlords, tellingly regards English cultural patterns as grotesque and "other"—as distant from his own world as those of a barbaric Indian tribe. Kearney's words virtually reinscribe the meaning of "civilization" and "barbarism" in the nineteenth-century discourse between England and Ireland.

The Martins of Cro' Martin

Lever's eighth novel, *The Martins of Cro' Martin*, published in 1854, in the decade after he abandoned Ireland for life in Europe, is no fictional masterpiece. Almost eight hundred pages of close print and a loose and baggy plot make its popularity among modern readers unlikely. Yet Lever's complex series of attitudes toward the approaching collision between Anglo-Irish and Catholic society represents an important literary treatment of the fall of the Big House. His study of the decline of Anglo-Irish power is, moreover, significant in the evolution of political fiction in Ireland. By transforming the abstractions of nineteenth-century Irish ideology into the felt life of social experience, Lever establishes himself as a serious historical novelist.

Too politically aware to ignore the historical processes that were to destroy his own caste, yet too bound to his Anglo-Irish heritage to welcome the new Ireland ushered in by O'Connell's Catholic coalition, Lever wrote as an astute observer of a transformation that he could not support. Much like Trollope, he registered, often with great dramatic conviction, those positions that he himself regretted: a Catholic politician's rancorous but prophetic speech, a successful Catholic businessman's measured judgment of the economic instability of the Big House, the chief secretary of Ireland's irrefutable prediction of Anglo-Irish defeat. Even as we struggle to negotiate the complicated plots and subplots of *The Martins of Cro' Martin*, we experience Lever's transformation of political abstraction into the dense texture of social life. On the panoramic canvas of his Big House novel, Lever demonstrates how changes at Dublin Castle or at the local polling places portend social disruption for the peasantry, the Catholic middle class, and the Anglo-Irish gentry.

The novel traces a family estate in Connemara from 1829, the year of the Catholic Emancipation Act, to 1848, when Cro' Martin falls into the hands of the courts set up by the Encumbered Estates Act. Lever loosely bases his novel on the fall of an actual Martin holding in Connemara, an estate so vast that Richard Martin, who built Ballinahinch Castle in the late eighteenth century, reputedly boasted to George IV that he had "an approach from his gatehouse to his hall of thirty miles length" (Bence-Jones 1978, 25). In the 1872 preface to the novel, Lever insists that he uses the historical Martin family and estate only as an allusive source, but his choice of a real family name and the actual geographical setting of their ancestral home suggests a powerful desire to legitimize his narrative by presenting fiction as meaningful history.

In *Tour In Connemara and the Martins of Ballinahinch,* Maria Edgeworth reports that the country people used to consider Richard Martin "not only the lord of all he surveyed, but the lord of their lives" (1950, 64). But she also perceives the breakdown of his semifeudal state, noting that with the advent of the law in western Ireland, Martin's son was "no longer the unrivalled King of Connemara. . . . There are hundreds who would start up out of their bogs to hazard their lives still for Mr. Martin. But he is called Mister now, and the prestige is over" (64). Edgeworth's letters about her visits and correspondence with the Martin family from 1834 to 1847, particularly her amused but affectionate description of Richard Martin's pedantic granddaughter Mary, support Lever's claim in his preface that the character of Mary Martin in his novel is "purely fictitious" (1895, 1:xi). He writes without seeking any mimetic accuracy about the Martins of Ballinahinch or, if we are to trust Edgeworth's eyewitness account, about the appearance of their ancestral home. Instead, he uses the general plight of the debt-ridden family of the "King of Connemara" to create a fictional depiction of the fall of one of Ireland's powerful Big Houses. If we compare his account of the Martin household with Maria Edgeworth's letters about the historical family—letters undoubtedly colored by her optimistic belief in the power of enlightened stewardship—we quickly realize how Lever's novel characteristically darkens her picture of the Irish landlord. (Harold Edgeworth Butler, the editor of his great-aunt's *Tour of Connemara,* rather disapprovingly notes in his epilogue that Lever's "actual story owes but little to fact" [Edgeworth 1950, 112].)

The Martins of Cro' Martin dramatizes the seemingly inevitable culmination of the political process whereby Irish landlords participated in their own destruction. An ambivalent morality play, it depicts the gradual loss of the Big House's power as a newly enfranchised Catholic majority begins to flex its political muscle. Lever wrote with an acute sense of the costs of social dislocations; history itself provides a sobering footnote to his tale. The fall of the actual Martin family brought loss and destitution rather than freedom from oppressive rule to the already impoverished peasants on the estate. When the Law Life Assurance Company bought the huge Martin property of Connemara, it evicted all small tenants and steadily increased rents. Failing to find work as laborers, many of the evicted tenant families were forced either to move to the workhouse or emigrate (Daly 1981, 36). The historical Mary Martin was left nearly penniless by her losses after the Great Famine, wrote several novels to support herself, emigrated to America in 1850 with her husband to improve her financial position, and died there in 1850 after childbirth (Edgeworth 1950, 111–12).

In Lever's novel the Big House is the center of a vast estate rumored to cover half the county, virtually a private kingdom in the west of Ireland.[4] As we first observe it, Cro' Martin is no decaying Castle Rackrent, no ramshackle Big House fast appropriating the condition of a native's hovel, but a castle in fact as well as in name. Rather than offering an eyewitness account of the Martin estate in Connemara—with dung heap and pig-sty—that Maria Edgeworth describes in her letters,[5] Lever envisions Cro' Martin Castle as an im-

4. Maria Edgeworth's account of the feeling of utter isolation she and other guests felt while visiting the vast Martin property—their fear that they should never again see their family and friends (1950, 49)—suggests that, in its sense of the geographic immensity of the Martin territory, Lever's novel is accurate indeed. According to the *Dictionary of National Biography* (1967–68), Mary Martin's father left an estate of nearly 200,000 acres. In its great size, the Martin estate was not a typical Big House holding.

5. Maria Edgeworth described the actual Ballinahinch Castle as the familiar Big House of Anglo-Irish fiction: "a rambling kind of mansion with great signs of dilapidation—broken panes, wood panes, and slate panes, and in the ceilings and passages terrible splotches and blotches of damp and wet" (1950, 39). Looking at "the castle" from the road, she found it to be very different from the flattering illustrations that she had seen; art had embellished life. "Ballinahinch is a whitewashed dilapidated mansion with nothing of a castle about it excepting four pepperbox-looking towers

posing monument to centuries of colonial expansion. Through his description of its grandeur and its layered architectural history—from Norman tower to opulent nineteenth-century residence—he emphasizes the break in historical continuity represented by the Martins' final loss of their home. "With few pretensions to architectural correctness, Cro' Martin was, indeed, an imposing structure. Originally the stronghold of some bold Borderer, it had been added to by successive proprietors, till at last it had assumed the proportions of a vast and spacious edifice, different eras contributing the different styles of building, and presenting in the mass traces of every architecture, from the stern old watch-tower of the fourteenth century to the commodious dwelling-house of our own" (1895, 1:2). By juxtaposing descriptions of Cro' Martin's grandeur with accounts of an impoverished peasantry, the novel also implies the injustice of the Martins' lives. "The spotless windows of plate glass, the polished floor that mirrored every chair that stood on it, the massive and well-fitting doors, the richly gilded dogs that shone within the marble heath, had little brotherhood with the dreary dwellings of the cottiers beyond the walls of the park; and certainly even Irish misery never was more conspicuous than in that lonely region" (1:3).

Lever's descriptions stress the luxury of the Martins' dwelling, which is filled with priceless furniture, carpeting, tapestries, and artwork, all in striking contrast to the abject poverty of the tenants beyond the park walls. Although Edgeworth's letters describe an ill-furnished Ballinahinch, with bare, drafty windows and poorly constructed doors that do *not* shut, Lever's insistence on the opu-

---

stuck on at each corner—very badly, and whitewashed; and all that battlemented front which looks so grand in the drawing is mere whitewashed stone or brick or mud, I cannot swear which. But altogether the house is very low and ruinous looking, not a ruin of antiquity—but with cow-house and pig-stye and dunghill adjoining, and a litter indescribable in a sunk sort of backyard seen at the end of the mansion—a man throwing dung about with *with no air of majesty,* and pigs and poultry" (1950, 44; emphasis mine). A short "History of Ballynahinch Castle" available at the reception desk of the current hotel-cum-fishing lodge notes that the castle was built as an inn by the father of Edgeworth's host—a fact that may have contributed to the lack of grandeur (but not to the dilapidated state) that Edgeworth described. Although Richard Martin's opulent lifestyle is much commented upon in the history, real grandeur seems to have come later to Ballynahinch. In 1924 the castle was purchased by His Highness the Maharaja Jam Sahib of Nawanagar (Ranji), who would purchase five motorcars upon arrival in Galway each June and distribute these cars to locals each October before his departure for India (Lally n.d., 10).

lent interior of Cro' Martin foregrounds its startling isolation from the surrounding bleakness of Connemara. Lady Dorothea Martin's library, for example, is "fitted up in the most luxurious taste,—with rarest gems of art, and cabinet pictures of almost fabulous value,— to supply which foreign dealers and connoisseurs had been for years back in correspondence with her Ladyship" (1:140). Again, by juxtaposing commentary on the cost of this glittering edifice with descriptions of tenant poverty, Lever underscores the ambivalent response he seeks to provoke from his readers. He writes about the Martins' Big House not with a welcome houseguest's amused affection for its failings, but with the outsider's mixture of awe and moral judgment; his view of the Big House is formed by visual icons that the actual eyewitness visitor declares to be unreliable works of art (see footnote 5).

Lever's imaginative re-creation of Cro' Martin—as a work of art destined to be stripped of those luxuries that Edgeworth tells us never actually existed at Ballinahinch—suggests the complex relationship between different narrative forms. The apparent contradictions between Edgeworth's eyewitness account of the Martins and Lever's fictional version of the Connemara family are not so much competing truths as they are alternative versions of family and national history. To tenants of the castle, for example, Ballinahinch would have been an opulent residence with or without window drapery to keep out the drafts. Although Lever wrote as a member of the middle-class Protestant ascendancy, he was not nearly so remote from the world of the Martins' drawing room as were their tenants. Yet he wrote of Cro' Martin with an outsider's perspective on the Big House myth of power and wealth, as a viewer of the flattering illustrations of the castle rather than of the actual dilapidated mansion that the family guest, Maria Edgeworth, saw.[6] Her description of the "extraordinary kindness, tenderness, generous hospitality" (1950, 79) of a Mr. and Mrs. Martin living in a ramshackle pile carries a very different charge than does Lever's indictment of an irresponsible landlord and his arrogant and vindictive wife. But Lever's fictional

6. Lever's fictional charaters can convey the author's complex relationship to the Big House. In *Lord Kilgobbin*, middle-class Joe Atlee, the son of a poor Presbyterian minister, who lives by his pen and his wit and who plays risky political games, probably expresses Lever's own social insecurity as an outsider to the world of the landed gentry. Ironically, Dick Kearney, whom Joe addresses in the following passage, lives

narrative of the course of Anglo-Irish history is by no means less useful than Edgeworth's letters in telling us about the mid-nineteenth-century Big House.[7]

To Lady Dorothea, the English mistress of all the luxury of Cro' Martin who travels to her estate "snugly encased in furs," the walls of the park estate are the boundaries of her prison. The beautiful grounds, the stately trees, the "battlemented towers of the princely residence" (1895, 1:135) evoke no feelings of appreciation—only boredom. Even Lord Godfrey Martin, whose Norman-Irish family has controlled this private kingdom for generations, responds to the beauty of his vast holding with neither pride of possession nor aesthetic pleasure, but simply with "dreamy, unremarking indifference" (1:135).

No less than Castle Rackrent, the Martin estate is doomed by the failures of its landlords: by the English Lady Martin's arrogance toward her native Irish tenants and the middle-class Catholic world of Oughterard; by Lord Martin's indolence, vanity, and self-indulgent refusal to accept the responsibilities of his position. In their luxuri-

---

from hand to mouth as the son of an overmortgaged landlord who is unable to escape the constant financial crises threatening Kilgobbin Castle.

> "Shall I make you a confession, Dick? I envy you all that! I envy you what smacks of a race, a name, an ancestry, a lineage." (Lever 1899, 102–3)

> "What would I not give," thought Joe, as he strolled along the velvety sward, . . . "what would I not give to be the son of a house like this, with an old and honored name, with an ancestry strong enough to build upon for future pretensions, and then with an old house, peaceful, tranquil, and unmolested: where, as in such a spot as this, one might dream of great things, perhaps might achieve them! What books would I not write!" (125)

7. Christopher Morash's essay on *The Martins of Cro' Martin* similarly focuses on "historical discourses outside the text" and emphasizes Lever's growing dissatisfaction with the way in which life and fiction fail to converge. In particular, Morash analyzes the differences between the Mary Martin of Lever's novel and the actual woman whom his essay recreates from her career, not only as a heroic daughter of the Big House, but also as a prolific writer of fiction. Morash observes that Lever's 1872 preface, in condemning contemporary society for failing to support his fictional Mary Martin's efforts to save the estate, reverses "the traditional expressive realist relationship between literature and society; instead of condemning the literary text because it fails to conform to reality, Lever denounces reality for failing to conform to fiction" (1992, 72).

ous setting, totally isolated from the lives of their tenants, the Martins display the worst characteristics of aristocratic hauteur. But more ominous than their failure to enjoy or value their land is their inability to accept the political and social change that is occurring in Ireland as a result of Catholic emancipation. They react with characteristic resistance to the emerging power of Dan Nelligan, the powerful shopkeeper of Oughterard who serves as an unofficial town banker and wields political power through his wealth. When Martin reminds his wife that Nelligan's son Joseph has won highest honors at Trinity College and warns her of the Nelligans' growing influence, her reply (and his comment on it) is telling:

> "A very shocking feature of the time we live in!". . .
> "So it may be: but there it is—just like the wet weather, and the typhus, and the sheep-rot, and fifty other disagreeable things one can't help."
> "But at least they can avoid referring to them in conversation, sir. There is no need to open the window when the look-out is a dreary one." (1:121)

Even the stripping down of the family estate, a recurring motif in the the Big House novel, appears in *The Martins of Cro' Martin* not as a slow process of loss and decay but as yet another assertion of the Martins' arrogance toward Catholic Ireland. In the chapter "A Country Auction" (1:328–42), Lever describes the sale of the estate's livestock when the Martins abandon Ireland. The magnificence of the stables—with ornamental fountains, copper sluices, and mahogany partitions—impresses the tenants and townspeople who come to view and to purchase. Lever's narrative intrusions call attention to the domestic loss represented by the breakup of a home, but the scene itself suggests how even in its decline the Big House retains its distance. During the day of the sale, the curious onlookers are kept from the house and herded into the stable yards. The easy intermingling of peasant and gentry that accompanies the fall of the Rackrents is absent here; in its defeat, the deserted Cro' Martin stands as a monument to snobbish exclusion rather than as a reminder of human loss. As they wander through the grounds, the country squires, shopkeepers, and small farmers are "all subdued into a kind of reverence for a spot from which they had been so rigidly excluded" (1:333).

While Lever's own political conservatism about Irish society never led him to advocate radical solutions to Irish social problems, his depiction of revolutionary Paris in 1830 suggests the complexity of his views. After the ignominious defeat of their Tory candidate by a liberal in the local elections of 1829, the Martins abandon their Irish estate in disgust. Finding solace in the elegance of Parisian society, a vengeful Lady Martin directs that her disloyal tenants be hounded: rents are to be called in, customary privileges abolished, evictions initiated. While in Paris, however, she and her family find themselves trapped between the the rebellious workers and the French army. In that cosmopolitan setting, Lever is able to sympathize with the radicalism that he rejects for Ireland.[8] The scenes at the barricades are not merely romantic adventures provided by a cosmopolitan author, but ominous reminders of the price of political isolation from the masses. Lady Martin's personal secretary and companion, Kate Henderson, escapes the values of her employer's world by embracing the ideology of Republican France.[9] Lever's admiration for Kate's personal solution to her situation as a dependent of the Big House is not translated into a thoroughgoing approval of political radicalism. Yet if French political solutions are never advocated for Ireland, Lever's characterization of Kate's ardent Republicanism and his depiction of the Parisian workers at the barricades—the canaille to Lady Martin—still reveal a powerful sympathy for a foreign underclass.

Beneath the wealth and power of the Martins' ascendancy class exists the world of the middle-class Catholic shopkeepers, lawyers, and estate managers, who gaze longingly and with growing hostility at Cro' Martin. In his depiction of this rising class that will, in the course of the novel, defeat the Big House and move toward political control of Ireland, Lever distinguishes and discriminates carefully. He both expresses and attempts to transcend his class-bound suspi-

8. The betrayals and the backbiting among the plotters of the 1798 rebellion in *The O'Donaghue*, for example, illustrate that Lever viewed nationalist politics as controlled by self-interest and personal ambition. But in *Lord Kilgobbin*, Lever's sympathetic portrayal of the head of the Fenian brotherhood, Don Donegan, suggests an enlarging sympathy for radical solutions to political crisis.

9. Kate's political means of escaping the constraints of Big House life is a strategy employed by several of Lever's most enterprising female characters. In *The O'Donoghue*, Kate O'Donoghue rejects the supremely eligible English military son of Marmaduke Travers and chooses to marry her cousin Mark, a fugitive United Irishman who joins the Catholic French army. In *Lord Kilgobbin*, the Kearneys' worldly niece rejects several eligible suitors (all of them rich and English), and elopes to

cions of Catholic Ireland. Unlike Maria Edgeworth, whose vulgar social climbers—Mrs. Raffarty in *The Absentee* and Jason Quirk in *Castle
Rackrent*—represent the social or moral failings of an emerging native middle class, Lever creates a thoroughly sympathetic Catholic
character. Joe Nelligan's meteoric rise from obscurity as the son of an
Oughterard shopkeeper to prominence as the chief justice of Ireland is achieved through intellectual brilliance, not political ambition. Joe's deepest embarrassments, in fact, lie in the way that many
of his fellow Catholics use his academic success for their own political
ends. "The fulsome adulation of some, the stupid astonishment of
others, but, worse than either, the vulgar assumption that his success
was a kind of party triumph,—a blow dealt by the plebeian against
the patrician, the Papist against the Protestant,—shocked and dis-
gusted him" (1:21).

Joe Nelligan's moral probity is grounded in a deeply ingrained
childhood loyalty to the Martin family and in his personal devotion
to Mary Martin, the Martins' niece. He handles Mary's lost glove as a
"relic" and adorns his chambers at Trinity with a single ornament: a
lithograph of Cro' Martin Castle. Even as he becomes a major political force in Catholic Ireland, he fails to display the hostility to the Big
House that would satisfy the more rancorous of his party. To the
viceroy of Ireland, who appoints Joe Nelligan to high political office
without consulting the Catholic leadership, Joe's political independence from Daniel O'Connell distinguishes him from other Catholic
aspirants. The search for an acceptable new Irish leader impels Lever
to create a curiously apolitical Catholic politician; clearly, social
change is best left to the moderate, an intellectual rather than a man
of action, a countryman with deep ties of affection to the Big House
and with a properly distant and humble adoration of its daughter. In
thus characterizing Joe Nelligan, Lever manages to have it both ways:
Joe is both the new Catholic hero of Ireland and the loyal admirer of
the neofeudal Big House.

The characterization of Maurice Scanlan, the Martins' electioneering agent, however, represents Lever's darker and more class-
bound view of the new Ireland—a view reminiscent of Edgeworth's

---

America with the fugitive head of the Fenians, Dan Donagon. Energy, intelligence,
and a sense of adventure lead Lever's most interesting heroines into radical political
alliances.

distaste for Jason Quirk and one that anticipates later characters by Somerville and Ross. Presented as an ambitious social climber and brilliant horse dealer, Scanlan uses his intimate knowledge of the peasant class to manipulate his fellow countrymen to his own will. He is depicted as a shrewd but vulgar parvenu, a sycophant to the Big House who makes himself ridiculous as he tries to advance his presumptuous designs on Mary Martin. Serving the Martins when they are ascendant, he switches allegiance to the Jewish moneylender who eventually gains control of the estate. With an eye to the main chance, he shrewdly warns the Martins against their stubborn adherence to reactionary political positions, but mistakenly confuses self-interest and cunning for wisdom. Self-congratulatory and irredeemably vulgar as he bows, sidles, simpers, and smirks before Mary, Scanlan is an object of contempt. Like later Anglo-Irish writers who become increasingly preoccupied with misalliance, Lever viewed marriage between the Big House and Catholic Ireland with alarm. While Joe Nelligan's humble, unspoken worship of the niece of the Big House is a sign of his delicate sensibilities, Scanlan's corruption is dramatized by his offer to save Cro' Martin from its creditor only if Mary Martin will be handed over to him as his reward.[10]

Less individualized than the middle-class Catholics in the novel are the Irish peasants whose major role is to suffer poverty, famine, and disease. In his descriptions of the Martin's tenants, Lever occasionally suggests a degeneracy that accompanies dire poverty. These descriptions represent the most ambivalent paragraphs in the novel, for in them Lever reveals his class fears, his guilt, and his uneasiness before an oppressed country people. Even as he sympathizes with the terrible poverty of the peasantry, he suggests a moral shiftlessness and genetic propensity for mindless submission that call into question the value of their feudal loyalty to the Big House.

> Nor would a follower of Lavater have argued too favorably of the
> prosperity of Irish regeneration, in beholding that arrar of faces,—low

10. Similarly, in *The O'Donoghue,* the land agent Hemsworth's villainy is clearest when he offers to save the young revolutionary, Mark O'Donoghue, from the gallows in exchange for the hand of Mark's cousin Kate. Whereas Yeats's harrowing vision of the results of misalliance in *Purgatory* represents an extreme Anglo-Irish position, Edith Somerville's anxious treatment of the theme in *Mount Music* (see 127) and Molly Keane's in *Two Days in Aragon* (see 176–81) indicate the ongoing eugenic pre-

browed, treacherous-looking, and almost savagely cruel, as many of them were in expression. . . .

Bronzed, blear-eyed, and weather-beaten, seamed with age and scarred with sickness, shrewd-looking, suspicious, and crafty in every lineament, there was yet one characteristic predominant over all,—an intense and abject submission, an almost slavish deference to every observation addressed to them. . . .

The expediency of misery had begotten the expediency of morals, and in all the turning and winding of their shifty natures you could see the suggestions of that abject destitution which had eaten into their hearts. (1:8)

In his 1872 preface Lever reveals his most conservative attitudes toward the changing relationship between tenant and landlord in nineteenth-century Ireland. Like Maria Edgeworth, writing her preface to *Castle Rackrent* to control her readers' responses to the novel, Lever used his preface to interpret his work retrospectively. As the recorder of a period of great change in Irish society, he informs his readers that he strove for a critical objectivity about political events; however, the preface reveals a nostalgia rooted in political conservatism.

Ireland, at the time I speak of, was beginning to feel that sense of distrust and jealousy between the owner and the tiller of the soil, which, later on, was to develop itself into open feud. The old ties that have bound the humble to the rich man, and which were hallowed by reciprocal acts of good will and benevolence, were being loosened. Benefits were canvassed with suspicion, ungracious or unholy acts were treasured up as cruel wrongs. The political agitator had so far gained the ear of the people, that he could persuade them that there was not a hardship or a grievance of their lot that could not be laid at the door of the landlord. He was taught to regard the old relation of love and affection to the owner of the soil as the remnants of a barbarism that had had its day, and he was led to believe that whether the tyranny that crushed him was the Established Church or the landlord,

---

occupations of ascendancy writers. Maria Edgeworth's sardonic remarks regarding the real Mary Martin's marriage at thirty-two to a poor man—rather than to the rich prince her family instructed her to seek in order to rescue herself from debt—suggest a typical Anglo-Irish view of unequal marriage as misalliance. "A Prince-Consort! Here is an Agent-consort! How lucky! How prudent! Nothing anti-romantic! after all the Princes! . . . So very sensible, Miss Martin, and well calculated and achieved!" (1950, 107)

there was a great Liberal party ready to aid him in resisting either or both, when he could summon courage for the effort. (1:viii–ix)

In such passages, written in 1872, two years after Gladstone's first land act, Lever announces his longing for a romantic feudal past, with the a warm, reciprocal, "hallowed" ties of affection between landlord and tenant. Despite his careful presentation of himself as the "cosmopolitan" nondidactic observer of the Irish social scene, he, one of the most politically acute of Irish novelists, shared with Maria Edgeworth a distrust of political solutions to Irish social problems. In the preface, which characterizes politicians as "agitators" who lead gullible peasants into a problematic future, Lever occasionally sounds like an early Charles Dickens, advocating human decency as the solution to all injustice: "I had not, I own, any implicit faith in Acts of Parliament, and I had a fervent belief in what kindness, when combined with knowledge of Ireland, could do with Irishmen" (1:xi).

Mary Martin is Lever's fictional mouthpiece for the hope that kindness combined with benevolent policies of land improvement—rather than political action—will preserve the Big House.[11] Called "the Princess of Connemara" by the peasant tenants, Mary struggles to protect them from the constant threat of unemployment, famine, and illness. Whereas Lord and Lady Martin view their property as a source of income, Mary's feudal relationship with the tenants assumes a system of mutual obligations. She initiates projects to build roads and to clear forests, organizes vast drainage schemes, has quarries opened, and founds schools and hospital dispensaries. The Edgeworths' reforming program is thus reinvented by Lever in the guise of an idealized old-style feudalism. Like a lady of the manor, Mary establishes a bond with the tenants that is personal, beneficent, and alternately stern and tender. She exists in the novel as a saintly anachronism, a sentimental reincarnation of the ideal feudal landlord. To the peasantry, Mary becomes an object of reverence, drawing around herself centuries of nostalgic longing for a lost Celtic community. "Oh, if courtiers could feel one tithe of the personal de-

11. Although he denies any acquaintance with the real Mary Martin, the daughter of Mr. and Mrs. Thomas Martin whom Maria Edgeworth came to know well, Lever coyly admits that his fictional character shares many traits with the "young lady of this very name—many traits of whose affection for the people and efforts for their well being might be supposed to have been my original." Moreover, he acknowledges that

votion to the sovereign that did these poor peasants to her they regarded as their chief, what an atmosphere of chivalry would breathe within the palace of royalty! There was nothing they would not have done or dared at her bidding" (2:309).

If Mary Martin, the Protestant scion of the Big House, dramatizes one vision of the ideal landlord or even the idealized memory of the Celtic chieftain, the variety of characters who speak against her program of reform suggests both the ambivalent position from which Lever wrote *The Martins of Cro' Martin* and the ways in which the novel—in contrast to his 1872 preface—is fraught with dissonance and doubt. His nostalgic longing for an age of social stability, represented by Mary's program, does not—or cannot—overcome his hard-headed political observations of a revolutionary century. Lever wrote, finally, without Maria Edgeworth's certainty that the "good" landlord would heal Ireland's wounds; even as he created his ideal figure, he undermined her.

Mary Martin represents the reconciliatory forces of an idealized feudal order, but her efforts are resented by those Catholics who recognize her dangerously reactionary power. Mary's detractors are not, for the most part, sympathetic characters. But neither are they total caricatures; they present their objections to her methods with some dramatic and political conviction. To one local politician, a follower of Daniel O'Connell, Mary's presence in the countryside is an alarming move backward in history motivated not by charitable impulses but by careful calculation.

> "She's trying hard to bring back the old feudal devotion to the Chief, which was the bane of Ireland. She wants the tenants to have no will of their own, but just to vote whatever the landlord tells them. She had the impudence to tell my 'august leader' that she had no need of him down there, that the country was too poor to waste its energies in factious squabbles. . . .

---

he was inspired by tales of her "devotion and her goodness" (1895, 1:xi). *The Dictionary of National Biography* (1967–68) reports that Mary Martin was so devoted to her father's tenantry that she was called the "Princess of Connemara." She borrowed large sums of money to relieve her starving tenants at the time of her marriage in 1847 and was unable to repay her debts in 1848 when she lost the estate. Lever blends fact and fiction freely.

"All policy, all scheming! . . . She sees how the family influence has declined, and is fast becoming obliterated in this country, by reason of their worthlessness, insolence, and neglect of the people; and she's just shrewd enough to see how far a little cajolery goes with poor Paddy; but as my 'august leader' observed, it is not a frieze coat, nor a pair of brogues, that can compensate for the loss of the freedom that is every man's birthright; and it is not by an ounce of tea, or a dose of physic, we'll ever see Ireland great, glorious, and free." (1:115)

On occasion, Lever describes Mary as she is viewed by her devoted peasant nurse: "the proud scion of a proud stock, who ruled over a territory rather than a mere estate." But to the local priest, Mary's good works among the poor threaten the growing political ascendancy of the Catholic Church over the Big House. "If she'd let the people alone about their religion I'd think better of her" (1:115). To Joe Nelligan's shopkeeper father, the sharpest business mind of Oughterard, her reforms at Cro' Martin are financially disastrous. "If what I hear be true, she is spending more money on the property than the fee-simple is worth" (1:115–16). To the Martins' parsimonious Scotch agent, she brings the dangers of education and higher expectations to a properly suppressed peasant class. He blames the momentous defeat of the Martins' Tory candidate in a local election on the dangerous changes Mary Martin has initiated. "I was not listened to. I foretold what it would all end in, this amélearating the condition of the small farmer—this raising the moral standard o' the people, and a' that. I foresaw that if they grow richer, they'd grow sturdier; and if they learned to read, they'd begin to reflact" (1: 298–99).

Lever characterizes most of Mary's critics—the politician, the priest, and the land agent—as self-serving men pursuing goals of personal advancement. Disavowing a society that failed to fulfill his vision of feudal harmony between tenant and landlord, in his 1872 preface he bitterly suggests that were Mary Martin to practice her benevolence in contemporary Ireland, the priest, the agitators, the national press, and the people themselves would be certain to warn "against whatever promised to establish peace and contentment to the land" (1:xi).[12] The most convincing arguments against Mary's ef-

12. See footnote 7 in this chapter for Christopher Morash's analysis of such a passage.

forts to reform the Big House emerge, however, directly within the text of the novel, from one of her strongest admirers and from one of Lever's most attractive characters. By creating the aging lawyer Valentine Repton, a former associate of Gratton and Curran in the golden days of the ascendancy, Lever provides his novel with a voice that is neither didactic nor idealizing. Inconceivable in an Edgeworth novel, Repton speaks with the worldly authority of unsentimentalized political experience. He evaluates the course of Anglo-Irish history with a tough-minded realism that avoids both cynicism and sentimentality. His admiration for Mary Martin's "noble career" and for her efforts to save the Big House does not mitigate his judgment that "the experiment comes too late" (1:172). One reader has suggested that through Repton, Lever speaks to a character much like Maria Edgeworth (O'Keefe 1977, 87).

> "It is too late to try the feudal system in the year of our Lord 1829, Miss Martin. We live in the age where everything is to be redressed by a Parliament. The old school compact between proprietor and peasant is repealed, and all must be done by 'the House.' Now, if your grandfather had pursued the path that you are doing to-day, this crisis might never have arrived; but he didn't young lady. He lived like a real gentleman; he hunted, and drank, and feasted, and rack-rented, and horsewhipped all around him; and what with duelling of a morning and drinking over-night, taught the people a code of morals that has assumed all the compactness of a system. Ay, I say it with grief, this is a land corrupted from the top, and every vice of its gentry has but filtered down to its populace!" (1895, 1:172)

To Repton the sources of Anglo-Irish decline are clear. With old families uprooted, and with the masses left without guidance, the Catholic Church, not the Big House, dominates a new Ireland. For Lever, the new order is sadly lacking in those human qualities that Mary Martin represents. Mary's old Irish nurse responds to change much as Thady Quirk does in *Castle Rackrent*. To both old family retainers, the new age of social mobility and improvement brings only loss.

> "There's change enough, and too many already. . . I remember the place upwards of eighty years. . . [t]here was no mill there then nor a

school-house, no, nor a dispensary either! Musha, but the people were better off, and happier when they had none of them. . . . Now it's all readin' and writin', teaching honest people to be rogues, and give them new contrivances to cheat their masters. . . Money is in everybody's heart. . . . Tis all money. . . To be rich they're all strivin." (2: 286–87)

Even Daniel Nelligan, the hard-nosed, budding capitalist shopkeeper of Oughterard, acknowledges the power of the past and the glamor of the Big House. He cannot refuse Mary's request that he ignore his partisan feelings and allow her to befriend his family. " 'It's more than a prejudice, after all,' muttered he, as he looked after her as she drove away. 'There's something deeper and stronger in it than that, or else a few words spoken by a young girl couldn't so suddenly rout all the sentiments of a lifetime! Ay, Ay,' added he, still to himself, 'we may pull them down; we may humble them; but we'll never fill their places' " (1:341).

By the end of *The Martins of Cro' Martin,* the old gentry is routed, but the peasants gain nothing from the fall of the Big House. Indeed, Mary Martin's place cannot be filled. When the Martins abandon their land and become absentee landlords, their tenants are left to their fate. Desolate and poverty stricken, they succumb to the depredations of famine and its accompanying horrors—slow starvation, cholera, and typhus. Lever's descriptions of Ireland in the 1830s as a wasteland of disease and hunger anticipate the Great Famine to come in the 1840s. "A dreadful malady walked the land, and its victims lay in every house! The villages were depopulated, the little clusters of houses at cross roads were stricken, the lone shealing on the mountain side, the miserable cottage of the dreary moor, were each the scenes of desolation and death. It was as though the land were about to be devastated, and the race of man swept from its surface!" (2:131–32).

Images of abandonment and death dominate the last sections of the novel. In her efforts to care for the dying tenants, Mary Martin herself contracts typhus and dies at Cro' Martin. Her uncle, Lord Godfrey Martin, now an absentee landlord leading a purposeless life in Paris and Baden-Baden, succumbs to a stroke. He imagines himself back in Ireland, and dying, calls out to the niece he abandoned.

The uncle and niece are buried together on the Irish estate, surrounded by their grieving tenants who can look forward only to a future of increasing bleakness.[13] Cro' Martin is briefly rescued from the bankruptcy of Lord Martin's profligate son by the revelation that the estate's true heir is Mary's father, the self-exiled Barry Martin, not the dead Godfrey. The complicated gothic plot machinations at the conclusion of *The Martins of Cro' Martin,* involving the unmaskings of true and false heirs, recall the end of Edgeworth's *Ennui* and suggest an insecure Anglo-Ireland's anxious preoccupations with bloodlines and orderly genealogical succession. Such melodramatic solutions are, however, merely temporary; the estate is ultimately claimed by the courts and lost by the Martins.

Torn between his political realism and his nostalgia, Lever created a novel of dissonance and contradictions; more able than Edgeworth to acknowledge the irrelevance of the Big House to Ireland's future, he nevertheless sought to preserve what was already lost. He finds hope for Ireland only in the idealized vision of Joe Nelligan, the brilliant son of Catholic Ireland who bears his sorrow at Mary Martin's death as the great "disappointment of his early life" (2:384). Thus

13. A funeral scene from *Julia Howard, a Romance* (1850), a contemporary sentimental novel about the dispossessed heir to a great estate in Connemara, demonstrates that Lever invoked the same feudal ideology as did the historical Mary Martin. *Julia Howard* was written by Mary Letitia Martin (Mrs. Martin Bell), the "Princess of Connemara" whose loss of Ballinahinch Castle lies behind the plot of her own novel as well as Lever's. In *Julia Howard,* the death of a chieftain landlord, caused by a fever caught when he visited a famine-ridden cabin, is mourned by his tenants. "They had often cut down his trees, poached his rivers, killed his red deer, and with wonderful ingenuity, had evaded the payment of their rents; yet as they thronged the chamber of death, they felt a regret sincere as it was profound, and unsullied by any sordid feeling . . . the men stood in reverent silence and all felt that their dark days were upon them, and that they were orphaned of their chief and their benefactor" (Bell 1850, 11). Lever's description of Mr. Martin's and Mary Martin's joint funeral echoes themes that the historical Mary Martin used in her novel: the gathering of the clan, the analogy of the chieftain–tenant bond to the parent–child relationship, and the overwhelming grief and "reverential awe" (Lever 1895, 2:370) of the tenants before their dead chief. Significantly though, *Julia Howard,* the novel written from within the Big House, is set in the eighteenth century, whereas Lever's *The Martins of Cro' Martin* insists on the persistence of feudal devotion well into the nineteenth century. (Christopher Morash's attention to *Julia Howard* and his notation of the loyal peasants' grief at the death of Julia, Mary Martin's "fictional substitute" for herself, led me to the novel in search of further parallels in the complex relationship between fictional and historical narratives [1992, 73].)

Joe is formed by the double strands of his national heritage—his vision of a hierarchical feudal world represented by the Anglo-Irish Big House and the reality of Catholic Ireland's displacement of the ascendancy. In *The Martins of Cro' Martin* the Big House survives only as an idealized moral force in Joe Nelligan's memory, a force that refines Joe and saves him from contamination by the rancorous political reality of a new world that Lever could not accept even as he exposed the rot in the old.

Ascendancy Guilt in the Anglo~Irish Gothic Novel

Charles Maturin and Sheridan Le Fanu

Although Charles Maturin's *Melmoth the Wanderer* (1820) and Sheridan Le Fanu's *Uncle Silas* (1864) are not written in the realistic tradition of Edgeworth's and Lever's fiction, these masterpieces of gothic terror exist in an allusive relationship to the Big House novel in Ireland, echoing but transforming the basic conventions of the form. The affinity between Maturin's and Le Fanu's gothic creations and other Anglo-Irish novels emphasizes compelling features of ascendancy life in postunion Ireland: preoccupation with a loss of position and prestige, with spiritual and physical decay, and with the guilt of an imperial class fast losing ground to Catholic political challenges. Living in a country that had recently ceded its identity through the 1801 Act of Union, and in a city filled with reminders of loss—where, for example, the former seat of parliament had become a commercial bank—Maturin and Le Fanu use gothic conventions to explore power and powerlessness. The predominance of the ruined or abandoned house in their novels suggests a growing confrontation with the insecure reality of postunion Protestant Ireland. Although *Melmoth The Wanderer* and *Uncle Silas* exist outside the major realistic tradition examined in this study, both novels evoke that atmosphere of guilt and desolation, that disquieting sense of loss and cultural isolation characteristic of nineteenth-century ascendancy fiction.

The masking of the social and political content in *Melmoth the Wanderer* and *Uncle Silas* by gothic conventions should not obscure the multiplicity of sources for the novels. On the one hand, both emerge from a literary tradition with recognizable conventions: decaying houses, disinherited heirs, haunting family portraits of doomed relatives, innocent but victimized heroines, guilt-ridden and demonic but tormented villains, and, in the case of Maturin's novel, virulent anticlericalism. But the novels are not merely brilliant apogees of a gothic tradition; they also represent complex literary responses to Anglo-Ireland's preoccupation with and negotiation of waning social and economic power structures. Central to each work are the latent subversive political implications of gothic literature that lend themselves so well to colonial Ireland.[1] In both novels, demonic villains act out both their guilty identification with systems of power and their tormented domination by them. Suggestions of the gothic appear covertly in Edgeworth's *Ennui,* in the description, for example, of Lord Glenthorn's estate, a description that implies the subversive power of an archaic and uncivilized Ireland. Even more pointedly gothic is the preoccupation in that same work (as well as in other Big House novels) with wrongfully disinherited heirs or hidden wills.[2] In Maturin's and Le Fanu's darker fiction, the gothic form becomes a means of exploring the costs of an oppressive colonial system—not only for its obvious victims, but for its perpetrators as well. In a preface to *Melmoth The Wanderer,* William Axton describes the inescapable enthrallment of the gothic hero-villain to the sources of his corruption. Axton's emphasis on the protagonist's guilty conscience suggests a congruence between the gothic form and the colonizer's predicament. "Equally a victim of despotism and an exploiter of it, he has been perverted by an authoritarian environment so that he both turns it to the gratification of his will for power and is twisted by his effort to break away from it or to undermine it. His individuality permanently threatened, he thirsts to realize himself in tyranny at the same time he is guiltily aware of his evil" (1961, x–xi).

Although they were both solidly entrenched in ascendancy life,

1. W. J. McCormack discusses, for example, the contradiction between the gothic genre's exposure of "the violence and corruption that lay behind authority" and its tendency "to glorify antique and elite values" (1991, 831). Such contradictory traits in a genre that was typically produced by Protestant writers in Ireland illuminate the anxieties of the nineteenth-century ascendancy's predicament.

2. Wronged heirs and crucial hidden documents appear, for example, both in Lever's *The Martins of Cro' Martin* (1895) or Somerville and Ross's *An Irish Cousin* (1903).

Charles Maturin and Sheridan Le Fanu, like Charles Lever, wrote from an urban, political, and literary Dublin world, rather than from the Big House. Maturin was a flamboyant but unsuccessful member of the Church of Ireland hierarchy, attempting to supplement his meager income, and Le Fanu, more than a generation later, a struggling literary entrepreneur. The self-consciously literary quality of *Melmoth the Wanderer* and *Uncle Silas* indicates that both novelists wrote as professionals seeking to satisfy public demand, not as proprietors bent on defending or reforming the social system that supported them.

As Julian Moynahan has noted (1982, 46), the French Huguenot ancestry of Maturin and Le Fanu suggests yet another biographical source for their distinctive use of Anglo-Irish themes in their novels. *Melmoth the Wanderer* was written during the early years of the Catholic struggle for emancipation in Ireland; although the novel echoes familiar anticlerical themes established by Maturin's gothic predecessors (most notably by "Monk" Lewis), it also suggests a deep rooted anxiety about Catholic power that far exceeds that of his Anglo-Irish contemporaries. Although in several of his works Maturin expresses strong sympathy for Irish cultural nationalism, his religious anxiety is perhaps best explained by his family's identification with the history of victimized French Huguenots rather than with the more secure Anglo-Irish Protestants. In their early fiction, however (for example, in Maturin's *Milesian Chief* or in Le Fanu's *Purcell Papers*), both authors express a covert sympathy with the native Irish gentry class, dispossessed and exiled by the Cromwellian intruders much as their own Protestant ancestors were dispossessed by the Catholic hegemony of seventeenth-century France. The harsh, if allegorized, attacks on the ascendancy's isolation from Catholic Ireland that can be found buried in both *Melmoth the Wanderer* and *Uncle Silas* suggest ways in which Maturin and Le Fanu use the conventions of gothic literature to both mask and release their complexly motivated political responses to Anglo-Irish society in a century of resurgent Irish Catholic nationalism.[3]

3. Although Maturin and Le Fanu are praised primarily for their creation of gothic masterpieces, a few critics have explored the social and political contexts of their work. Henderson argues against the traditional emphasis on Maturin's gothic traits and proposes a convincing reinterpretation of him as a commentator on Ire-

Charles Maturin's *Melmoth The Wanderer*

Like much of Charles Lever's postunion fiction, Maturin's wildly extravagant fictional construction *Melmoth The Wanderer* is resolutely unprovincial. The collection of six interwoven plots, set in Ireland, Europe, and even India, is centered on the damned Melmoth, who must wander the world searching for a victim who will release him from a Faustian pact. In exchange for one hundred and fifty years of youth and supernatural powers, Melmoth barters his soul with the devil. But, unlike Faust, he can free himself from eternal torment if he finds a substitute victim, one who will succumb to his temptations, enter into the satanic pact, and exchange destinies with him. Thus, Melmoth is Faust and Mephistopheles in one, traversing the earth in search of his reprieve. This guilt-ridden, tormented villain has his roots in the tradition of romantic satanism but emerges most directly, Maturin tells us in his preface, from one of his own sermons:

---

land's social condition in the early nineteenth century (1980). Henderson's reading of *Melmoth the Wanderer* as a spiritual and social allegory rather than simply as another gothic sensation novel is echoed by McCormack's radical reinterpretation of Le Fanu's *Uncle Silas* as an allegory of Anglo-Irish guilt (1980). Lougy emphasizes the Tory, Protestant identity that left Maturin both permanently estranged in his native country and preoccupied with recording that estrangement through his characters (1975, 86). Moynahan's suggestive article, "The Politics of Anglo-Irish Gothic: Maturin, Le Fanu, and 'The Return of the Repressed' " (1982) (much of it reprinted as chapter 6 of *Anglo-Irish: The Literary Imagination in a Hyphenated Culture*, 1994), notes how Maturin viewed early nineteenth-century Ireland as essentially a "living Gothic." Moynahan explores the affinity between gothic literary conventions and the earliest major Anglo-Irish novel.

> With a little creative misreading one could claim that the Gothic strain in this literature is a major one all the way through. For is not *Castle Rackrent*, which focuses on a decayed but titled house, on decline and fall, on visiting the sins of the "old ones" on later generations, a Gothic romance in the Faulknerian if not the Radcliffian mold? It is indeed, except that the thing is worked as a sly and bracing middle-to-low comedy and the story lacks anything remotely resembling a broody Gothic hero of relentless will and suicidal tendency. (1982, 44–45)

In his overview of Irish gothic writing for the *Field Day Anthology of Irish Writing*, McCormack characterizes Maturin's sadomasochism as "bound up with colonial exploitation" and as a "symptomatic feature, not a literary achievement." Thus, McCormack also emphasizes how Irish gothic fiction is attached to and arises from contemporary history and politics (1991, 832–33).

"At this moment is there one of us present, however we may have departed from the Lord, disobeyed his will, and disregarded his word—is there one of us who would, at this moment, accept all that man could bestow, or earth could afford, to resign the hope of his salvation?—No, there is not—not such a fool on earth, were the enemy of mankind to traverse it with the offer!" (1977, 37). Maturin presents Melmoth, then, as a warning of the extraordinary man's capacity for total corruption; Melmoth's failure to find reprieve for his sin, as evidence of the faith of the rest of humanity.

By framing his narrative of sin and damnation with a description of a decaying Anglo-Irish estate and by presenting his protagonist as an absentee landlord, Maturin creates a gothic version of ascendancy fiction. The novel begins in 1816 when young John Melmoth, the impoverished scion of a declining landed Anglo-Irish family, is summoned to the deathbed of his only living relative. This uncle is a miserly and reclusive old man whose fear of poverty and paranoiac suspicion of his Irish retainers have reduced his country seat to desolation: ". . . penury had been aggravated and sharpened into downright misery" (43). His lodge is in ruins; the approach has been transformed into a miry road; the kitchen fare is squalid. The uncle's lifelong "oddities and infirmities" have led to collapse of authority and affection. As he lies dying, his obsequious and brutalized retainers reward his mistrust by stealing his liquor and food under the guise of mourning his approaching death.

The introductory and concluding sections of *Melmoth The Wanderer,* the framework for an intricate series of five gothic stories of terror, provide the novel with a powerfully realistic backdrop in Ireland. Set easily within memory of the Act of Union, when the Protestant ascendancy was accused of selling its country for a handful of titles, the story of Old Melmoth's death is essentially a study of Anglo-Irish guilt. Gone are all illusions of the feudal bond between landlord and tenant, which Lever elegized in *The Martins of Cro' Martin.* The old miser fears his retainers' depredations of his property, and although he dies a rich man, leaving his nephew a handsome patrimony, his last words attest to his obsessive suspicions. He shocks his nephew by begging that he intercede with the minister for a parish coffin, and, as the housekeeper attempts to clothe the dying man in a clean shirt and nightcap, he cries out desperately: "They are robbing me,—robbing me in my last moments,—robbing a dying man. John won't you assist me,—I shall die a beggar; they are taking my last shirt,—I shall die a beggar" (57).

Maturin provides no direct explanation for the miser's terrors, but the story of his family history, which the nephew learns after the old man's death, suggests a familiar historical basis for the Anglo-Irish landlord's guilt, insecurity, and paranoia. At first, John Melmoth's darker musings about his uncle's fears lead him to assume a criminal past, some personal culpability toward his tenants. "If his uncle was not superstitious, might he not have been guilty, and might not his strange and sudden death, and even the terrible visitation that preceded it, have been owing to some wrong that his rapacity had done the widow and the fatherless?" (61–62) The housekeeper's answer to his inquiries is reassuring, however, for she convinces him that, though his uncle was harsh, he was honest. "He would have starved all the wrong, but he would not have wronged it for a farthing" (62). Old Melmoth's sense of guilt, then, has more complex sources. Finally, the young heir seeks information about his family's history from a witchlike peasant sibyl and meditates on her revelations.

Sitting in the derelict Big House amidst the symbolic squalor of his family's decline—an almanac of the penal law days, a "dumb" clock that cannot record history or time, and a useless, rusty gun—young Melmoth overlooks the miser's neglected garden of broken-down walls, nettles, and weeds through the shattered windowpanes of the decaying house. He recalls what he has just learned, "with the air of a man who is cross-examining an evidence, and trying to make him contradict himself" (64). In his family's history, he hears a familiar story of Anglo-Irish injustice and expropriation. Unlike Glenthorn in Edgeworth's *Ennui*, who learns from an old peasant woman of a noble family history, Melmoth hears of his family's guilt. His peasant informant reveals that the first Melmoth who settled in Ireland was an officer of Cromwell's army who was given land confiscated from a native Irish family. But, more ominously, he hears of a mysterious, satanic elder brother of that first settler, a "damned magician," an ageless specter who traveled abroad in his youth and who returns to Ireland to haunt the deathbeds of those family members known to be "of evil passions or habits" (65). The threatening peasant usurper of the traditional Big House novel—Edgeworth's Jason or Lever's Scanlan—is thus transmuted into the insider, the ominous personification of a guilty Anglo-Irish conscience who haunts the corridors of the decaying estate.

The setting for these revelations suggests that the condemned ancestral Melmoth, the personification of evil who dominates the subsequent four hundred pages of the novel, is a figure with roots not only in the Faustian legends of Europe and in the tradition of romantic hero-villains, but also in a particularly Anglo-Irish vision of guilt. Old Melmoth's paranoiac fear of dispossession by his Irish tenants, as well as his miserly withholding of money and care from them, suggests those "evil passions or habits" that warrant the visitation by his satanic ancestor.

The above reading of the framing tale of *Melmoth The Wanderer* only begins to touch the richness of the multilayered novel. Maturin's insistence on the Anglo-Irish nationality of his doomed protagonist indicates his attempt to create not only an archetypal figure of tormented pride and damnation, but also, through the frame story, a more localized vision of sin. Although Melmoth represents an incarnation of Anglo-Irish guilt, Maturin's virulent attacks on the Catholic hierarchy throughout the subsequent tales complicate any simple allegorical readings of the novel. But, Maturin's anti-Catholicism during a period of rising Catholic pressure for emancipation does not lead him to excuse the failures of the Protestant ascendancy. He frames his novel within a narrative of the breakdown of reciprocity between Irish tenant and landlord, and by depicting the tenants on the old miser's estate much as Lever often did—as the illiterate, obsequious victims of neglect and exploitation—the Church of Ireland clergyman lashes out at the failures of his own class to rescue the Catholic peasantry from superstition and ignorance.

If we push the allegorical reading of the novel further, then Melmoth is the quintessential absentee landlord, wandering through Europe searching for his own reprieve, while his family estate slides into decay. On one occasion Maturin calls attention to Melmoth's Irish origins as he wanders the streets of Madrid, as if to counteract any impulse to view him solely as a transcendent figure of doom, free from any specific human or national history. "He is said to be a native of Ireland—(a country that no one knows, which the natives are particularly reluctant to dwell in from various causes)" (433). Or again, when Immalee, the innocent young woman Melmoth possesses and destroys, recalls him, she remembers "those wild and sweet songs of his country which he had taught her in his happier moods" (442).

When Melmoth fails to find his sacrificial victim, he returns for his punishment from the gothic world of Catholic Spain to the Irish Big House, to the decaying family lodge that he had deserted one hundred and fifty years ago. There, before the horrified eyes of his descendant, young John Melmoth, the Wanderer reappears. "Your ancestor had come home . . . his wanderings are over. . . . In this apartment . . . I first drew breath, in this I must perhaps resign it,—would I had never been born!" (696, 701). Even in Melmoth's actual death, when he is presumably dragged over a cliff by the forces that pursue him, Maturin carefully distinguishes between florid literary visions of damnation and the cold, grey landscape of the Wanderer's actual end in Ireland. Melmoth spends his last night in a spiritual terror that is expressed in conventional Christian terms.

> He dreamed that he stood on the summit of a precipice whose downward height no eye could have measured, but for the fearful waves of a fiery ocean that lashed, and blazed, and roared at in bottom, sending its burning spray far up, so as to drench the dreamer with its sulphurous rain. The whole glowing ocean below was alive—every billow bore an agonizing soul, that rose like a wreck or a putrid corse on the wave of the earth's ocean—uttered a shriek as it burst against that adamantine precipice—sunk and rose again to repeat the tremendous experiment! (697–98)

Melmoth's actual death struggles, accompanied by cries of supplication or blasphemy—his terrified listeners cannot distinguish which—occur not by the "fearful waves of a fiery ocean," but by the shore of the Irish sea. Young Melmoth and his companion follow a path through a field that looks "as if a person had dragged, or been dragged, his way through it" to the edge of a summit of rock among the cliffs of the Wicklow coast. The ocean by which they find the Wanderer's handkerchief—"the wide waste, engulphing ocean!" (703)—is, in its representative Irish particularity and its gray, gaping desolation, as terrifying as the most florid gothic nightmare of eternal doom. The return to an abandoned Ireland is a return to a desolate punishment.

Sheridan Le Fanu's *Uncle Silas*

Although Sheridan Le Fanu's *Uncle Silas,* another major gothic creation of nineteenth-century Irish fiction, was written almost a half-century after Maturin's *Melmoth The Wanderer,* the two novels share a similar preoccupation with ascendancy guilt. Le Fanu's complex relationship to Anglo-Irish political life suggests why *Uncle Silas,* like *Melmoth The Wanderer,* should be read not simply as a gothic sensation novel, nor as an exploration of psychic repression and projection, but also as an exploration of the beleaguered, isolated, and culpable position occupied by the Anglo-Irish Protestant class in the nineteenth century. Le Fanu's life reveals a profoundly ambivalent relationship to his own background. His biographer, W. J. McCormack, traces Le Fanu's childhood as the son of an early nineteenth-century Church of Ireland clergyman who was fast losing both income and prestige because of Catholic resistance to the tithe. As a child, Le Fanu witnessed attempted violence against his own family, and as an adult he strongly opposed Daniel O'Connell's Catholic leadership and the Whig alliance with O'Connell. Yet Le Fanu's growing dissatisfaction with Tory solutions to the erosion of Protestant power led to his flirtation with the reconciling cultural politics of the United Irishmen and to subsequent feelings of betrayal at finding himself closely linked with the revolutionary Anglo-Irish figure of William Smith-O'Brien in the abortive revolution of 1848. After this political crisis in his life Le Fanu abandoned his early historical fiction, in which he identified, like Maturin, with the decaying remnant of a safely defeated and exiled Jacobite gentry class. He turned instead to the masked and symbolic exposure of Protestant Anglo-Ireland guilt that we see in *Uncle Silas* (McCormack 1980, chs. 2–3 passim).

Uncle Silas exists, like *Melmoth The Wanderer,* at many removes from the social realism of much of Edgeworth's and Lever's fiction. Without any direct reference to Irish politics, with a setting in nineteenth-century England rather than in Ireland, and with the plot of a conventional novel of terror, *Uncle Silas* has tenuous links with the Big House form established by *Castle Rackrent.* Read with an awareness of its historical contexts, however, the novel stands as a powerful symbolic assault on the ascendancy from within the culture itself. As its subtlest commentator, William McCormack, demonstrates, *Uncle Silas* demands an apprehension of symbolic patterning and a willingness to engage in allegorical interpretations. The above reading of Maturin's *Melmoth The Wanderer* suggests that such modes of criticism enrich the traditional interpretations of these Anglo-Irish novels as major achievements of gothic fiction.

The problem of setting—in England rather than in Ireland—is

easily dissolved. Although *Uncle Silas* was written in 1864, it is closely based on an 1838 short story Le Fanu included in *The Purcell Papers*. In "Passage in the Secret History of an Irish Countess," one of his earliest works set in a Protestant Big House, an eighteenth-century Anglo-Irish woman tells the terrible story of her youth. Raised by a cold but duty-bound widowed father, she was left after his death with her uncle, an isolated landlord living under an unproved but powerful charge of murder. The narrator's father resents the society's suspicion and ostracism of his kinsman, and to prove his faith in his "deeply injured" brother, he appoints him guardian to his daughter. By leaving him her fortune in the event of her premature death, he unwittingly places his unprotected child in the clutches of a violent criminal with powerful motives to see her dead. In her new guardian's decaying mansion house of Carrigvarah in County Galway, the orphan is terrorized by the marital aspirations of her loutish cousin who seeks her fortune, and, after she angrily rejects her cousin, by the threats of her uncle. Imprisoned within the demesne walls, threatened with the madhouse for her terrors, she fearfully awaits her uncle's move and finally escapes his brutal attempt to murder her (Le Fanu, 1979, 1–102).

The Irish setting of this tale of terror and its preoccupation with decay and corruption on the Galway estate reveal Le Fanu's interest, as early as 1838, in questions of guilt within the ascendancy class. Although "Passage in the Secret History of an Irish Countess" only hints at the psychological complexity of *Uncle Silas,* the early story serves as a plot outline for the novel. Moreover, it clearly establishes the novel's original venue, which was changed to England because of the demands of Le Fanu's English publishers (McCormack 1981, xvii). Like Edgeworth, Lever, and Maturin, Le Fanu was constantly subjected to pressures by London publishers to write for English audiences only superficially acquainted with Irish society. In an essay written in 1946, Elizabeth Bowen responds to the familiar Anglo-Irish characteristics of the novel.

> *Uncle Silas* has always struck me as being an Irish story transposed to an English setting. The hermetic solitude and the autocracy of the great country house, the demonic power of the family myth, fatalism, feudalism and the "ascendancy" outlook are accepted facts of life for the race of hybrids from which Le Fanu sprang. For the psychological

background of *Uncle Silas* it was necessary for him to invent nothing. Rather, he was at once exploiting in art and exploring for its more terrible implications what would have been the norm for his own heredity. (1986, 101)

In *Uncle Silas* Le Fanu reconstructs several of the conventions of the Anglo-Irish Big House novel. The setting of a gloomy country estate, isolated and beleaguered, exists both at Knowl, the seemingly "safe" childhood home of the narrator, Maud Ruthyn, and in the second half of the novel, at the more terrifying prison of Bartram-Haugh, her Uncle Silas's vast, crumbling Derbyshire mansion where she must live after her father's death. Knowl's dark wainscoting, its "grim and pale" portraits, and shadowy corridors are balanced by its cheerful fires, its "pretty" and "graceful" paintings, and by the loving servants who surround Maud. But the specter of death haunts her first home as well as her second. The tapping and sighing ghosts who frequent the corridors of Knowl foreshadow terrifying human violators who will threaten Maud at Bartam-Haugh. In both *Melmoth The Wanderer* and *Uncle Silas,* the intruders are no longer outsiders—ambitious Catholics acquisitively eyeing the Big House—but threatening family presences, tormented villains living in the private hell of personal damnation. Thus, in Maturin's and Le Fanu's psychological explorations of Anglo-Irish guilt, the traditional gothic specters become emblematic of ascendancy crimes.

Bartram-Haugh's appearance is wilder and darker than that of the well-maintained Knowl. The symbolic pattern of enclosure and constriction surrounding this ancient family estate is clear as Maud first enters her new home.

[W]e wheeled into a wide semicircle formed by the receding park walls, and halted before a great fantastic iron gate, and a pair of tall fluted piers, of white stone, all grass-grown and ivy bound, with great cornices, surmounted with shields and supporters, the Ruthyn bearings washed by the rains of Derbyshire for many a generation of Ruthyns, almost smooth by this time, and looking bleached and phantasmal, like giant sentinels, with each a hand clasped in his comrade's, to bar our passage to the enchanted castle—the florid tracery of the iron gate showing like the draperies of white robes hanging from their extended arms to the earth. (Le Fanu 1981, 182)

The seemingly inaccessible "enchanted castle" is soon transformed into a walled prison, with barred windows and an enclosed courtyard; the Ruthyn coat of arms no longer bars passage into the castle but prevents Maud's escape. The gates are locked against her flight, the orphan is drugged, the murder of the innocent is planned.

Bartram-Haugh is occupied but not owned by Silas Ruthyn, whose dissipated life and tarnished reputation have reduced him to poverty and financial dependence on his brother, Austin. A terrifying figure of scorn and anguish, Silas shares with Melmoth the baleful, glaring eyes of the damned soul. As oppressors and guilt-ridden victims, both men illustrate how the characterization of the gothic villain can reflect a subversive and covert political attack on the colonial system. Silas neglects and despoils his home, an ancient and magnificent family estate. As Maud arrives, she sees giant trees uprooted by a recent storm and weed-filled avenues that give Bartram-Haugh "a forlorn character of desertion and decay, contrasting almost awfully with the grandeur of its proportions and richness of its architecture. . . . It was plain that not nearly a tithe of this great house was inhabited; long corridors and galleries stretched away in dusts and silence, and were crossed by others, whose dark arches inspired me in the distance with an awful sort of sadness" (183, 196). As the romantic young girl wanders about Bartram Haugh, she is reminded with a "pleasing terror" of the gothic settings of Mrs. Radcliffe's romance (196). Through literary analogy Maud seeks to protect herself from terrors that are finally more malignant than any conceived of by Mrs. Radcliffe.

The personal luxuries with which the degenerate Silas surrounds himself—his jeweled pencil case, his silk hangings, fine wines, and chains and seals—are the spoils of his abuse of his brother's trust, for he is engaged in illegally deforesting his niece's property. The opulence of the great house is no longer associated with aristocratic hauteur, as in *The Martins of Cro' Martin*, but with criminality. The trunks and limbs of ancient oak trees that lie about the estate numbered for sale are reminders of his greed, but to the romantic imagination of his niece, they suggest the tragic fall of the Ruthyns. "I sighed as I passed them by, not because it was wrongfully done, for I really rather leaned to the belief that Uncle Silas was well advised in point of law. But alas! here lay low the grand old family decorations of Bartram-Haugh, not to be replaced for centuries to come, under whose spreading boughs the Ruthyns of three hundred years ago had hawked and hunted!" (323) Like Thady Quirk in *Castle Rackrent,* Maud mourns what she perceives as the poignant decline of a once great family. Until faced with the actual plot against her life, she refuses to accept her trustee's account of her uncle's illegal business dealings—and thus refuses to acknowledge her family's guilt. Romantic nostalgia blinds her.

The two country estates portrayed in the novel, Austin's Knowl and Silas's Bartram-Haugh, evoke the dark, isolated splendor of traditional gothic settings, but without that covert affirmation of disorder that we find, for example, in Maria Edgeworth's contrast between the orderly English estate and the wild Irish castle in *Ennui.* Edgeworth's use of the gothic setting in *Ennui* suggests a subversive freedom, not a constriction; a potential for disorder, but also for health and renewed life for Lord Glenthorn. But Knowl and Bartram-Haugh are both simply houses of terror; they first represent barriers, and then solitary confinement—imprisonment, not freedom—for the young heroine. On each estate Maud is isolated and abused: kept from her loving aunt; subjected to the sadistic control of a grotesque French governess, Madame de la Rougierre; and then exposed to the terrifying attacks of her cousin. The distinctions between her childhood with a seemingly loving father and the terrifying months of her youth with her Uncle Silas begin to collapse when we realize how the events of the first half of the novel foreshadow and anticipate the violence of the second. As McCormack puts it, "The recurring plot of Le Fanu's fiction is the recurrence of history in the present, the past re-enacting itself" (1981, xviii).

The doting servants at the well-maintained estate of Knowl are certainly different from the disreputable and violent band of attendants that Silas gathers around him in his decaying mansion, but Maud is a victim in each of her domiciles. At Knowl, she suffers from her father's brooding isolation; from her terror of the ghosts that haunt the dark corridors; from Austin's melancholy and hints about his impending departure, and from her nightmares; in one of which her father appears to her as her Uncle Silas later will, "white and malignant," pronouncing the word "death" (Le Fanu 1981, 30). When her loving Aunt Monica angrily leaves Knowl after Austin rejects her sensible warnings about Maud's sinister governess, Maud's comment on her home is revealing. "Knowl was dark again—darker than ever" (74).

Knowl's manicured gardens and wooded demesne are not exempt from the terrifying violence that Maud will later endure at Bartram-Haugh. While picnicking on the grounds of her father's estate with Madame de la Rougierre, she is accosted, insulted, and barely escapes being kidnapped by unknown ruffians—later revealed as agents of her Uncle Silas, who work in league with her governess. Among them is Silas's son Dudley Ruthyn, whose brutish vulgarity, when coupled with his father's refined viciousness, attests to the degeneracy of the Anglo-Irish family line. Le Fanu's preoccupation with violent attacks on a helpless girl may have roots in his childhood terrors during the tithe wars, as well as in the conventions of gothic literature, but in *Uncle Silas* violence and sexual threats to the young come from within Anglo-Ireland rather than from without. Because Maud is accosted by agents of her own family, her father's initial fury at the mysterious assault quickly subsides. He accepts with equanimity the escape of the attackers, an escape that will spare Maud unwelcome "publicity and annoyance" (88).

Austin's insistence on "solitude and silence" (102), his absolute psychological domination of Maud and the household staff (even his daughter seldom dares to address him before being addressed), his Swedenborgian religion that isolates him from his community, and his obsessive preoccupation with vindicating his family name all suggest the psychic condition of a beleaguered social class. In an allegorical reading of *Uncle Silas*, Austin represents an Anglo-Ireland that is fast losing ground to historical change, unable to transcend its obsessive paranoia and thus spare its posterity, represented in the novel by a victimized and helpless daughter. Austen's culpability for Maud's future suffering is unmitigated by the abstract idealism of his intention, for he makes Maud a living sacrifice to his family name.

> "It may cost you something—are you willing to buy it at a sacrifice? Is there—I don't speak of fortune, that is not involved—but is there any other honorable sacrifice you would shrink from to dispel the disgrace under which our most ancient and honorable name must otherwise continue to languish? . . . I believe it to be a duty to take care of others beside myself. The character and influence of an ancient family is a

peculiar heritage—sacred but destructible: and woe to him who either destroys or suffers it to perish." (102–4)

Austin and Silas Ruthyn are proud and alienated men, landlords cut off from their surroundings, living in smoldering resentment against the gentry neighbors who will not forget the unsolved murder of a guest in Silas's home. Between Austin and Silas, Le Fanu portrays virtually every possible failing of the ascendancy, achieving a specificity of attack that Maturin's far more abstract vision of Anglo-Irish culpability does not even attempt. The Ruthyns are of an ancient lineage "who had refused a baronetage often, and it was said even a viscounty, being of a proud and defiant spirit, and thinking themselves higher in station and purer of blood than two-thirds of the nobility into whose ranks, it was said, they had been invited to enter" (1).

Austin's unsuccessful attempts to enter political life lead him to a life abroad of connoisseurship and study. Returning to Knowl, he chooses to live in "remarkable seclusion" and in proud aloofness from the concerns of his country. Silas represents a far darker pattern of Anglo-Irish life, embodying the explicit criminality that the young John Melmoth dreads to hear about his dying uncle and discovers in the legend of his fearful ancestor, Melmoth the Wanderer. Silas marries beneath him, games away any money he has, and finally lives as a social outcast. Filled with rage against those who turn against him, he disguises his unregenerate impulses in the trappings of piety and comforts himself with opium. Whereas earlier Big House novels emphasize the failures of the proprietor as landlord to his tenants, Le Fanu adds a true gothic dimension to his attack on Anglo-Ireland. He explores a deep personal moral degeneracy within the ascendancy class: the crippling pride that encourages Austin to sacrifice his innocent daughter to his blind faith in family; the criminal greed that provokes Silas's murderous attempt on his niece.

Austin's single-minded preoccupation with family lineage and his refusal to see beyond his own obsession to the real needs of others—what McCormack refers to as the gentry class's "reduced apprehension of reality" (1981, xvi)—is a common theme in Anglo-Irish literature. We need only look back to Lever's portrayal of an isolated landlord class in *The Martins of Cro' Martin* or forward to Somerville's depiction of the foolishly irrelevant Talbot-Lowrys in *Mount Music* to find the same pattern of genealogical obsession and decline that Le Fanu explores, albeit in a masked and symbolic form.

McCormack's interpretation of *Uncle Silas* stresses the simultaneity of the two parts of the novel; for the critic, Silas is virtually a reincarnation of potentials within the seemingly good father. From this dualistic reading of the novel comes that brilliant insight that places *Uncle Silas* centrally in the tradition of Anglo-Irish Big House fiction. If Knowl, the childhood home of the past, cannot be evoked as the image of harmonious order and safety, then the whole notion of a once coherent ascendancy culture begins to collapse.

> It is tempting to read the two-part structure of *Uncle Silas* in terms of a simplified literary sociology in which Austin and Knowl are images of an orderly eighteenth-century hegemony, Silas and Bartram-Haugh as its degenerate or betrayed inheritance in the Victorian age. . . . The temptation is best answered by a return to the novel and the reciprocity with which Le Fanu fully relates the two settings to each other. . . . Le Fanu offers no view of an Edenic past or of a serene history; if the present is a vicious falling away from previous harmony, then it is the past which is exposed as inadequate or treacherous or illusory. (1981, xvii–xviii)

McCormack's reading of *Uncle Silas* as an exposure of the myths of a feudal stability is relevant to virtually every Big House novel discussed in this study. The ideal of a beneficent feudal landlord is merely an illusion of the abandoned retainer, like Thady Quirk in *Castle Rackrent,* or of the defeated Big House lady, like Mary Martin in Lever's *The Martins of Cro' Martin.* In *Uncle Silas,* Maud's idealization of her father and uncle—representing her wish fulfillment rather than a realistic assessment of her guardians—almost costs her life. In Anglo-Irish fiction the proprietors of the Big House are improvident and irresponsible at best (the Rackrents); more typically they are exploitative of their dependents or are blinded by class pride (the Melmoths or the Martins). Le Fanu goes further than any of his predecessors in assigning culpability to the Anglo-Irish landlord. In *Uncle Silas* the Big House turns upon itself; Austin Ruthyn's pride in family and Silas Ruthyn's vicious greed condemn Maud to suffering and nearly to death. Not until Molly Keane's *Good Behaviour,* written more than century after *Uncle Silas,* do we again see such an exposure of the illusions sustaining the Big House, such an unmerciful depiction of how a beleaguered society savagely destroys its own young.

The Big Houses of
Somerville and Ross

To move from the world of mid-nineteenth-century Anglo-Irish fiction—from Charles Lever's depiction of the waning of a powerful landlord class or Le Fanu's gothic allegory of Anglo-Irish guilt—to the late nineteenth- and early twentieth-century world of Somerville and Ross is to move to a society not merely in decline, but in the advanced stages of disintegration. The viability of the Big House and traditional systems of land tenure came under specific attack in the late nineteenth century, when Edith Somerville and Violet Martin embarked on their literary partnership. By the 1890s, parliamentary legislation had begun to shift control of Irish land from the ascendancy class to the tenantry. Finally, the Wyndham Land Act of 1903 encouraged landlords to sell their property to tenants by reducing the interest rate on loans and by extending the time of repayment to sixty-eight years. Although many Irish landlords welcomed the legislation for relieving them of the costs of maintaining burdensome estates, others were bitterly resentful. Owners who wished to retain their holdings felt that England had abandoned them; they were, in effect, now forced to sell their land to their tenants and abandon their hereditary roles. *The Big House of Inver,* the last major work published under the names of Somerville and Ross, was produced in 1925, after the War of Independence, the Civil War, and the burning of more than two hundred Big Houses. Anglo-Irish political ascendancy had ended.

During that period of crisis for the landowner, Somerville and Ross emerged as writers from gentry society, not from the unlanded, professional, urban Protestant class that produced Lever, Maturin, and

Le Fanu. Violet Martin, the Ross of the literary partnership, belonged to a powerful Connemara clan, one of the Tribes of Galway, whose family decline provided the loose framework for Charles Lever's *The Martins of Cro' Martin*. Norman-Irish in origin, the Martins came to Ireland with Strongbow and converted from Catholicism a few generations before Violet Martin's birth. Her family home, Ross, near Oughterard in County Galway, was the first of four Martin houses to be built in Connemara. Smaller than the 200,000-acre property of Ballynahinch, which was constructed by her great-grandfather Richard Martin and became the setting of Lever's novel, Ross survived as a family property longer than any of the other Martin homes.

Edith Somerville's family lineage was marginally less distinguished than her literary partner's. She was, like her second cousin Violet Martin, a descendant of the incorruptible Charles Kendal Bushe, the lord chief justice of Ireland who voted against the union; the Somervilles were, however, much smaller landlords than the Martins. Because they depended for income primarily on trade and army commissions rather than on land, their position was not seriously affected by the Famine, which ended the Martin family's ownership of Ballynahinch and which permanently changed the semifeudal relationship between tenant and landlord at Ross. The Somerville family's nationalist sympathies were unusual; in 1858, Edith's grandfather, a friend of the Fenian leader O'Donovan Rossa, hid two Fenians fleeing to America. Even earlier, during the tithe wars, the same grandfather distinguished himself by defending his tenants against government forces (Lewis 1985, 20).

Their Anglo-Norman origins, their families' long associations with ascendancy Ireland, and the security of their social positions among the Anglo-Irish gentry all suggest that these literary partners—who took Somerville and Ross as their pen name—would speak from a deep loyalty to their class and background. And often they did. Their nostalgic memoirs of their ancestral heritage, which Edith gathered together in *Irish Memories* and *Wheel-Tracks* after Violet Martin's death in 1915, reveal the powerful appeal that Anglo-Irish tradition held for them. In Martin's history of her family, the political silences of premodern Ireland are celebrated with an elegiac nostalgia. She wrote of the semifeudal life at Ross in 1846, the first year of the Famine, without any self-consciousness about the human costs of such patterns of life for the country people.

The quietness of untroubled centuries lay like a spell on Connemara, the country of his ancestors; the old ways of life were unquestioned at Ross, and my father went and came among his people in an intimacy as native as the soft air they breathed. On the crowded estate the old routine of potato planting and turf cutting was pursued tranquilly; the people intermarried and subdivided their holdings; few could read and many could not speak English. All were known to the Master, and he was known and understood by them, as the old Galway people know and understood; and the subdivisions of the land were permitted, and the arrears of rent were given time, or taken in boatloads of turf, or worked off by day-labor, and eviction was unheard of. It was give and take, with the personal element always warm in it: as a system it was probably quite uneconomic, but the hand of affection held it together, and the tradition of centuries was at its back. (Somerville and Ross 1918, 4)

Martin's bitterness at the wounding separation between proprietor and tenant that she saw as a result of the late nineteenth-century land acts suggests her unequivocal resistance to the rising nationalist movement. She wrote of the mutual dependence of landlord and the country people as "a delicate relation, almost akin to matrimony, and like a happy marriage, it needed that both sides should be good fellows" (26). Legislation designed to protect tenants was perceived as a superfluity. "In 1870 came Gladstone's Land Act, which by a system of fines shielded the tenant to a great extent from 'capricious eviction.' As evictions, capricious or otherwise, did not occur at Ross, this section of the Act was not of epoch-making importance there" (26).

Such attitudes suggest why the Martins were unprepared for the 1872 election, when the tenants of Ross turned against the Big House candidate and inflicted a "personal wound" on Violet Martin's father (27). Like the defeat of the Edgeworth family's candidate forty years earlier, such recurring political shocks to nineteenth- and early twentieth-century Big House society demonstrate how easily landlords mistook their tenants' repressed hostility—or, at least, their ambivalent subservience—for passive feudal devotion. Writing about Martin's memoir of Ross, Somerville accurately implied that an Edenic fantasy governed her collaborator's version of Big House life. "Martin has, in her memoir of her brother Robert, given a sketch of life at Ross as it was in the old days, in its patriarchal simplicity, its pastoral abundance, its limitless hospitality, its feudal relations with peasants. Its simplicity was, I imagine, of a more primitive type than can be claimed for any conditions that I can personally remember in my own county" (62).

The choice of language here is significant. By calling Martin's piece a sketch, Somerville emphasizes its pictorial and personal re-creation of mood and ambiance rather than its historical accuracy. Her language of critical praise reveals how an aura of nostalgia surrounds Martin's vision of Ross in its "pastoral abundance" and "feudal relations." In its recognition of the role of nostalgia in shaping memory, Somerville's memoir of her own ancestral home is significantly different from Martin's. Her essay "Drishane" involves a more self-conscious acknowledgment of the difference between the forgotten "details" of the past and nostalgic "impressions" (1923, 1). She begins her description of Drishane by acknowledging the power of childhood memories to evoke nostalgia, rather than dispassionate perception. Somerville's distinction between the lost "details" and the glowing "impressions" by which the details are replaced anticipates the hard-headed capacity to transcend nostalgia that characterizes the best writing she did about the Big House, after Violet Martin's death in 1915.

An Irish Cousin

Published in 1889, Somerville and Ross's *An Irish Cousin* is generally dismissed as an awkward piece of gothic apprentice work, of interest primarily because of their later success in the mode of social realism. Yet, by recreating the gothic novel in a specifically Irish setting, *An Irish Cousin,* unlike the earlier *Melmoth the Wanderer* or *Uncle Silas,* no longer encodes or disguises the society that it exposes. The obvious flaws in this early fiction—its abrupt and unconvincing happy ending, the creakiness of its plot mechanisms, the occasional embarrassments of its gothic excesses—are the faults of inexperience and of a desire to satisfy the demands of the literary marketplace.[1] But in their first sustained work, Somerville and Ross employ traditional gothic conventions to create a powerfully subversive vision of their own culture.

Significantly, authors who were both deeply rooted insiders in as-

1. As economically dependent young women, Edith Somerville and Violet Martin began the novel eager to find a source of income. Edith's account of their efforts to

cendancy society chose as their first-person narrator a similarly well-born figure. Nevertheless, Theodora Sarsfield is, as she describes herself, "a stranger in a strange land" (Somerville and Ross 1903, 163), the innocent outsider capable of judging Big House society with new but socially reliable eyes. Born abroad and raised in Europe by her widowed mother, Theo arrives in Ireland to visit Durrus, her dead father's childhood home, which is now occupied by her father's younger brother, Dominick, and by his son, her Irish cousin Willy. The novel begins with her entrance, as a complexly connected outsider, into a new world whose secrets she will expose. Both like (by nature) and different from (by nurture) the other Anglo-Irish characters, Theo is a reliable judge of them.

Suspecting that all Irishmen wear knee breeches and greet strangers with the "national salutation, 'Begorra!' " (5) Theo knows nothing of the dense and festering Anglo-Irish world of her father's family. Nevertheless, her cool and discriminating voice conveys authority. Purged by an unpleasant sea journey of her memories, she enters a disordered and bewildering society that, for all its surface social decorum, is filled with primitive passions: sexual obsession, greed, madness, and criminality. Theo's gradual awakening to the truth about her family history forms the dramatic center of a work that, according to Somerville, first became alive for its authors after their visit to a Townshend cousin living in a lonely Big House by the sea. Edith reports that after that experience, "realities" asserted themselves.

> The sunset was red in the west when our horses were brought
> round to the door, and it was at that precise moment that into *The Irish*
> *Cousin* some thrill of genuineness was breathed. In the darkened fa-

---

produce *An Irish Cousin* suggests that as apprentice writers they lacked the confidence or support they needed to conceive of themselves as the serious artists they were. She makes light of their efforts and describes how they tolerated their families' derisive references to the manuscript as "the shocker" (a term they themselves used in referring to it) as well as an overt hostility to claims on their time made by their writing (Somerville and Ross 1918, 131–34). Although my analysis of *An Irish Cousin* seeks to legitimize their use of gothic conventions, the book does suffer on occasion from their awkward piling up of gothic horrors in the tradition of popular sensational literature. Mad Moll's "dreadful" midnight dance and supplicating prayer under Theo's window is the most glaring example of such excess (1903, 45–46).

cade of the long grey house, a window, just over the hall-door, caught our attention. In it, for an instant, was a white face. Trails of ivy hung over the panes, but we saw the face glimmer there for an instant and vanish.

As we rode home along the side of the hills, and watched the fires of the sunset sink into the sea, and met the crescent moon coming with faint light to lead us home, we could talk and think only of that presence at the window. We had been warned of certain subjects not to be approached, and we knew enough of the history of that old house to realize what we had seen. An old stock, isolated from the world at large, wearing itself out in those excesses that are a protest of human nature against unnatural conditions, dies at last with its victims around its death-bed. Half-acknowledged, half-witted, wholly horrifying, living ghosts; haunting the house that gave them but half their share of life, yet withheld from them with half-hearted guardianship, the boom of death. (Somerville and Ross 1918, 130–31)

Their response to the visit to the Townshend house suggests Somerville and Ross's early awareness of disorder behind the façade of an ascendancy society they embraced and supported both through their writing (in, for example, their affectionate Resident Magistrate tales and their memoirs) and through their lifelong commitment to the economic survival of their respective Big Houses. The apparition of the white face in the window both recalls and anticipates recurring subversive themes in Anglo-Irish fiction. Through that face peering out, two young Anglo-Irish women inscribed the costs of an imprisoned, imprisoning, and isolated culture: most obviously its overbred, incestuous old stock and sequestered, half-witted relatives. Miss Pidgie in Molly Keane's *Two Days in Aragon* is just such an eccentric maiden aunt, expelled to the attic of the Big House; in the context of *An Irish Cousin*, the face in the window specifically evokes the Durrus lodgekeeper's mad wife, Moll Hourihane, who is Uncle Dominick's illegitimate cousin and mistress. Moll's life embodies the ascendancy's sexual exploitation of native Irish women and exposes the recurring patterns of incest that emerge from the past. Her demented haunting of the Big House in *An Irish Cousin* embodies an explicit condemnation of ascendancy relationships with the native Irish.

Somerville and Ross's first novel should be read as a politically charged exploration of social disorder, not simply as an awkward and flawed experiment with gothic sensationalism. Placed within the tradition of other Anglo-Irish novels set on country estates, works that convey both the fear and desire inherent in the colonizer's relationship to the colonized, *An Irish Cousin* is a significant achievement. In it, two apprentice writers transform stock gothic conventions into the political matter of Big House fiction. Dominick Sarsfield's long, lonely house by the sea (certainly suggested by the Townshend home) is the classic gothic mansion of terror, but now overlaid with a familiar vision of Anglo-Irish domestic disorder.[2]

Durrus is, indeed, both a house of terror out of Le Fanu and a familiar, declining, Rackrent-like Big House. Lights flicker and extinguish themselves in its long dark halls; "claret-colored ancestors" stare down from dirty portraits on the walls; furnishings and paintings are covered with a thick coating of dust; gates remain unrepaired; donkeys and calves roam throughout the stableyards. Yet poverty does not wholly account for all this neglect. Theo observes that the stable is well equipped and that stable helpers and hangers-on populate the barnyard. She is endlessly bewildered by the "mixture of prosperity and dilapidation" (Somerville and Ross 1903, 48) that she encounters wherever she turns, and does not yet understand the depths of moral—not simply economic—decline that is signaled by such disorder.

In *An Irish Cousin,* Somerville and Ross link Edgeworth's motif of bad housekeeping with a threatening moral degeneracy rather than with mere sloppy improvidence. Theo constantly encounters examples of slipshod domestic arrangements and initially reacts to such slovenliness with an Edgeworthian dismay. Entering her cold, smoke-filled room, she finds a window with a broken pulley held open by her hairbrush, and reflects on the change her life has undergone— from an ordered childhood to this perplexing disorder. "I leaned

2. John Cronin's accurate if dismissive description of the atmosphere of Durrus as "compounded of equal parts of Brontean Gothic, Le Fanu-like mystification, and Rackrentish disorder" (1972, 27) suggests the many literary echoes in the novel but implicitly devalues the political charge of any of them. Cronin reads *An Irish Cousin* as a "social novel stuggling to break through the book's overlay of Irish Gothic" and, following Edith Somerville's own suggestion, divides the novel between "the absurdly romantic and the convincingly realistic" (27). Thus, Cronin dismisses Uncle Dominick and Mad Moll and praises those characters, like Willy, who anticipate later, realistic characters. Hilary Robinson is far more sympathetic to the gothic element in the novel, but she emphasizes the working out of literary conventions rather than the subversive political implications of the form (1980).

against the shutter and looked about beset by poignant reflections of a time when life without my mother seemed an impossibility, and when Durras was no more to me than a place in a fairy tale" (44). Visiting a neighboring Big House where the floors are polished and the furniture dusted, she realizes how quickly she has become "inured to untidiness" (117). But suggestions of the ominous moral implications of such domestic disorder gradually flood the novel. The dilapidated and neglected garden filled with unpruned apple trees resembles a fallen Eden, and branches of a peach tree thrust themselves out of the decaying window sashes and broken panes of a hothouse "as if breaking loose from imprisonment" (233).

The dark fairy-tale world at Durrus rapidly becomes a nightmare of terror, like Le Fanu's Bartram-Haugh. When she first enters her own "gaunt apartment," Theo uneasily notices a suspiciously disguised door, papered over to blend in with the wall. The door opens into a mysterious room with uncurtained windows, an uncarpeted floor, and a few pieces of furniture that are, appropriately enough, "shrouded in sheets and huddled in one corner" (18). In this chamber—Owen Sarsfield's boyhood room and the site of his lonely death—she later discovers the journal that her father wrote as he lay dying as well as his stamped but unmailed letter to her mother; these papers suggest the existence of a stolen will and an unjust disposition of the family property by her Uncle Dominick. The traditional gothic emphasis on ancient documents—lost wills exposing unjust inheritances—becomes more than a literary convention.[3] Theo's discovery of her own dispossession politicizes that gothic convention in a society preoccupied—after centuries of dispossessions—with the dubiousness of seemingly lawful transmissions of property. Although Somerville and Ross are far too committed to their own rural Anglo-Irish society to contemplate the injustices of early dispossessions in Irish history, their preoccupation with orderly lines of succession encodes a central source of Anglo-Irish anxiety at a time of new land legislation and tenant challenges to "lawful" ascendancy tenure.[4]

3. Similar preoccupations with the legitimacy of lines of succession appear in Edgeworth's *Ennui* and Lever's *The Martins of Cro' Martin*.

4. *An Irish Cousin* appeared in 1889, shortly after a period of particular crisis for Big House landlords. By the late 1870s the continuing economic insecurity of Irish tenants encouraged vigorous mass actions organized by the newly formed Land League—specifically, boycotting and the resumption of rural outrages as a reaction

Theo responds with despair to the horrors she discovers in her father's old room. She reacts not only to her economic loss, but also to the revelation of an almost palpable evil she can express only in theological language. "I sat down by the window and covered my face with my hands, afraid of those dark places of guilt in which I found myself" (296). In such a scene Somerville and Ross imply a pervasive moral stain on the Big House, a taint anticipating the indelible memory of cruelty that destroys an Anglo-Irish family in William Trevor's *The Silence in the Garden,* written a full century later.[5] Like other Irish gothic fiction, Somerville and Ross's first novel views the ascendancy landlord within moral rather than merely social categories. Dominick Sarsfield is no longer simply an improvident and irresponsible landlord who must be reformed (as he would be in Edgeworth's fiction); he is, rather, like Uncle Silas or Melmoth, a criminal, a guilt-ridden sinner, a moral outcast for whom suicide, not reeducation and reform, is an appropriate fate.

Behind the familiar domestic disorder that ascendancy novelists repeatedly evoke to signify Big House decline, lies the psychic burden of Anglo-Irish culture. Like Faulkner, whose fiction obsessively returns to the effects of past miscegenation on the descendants of slave owners and slaves alike, Somerville and Ross examine the costs of ascendancy sexual exploitation to both the Sarsfields and their tenants. Theo discovers that a beautiful peasant girl in the lodge house—Mad Moll's daughter, Anstey—is her cousin Willy's half-sister and discarded mistress. She learns that Moll, who haunts Owen Sarsfield's deserted room in Durrus, is herself an illegitimate child of the Big House, her uncle Dominick's former mistress, Willy's foster mother, and possibly the murderer of her own father. Finally, after a series of overly cryptic clues, hints, and terrifying encounters with Moll, Theo discovers that Owen was cheated of his inheritance by her Uncle Dominick, who left his elder brother to die, and then, with his mistress's help, secretly disposed of his body. This cauldron of Big House guilt, of greed and sexual exploitation, embodies a melodra-

---

to eviction (Lyons 1973, 165). The agricultural depression of the 1880s lowered rents; thus, small farmers became debtors, threatened by foreclosures of mortgages. Squeezed between inflexible costs and declining rent rolls, landlords suffered major losses along with their tenants (Solow 1971, ch. 5 passim). A series of land reforms attempted to deal with the increasing hostility of Irish tenants toward the landlord class, a hostility which erupted into a land war between 1879 and 1882.

5. See the discussion of Trevor's novel on pp. 230–33.

matic vision of cultural decline by two young cousins whose lives appeared to be deeply committed to their gentry society.

Critics have noted resemblances between *An Irish Cousin* and *Uncle Silas*,[6] certainly, the story of an orphan girl's discovery of criminal malevolence in a great house is heavily indebted to the gothic terrors of Le Fanu's masterpiece. But despite similarities between the two books, Theo is never a helpless victim like Maud. Throughout *An Irish Cousin*, she retains control over the importunate advances of her cousin and the more hostile pressures of her uncle, who demands that she rescue Willy from a ruinous liaison. Dominick's villainy and snobbery, however, rival the worst traits of Le Fanu's landlords: the criminal dispossession of his brother and complicity in his death, the sexual exploitation and corruption of Moll, an obsessive preoccupation with social class (and subsequent terror that his neglected son will marry a peasant girl whom he himself probably fathered).

Through the characters of Moll Hourihane and her daughter Anstey, Somerville and Ross reveal the limits of their empathy with a Catholic tenantry. As peasant women who provide sexual services to ascendancy landlords, Moll and Anstey are initially presented as victims. Although the details of Moll's past are inadequately revealed, her madness is presumably a response to her exile from Dominick's bed and household, as well as to her arranged marriage to the lodge-keeper, Michael Brian. Her daughter Anstey is initially treated with considerable sympathy as the passionate lover of Willy Sarsfield, a son of the Big House. Ashamed of his mistress, however, Willy is desperate to escape her clutches and rescue himself by marrying his cousin Theo.

But if *An Irish Cousin* manages to expose the victimization of those two women, it never seriously undermines hierarchical assumptions of class and caste, even as it stigmatizes the violent snobbery of Dominick Sarsfield. In one telling scene Dominick argues with a more democratically inclined neighbor, who maintains that his tenants' degradation is the result of injustice, not inherent inequality. Dominick's angry rejoinder reflects both his immediate fears for his son and his acceptance of class hierarchy as a "natural arrangement." "If

6. Hilary Robinson, for example, acknowledges that *An Irish Cousin* is "uncannily similar to Sheridan Le Fanu's *Uncle Silas*" but insists on the superiority of Somerville and Ross's work to Le Fanu's unserious "supernatural tale written for effect" (1980, 59). By failing to appreciate the encoding of Anglo-Irish anxieties in *Uncle Silas,* she fails to explore more than the surface similarities between the two gothic novels.

you were to marry your coachman, as, according to your theories of equality, I suppose you would not hesitate to do, do you think these latent instincts of refinement that you talk about would make him a fit companion for you and your family? You know as well as I do that such an idea is preposterous. It is absurd to suppose that the natural arrangement of things can be tampered with" (103).

By putting the defense of class distinction into the mouth of the novel's most corrupt character, Somerville and Ross appear to support the arguments of Dominick's gentry antagonist, who argues for a less rigid calculation of social position. Yet the two women who dare to make claims on men above their station are viewed with growing uneasiness and distrust. Anstey virtually disappears from the novel, and her marriage to Willy is presented wholly from his point of view as a tragic case of the entrapment of a young man, never as a fulfillment of her passion or love. (A scene in which Anstey's putative father drunkenly threatens Willy reinforces our sense of this entrapment.) He imagines that his life is destroyed by his marriage, although his newly developed capacity to defy his father suggests a growing independence. Just as Anstey's claims for our sympathy erode as she disappears from the novel, Mad Moll's role as victim is gradually undermined as we discover her criminal contrivances in the death of Theo's father, the secret disposal of his body, and her failure to send the dying man's letter to his wife. Somerville and Ross's shifting attitudes toward Moll and her daughter suggest their uneasiness before any easing of social barriers, even as they begin to acknowledge the deep moral culpability of their own class.

Dominick Sarsfield's alcohol-related madness and subsequent suicide occur in a setting new to Big House fiction, a gothic landscape of the mind that anticipates future reworking of the tradition as a psychological rather than a sociological literary form. Dominick's death in the woods of his demesne introduces a new psychic territory: neither the well-ordered grounds of a great house, nor the invigorating "primitive" world of a feudal estate in the west, nor the familiar slack disorder and improvidence of a Castle Rackrent. Searching for her mad guilt-ridden uncle after a storm, Theo finds herself in a nightmare setting; she is surrounded by dead bracken, muddy pits, torn-down branches, uprooted vegetation, a landscape suggestive of her deepest response to the collapse of her family's patriarchal line. The terrifying keening she hears implies, moreover, the new ascendancy of the peasant woman's voice over the country-side.

> Since yesterday afternoon blow upon blow had been dealt me, and the stupor of accumulated fatigue had fallen upon me. There was a weight in the air, the sky was low and foreboding, and a watery streak of yellow lay along the horizon behind the bog. A rook rustled close over my head with a subdued croak; I dully watched him flying quietly home to the tall elms by the lodge; he was still circling round them before settling down, when a long wavering cry struck upon my ear, a sound that once heard is never forgotten, the cry of a woman keening. It came from the bog; every pulse stood still as I heard it, and I clung to the gate for support, while the varying ominous cadences filled the air, I knew, above and beyond reasoning, that it meant the end. (303–4)

Mount Music

The marginally different political backgrounds Somerville and Ross brought to their writing had far-reaching consequences. The literary partners' earliest novel, *An Irish Cousin,* offers its harshest judgment of Anglo-Ireland through gothic conventions that distance readers from the density of social and political experience that appears in Somerville's later fiction. Although most critical opinion argues that Violet Martin was the more subtle stylist and sophisticated thinker in the partnership, the level of political conservatism evident in her nonfiction helps explain why Edith wrote *The Big House of Inver,* her most historically resonant novel about ascendancy decline, a full decade after her collaborator's death.[7]

Mount Music, Somerville's first major work after Violet Martin's

7. In choosing those novels that Edith Somerville wrote after Martin's death as the central texts for this chapter I am implicitly questioning the received critical judgment that Violet Martin is the better writer. Hilary Mitchell suggests that with Violet Martin's death "the partnership lost its finer, more literary mind" (1968, 37). Hilary Robinson's chapter on the collaboration, although it insists always on the joint enterprise of the writing and withholds any specific value judgment, approvingly summarizes Cresap Watson's unpublished thesis on the subject: Martin illustrates more "profound thought"; she is the "poet," Edith the "painter" (quoted in Robinson 1980, 38–39). In his discussion of Somerville and Ross in *Anglo-Irish: The Literary Imagination in a Hyphenated Culture* (1995), Julian Moynahan includes an extensive laudatory analysis of Violet Martin's writing without Edith, but fails to discuss *The Big House of Inver.*

death, is indebted to her nostalgic memories of her earliest years at Drishane, "that most wonderful and splendid old house" (1923, 1). But the novel is also committed to registering the life of the Big House in the context of late nineteenth- and early twentieth-century Irish politics. In its strongest moments, it transcends nostalgia and achieves historical objectivity and tough-minded judgment of an Anglo-Irish society that attempted to ignore history. Edith Somerville wrote *Mount Music* and *The Big House of Inver* between 1915 and 1925, decades in which Yeats composed poems—"Coole Park" and "Meditations in Time of Civil War," for example—in which the beleaguered Anglo-Irish country house came to represent lost aesthetic and aristocratic values. In the contemporary Big House, particularly in Lady Gregory's Coole Park and his own tower home in Galway, Yeats found the sustained trope through which to evoke his idiosyncratic vision of ascendancy history—whose claim for validity lay in a conservative theory of art and society.[8] Only in *Purgatory*—his last major statement on the Big House, published fourteen years after *The Big House of Inver*—did Yeats turn to a more corrosive view of Anglo-Ireland, one that was shared by many novelists. Much of the disturbing power of *Purgatory* lies in its narrative disgust with the failures of ascendancy culture, with the corruption of blood and genealogy that lead, as they do in so many novels, to greed, violence, decay, and defeat.

Unlike Yeats's earlier work, *Purgatory* conveys a revulsion against contemporary Anglo-Ireland that Standish O'Grady, the father of the Literary Revival, was expressing as early as the 1880s. As he watched the landlords of Ireland steer themselves into certain extinction, O'Grady articulated—albeit with greater rhetorical fervor—the judgment of Big House society being delivered by Anglo-Irish novelists. "Alas! I believe there never will be, as I know there never has been within the cycle of recorded things, an aristocracy so rotten in its seeming strength, so recreant, resourceless, and stupid in the day of trial, so degenerate, outworn, and effete. You have out-

8. Yeats's choice of Coole Parke, for example, as a recurring trope for spiritual ascendancy ignores the estate's association with Anglo-Ireland's most infamous contribution to the evictions and death of Irish country people during the Great Famine. The 1847 Gregory clause, an amendment to the Whig poor-relief bill, denied assistance to any tenant holding more than a quarter-acre of land. The act was named for William H. Gregory, heir to Coole Park and future husband of Lady Gregory.

lived your day" (1886, 213). Edith Somerville's *The Big House of Inver* conveys a similarly dark judgment of late nineteenth-century and early twentieth-century Anglo-Irish prodigality, but, unlike O'Grady or Yeats, Somerville is far less insistent on the "greatness" of earlier inhabitants of the Big House. In *The Big House of Inver,* her devaluation of the Anglo-Irish reaches far back into the eighteenth century itself—the period that Yeats celebrates as the pinnacle of the ascendancy's achievement.

Committed to the circumstantial realism of the novel form, Somerville chose to turn, not to a culturally evocative Big House like Coole Park (which served as the center of the Literary Revival), but to the far more ordinary fictionalized estates of Mount Music and Inver, modeled on houses she knew. These were houses, grand and not so grand, whose contemporary owners were isolated from culture, unaware of the art treasures they may have inherited, preoccupied with horses or fox hunting not with books and ideas. (O'Grady's comment on his fellow Anglo-Irish is telling: "Christ save us! You read nothing, know nothing" [1886, 240].) Like Yeats, Somerville feared misalliance between the Big House and the native Irish—a preoccupation that was undoubtedly influenced by early twentieth-century interest in eugenics and possibly by her class's obsession with the breeding of horses and dogs for its blood sports. But like her nineteenth-century predecessors Edgeworth and Lever, Somerville used the Big House form not to idealize a dying culture but to register those steps by which the ascendancy negotiated its own defeat.

Published in 1919, more than a century after Jane Austen's last novel, *Mount Music* examines a country house and village society that seems as deliberately narrow as the rural world that was Austen's recurring subject. Somerville follows Austen's advice about successful composition. "You are now collecting your People delightfully, getting them exactly into such a spot as is the delight of my life;—3 or 4 Families in a Country Village is the very thing to work on" (1952, 401). Like England's greatest country house novelist, Edith Somerville wrote about the nuances of a small social hierarchy, about the social discriminations and snobberies in village life, with the ease and assurance of a master.

But political change plays a significantly different role in English and Anglo-Irish country house novels. In Austen's *Persuasion,* for example, Sir Walter Elliot heads a declining landed gentry family. Meanwhile a new class of self-made men, such as the post-Napoleonic British naval officers Admiral Croft and Captain Wentworth, are renting the estate that Sir Walter can no longer afford to maintain or are marrying into his family. In Austen's fiction, the economic expansion and social transformations of a newly rising class exist as the backdrop for a narrative emphasis on the moral discriminations by which the inhabitants of a changing society are judged. In Somerville's Big House novels, however, the decline of the Anglo-Irish landed class is the foregrounded thematic focus, not just a historical context of the fiction.

An examination of Austen's work also reveals how social change in Ireland is far more polarized, characterized by far more conflict and radical loss for the landed class, than it is in England. In her social landscape, an aristocrat like Darcy in *Pride and Prejudice* easily befriends young Bingley, whose family has acquired its wealth in trade and who is seeking to purchase his own estate. In *Emma,* Mr. Weston gradually moves up the social ladder into the world of the landed gentry. Although a sense of strong class demarcation controls Austen's settings, the rigidity of such division is gradually eroding. As Raymond Williams demonstrates, her novels depict a society in the midst of assimilating itself to social mobility and shifting class distinctions (1973, 113–19). Those characters who are most insistent on halting the breakdown of strict social barriers are the most flawed; like Lady Catherine De Bourgh or Sir Walter Elliot, they are presented as caricatures rather than as fully developed personalities. In Anglo-Irish fiction, however, social change brings acute political loss to the Big House. Change is portrayed not as a series of gradual shifts in the systems of economic distribution and social status, but as potentially radical and occasionally violent transformations of political institutions. Such transformations enfranchise and enrich the Catholic majority, but rapidly eclipse the power and privileges of the ruling Anglo-Irish class. Thus, social change in Anglo-Irish literature appears as far less gradual and organic than in English fiction, and from the perspective of the Big House, the bearer of such change emerges from a hostile and alien social group.

A specific sense of social and political history is always in the foreground in *Mount Music,* a novel written from the point of view of the Irish Big House in the late nineteenth and early twentieth centuries.

Spanning the years from 1894 to 1907, when the land acts were taking effect, it depicts a period of acute crisis for the Anglo-Irish landlord. Political turmoil—remote from the surface of Austen's early nineteenth-century novels, and still only the ominous shadow of World War I and encroaching suburban values in Forster's *Howards End*—constantly intrudes on the lives of the characters in *Mount Music*. For the Big House children who dread returning to school after the holidays, "there was always a hope of a 'rising,' in which case it would be the boys' pleasing duty to stay at home and fight," either against the Land Leaguers or "the English oppressors of a downtrodden Ireland" (Somerville and Ross 1920, 8). The novel's lovers— Christian Talbot-Lowry, who professes her loyalty to the king, and Larry Coppinger, who asserts his Home Rule convictions—include political argument in their repertoire of love talk and almost lose each other because of political differences.

At the pinnacle of society in *Mount Music* are the Talbot-Lowrys, the owners since the Elizabethan settlements of an Irish estate that gives the novel its title. Their Catholic cousin Larry Coppinger owns the adjoining estate. The Talbot-Lowrys and the Coppingers live in the days when "the class known as Landed Gentry was still pre-eminent in Ireland. Tenants and tradesmen bowed down before them with love sometimes, sometimes with hatred, never with indifference" (11). Larry's religion, a disturbing result of his English Catholic mother's powers of persuasion over her Irish Protestant husband, mars the clarity of social discriminations in late nineteenth-century Anglo-Irish society. The feudal loyalty of the Roman Catholic servants and tenants who work as domestics, stable hands, and farmers on the grounds of Mount Music and Coppinger Court undergoes a perceptible shift in the course of the novel. Finally, in the neighboring village of Cluhir reside the Mangans, the middle-class Catholic family whose ascent to property and power parallels the descent of the Talbot-Lowrys. By the end of *Mount Music,* Dr. Mangan, the clever and manipulative family patriarch, gains control of mortgages against the Talbot-Lowry's estate and arranges a marriage between his daughter and Larry Coppinger. At his death he is plotting to push his son into marriage with Christian Talbot-Lowry, the youngest daughter of the Big House.

A sectarian rift between the occupants of the Big House and Catholic Ireland provides the major source of division between groups of characters in *Mount Music.* "Religion, or rather, difference of religion, is a factor of everyday Irish life of infinitely more potency than it is, perhaps, in any other Christian country. . . . It is, no doubt, possible to write of human beings who live in Ireland, without mentioning their religious views, but to do so means a drastic censoring of an integral feature of nearly all mundane affairs" (19). The novel's intelligent heroine characterizes the Irish "Spirit of Nation" as "Religious Intolerance" (129), and Somerville carefully delineates the shades of anti-Catholic feelings among the various members of the gentry class. Faced with the erosion of their wealth and social position, the Big House occupants use religion as a means of maintaining their sense of superiority. But Larry Coppinger's role in the novel suggests narrative anxieties about the erosion of sectarian and class barriers; as a Catholic member of the gentry, Coppinger becomes a magnet for middle-class Catholic social aspirations. Somerville thus invests Larry's personal charms with a certain shallow gullibility. Against his best interests (his love for Christian Talbot-Lowry), Larry is drawn both into a disastrous romantic involvement with Dr. Mangan's vulgar daughter and into nationalist politics. Practically destroyed by his attempt to break down the barriers between the Big House and the "other" Ireland, he must be rescued from the Mangans' Catholic world by a series of improbable plot devices.

Mount Music is most successful on its social, sectarian, and political levels, as a portrait of an isolated Anglo-Ireland accelerating its own decline and in its expression of the class fears of a new Ireland. With its occasional coy verbal mannerisms, its sentimental attachment to the heroine, and its preposterous deus ex machina that restores the rightful Big House lovers to one another, the novel never achieves the control of character and plot evident in the best of Edith Somerville's works, *The Big House of Inver.*

In her essays Somerville could, on occasion, idealize the Big House as a symbol of a golden age, a modern version of the medieval Irish monastic centers that preserved a civilization under siege. Writing of Violet Martin's efforts to restore Ross, she lapses into elegy. "Ireland, now, is full of such places as Ross was then. 'Gentry-houses,' places that were once disseminators of light, of the humanities; centres of civilization; places to which the people rushed, in any trouble, as to Cities of Refuge. They are now destroyed, become desolate, derelict" (Somerville and Ross 1918, 154–55). But in her fiction Somerville's eye was colder. For all its lingering evocation of what has been lost, *Mount Music* maintains an unsentimental view of a dying class. The house at the center of the novel is an ancient Elizabethan structure, "large, intensely solid, practical, sensible, of the special type of old Irish country-house that is entirely remote from the character of the men who originated it" (Somerville and Ross 1920, 12). Its solidity is English rather than Irish and it has been kept up because its present owner, Major Richard Talbot-Lowry, has married an English heiress, the daughter of an earl who comes equipped with a careful financial trustee in London.

Early in the novel, the house indeed appears as the nostalgic center of childhood memories, much like the childhood home evoked in Somerville's memoirs. Mount Music's charm is a function of that Anglo-Irish quality of casual living that fills the architecturally solid structure "gloriously with horses and hounds, and butts of claret, and hungry poor relations unto the fourth and fifth generations" (13). However, such charm is also associated with disorder, with cluttered drawing rooms where priceless objects jostle against rubbish and with rat- and cockroach-infested back stairways and kitchens. In such descriptions, Somerville echoes Edgeworth's recurring theme of bad housekeeping in the Big House and anticipates Molly Keane. *Mount Music* suggests the ways in which the pleasantly easy-going habits of the Talbot-Lowrys slide into a slovenliness that serves them ill in the 1890s. The ease and charm of their lives rests on the assumption of the loyalty of their retainers; they are at a loss when the smiles, welcoming bonfires, and homecoming gifts disappear. Major Talbot-Lowry is bewildered by the resistance of his tenants when he refuses to sell his property to them under the Wyndham Land Act. He is then enraged at their response to this refusal: the burning of his favorite covert; the denial of his hunting rights; and, finally, an outright attack on his daughter as she hunts.

Somerville's affection for the vague and ineffectual Lady Isabel Talbot-Lowry and her blundering husband is clear, but the narrative expression of such affection is tempered by an unsparing depiction of their limitations. Talbot-Lowry is "gallant in resistance, barren in expedient" (156), and doomed by his political conservatism. "The common lot of Irish landlords, and Pterodactyli, was upon him, and he was in the process of becoming extinct. It was his fate to see his income gradually diminishing, being eaten away, as the sea washes away a bulwark-less shore, by successive Acts of Parliament and the machinery they created . . ." (156). Nor does Somerville's regard for Talbot-Lowry's "fidelity" mitigate her tough-minded analysis of his pig-headed conservatism. "He had . . . the desire to disparage and disprove new ideas, that is a sign of a mind incapable of originality, and anxious to assert itself negatively, since it must otherwise remain silent" (178). The landlord's feudal attitudes toward his servants and tenants are subjected to as unsentimental an analysis as is his political conservatism. His tenants are to assent to his bullying because he owns them: ". . . the Mount Music tenants were his, as they had been his ancestors', to have and to hold, to rule, to arbitrate for, and to stand by, as a fond and despotic husband rules and stands by an obedient wife, loving her and bullying her (but both entirely for her good)" (178). Such an ironic image of a loving "marriage" between tenant and landlord unmistakably distinguishes Somerville's political perspective from that of her former literary collaborator.

Mount Music also dispels the heroic aura of high culture and ceremony with which Yeats endowed the Big House in the early decades of the twentieth century. The intellectual vacuity of Anglo-Ireland is never made more explicit than in the characterization of the pig-headed stupidity of the major and the vapid helplessness of Lady Isabel before their daughter's intelligence. Though Mount Music's comfortably cluttered drawing room is "a place full of the magnetism that is born of happiness" (159), it exists quite without intellectual content. "The claims of literature were acknowledged, but without enthusiasm. A tall, glass-fronted cupboard, inaccessibly placed behind the elongated tail of an early grand piano, was filled with ornate miniature editions of the classics, that would have defied an effort— had such an effort ever been made—to remove them from their shelves, whereon, they had apparently been bedded in cement, like mosaic" (159).

Although Somerville acknowledges the power of tradition in *Mount Music,* her portrayal of the Talbot-Lowrys as limited and doomed conservatives undercuts the novel's nostalgic celebration of Anglo-Irish life. Our last vision of them is devastating in its irony. Hounded by creditors, they determine to retreat to an English suburb and rent Mount Music to a mythical rich Englishman. Their hasty departure, without dignity or awareness of their irrevocable loss, allows them to betray their ancestral home with characteristic mindlessness. They are ". . . too agitated by their coming journey to have a spare thought for sentiment; too much beset by the fear of what they might lose, their keys, their sandwiches, their dressing-boxes, to shed a tear for what they were losing, and had lost" (313).

With her description of the rising fortunes of Dr. Magnan, which accompanies the accelerating losses of the Talbot-Lowrys, Somerville exposes her deepest ambivalence about social change. An obvious descendant of Edgeworth's Jason Rackrent or Lever's Maurice Scanlan, Dr. Mangan manipulates and plots until he owns Mount Music. In Anglo-Irish fiction, a rising man from a lower social class is not, like Bingley in Austen's *Pride and Prejudice,* a friend and potential fellow landlord, but rather an alien usurper and enemy. Mangan's ambitions, moreover, are not limited to financial control; from the beginning of the novel he works to arrange a marriage between his daughter and Larry Coppinger, and later between his son and Christian Talbot-Lowry. Mangan is, however, a warm and generous man—a pillar of the Catholic community. His single-minded ambitions to raise the status of his family are seen always in the context of his role as loving father and husband. The vulgarity of his wife, rumored to have been his cook, is more than balanced by her good nature, beauty, and genuine affection for him. Somerville seems helpless before the genial hypocrite she has created, a usurper who gently and ruthlessly strips the Big House owner of his property. The author's solution—to kill off Dr. Mangan as he selflessly travels to visit a sick patient—suggests her unwillingness to face both the inevitable working out of her own plot—and of her nation's historical process. With the death of Dr. Mangan and the equally unexpected elopement of his daughter—Larry Coppinger is free to marry Christian Talbot-Lowry. Thus, *Mount Music* ends in wish fulfillment—not with the expected loss of the Big House, but with its unlikely restoration by a new and wiser generation.

The Big House of Inver

The Big House of Inver anatomizes the death of a social class: the final destruction of Anglo-Irish culture. In this, the most successful of Edith Somerville's novels, the house itself is consumed not by the fires of class warfare but by the wanton carelessness of its owners. As several critics have noted (Power 1964, 51; Martin 1982, 47; Cronin 1985, 7–9), the novel is a twentieth-century retelling of *Castle Rackrent;* its appearance in 1925 suggests the persistence of a genre and the continuity of its themes. Whereas Somerville and Ross's earlier collaborative work, *The Real Charlotte* (1894), also invokes Anglo-Irish eccentricity and passivity in its portrayal of the overbred Dysarts, the Big House as setting and theme is primarily peripheral to that brilliant novel of class fluidity in rural Ireland.

Although set in 1912, as Anglo-Irish landlords were slowly succumbing to the pressures of Irish nationalism, *The Big House of Inver* constantly moves backward, and finally becomes a book about Irish history, like *Castle Rackrent* or *The Martins of Cro' Martin,* focusing on the slow decay of a once powerful family. At the center of the novel hovers the empty and abandoned but still splendid Big House, dominating the landscape, clammy with damp, overgrown with vines. No longer occupied by its Prendeville owners, it stands looming over the sea, a reminder of the incommensurability of the heroic architectural image and its debased human inhabitants.

The genesis of the novel is clear, for as its epilogue Somerville reprints extracts from a letter written to her on March 18, 1912, in which Violet Martin recounts a visit to the abandoned Tyrone House in County Galway.

> Yesterday I drove to see X— House. A great cut stone house of three stories. . . .
>
> Perfectly empty . . . It is on a long promontory by the sea, and there rioted three or four generations of X—s, living with country women, occasionally marrying them, all illegitimate four times over. . . . About one hundred and fifty years ago a very grand Lady—married the head of the family and lived there, and was so corroded with pride that she would not allow her two daughters to associate with the neighbors of their own class. She lived to see them marry two of the men in the yard. . . .
>
> Yesterday, as we left, an old Miss X, daughter of the last owner, was at the door in a little donkey-trap. She lives near in an old castle, and since her people died she will not go into X— House, or into the enormous yard, or the beautiful old garden.
>
> She was a strange mixture of distinction and commonness, like her breeding, and it was very sad to see her at the door of that great house.
>
> If we dared to write up that subject—! (Somerville and Ross 1978, 313)

Thirteen years after receiving Martin's letter, and ten years after her literary collaborator's premature death in 1915, Edith Somerville finally fulfilled the suggestions voiced in Martin's fleeting impressions of Tyrone House, the seat of the St. George family. Martin's letter summons up the evocative power of the ruined Big House and the degeneration of the family line that is such a familiar theme in Anglo-Irish literature. The relationship between St. George family history and the novel that Edith Somerville wrote, however, is complex and ambiguous, for history in Ireland is often more spectacular than fiction itself. Martin's letter reflects only the outsider's impressions of a derelict, abandoned mansion and the rumors of family degeneration; the actual story of the decline of the St. Georges reads, on occasion, more melodramatically than the novel it inspired.

Although family members argued that the St. Georges had not come down in the world nearly so much as Martin imagined in her letter (see Mark 1976, 62), the historical record is revealing. The St. Georges' decline from a position as one of the leading landed families in County Galway was, according to some accounts, accompanied by the same eccentricity and promiscuity that Somerville evokes in her novel (manuscript of Louisa Beaufort's journal, quoted in Mark 1976, 23). The grandeur of the fictional Inver House mirrors the lavish eighteenth-century mansion of the St. Georges, just as the scale of Big House life depicted in the novel reflects descriptions of St. George christening parties for eight hundred guests and funerals attended by a thousand tenants (Mark 1976, 27; 54). Similarly, reports of late nineteenth-century St. George descendants living as virtual squatters in various corners of the mansion, cooking over an open fire in a top-floor room, suggest how accurately Somerville's fictional account of Anglo-Irish decline mirrors a historical reality. But two episodes of St. George family history are conspicuously missing from the novel: the family's embroilment in charges of "relentless severity" in evicting destitute peasants from the estate during the Great Famine—charges vigorously denied by the St. George landlord in an 1848 speech to Parliament (*The Times,* 5 April 1848; quoted in Mark 1976, 35–41), and the 1920 destruction of the uninhabited and unfurnished Tyrone House by the "savage rage of the infuriated rabble" according to a contemporary newspaper account (quoted in Mark 1976, 57). Edith Somerville's secondhand, fictional evocation of Tyrone House (she never saw the mansion herself) depicts the costs of Anglo-Irish profligacy and irresponsibility with an unsparing eye. But her account of Anglo-Irish decline in *The Big House of Inver* avoids the full acknowledgment of bitter class and sectarian conflict that the historical record itself provides. (In Somerville's work, the mistress of the estate dies of famine fever as a result of her efforts to feed the poor.)

In *Mount Music,* Somerville depicted the family estate as the center of nostalgic memories of childhood idylls. Inver House, however, is initially presented, much like Lever's Cro' Martin Castle, as a showcase, a monument to the arrogance and pride of the Anglo-Irish Prendeville family. The first chapter of the novel is a tour de force; beginning with its initial sentence, it provides a rapid history of the Prendevilles' exuberant prodigality. "The Big House of Inver stood high on the central ridge of the promontory of Ross Inver, and faced unflinchingly the western ocean" (Somerville and Ross 1978, 7). The arrogance of the family is reflected in Robert Prendeville's choice of a site for his mansion. Aloof from the village, unsheltered from the elements, in view of a tall and square tower built by the earliest Norman Prendeville settlers in Ireland, the site was chosen to allow an unobstructed view of Prendeville ships smuggling claret into Ireland from France. The description of Inver House evokes the balanced and harmonious vision of neoclassic Georgian England; thus, the Anglo-Irish Big House, built of native limestone in alien architectural forms, is the monument of a conquering race. It suggests that grace or "civilization" is born of lawless arrogance. "Inver House embodied one of those large gestures of the minds of the earlier Irish architects, some of which still stand to justify Ireland's claim to be considered a civilized country. It was a big, solemn, square house of three stories, built of cut stone, grandly planned, facing west in two immense sweeping curves, with a high pillared portico between them and stone balustrades round the roof" (9).

Certain architectural details reveal the self-confidence of its builders. Over the door of the house are carved the family crest and the family motto, "Je Prends." In 1912, the nouveau riche purchaser of Inver House, Sir Harold Burgrave, gazes enviously at the marriage stones taken from the original family home and inserted into the steps of the eighteenth-century mansion. " 'Prendevil-Martine, 'Prendevill-O'Rorke,' 'Prendevilles-Devannes.' The names with their archaic spelling, and the roughly-carved coats, blurred and lichened by age, deepened in Burgrave the sentiment of respect for the old house and jealousy for its owners. He thought of his father, and of how he had paid a whacking price to the College of Heralds for the coat-of-arms, and the crest that now adorned the back of his watch. These people, these Prendevilles here, had 'em for nothing" (171–72).

In Somerville's novel, civilization is ironically equated with physical beauty—of houses and horses and people—and with debased moral standards. The eighteenth-century Robert Prendeville's son, Beauty Kit, is a "bad boy, dissolute and drunken" (9), but so handsome and rich that he marries Lady Isabella, the beautiful daughter of the marquis of Breffny. The shadow of her defeated pride hovers over subsequent generations of Prendevilles. To Inver House, Lady Isabella brings a post-chaise full of Italian artisans to decorate the mansion ceilings and thereby create a perfect specimen of Irish Georgian architecture. However, like the aristocratic Lady X obliquely referred to in Martin's 1912 letter, Lady Isabella arrogantly isolates herself from the local gentry. Turning herself into "an iceberg of pride" (10) and refusing to allow her children to associate with their neighbors, she must suffer the shame of watching her son marry the daughter of the estate gamekeeper and her daughters go off with the grooms.

This "pollution" of the family lineage mirrors the dissipation of Anglo-Ireland that Edgeworth evoked more than a century earlier in *Castle Rackrent*. "Five successive generations of mainly half-bred and wholly profligate Prendevilles rioted out their short lives in the Big House, living with country women, fighting and drinking, gambling" (Somerville and Ross 1978, 10–11). In passages reminiscent of the Rackrent family history, the narrator describes the haphazard means by which the family inheritance is squandered and depicts the breakdown of orderly systems of inheritance and succession. "The legitimacy of the succession was secured by means and stratagems that need not be recorded. Somehow out of the mire an heir would be evolved and acclaimed, and the process of drinking and dicing away the lands of Inver would be carried on with all the hereditary zest proper to a lawful inheritor" (11). Somerville's equation of intermarriage between the Prendevilles and Catholic Ireland as misalliance suggests not only class anxiety in the face of social and economic decline, but also a growing preoccupation with bloodlines and eugenics in early-twentieth century Anglo-Ireland.

Jas Prendeville comes into his ascendancy early in his life, on his tumultuous christening day. After Jas is christened at a church on the strand, his father rushes from the church to fight a duel, wading with his opponent and seconds into the sea to escape the police. The mortal combat, witnessed with delight by hundreds of onlookers, evokes the lawless and exuberant wastefulness that runs as a thematic strand through all Big House fiction since *Castle Rackrent.*

> One wonders, if anywhere, save in Western Ireland, could such a sight have been paralleled. The four young bloods waist-deep in the shining sea, with the blue sky of June above them, and the seagulls squealing over their heads, and young Madam Prendeville, with the newly christened Jasper and his retinue of nurses, sitting in her yellow chariot by the edge of the tide. The sands, right and left of her, were thronged with the people of three parishes; fish-women and fishermen from the near-by village of Cloon, and wild men, Prendeville tenants, from back in the bogs of Iveragh and Moyroe, all gabbing in Irish their views as to the merits of the combatants, betting on the result, enjoying to ecstasy such nerve-strain as they were capable of feeling. (12–13)

Jas is a fitting heir to his dissolute ancestry; combining improvidence with carelessness, he wastes away his life and remaining fortune drinking with the local fishermen. He enters into an affair with the daughter of a compliant owner of a favorite public house, who "was sufficiently medieval . . . to accept with composure, a certain *Droit de Seigneur,* that was, as a rule, based rather on might than right" (23). After unsuccessfully attempting a military career, Jas retreats to the Norman tower beside the roofless Inver House and gradually sinks to the level of his fishermen companions.

Shibby Pindy, Jas's illegitimate daughter and one of the many offspring of Prendeville breeding with the country people, is Edith Somerville's great creation in *The Big House of Inver.* She emerges from the morass of Anglo-Irish history that lies behind the contemporary action of the novel. Her surname, Pindy, is the local appellation for those Prendeville descendants with an ambivalent relationship to the family line; her given name, Isabella, corrupted to Shibby by generations of tavern usage, suggests how "the much blotted family escutcheon" (38) perpetuates the social shame of Lady Isabella more than one hundred years after her daughters abandoned their own class and disgraced their family name. Shibby becomes a family retainer, a quasi-servant, and a powerful maternal force, residing with her father and her legitimate half-brother and -sister in the Norman tower of Inver. Indomitable, handsome, wily, and, on occasion, ruthless, Shibby dreams of reinstating her beautiful half-brother Kit—the image of his profligate eighteenth-century ancestor, Beauty Kit—into Inver House. Her struggles to reassert the Prendeville line are brilliantly dramatized: she haunts local auctions, for example, to fill the mansion's decimated rooms with tawdry Victorian furniture bought with her own savings; she schemes endlessly to provide Kit with the education, and failing that, the marriage he needs to reinstate himself into his patrimony.

The forces of history and genetic weakness, however, conspire against Shibby, for her half-brother's startling beauty and grace are accompanied by all the deficiencies of the male Prendeville line. Lazy, pleasure-loving Kit loses his only chance to reclaim the Inver demesne from the Weldons, his family's land agents whose steady rise to social eminence mirrors the fall of the Prendevilles. Shibby contrives to arrange a marriage between Kit and the Weldons' daughter, Peggy, and thus recover the demesne lands of Inver that have been dubiously, if legally, appropriated from a drunken Jas by Peggy's wily grandfather. Instead of pursuing Shibby's plans, however, Kit cheats at horse races and consorts with the debauched local daughter of a shebeen-keeper, a girl who refuses to accept with proper silence and equanimity the fate that Irish history has traditionally allotted to the victim of the *droit du seigneur.* Thus Kit's chances to reclaim his family lands are doomed, for his wild behavior frightens off the respectable middle-class Protestant Weldons, who turn to safer English matrimonial material for Peggy.

A character as memorable in her own way as Defoe's Moll Flanders or Hardy's Tess Durbeyfield, Shibby Pindy embodies, with an exacting literalness, an archetypal pattern of fictional significance. A brilliant vision of false consciousness, she is trapped by her sex and ancestry into worshipping Kit's beauty and Prendeville blood, that very strain of aristocratic lineage that defiled her own hapless mother. She devotes herself single-mindedly to her cause: "The King shall have his own again! Inver should once more worthily house a reigning Prendeville! Her boy should live as a gentleman should, as his ancestors did" (51).

Shibby's majestic presence and shabby life suggest the costs of colonial occupation for its victims. She is driven by the fiercely proud ambitions of Lady Isabella, her eighteenth-century ancestor whose portrait she so strikingly resembles. At once the crafty and ruthless peasant mother who dreams, for example, of poisoning Kit's village mistress, and the dark and haughty aristocratic lady who can terrify her neighbors with her baleful glances, Shibby lives her life enthralled to the very forces that have destroyed her chances for happiness. Unable to forget her shameful heritage as Jas's illegitimate daughter, she refuses all marriage offers, even one from a respectable doctor whom she loves, and lives instead as "the one faithful though unacknowledged daughter" of the Big House (50). She becomes, as it were, an acolyte to Kit's beauty, devoting herself to preserving his patrimony from further defilement, somehow finding the money to repair its roof, patch its leaks, and refurbish it in preparation for Kit's ascendancy. The magnificent drawing room of Inver House, with its heavy teak doors, its chipped but still elegant marble fireplaces, its century-old portraits of Lady Isabella and Beauty Kit, becomes her "secret temple" (50). With her untutored taste (for Somerville, the unmistakable mark of her peasant blood), she furnishes it with Victorian clutter.

In creating Shibby as a powerful but victimized woman, Somerville draws, not only upon the traditions of Anglo-Irish literature, but upon those of Celtic Ireland as well. If Shibby is the reincarnation of Lady Isabella Prendeville and of a series of ruthless Big House ladies (Lady Dorothea, for example, in *The Martins of Cro' Martin*), she is also her mother's daughter: the Irish victim of her own Anglo-Irish inheritance. Thus, Somerville boldly appropriates for the Big House novel the Celtic tradition of the *Shan Van Vocht,* the old woman of Ireland whose adherence to a lost cause and whose personal victimization symbolizes the victimization of a nation. The "nation" Shibby loses, however, is the Anglo-Irish nation that oppressed her maternal ancestors. Other victims of this arrogant pattern of oppression recur in the novel; not only is Shibby's own mother deserted by her father, Jas, but Kit also abandons his disreputable, pregnant mistress, Maggie Connor, whose mad despair leads to her death. Shibby is never aware of the larger historical patterns of colonial occupation that have victimized her and others like her; she sees Maggie Connor, for example, solely as an obstacle to her dreams for Kit, never as a victim like her own mother. In her loyalty to her worthless halfbrother and to her own Prendeville blood—bequeathed to her by a father who never acknowledges her and who had once offered her servant's wages—Shibby's tragedy is absolute. Learning that Kit has lost his chance to marry Peggy Weldon and has colluded with Jas to sell Inver House to Peggy's rich English fiancé, she confronts her loss. " 'The curse of God is on me!' she said in a low voice, 'what use is there to strive? Laugh away, boy! You're easily pleased! Your sweetheart has left you for another man and your fancy-girl is drowned, and now your house is sold!' " (302) As Shibby walks from the Big House, her look of despair attracts the attention of the local people. Unlike Cathleen Ni Hoolihan, the Celtic *Shan Van Vocht* whom Yeats transforms from a withered crone into a young girl with "the walk of a queen" (Yeats 1952, 57), Shibby goes down to defeat with Anglo-Ireland. "God! As bad as she was before, she looks dead altogether now!" (Somerville and Ross 1978, 303).

One reader suggests that Shibby's unconsciousness of her place in Irish history and of the implications of her own tragedy is the fatal flaw of *The Big House of Inver.* Such a flaw, then, relegates the novel to the status of Corkery's "colonial" literature, an alien literature exploiting Ireland for an English audience and failing to achieve any vision of a truly "Irish" (i.e., nationalist) experience (Martin 1982, 52). In the context of such criticism, Shibby's enthrallment to the Big House reflects the limitations of her creator's historical perceptions. Thus, Somerville herself is seen as trapped in the limited vision of her character, whose blind loyalty to ascendancy culture prevents her from transcending her false consciousness.

Writing from within Anglo-Ireland, however, Edith Somerville offers a tough-minded vision of how history actually works itself out for all victims of colonialism. The arrogant power of Big House glamour, both in its ascendancy and in its decline, can bind to it even those whom it destroys. Critical revivals of Corkery's distinctions between "colonial" and "Irish" literature, or Seamus Deane's arguments against the existence of a genuinely aristocratic ascendancy, seem beside the point of discussions of *The Big House of Inver.* Through its exposure of the wasteful and prodigal glamour of the Big House (a glamour embodied in images of architectural grandeur and in the ignorant and dissolute violence of Yeats's "hard-riding country gentlemen"), and through its simultaneous refusal to deny the power of such glamour, the novel represents a masterly exploration of the complexity of Irish history as it actually existed for some, rather than as it perhaps should have existed.

Edith Somerville published the *The Big House of Inver* in 1925, a few years after scores of Anglo-Irish houses, including the St. George mansion that inspired the novel, were torched by Irish nationalists as symbols of colonial oppression. In *The Big House of Inver,* however, this Anglo-Irish writer, like her literary predecessors, blames her own class for its decline. Old Jas Prenderville's accidental burning-down of the house, which he has just sold, is an effective symbolic conclusion for the novel. But the Big House is already dead. It has been destroyed, not by the new class of Irishmen represented by the Prendevilles' small-minded Protestant agent, Johnnie Weldon, the Jason Rackrent of the twentieth century, who will collect insurance for the new owner he has found for the house, but by the generations of Prendevilles who have squandered their heritage.

Stages of Disloyalty in
Elizabeth Bowen's Irish Fiction

I regard myself as an Irish novelist. As long as I can remember, I've been extremely conscious of being Irish—even when I was writing about very un-Irish things such as suburban life in Paris or the English seaside. All my life I've been going backwards and forwards between Ireland and England and the Continent, but that has never robbed me of the strong feeling of my nationality. I must say it's a highly disturbing emotion. It's not—I *must* emphasize—sentimentality. ("Meet Elizabeth Bowen," by The Bellman. *Bell* no. 4 [September 1942].)

Of all Irish novelists, Elizabeth Bowen is most complexly associated with the waning ascendancy culture that shaped her sensibility. Bowen's brooding vision of the past—revealed as her fictional children and adolescents experience the desolation of a fallen world—conveys that sense of loss and guilt that is inseparable from the Anglo-Irish experience. Her early personal history reads, moreover, as a painful recapitulation of the cultural dislocation suffered by her and by her parents' generation. Deserted twice as a child, once by her father, whose mental breakdown forced her mother to take a seven-year-old child from Ireland to England to live, and later, at thirteen, by her mother's unexpected death, Bowen returned obsessively in her fiction to parents who fail their children and to orphaned children in search of love. Her recurring plot posits a world without security or permanence, where her quintessential protagonist, the orphaned child thrust out into a void, longs for the imagined security of a lost home. As Howard Moss notes, "she grasped early the colonial mentality from both sides, and saw how, in the end, it was a mirror image of the most exploitative relationship of all: that of the adult and the child" (1986, 236).

Even her famous dictum that verisimilitude in fiction begins always with place or "topography" (1975, 34) arises from a simultaneous idealization and rejection of the rootedness in place and nation that her own family and class history promised and denied her. Thus, Bowen's persistent explorations of women's struggles for selfhood are inseparable from her recurring depictions of domestic spaces— not only Anglo-Irish country estates in *The Last September, The Heat of the Day,* and *A World of Love,* but also suburban villas, London townhouses and flats, country cottages, and seaside retreats that appear in her other fiction. Her heroines both flee from and seek houses that function as symbols of a psychic shelter that defines and threatens them. Simultaneously struggling against the confines of traditional roles as nurturing mothers, submissive daughters, or loving wives, and reacting fearfully to their flight from these roles, Bowen's protagonists inhabit and reject a variety of domestic settings that present themselves as possible solutions to a sense of homelessness.

The persistence of the ur-house in Bowen's fiction reflects her complex identification with her own family home, Bowen's Court, as well as her earliest memory of a domestic space that both established and circumscribed personal and cultural identity. In her fiction, this ancestral home and other sorts of dwellings—for example, the ominous house in Paris, the temporary rented villa in St. John's Wood (*To the North*), the carefully decorated and coldly rejecting London townhouse (*The Death of the Heart*), and a series of more fragmentary retreats—cannot sustain her characters. Each of her fictional houses embodies a desire for wholeness and safety, which was promised but never wholly delivered by the Big House in Cork that she celebrated during World War II in *Bowen's Court.*

A study of Bowen's work should therefore include—even begin with—an exploration of the house that, in one form or another, she repeatedly transformed into literary text. Not only in her major works about Anglo-Ireland—in her early novel, *The Last September,* and in her later account of her family's history, *Bowen's Court*—but recurrently in her fictional depictions of domestic space, the image of her family home offers a promise of identity and security. The emblematic Anglo-Irish Big House, or diminished versions of it, hovers before her characters, yet repeatedly fails them. Bowen's fiction embodies the tensions and discordances of her Anglo-Irish experience as that experience—or history—becomes a subject of her art.

In "The Bend Back," an essay written late in her life in 1950, Bowen suggests that history and fiction are very different sorts of narratives. History, she implies, is the "raw" data, whereas art is comforting and even false "illusion."

> We must not shy at the fact that we cull the past from fiction rather than history, and that art, out of the very necessity to compose a picture, cannot but eliminate, edit—and so falsify. Raw history, in its implication, is unnerving; and, even so, only chronicles the survivors. . . . As things are, the past is veiled from us by illusion—our own illusion. It is that which we seek. It is not the past but the idea of the past which draws us (1986, 57–58).

But in the very year that she offered the above explanation of fiction as inevitable nostalgia, Bowen also insisted that the artist must resist the urge to sustain such illusion. In the essay "Disloyalties," she describes the powerful effect of a regional background or of "ancestral pieties" on an intuitive writer like herself. Yet she suggests that serious writers must disengage themselves from the "hereditary influences" of childhood—"racial, local or social"—that they feel most dearly; they must, in fact, go through a crisis of pain, loneliness, and loss in order to shed the haunting power of past loyalties (1986, 62). With approval, she quotes Graham Greene: "Isn't disloyalty as much the writer's virtue . . . as loyalty is the soldier's?" (Bowen 1986, 60)

In insisting that serious writers "test" and "tax" themselves only when they free themselves from hereditary influences and enter a new and harsher relationship with their material, "Disloyalties" offers a standard of judgment, a way to evaluate the writer's relationship to her past. Bowen's own successful achievement of the necessary, "disloyal" distance from the assumptions of her own culture may, therefore, legitimately operate as a self-imposed yardstick of her artistic growth. Using the standards Bowen articulates, a reader can examine how each of her works illustrates the observation she made in 1946: "It is not only our fate but our business to lose innocence, and once we have lost that it is futile to attempt to picnic in Eden" (50). In her fiction, however, Bowen moves from a painful disloyalty toward past sanctities in her early work, *The Last September* (1928), to a far more conservative perception of Anglo-Irish Big House culture in the later *The Heat of the Day* (1949). Although that novel subtly explores the psychological landscape of wartime betrayal, its depiction of Ireland suggests Bowen's recourse to nostalgia. Finally, in *A World of Love* (1955), her last Irish novel, she returns to a Big House setting but attempts the difficult task of simultaneously affirming and condemning human recourse to illusion. In this psychological fiction Bowen abandons—at considerable artistic cost—an explicit depiction of the tension between the individual and a larger political and social history that shapes both *The Last September* and *The Heat of the Day.*

Born into a gentry family from county Cork, Bowen's inherited baggage was formidable: a family history of Cromwellian settlers from Wales; an austere Georgian mansion, Bowen's Court (of which she was the first female heir); and all the colonial assumptions of the Anglo-Irish that assured their isolation from the native Irish—and, finally, by the early twentieth century, from the modern world itself. In the autobiographical *Seven Winters,* she describes how, to an Anglo-Irish child growing up in professional Dublin society and summering in Cork at Bowen's Court, Catholics were aliens whose predisposition to "frequent prayer bespoke . . . some incontinence of the soul. . . . They were simply 'the others' whose world lay alongside ours but never touched" (1942b, 52).

Bowen's autobiographical pieces expose her class's isolation from native Catholic Irish society. Her early vision of Ireland was confident and even arrogant, evoking in its certainties and its misapprehension the insularity and the poignant self-centeredness of the child—and of the Anglo-Irish class. She speaks, for example, of her "endemic pride" in her country, which was founded on a child's mistaken conflation of the words "Ireland" and "island." Assuming that all countries surrounded by water were named after her native land, she congratulated herself on living in a country that was a prototype, not merely an imitation, like England (12). In *Seven Winters* she also observes that growing up as a child in Dublin she did not understand "that we Protestants were a minority, and that the unquestioned rules of our being came, in fact, from the closeness of a minority world" (51). Disenchantment, implies the detached adult writer of these reminiscences, is inevitable.

Bowen's three novels dealing with the Anglo-Irish Big House differ in their use of that setting and motif. Her shifting tone toward a highly-charged subject—the survival of the pattern of life that Bowen's Court came to represent for her—reveals her ambivalent attitude toward her culture. A virtual orphan from the age of thirteen, her adolescent life as an absentee from Ireland accentuated the normal Anglo-Irish sense of being hybrid. For Bowen, however, the disloyalty toward the fixed patterns of the past that she came to see as the mark of artistic breakthrough and growth struggled against formidable obstacles. The very creation, for example, of a history of her ancestral home represents an act of piety and an attempt at self-definition through the past.

Bowen's Court, the nonfictional text that expresses many of the assumptions implicit in her fiction, was written between 1939 and 1941, more than a decade after the publication of *The Last September* and before *The Heat of the Day* and *A World of Love.* In it Bowen conceives of her Irish home as a symbol of permanence and continuity, as a refuge from the chaos of her London residence during the bombing raids of the Nazi offensive. She celebrates the survival of Bowen's Court in Ireland—"this . . . country of ruin" (1979, 15)— and sees her Georgian house, built of native limestone by an alien power, as finally integral to—even harmonious with—the grey gleam of the Irish landscape.

> This is Bowen's Court as the past has left it—an isolated partly unfinished house, grandly conceived and plainly and strongly built. Near the foot of mountains, it has little between it and the bare fields that run up the mountain side. Larger in manner than in actual size, it stands up in Roman urbane strongness in a land on which the Romans never set foot. It is the negation of mystical Ireland: its bald walls rebut the surrounding, disturbing light. Imposed on seized land, built in the rulers' ruling tradition, the house is, all the same, of the local rock, and sheds the same grey gleam you see over the countryside. So far, it has withstood burnings and wars. (31)

The ironies of Anglo-Irish history being what they are, Bowen's Court, even if of "native rock," survived fewer than fifteen years after World War II. Having struggled unsuccessfully to support the house, Bowen sold it to a farmer in 1959, never anticipating his destruction of it within a year. Writing during the war, while Bowen's Court still stood, she celebrates its builder, her ancestor Henry Bowen, or Henry III as she audaciously names him to differentiate him from his predecessors and successors. Royal in vision if not position, in 1775 Henry created an austere and spacious limestone building, a house filled with light and space, that represented, according to his descendant, an exaltation and an obsession. "The stern and cold force of his unconscious nature perpetuated itself in stone as the house went up. But Henry was, at the same time, a man of his time's Renaissance: his sense of what was august in humanity made him make his house an ideal mould for life. He was more than building a home, he was setting a pattern" (169).[1]

In "The Big House," an essay written in 1940 while she was working on *Bowen's Court,* Elizabeth Bowen expanded on this Anglo-Irish pattern. She asserts that "the idea" from which the Big House sprang "was before everything, a social one. . . . Society—or, more simply, the getting-together of people—was meant to be at once a high pleasure and willing discipline, not just an occasion for self-display" (1986, 29). The Big House, with huge public rooms and staircases, was designed, then, for an idea of society. "The most ornate, spacious parts of these building *were* the most functional—the steps, the halls, the living-rooms, the fine staircases—it was these that contributed to society, that raised life above the exigencies of mere living to the plane of art, or at least style." (26–27). Bowen also notes—quite without self-consciousness—how the "functional" parts of the house, such as the kitchen or farm buildings, were sunk underground or otherwise concealed. In the Anglo-Irish pattern that she celebrates, servants' lives were to be screened from or literally buried out of the sight of the social spaces of the house. Of the outbuildings only the stables—"for horses ranked very highly" (26)—were visible.[2]

The pattern set by Bowen's Court had far-reaching effects on Henry's descendants. "If a Bowen . . . made Bowen's Court," her fam-

1. Virginia Woolf's 1934 diary entry about an April visit to Bowen's Court is a useful reminder that the aristocratic ideal which Bowen saw embodied in her house was not necessarily visible to all observers. While Woolf finds "character and charm" in the house, she also notes the "desolation" of its "cracked grand pianos, faked old portraits, stained walls." With her own brand of English snobbism Woolf hones in on the pretentions of Anglo-Ireland: ". . . & it was all as it should be—pompous & pretentious & imitative and ruined" (1982, 21).

2. The survival of the lofty barrel-vaulted stables, as well as the gloomy underground passages for house staff, at Strokestown Park House in county Roscommon graphically indicates the relative care lavished on horses and native Irish servants.

ily history relates, "since then with a rather alarming sureness, Bowen's Court has made all the succeeding Bowens" (1979, 32). In this study of her family and her house, virtually synonymous concepts in her book, Elizabeth Bowen described the life of a minor Anglo-Irish dynasty and interwove her narrative with passages from the history of Ireland. She insisted on the part her family played, if unconsciously, in the "drama outside themselves" and thus conceived of their history as representative of their class. We are reminded here of the other major twentieth-century elegist for the Anglo-Irish, and in particular of Yeats's claims in "Pardon, Old Fathers" that his Anglo-Irish predecessors were significant men of gentle birth: "Merchant and scholar who have left me blood / that has not passed through any huckster's loin. . ." (1956, 99).

Bowen's Court is a persuasive work, presenting a representative Anglo-Irish family as neither particularly eccentric nor improvident, insisting always on the decencies of ordinary well-born provincial men and women who were projected by history into positions of moderate power and moderate wealth. Although her ancestors were occasionally flawed as landlords and householders—for example, in their self-destructive and obsessive forays into litigation to regain a lost family property—they are also presented as humane and even heroic in their relief exertions during the Great Famine. *Bowen's Court* depicts few of the wildly dissolute or irresponsible Anglo-Irish landlords found in the eighteenth-century memoirs of ascendancy life by Jonah Barrington and in many Big House novels. With one minor exception (Henry IV), Bowen landlords were neither absentees nor debauched sensualists; the drunken prodigality of Edgeworth's Rackrents or Somerville's Prendevilles is absent from this version of history, as is the vindictive treatment of the peasantry by the Big House that Lever depicts in *The Martins of Cro' Martin*.

Bowen's Court describes declining postunion Anglo-Irish culture, which found itself gradually eased out of political ascendancy. "Property was still there, but power was going" (1979, 258). In her family history, Bowen traces the growing eccentricity, obsessiveness, and darkening gloom of Big House society, its response to an emerging sense of dislocation. Fantasies of living solely as feudal lords of the manor began to replace serious confrontations with political realities. One neighboring landlord, with power over three counties, was unable to face his tenants' refusal to vote for his political candidate in the 1825 elections. Gathering them all around him in his great hall, he went mad before the assembled crowd.

> It was democracy, facing him in his gallery, that sent Big George mad. In other cases, the line between sanity and insanity was less perceptibly crossed; many gentlemen only became 'interesting'; the cult for the glen and tear made a market for lyrics; the tendency to darken houses began. Anglo-Ireland began to claim and patent the everlasting Irish regret. Society—which can only exist when people are sure of themselves and immune from fear—was no longer, in the Anglo-Ireland I speak of, in what I call the magnetic and growing stage; it was on the decline; it was breaking up. (258)

Bowen identifies the decline of her people with the absence of political judgment that proved fatal to all the Anglo-Irish and that was personally evident, she implies, in her own childhood "endemic pride" of country. For the "new Irish" formed by the Cromwellian settlement, the grafting on to an alien land had seemed successful. They were mistaken. "If Ireland did not accept them, they did not know it—and it is in that unawareness of final rejection, unawareness of their being looked out at from secretive opposed life, that the Anglo-Irish naive dignity and, even, tragedy seems to me to stand" (160).

Bowen's Court unflinchingly faces the injustices of her family's ascendancy, acknowledging that they "got their position and drew their power from a situation that shows an inherent wrong" (453). But the book, measured and qualified as it is in its praise of the Bowens, is finally an elegy to an idea of "reason, order and light," to "a house that should be certain to elevate" (31), and above all, to a vision of society that could be fully realized only when the ascendancy was unchallenged by democratic forces. Written when the modern world seemed to be collapsing under the threat of fascist aggression, *Bowen's Court* represents a deeply conservative commitment to the idea of property. For Bowen, the eighteenth-century gentry homes of Ireland were monuments to an ideal of civilization, hierarchical and stable, an ideal that was preferable to the social fragmentation of the twentieth century. She quotes Arthur Young's observation in 1776 (the year in which Bowen's Court was officially occupied) that the monumental building program occurring in Ireland could not fail to impress new ideas and a feeling of respect and love onto a country changing "from licentious barbarity into civilized order" (Bowen 1979, 208). Although she dryly points out that Anglo-Ireland's failure to provide such an idea of order for all of Ireland's people contributed to the rise of democracy and the decline of the ascendancy, Bowen still argues, almost as if for an abstract good, for the civilizing effects of property.

> One may say that while property lasted the dangerous power-idea stayed, like a sword in its scabbard, fairly safely at rest. At least property gave my people and people like them the means to exercise power in a direct, concrete and therefore limited way. I have shown how their natures shifted direction—or the nature of the *débordement* that occurred—when property could no longer be guaranteed. Without putting up any plea for property—unnecessary, for it is unlikely to be abolished—I submit that the power-loving temperament is more dangerous when it either prefers or is forced to operate in what is materially a void. We have everything to dread from the dispossessed. In the area of ideas we see more menacing dominations than the landlord exercised over land. (455)

If *Bowen's Court* is an intelligent and measured history of Anglo-Irish society, it is nevertheless bound by those conservative values that prevent its author from questioning the deepest assumptions of her culture that caused its decline. Unpropertied Catholic Ireland is strikingly absent from the book; we are told that in Bowen's Court Catholics were treated with respect, tolerance, and distance; the lives of the vast majority of Irish did not impinge on Anglo-Irish society. Property rights of the ascendancy class, even though they were admittedly based on expropriation, were sacred.[3] Bowen admired the enlightened or "rational" unionism of her father, Henry VI, who

3. George O'Brien's *The Village of Longing*, an autobiographical account of growing up Catholic in a village near Bowen's Court, offers an alternate reading of the meaning of property for the ascendancy. For O'Brien, the conquerors of his land were rapidly brutalized rather than civilized by the land they seized. "They freely thought the world their plaything; there was nobody to put a check on their avarice. The mind they fostered was called 'property.' Once mindfulness was installed, once a scale of values was introduced (whether consciously as an intellectual habit or just as a means of attempting to calibrate lust), once ownership became a synonym for living—then the beauty turned terrible" (1989, 83).

sought (like the Edgeworths) to base such rights on "morals and discipline" (398). Neither through irony nor political speculation does Bowen achieve that questioning stance toward Anglo-Irish culture that would seem to lead to the disloyalty toward ancestral pieties that she herself established as the mark of major artistic achievement. The power of *Bowen's Court* resides in its elegiac resonances, its intelligent and graceful merger of the narrative of the Bowens' lives with the history of Ireland, and in its powerful argument for the conservative view of life as embodied in the Anglo-Irish Big House. The book represents, finally, a statement of loyalty to the past rather than the painful task of disloyalty.

The Last September

Bowen's first novel set in Ireland, written in 1928, more than a decade before *Bowen's Court,* is another matter. In *The Last September,* the Big House is destroyed in the holocaust depicted on the final page of the book. Danielstown and other neighboring Anglo-Irish homes light up the sky of the district, and Irish Republican Army soldiers silently drive their cars out of the gates of the estates they have destroyed. Alternately anticipated, dreaded, yearned for, and denied, the burning of Danielstown evokes complex responses from the reader. Amidst the expected shock and regret at the destruction of a beautiful artifact emerges a sense of necessary completion, and even fulfillment.

The politically motivated burning of Danielstown, that highly charged symbol of Anglo-Irish ascendancy, is a more powerful image of cultural waste than are holocausts in earlier Big House novels—when, for example, Christy O'Donoghoe accidentally sets fire to his ancestral home in Edgeworth's *Ennui* (proving the inappropriateness of a peasant upbringing for aristocratic life), or when Somerville's Jas Prendeville unintentionally ignites the magnificent house that he has mortgaged away and finally sold. Reading accounts of earlier destructive fires, we realize how our responses to them are conditioned by modern Irish history, how the burning of two hundred Big Houses during the twentieth-century Civil War has become the event that reduces all previous fires to foreshadowings, anticipations, and prefigurations of the great conflagration that was to come.

In February, before those leaves had visibly budded, the death—execution, rather—of the three houses, Danielstown, Castle Trent, Mount Isabel, occurred in the same night. A fearful scarlet ate up the hard spring darkness; indeed, it seemed that an extra day, unreckoned, had come to abortive birth that these things might happen. It seemed, looking from east to west at the sky tall with scarlet, that the country itself was burning; while to the north the neck of mountains before Mount Isabel was frightfully outlined. The roads in unnatural dusk ran dark with movement, secretive or terrified; not a tree, brushed pale by wind from the flames, not a cabin pressed in despair to the bosom of night, not a gate too starkly visible but had its place in the design of order and panic. At Danielstown, half-way up the avenue under the beeches, the thin iron gate twanged (missed its latch, remained swinging aghast) as the last unlit car slid out with the executioners bland from accomplished duty. The sound of the last car widened, gave itself to the open and empty country and was demolished. Then the first wave of a silence that was to be ultimate flowed back, confident, to the steps. Above the steps, the door stood open hospitably upon a furnace. (Bowen 1942a, 206)

Bowen's imagery implies the fatedness or "design" of a political "execution" of the Big House. The "open and empty" countryside, upon whose bosom of night the cabins "pressed in despair" is neither nurturing nor comforting. Nature itself becomes disarrayed as "the unnatural dusk" and wind from the flames create the illusion of daylight at night; an "extra day" is issued in. The flames that transform the formerly hospitable hall into a fiery furnace announce the "abortive birth" of a new dispensation; they imply the necessary terror of unloosed anarchy evoked by Yeats in "The Second Coming," a poem that emerged from the same period of Irish history. The "first wave of silence" after the executioners depart prefigures the lasting silence of Ireland's new ruins. "Sir Richard and Lady Naylor, not saying anything, did not look at each other, for in the light from the sky they saw too distinctly" (Bowen 1942a, 206).

The meaning of political events in *The Last September,* set for the most part in the late summer of 1920, is so integrated into the social and psychological texture of the book that the violence of these events seems to emerge as much from the unconscious needs of those living at Danielstown as from Irish political history. Unlike *Bowen's Court,* this early novel is subversive of ancestral pieties; it arrives with painful inevitability at that state of "disloyalty" Bowen praised. By February 1921, Danielstown is ripe for burning. Sir Richard and Lady Naylor administer their estate with the benevolent condescension of nineteenth-century landlords, while twentieth-century Ireland invades their demesne. Purposeful men in trenchcoats walk through the shrubbery, searching, perhaps, for weapons buried on Danielstown land. The "furtive" sound of armored British lorries menaces the after-dinner conversation of guests sitting on the steps of the Big House. The Naylors' young niece and a houseguest are threatened by a gunman in a deserted mill on the property, and a neighboring estate is invaded by rebels looking for firearms.

During the major political crisis of modern Ireland, the Naylors adopt the strategy of denial, preferring not to hear, not to countenance rumors of hostilities that usher in the Anglo-Irish Treaty and their own extinction as an ascendant class. With characteristic ambivalence, they are torn between their traditional hospitality toward the occupying British garrison and their vision of themselves as benevolent landlords of a loyal feudal community. As one reader observes, however, the benevolence that the Naylors direct toward their own tenants allows them to ignore the larger grievances of the Irish (Scanlan 1985, 71). Sir Richard, reacting to reports of rebel guns buried on his property, attempts to avoid the actualities he cannot face. "I will not have the men talking, and at all accounts I won't have them listened to" (Bowen 1942a, 25). Instinctually loyal to his Irish tenants, he accuses the British army of doing nothing but socialize with the gentry and terrorize old women in its search for weapons. His wife, reflecting a similar belief in her feudal bond to her tenants, whether or not they are IRA soldiers, also adopts a strategy of evasion. "From all the talk you might think almost anything was going to happen, but we never listen. I have made it a rule not to talk, either" (26). (Lady Naylor's uneasiness with the British forces sent to protect her class from Irish rebellion is fraught with her snobbish perception of the changes the Great War has brought to the English army. After the slaughter of a generation of young men in the war, the ranks of officers are now, she insists, filled with middle-class recruits.)

A painfully accurate assessment of the Anglo-Irish situation comes from a Naylor houseguest, Hugo Montmorency, a deracinated former landowner who has sold his home, and even before the political collapse of Anglo-Ireland, has failed to find a role for himself. When asked by a fellow guest, "How far do you think this war is going to go?

Will there ever be anything we can all do except not notice?", he replies with a devastating assessment of his society. Bitter, purposeless Hugo not only suggests that his class has no legitimacy, but implies that such legitimacy never existed. " 'Don't ask *me*,' he said, but sighed sharply as though beneath the pressure of omniscience. 'A few more hundred deaths, I suppose, on our side—which is no side—rather scared, rather isolated, not expressing anything except tenacity to something that isn't there—that never was there' " (82).

Danielstown itself, the austere stone house clearly modeled on Bowen's own family home, is presented through images that suggest a darker vision of Anglo-Ireland than that expressed more than a decade later in *Bowen's Court*. Filled with light and space, the house nevertheless diminishes the individuals occupying its vast rooms—forcing them into the patterns of dignity and aloofness it projects. In "The Big House," published thirteen years after *The Last September*, Bowen writes admiringly of the conception of life implicit in eighteenth-century Irish country house architecture and praises a culture that could value society over personality. "What is fine about this social idea is that it means the subjugation of the personal to the impersonal. In the interest of good manners and good behavior people learned to subdue their own feelings. The result was an easy and unsuspicious intercourse, to which everyone brought the best that they had—wit, knowledge, sympathy and personal beauty" (1986, 29). At Danielstown, however, where the sense of the past is alive and oppressive, the social idea dwarfs and silences the individual. While never going as far as Molly Keane in anatomizing the devastating effects of "good behaviour" in the Big House, in *The Last September* Bowen suggests the personal costs of life devoted to the ideals of an aristocratic society. Sitting beneath the family portraits at dinner, the family members and guests are transformed into "thin, over-bright" unconvincingly painted images—"startled, transitory." They dwindle personally in the overwhelming space of the room while above, the "immutable figures" of the family portraits "cancelled time, negatived personality and made the lower cheerfulness, dining and talking, the faintest exterior friction" (1942a, 24).

In *The Last September*, individuals are subsumed into the patterns of the past. The Naylors' nineteen-year-old niece, Lois Farquer, for example, is perceived through the lens of her family history; ideally, she will look as well and behave better than her rebellious and beautiful mother who broke with the family, married disastrously, and died young. Lois's romantic fascination with Hugo Montmorency, her mother's rejected suitor, suggests her own acceptance of the power of the past over her life. Similarly, Marda Norton, another Danielstown house guest, is fated for endless disasters because of a childhood accident at a Danielstown party. And Lady Naylor turns against Lois's suitor, a young English subaltern, because she can discern no acceptable family pattern in Gerald's English middle-class background. Unlike the Anglo-Irish who are all related to each other, Gerald exists outside any recognizable network—and is thus dismissed as "villa-ry." Lady Naylor's malignant snobbery in humiliating Gerald recalls the manipulative talents of Lever's Lady Martin and anticipates Molly Keane's countless vicious mothers, women whose lives are reduced to fulfilling the empty forms of power when real power is gone. Oppressing the young becomes the most accessible outlet for waning authority.

At Danielstown Lois feels either lonely and excluded or spied upon by the older generation. Life with her aunt and uncle in the Big House represents a state of impermanence, and as she watches night come to the guests lounging on the steps of the house, she senses that everyone waits for some unknown event. Fearing definition by the Naylors and their house guests, she covers her ears rather than hear herself being discussed in the cavernous anteroom of the second floor of Danielstown, a house whose perfectly proportioned open spaces afford little privacy. "She didn't want to know what she was, she couldn't bear to: knowledge of this would stop, seal, finish one" (1942a, 60). Lois alternatively longs to be related—"I like to be in a pattern" (1942a, 98)—and, like a Chekhovian heroine, to be free and purposeful—"What they never see . . . is, that I must do something" (1942a, 186), but she ambivalently fulfills the social roles Danielstown imposes on her. Too dependent on her position as obedient niece of the Big House to rebel as her dead mother did, Lois is trapped by the privileges and reassurances of the pattern Danielstown represents.

The Big House imposes itself on the countryside, just as it dominates its human inhabitants. Surrounded by lawns giving way to dark lines of trees, the house "was highest of all with toppling immanence, like a cliff" (1942a, 30). However, when she looks down at Danielstown from the road above, Lois feels that they live in a forest. "She wondered they were not smothered; then wondered still more that they were not afraid. Far from here too, their isolation became apparent. The house seemed to be pressing down low in apprehension, hiding its face, as though it had her vision of where it was. It seemed to gather its trees close in fright and amazement at the wide, light, lovely unloving country, the unwilling bosom whereon it was set" (1942a, 66). In such a passage Bowen is most explicit about the claustrophobic, smothering quality of the Big House, whose inhabitants are isolated not only by location but also by religion and class from easy social intercourse with an unloving Mother Ireland whose bosom it has ravished with its alien limestone structures. The imagery of this passage prefigures Danielstown's fate, when the "bosom" of Ireland again offers no comfort to those who witness the terror of the final holocaust.

For Lois the events of Irish politics as they touch her life release the real, "the actual," into the rigidified world of social convention and snobbery at Danielstown. In her desire for experience—social, political, and sexual—she cries out to her inadequate and conventional suitor against her situation. "How is it that in this country that ought to be full of such violent realness, there seems nothing for me but clothes and what people say? I might just as well be in some kind of cocoon" (49). After a stifling dinner at the Big House, Lois walks alone into the dark shrubbery, from where she views the family party as encased, even fossilized, in Danielstown's luxurious cocoon. Standing in the darkness, Lois is startled by the figure of a man in a trench coat resolutely striding through her uncle's demesne. His physicality and purposefulness awaken her. Suddenly, "not to be known seemed like a doom: extinction" (1942a, 34).

Several readers have noted Lois's sexual reaction to intruders in the Danielstown demesne (Blodgett 1975, 41–43; Heath 1961, 39–40; Tracy 1986, 8–12). Lois is convinced that the the young man who strides past her with "contemptuous unawareness" is inspired by intentions—which "burnt on the dark like an almost visible trail" (Bowen 1942a, 34). Her assumption of his exalted selflessness reminds her of her own drifting life and inability to love. "Here was something else she could not share. She could not conceive of her country emotionally" (1942a, 34). Running to report her experience, she sees Danielstown in the dark; the encapsulated safety of its drawing room now seems "excluded, sad, irrelevant" before the power of the fuller life she has just witnessed. With a new fear and a contempt for the ordinary, patterned routines of the Big House, she decides to keep her experience to herself. "Conceivably, she had just surprised life at a significant angle in the shrubbery" (1942a, 34).

Lois's second encounter with political Ireland occurs when she and Marda Norton encounter and awaken a gunman sleeping in a decaying mill on the estate. Like Elizabeth Bowen herself, Lois and Marda are both Anglo-Irish women with strong ties to England, virtually absentees in Ireland. Nineteen-year-old Lois has been raised in England by her mother and has returned to Ireland as an orphan after completing her education. Twenty-nine-year-old Marda, after breaking off several engagements, has resolved to marry a rich Englishman. The scene at the mill, a dramatic focus of the novel, represents a powerful initiation of both women into the life of their own country. In fusing sexual and political imagery, Bowen integrates two narratives: the story of a young woman's attempted passage into adulthood and an account of Ireland's historical transformation into the twentieth century.

Lois's horror at the decaying mill invites interpretation. For Hugo, these dead mills embody Ireland's political grievance against England's strangulation of the colony's trade. Roofless, floorless, tottering, with hinges that bleed rust, the "dead mill now entered the democracy of ghostliness, equaled broken palaces in futility and sadness" (1942a, 123). As a prefiguration of the destruction of Danielstown, the mill provides a richly symbolic historical setting, but it serves as well to evoke Lois's nightmare of " brittle, staring ruins" (123). It reminds her, as Robert Tracy notes, of that terrifying image of sexual horror and family decay suggested by Poe's House of Usher (1986, 12).

A desire for adventure leads the two women into the decaying mill where they disturb a sleeping gunman. Although the scene dramatizes what is, essentially, a dangerous political confrontation between an armed rebel and two Big House inhabitants, Bowen insistently foregrounds the sexual impact of the encounter for Lois and Marda. Most striking are the women's embarrassment before the sleeping gunman, their insistence on protecting him, and their subsequent bonding together against the deracinated and sterile Hugo—from whom they had escaped by entering the mill. The terror of their experience—Marda's hand bleeds from the gunman's accidental shot—releases their desire for love and fecundity. After rebuffing Montmorency's frantic attempt to enter the mill to investigate the gunshot, the women, both purportedly virginal, retreat into a female intimacy in which they nervously confess that their behavior was "goatish," not girlish. Marda, seemingly inconsequentially, expresses her desire for children—"I should hate to be barren" (1942a, 128)—while Lois, at this moment of greatest danger, thinks that she must marry Gerald. The scene provides a sexual initiation of sorts for Lois, as she firsts perceives the aborted relationship between Hugo, her mother's one-time admirer, and Marda.

Bowen juxtaposes Lois's liberating encounters with potential violence against the Big House with a portrayal of the oppressive life that Danielstown imposes on its young. Lady Naylor's nephew, Laurence, a bookish undergraduate who is discontentedly vacationing from Oxford, crassly expresses a realism that no one else will face. He shocks Mr. Montmorency by his desire to smash the decorum of Danielstown's illusions. "I should like something else to happen, some crude intrusion of the actual. . . . I should like to be here when this house burns. . . . And we shall all be careful not to notice" (44). Lois's *schadenfreude* is less overtly political, but as she contemplates the pattern on a fading rug in glamorous Marda's bedroom, she "hoped that instead of fading to dust in summers of empty sunshine, the carpet would burn with the house in a scarlet night to make one flaming call upon Marda's memory" (98). In pitting the unfulfilled young, who dream of an apocalyptic future, against the defeated or self-deluding old, Bowen's *Last September* is strikingly disloyal to the conservative tradition that is later elegized in *Bowen's Court*.

In this early novel, Bowen's vision of Ireland, a vision characterized by the purposeful intruders on the Danielstown demesne, recalls the subversive strand in Maria Edgeworth's *Ennui* that obliquely celebrates primitive sources of power in Ireland. Although in Edgeworth's novel the savagery and dissoluteness of native Ireland must be reformed, the ennui-ridden Lord Glenthorn is still revitalized by his encounter with a disordered and unsubdued nation. The savage splendor of his Irish castle represents a healing release from the well-bred perfections of his English home. Life in the twentieth-century Big House no longer offers a psychic alternative to English "civilization." Behavior at Danielstown has become so attenuated, so controlled by social ritual and political denial, that only when Lois brushes against the violence that aims to destroy her society does she begin to feel and indirectly express desires that might take her beyond the cloistered life of Anglo-Ireland. Not that Bowen offers us a vision of Lois's successful negotiation of her adolescent dependencies and longings; neither the Naylors' patterns of unthinking conservatism nor the unimaginative devotion Gerald offers her can satisfy Lois's longings. (Gerald's death in an IRA ambush is less Lois's tragedy, more a fulfillment of the pattern of violence that has been developing at Danielstown, where the Anglo-Irish failure to choose between England and Ireland assures the victimization of both sides. Lois has rejected Gerald's love before he dies.) Only in her decision to remain silent about her two encounters with Irish rebels does she momentarily attain some measurable independence from the oppressive Big House and some fidelity to her own impulses.

Lois's two encounters with Ireland—in which sexual and political longings unconsciously emerge—dramatize the isolation from "the actual" that the Big House has imposed on her. The forbidden Irish rebels are the only sexually potent figures in *The Last September,* but they represent possibilities of life that remain inaccessible to her. Like most Anglo-Irish writers, Bowen does not contemplate a social or sexual bonding between the Big House and the cabin, but the potential for such community emerges in Lois's unconscious reactions to the hidden and forbidden Ireland.

The Heat of the Day

When Bowen began to write *The Heat of the Day* in 1944, the apparent breakdown of European culture under Axis aggression engendered a more nostalgic vision of the Big House. In this novel set during World War II, the Big House represents an idyll of order and stability in a fragmented world. For Stella Rodney, the English protagonist of *The Heat of the Day,* the Irish estate her son inherits becomes a temporary psychic retreat: from her sense of her generation's responsibility for the political collapse of Europe, from her lover's betrayal of his country, from the bombings and tensions of wartime Britain. The smothering forces of tradition that oppressed Lois at Danielstown still exist, but they are transformed first into respite, and then into simple moral order.

Admittedly, Bowen's major achievement in *The Heat of the Day* is to depict the fragmentation of society—not to evoke a pastoral alternative to urban collapse. She portrays a fractured garrison city where the individual is subject to forces that control and betray. The novel's characterization of wartime London as a vast spy network should be of increasing interest to post-Foucaultian critics. Bowen's own role as a secret agent in neutral Ireland for the British Ministry of Information, as well as her friendship with many of the players in the climate of treason surrounding the British war effort,[4] suggest ample biographical sources for the novel's obsession with doubt, ambiguity, and falsehood. Like her creator, Bowen's protagonist finds herself drawn into a paranoiac network of surveillance. Forced to spy upon her lover, Stella is also the object of a would-be lover's—the blackmailer Harrison's—snooping. One critic notes how the convergence of names in the novel—both Harrison and her lover are named Robert—suggests the indeterminacy of identification in a wartime world (McCormack 1993, 227). But the settings of the novel, in fact, release even deeper ambivalences, for the two Roberts share their name with Bowen's grandfather—the last secure owner/occupant of Bowen's Court. Thus Bowen's choice of names for these two betrayers undermines the novel's strongest image of order and stability—the Big House in Ireland.

In London, all personal relations—and even sexual love—are reduced to spying, as the individual is relentlessly manipulated by propaganda and surveillance. Besieged Londoners are warned against loose talking; even the appearance of thinking silently in public exposes one to "the sense of having been watched" (Bowen 1962, 14); an exaggeratedly quiet voice on the phone hints "at some undefined threat" (22–23). Stella's blackmailer and would-be lover, the counterspy who risks his career for her, has no experience of love, only of having "watched quite a lot of it" (43). Her working class counterpart, Louie Lewis, discovers that she has a point of view, an identity, only when she reads the newspaper and finds herself described: "Was she not a worker, a soldier's lonely wife, a war orphan, a pedestrian, a movie-goer, a woman of Britain, a letter writer, a fuel-saver, and a housewife?" (152) Tellingly, Louie regrets only those aspects of

4. Bowen's wartime service as an air-raid warden, her secret investigations of Irish neutrality for the British Ministry of War, her friendship with figures like Goronwy Rees (invited by Guy Burgess to be a double agent), and her affair with Canadian diplomat Charles Richie are discussed by Jordan (1992, 98–105; 155) and McCormack (1993, 212–13). McCormack suggests that in the period before writing *The Heat of the Day* "the author was enmeshed in several overlapping webs of deceit and implicit treachery" (1993, 212).

herself that do not fit into the newspaper's image of the model citizen.

In *The Heat of the Day,* human relationships are formed without the protective layer of known accretions of personal history. Thus, Stella enters an affair with Robert Kelway without any knowledge of his past (his family or his home). During the suspended world of the London Blitz, she herself inhabits a "hermetic world" (90): a rented, furnished flat in London in a building occupied by commercial offices during the day, but totally empty at night. As the setting for her affair with Robert Kelway and for Harrison's ominous revelations, the apartment is most striking in its absolute anonymity and lack of a personal history. When complimented for the pretty things with which she surrounds herself, Stella is quick to deny ownership: " 'It's not mine' she flickered. 'Nothing in this flat is' "(28). Sealed off from the city by blackout curtains, the rooms are more deeply sealed off from time; they become the anonymous setting of wartime liaison in a garrison world, a social vacuum in which "one knew people well without knowing much about them" (95). Similarly, Louie Lewis lives anonymously in London, orphaned since German bombs obliterated her childhood home and her parents in Kent. Like Stella's flat, Louie's London apartment is a temporary dwelling that serves as a place for furtive relationships with the lonely soldiers she picks up to replace her absent husband. His departure for battle makes her feel, in London, "like a day tripper who has missed the last night train home" (145).

The moral resonances of dwellings and houses, particularly their architecture and decoration, loom large in *The Heat of the Day,* a novel in which bad taste is equated with deep failings of character. In an effort to learn more about Robert, Stella accompanies him to his childhood home, Holme Dene, the novel's awful reminder of the modern disintegration of taste and tradition. A suburban version of an old manor house, with imitation oak beams and gables, Holme Dene is described with such contempt by Bowen, that describing it, she lapses, on occasion, into overwriting that is close to diatribe. Built purely as an investment property, listed for sale on the estate agent's books since its purchase by the Kelways, Holme Dene suggests a transient society in which the sense of place is transformed into a vulgar quest for profit. Although the Kelways' house represents Bowen's version of middle-class English vulgarity, its Irish antecedents are clear. Like Edgeworth describing the flamboyant

Raffarty household in *The Absentee* or Yeats expressing his scorn for the Catholic middle class, Bowen writes with the conservative's distrust of class mobility.

Architecturally, Holme Dene is the antithesis of the rationally proportioned, austere Georgian house described in *Bowen's Court* or *The Last September*. In an effort to manufacture history and dignity, the builder created a series of vulgar elaborations and complications of architectural style. "Upstairs, as elsewhere, it had been planned with a sort of playful circumlocution—corridors, archways, recesses, half-landings, ledges, niches, and balustrades combined to fuddle any sense of direction and check, as far as possible, progress from room to room" (256). The house is gabled and trimmed, draped with blood-red Virginia creeper, surrounded by "a tennis pavilion, a pergola, a sundial, a rock garden, a dovecote, some gnomes, a seesaw, a grouping of rusticated seats and a bird bath." Unlike the Anglo-Irish country house with its great open spaces, Holme Dene is designed to discourage social contacts rather than facilitate them. The primary activity of its formidable matriarch, Mrs. Kelway, is to oversee and condemn everything about her. The head of a "man-eating house," she provides Robert with memories of "unstated indignities suffered by [his] father" (259). Mrs. Kelway's position at tea, in the house's dark, stuffed lounge, seems "strategic" and gives her command of all the windows of the room. Failing to dispense affection or respect, she instead spies on and dominates her children.

Bowen's description of Holme Dene legitimizes the counterspy Harrison's belief that wartime life reflects normal social patterns: "War, if you come to think of it, hasn't started anything that wasn't there already" (33). Thus, the two upper floors of Robert's childhood home are packed "with repression, doubts, fears, subterfuges, and fibs" (256). Passages are filled with twists so that family members can avoid embarrassing each other by inadvertent meetings. Although their private hours are spent "nerving themselves for inevitable confrontations," the family "intelligence service" is unrelenting. Taking a private walk is deemed "hiding"; outgoing letters slipped into the mailbox rather than left to be scrutinized on the hall table are unacceptably furtive. Holme Dene demands control over all behavior and breeds self-righteousness, smugness, and apparently, in Robert, a self-hatred that leads to treason.

In her creation of Robert's house and family, Bowen seems guilty of that snobbery of which Elizabeth Hardwick accused her shortly af-

ter the publication of *The Heat of the Day*. Suggesting that Robert Kelway's treason is reduced to a matter of bad breeding and vulgar middle-class values. Hardwick found

> a complicated theology of objects [by which] the noble and the lost
> soul are defined. . . . Peace is a well-lit drawing room, purity is light,
> airy, spacious. . . . The guilty lead an uneasy existence among the
> thick, dark, impersonal objects in a furnished room (Eddie in *The
> Death of the Heart*) . . . or bear upon their souls the terrible scar of one
> of those boy's dens in which the coins, birds' eggs, trophies and snap-
> shots of youth are kept intact by a vulgar family (Robert Kelway in *The
> Heat of the Day*). (1949, 1116)

In *The Heat of the Day*, where Bowen's revulsion against contemporary society engenders a powerful nostalgia, her hierarchy of values
often slides into a familiar Yeatsian worship of social lineage and inherited property. To be middle-class like the Kelways is to be "suspended into the middle of nothing" (Bowen 1962, 114). Stella's own
good breeding—she is the descendant of faded landed gentry—distinguishes her from Robert's vulgar heritage. Among her memories
are "a handsome derelict gateway opening onto grass and repeated
memorials round the walls of a church" (115); such memories provide her with a certainty of and, thus, indifference to position that
frees her from the desperate social climbing and financial scram-
blings of the middle class. "How can they live, anyone live," she asks
Robert of his family, "in a place that has for years been asking to be
brought to an end?" (121).[5]

5. In her autobiographical essay, "Pictures and Conversations," written in the last
year of her life, more than twenty years after *The Heat of the Day*, Bowen recollects her
childhood sense of the difference between England and Ireland. In the following
passage we again hear the traditionalist's preoccupation with the dangers and vulgar-
ities of the new (now associated with England), which Stella articulates in her earlier
description of the Kelways. "Everything, including the geological formation, struck
me as having been recently put together. . . . And this *newness* of England, manifest in
the brightness, occasionally the crudity, of its colouring, had about it something of
the precarious. *Would* it last? . . . How much *would* this brittle fabric stand up to"
(1975, 25). Again in *A World of Love*, with the appropriately named Lady Latterly's attempt to restore an "unusually banal Irish castle" (1983, 57) with Mayfair decor and
vast expenditure, Bowen reveals her contempt and suspicion of the nouveau riche
English. "The evening reeked of expense; everything cost, nothing was for nothing"
(1983, 51).

The Anglo-Irish Big House, Mount Morris, that her son inherits becomes part of a larger pattern of valuation in *The Heat of the Day*. The continuity of inherited land is a saving force in a world where houses are built for financial speculation, not to be lived in and passed on from generation to generation. Possessing Mount Morris gives Stella's fatherless son a "historic future" and meets his "capacity for attachment" (50). Roderick is deeply traditional, a simple and conventional young man seeking the "authoritarianism," or customs and habits, of a home life that Stella's unconventional role as a divorced mother denied him. As a child, she remembers, he idealized pattern and order. "He liked going out to tea with families who had a brook through their garden, hypothetical snakes in their uncut grass, collections of any kind in cabinets, a haunted room, a model railway, a funny uncle, a desk with secret drawers" (61). Like Gerald in *The Last September*, unimaginative but solid, Roderick represents and seeks traditional virtues. Whereas Gerald is clearly too limited and unimaginative to bring Lois to a resolution of her situation, Roderick exists in *The Heat of the Day* as a successful reassertion of tradition. In inheriting Mount Morris, he has, as his mother understands, "been fitted into a destiny; better it seemed to her than freedom in nothing." (175). He thus finds in the Big House the social coherence that Robert Kelway seeks in fascism.

The Big House in *The Heat of the Day* endows men and women with a historical context, with a role and a social position in life. Mount Morris transforms Stella from an unconnected divorcée in London into "the master's mother." Studying her face in a mirror in the shuttered drawing room, she "became for a moment immortal as a portrait. Momentarily she was the lady of the house" (173). Feeling that her generation had broken "the fatal connection between the past and the future" (176), Stella envisions her son as redeeming the "broken edges" of that connection that "she felt grating inside her soul" (176). Suddenly, for example, she imagines him bringing his bride to the house. Roderick, too, becomes aware of his role in the future for first time when he visits Mount Morris; contemplating the possibility of his death, he realizes his lack of a real heir, his lack even of a will.

For both mother and son, visiting neutral Ireland in wartime means entering into another world, experiencing an enclosed society so certain of its historical continuity as to be indifferent to the passage of time. The future was not an ominous void to eccentric Cousin Francis, the last owner of Mount Morris, but rather a certainty, an event as it were, to be anticipated and planned for. Thus he leaves careful directions, "injunctions, admonitions, and warnings," for the stewardship of his home.

> *Clocks,* when and how to wind . . . *Fire Extinguishers,* when and how to employ . . . *Locks and Hinges,* my method of oiling . . . *Live Mice* caught in traps, to be drowned *Not* dropped into kitchen fire . . . *Tim O'Keefe, Mason,* not to work here again unless he does better than last time. *Beggars,* bona fide 6d., *Old Soldiers* 1s, *Hysterics, Puppies,* in case of . . . In case of *Blocked Gutters.* . . . In case of *Parachutists* . . . *Birds in Chimney,* in case of . . . In case of *Telegrams* . . . In case of *River* entering *Lower Lodge* . . . In case of *My Death.* (164)

Reading his instructions for the future, Stella regrets that she had not "any such clear directions as to her own life" (164), and half longs to remain in Ireland to assume the clearly defined role the Big House imposes on her. Awakening on her first morning in Ireland from a trance-like deep sleep, she walks to the river and experiences a peace "of the moment in which one sees the world for a moment innocent of oneself" (177). Stella's epiphanic experience is described as her recognition of "a rapture of strength," "a breathless glory," "an unfinished symphony of love" in the world about her (177). These vague expressions of fulfillment are followed by news of a turn in the Allied war effort—Montgomery has broken through in Egypt. Forever in Stella's memory Mount Morris is connected with a "mirage of utter victory" (179).

Upon arriving at Mount Morris, Roderick also experiences an epiphany, a mystic identification with his land. In taking possession of his inheritance, he is possessed by it. "The place had concentrated upon Roderick its being: this was the hour of the never-before—gone were virgin dreams with anything they had of himself in them, anything they had of the picturesque, sweet, easy, strident. He was left possessed, oppressed and in awe. He heard the pulse in his temple beating into the pillow; he was followed by the sound of his own footsteps over his own land" (312). The imprecision of such dreadful prose, evoking ecstatic mystical experiences with vague and sentimental language (what is an "unfinished symphony of love" or a "picturesque, sweet, easy, strident" virgin dream?), suggests how problematic Bowen's writing becomes under the influence of nostalgia.[6] In view of the political history of the Anglo-Irish Big House, the young Englishman's solemn insistence on using the trope of possession—"his own footsteps over his own land"—is, moreover, striking in its absence of irony.

The Irish sections of *The Heat of the Day* do little to place Mount Morris in a social or political context. The dismay of Cousin Francis, its former owner, over Irish neutrality is noted but never fully explored. In fact, the very qualities of the inviolate Big House to which Stella and Roderick respond most positively—its peacefulness and isolation from war-torn England—emerge from Ireland's refusal to participate in the Allied war effort. Bowen's concern with Ireland's neutral stance in World War II is evident in an apologetic defense of neutrality she wrote for *The New Statesman* in 1941 (Bowen 1986, 30–35). But in *The Heat of the Day,* neutrality is merely the necessary condition that ensures Ireland's actual and symbolic isolation from the modern world.

In evoking the twentieth-century Big House, Bowen, like Yeats, praises an institution with little remaining social or political substance. Its reality is grounded in its aesthetic evocation of an idea of order and hierarchy that arose in Anglo-Ireland only as real power declined. And, whereas the Big Houses that Yeats knew and elegized in his poetry—Coole Park and Lissadell—represent an ideal of aristocratic high culture and service, Bowen, with characteristic ambivalence, even in her celebration, makes no comparable claims for

6. In focusing on Bowen's language, I join several earlier critics. With its abundant use of negatives, its "astonishing absence of referentiality" (Chessman 1987, 130), and its enmeshment in a world "where language dominates yet communication is impossible" (Heath 1961, 119), the texture of *The Heat of the Day* has long elicited significant critical response. William McCormack defends the willful distortion of syntax and "edgy repetitions" of the novel, claiming that Bowen's nervous style reflects a Joycean vigilance before the dead linguistic currency of a world defined by systems of betrayal. "Betrayal and linguistic deadness cohabit" (1993, 219). Despite McCormack's insistence that "the highly distinctive language of *The Heat of the Day* is required to convey a quality of absence or negativity special in the novel and its theme" (1993, 224), I find the fractured syntax to be far less controlled and purposeful than the critic's Joycean analogy implies. The passages I have questioned above in the text arise from Bowen's effort to convey a world of commitment, not betrayal, of continuity, not chaos. But here too the language is problematic—fulsome, vague, imprecise. Bowen's uneasy nostalgia about Ireland and the Big House leads her, I argue, to a loss of control over language rather than to the eccentric mastery over it that more forgiving critics ascribe to her.

Mount Morris. There, mere survival in a timeless world is sufficient. The library, filled with hundreds of books, is quite "without poetry" (Bowen 1962, 163). The cold, dark drawing room—mirrored, veneered, and ornately furnished—evokes "virtue and honor" but has driven former mistresses mad with its empty echoes and its insistence on eternity. Bowen emphasizes how, in spite of its centuries of social life, the Mount Morris drawing room projects upon its occupants an aura of silence and perpetuity. For the former ladies of Mount Morris, "conversation was a twinkling surface over their deep silence" (175). Yet the very dominance of the past, which oppresses conversation and stifles the young at Danielstown, is a saving force at Mount Morris.[7]

In *The Heat of the Day,* continuity is enough. In a world where history is quite literally collapsing about him, Roderick turns with relief to a country that has encapsulated the past. Mount Morris is the real thing; Holme Dene is the crass imitation. Mount Morris represents a level of breeding and social certainty to which the vulgar middle-class world of the Kelways' England cannot aspire. At its most destructive, Mount Morris breeds private grief like Cousin Nettie's madness, but it also produces eccentric Cousin Francis' loyalty to the Allies. Holme Dene, on the other hand, creates Robert Kelway's treason. In *The Last September,* those characters who remain committed to the neofeudal ideals represented by Danielstown are doomed by their fantasies to experience catastrophic loss. But in *The Heat of the Day* Bowen strains to transform the isolated Big House—the symbol of a dying social order—into a representation of social permanence. The price for such a transformation is evident in the language of Stella's and Robert's epiphanies and in the disturbing hierarchy of social values that the novel presents.

7. Bowen's portrayal of Mount Morris as the source of a traditional order is presented with some characteristic ambivalence. Phyllis Lassner's reading of the Mount Morris section of *The Heat of the Day* emphasizes the costs to women of a narrative of traditional life—"the myth of the ancestral home"—implied by the Irish subplot (1990, 135). Certainly, the former owner's mad wife, Cousin Nettie Morris, sequestered in her asylum after refusing to return to her husband and home, evokes the terrors of a patriarchal order that isolated generations of women in the silence of the Irish country estate. In paralleling Nettie's story with Stella's—both women abandon traditional domestic roles—Lassner foregrounds subversive undercurrents in Bowen's view of Ireland. But Stella's identification with the passive women trapped in the drawing room of Mount Morris includes at least as much desire as fear. And her image of the next mistress of the Big House—her son's future wife—is of a woman of "fluid autonomy," with eyes "unspent and fearless" (Bowen 1962, 175).

Stella's inability to enter into the world her conventional son embraces (she disappears from the last key scenes of the novel) suggests Bowen's recognition that a traditional domestic role is inadequate for her fictional alter-ego. Although Stella's deracination and Cousin Nettie's madness are convincing responses to the pervasive world of surveillance and control depicted in *The Heat of the Day*, the novel concludes with strikingly traditional resolutions: Roderick's ascendancy as landlord of the Big House and Louie's return to the site of her childhood home and apotheosis into motherhood. In failing to achieve a disengagement or "disloyalty" from the past, in turning at a time of crisis to the answers provided by ancestral pieties, Bowen undermines her most complex and resonant novel.

A World of Love

Bowen's ambivalence about her Anglo-Irish identity is written into the structure, theme, and language of the last novel she wrote before she sold Bowen's Court in 1959. Most readers view *A World of Love* (1955) as one of her lesser works; it is criticized both for not knowing what it wants to be and for straining to be too many things at once (a ghost story, a modernist subjective novel, a "poetic," open-ended romance) (Kenney 1975, 78; Lee, 1981). Praised by Blodgett and Leray for its symbolic unity, it is also attacked for its obscurity, its overuse of exposition, its fractured syntax.[8]

Critics generally fail to read *A World of Love* as a novel about Ireland.[9] Although it is set in that country, for most readers its real plot turns inward to the workings of three women's minds, and explores their delusions and emergence from delusion. The Big House exists,

8. The novel has been judged least successful of her works by Austin (1989, 55) and Kenney (1975, 78); it has received far less critical attention than have her other Irish works. Heath views it as the most intellectually ambitious of her novels, "but artistically one of the least convincing" (1961, 143). Although two close readings of the novel call attention to sustained patterns of imagery and metaphors (Blodgett 1975, 45–52; Leray 1991, 170–75), the more critical responses by Lee, Austin, and Kenney are not adequately addressed by Blodgett and Leray. Significantly, except for a few comments, Lassner's study of Bowen as a woman writer (1990) neglects this novel, which is centered on the lives of three women.

9. Leray declares that although the novel "is set in Ireland, . . . it it not a novel about Ireland" (1991, 165). Austin's hesitant suggestion that the novel "may be the author's covert criticism of Ireland" (1989, 60) is an exception to the general refusal to consider *A World of Love* in its Irish setting.

thus, as a receptacle of illusion, as a richly evocative symbol of its occupants' encapsulation in the past. Although the setting of *A World of
Love* is a typical decaying Anglo-Irish gentry estate, located somewhere in the south of Ireland in the postwar years, the novel avoids
confronting its own social and political context. Major characters are
exclusively Anglo-Irish or English, and the tension between a declining ascendancy and a restive native Irish society—the central political conflict of most Big House literature—is absent. For most
readers, then, *A World of Love* exists in the shadow of Virginia Woolf
rather than of Somerville and Ross.

But the critical emphasis on Bowen's innovations as a psychological novelist in *A World of Love* has led to a neglect of its more traditional elements. This novel, too, is unmistakably a product of its
author's preoccupation with her Anglo-Irish heritage, a preoccupation now dominated by her growing fears that the Big House would
have no sustainable role in modern Ireland. Even in its first paragraph, which describes a decaying Big House with a self-referential
allusion to "the heat of the day," Bowen draws attention to the connection between *A World of Love* and her previous work. She thus
makes clear her need to return again to the problematic idealizations Ireland had represented for her in 1949 when she completed
The Heat of the Day.

Bowen responded to World War II by valorizing all that it threatened. In the preface to her collection of war stories, *The Demon Lover*
(1945), she pointed out that even as writers outwardly accepted that
their individual destiny "counted for nothing" in wartime, they became obsessed with its preservation. "Every writer during this time
was aware . . . of the passionate attachments of men and women to
every object or image or place or love or fragment of memory with
which his or her destiny seemed to be identified, and by which the
destiny seemed to be assured" (1986, 97). Thus, in *The Heat of the Day,*
Bowen turned to the isolated Irish Big House of her childhood to escape the rootless cosmopolitanism of wartime London. The unsatis-
factory nature of the Irish sections of the novel suggests that they
were conceived by a writer who—against powerful critical instincts—
succumbed to a temptation to picnic once more in Eden, or more accurately, in an untroubled Ireland she imagined to exist outside the
fallen world of history.

Bowen's own fear of succumbing to a dreary attachment to the past, however, remained with her throughout the postwar era, as evidenced by her 1951 essay, "The Cult of Nostalgia," which decries those who cannot live except through the past. By turning to the Big House in *A World of Love*, Bowen once more struggles to reconcile her search for sustaining images of order with her suspicion of easy retreats from the fractured modern world. Bowen's biographer argues that the novel, written in the decade when its author sold Bowen's Court, registers anxieties about the heritage she was soon to abandon (Glendinning 1993, 200). Certainly, *A World of Love* emerges from two competing impulses: a nostalgic desire to preserve and celebrate the illusions that make life possible and an equally compelling need to expose the lies contained within those illusions. In *A World of Love*, Bowen returns for the last time to the Anglo-Irish Big House, the site of the childhood Eden that her fiction alternately resurrects and undermines.

A World of Love describes a few hot June days in the 1950s at Montefort, a decaying Anglo-Irish estate owned by Antonia, the heir and cousin of its former proprietor, Guy. Montefort is now occupied and farmed by their illegitimate cousin, Fred Danby, and his unhappy English wife, Guy's former fiancée, Lilia. In the course of the novel, Fred and Lilia's elder daughter, Jane, discovers a cache of Guy's love letters in the Montefort attic. Jane's subsequent infatuation with Guy precipitates a series of crises. All three women, Jane, Lilia, and Antonia, are forced to confront their own enthrallment with Guy's memory and, finally, to move beyond their imagining of an Edenic past.

Written toward the end of the realistic ascendancy tradition, *A World of Love* anticipates Jennifer Johnston's repositioning of the Big House novel into the genre of psychological fiction. Moreover, in its versions of characters who are encapsulated in the past (the three female protagonists are visited by apparitions of the long-dead Guy), Bowen also anticipates John Banville's neogothic *Birchwood* and his parodic *The Newton Letter*. Just as a ghost from the past, rather than a living character, precipitates the major crises of the novel, so the house exists most often with a certain disembodiment, as a form of the Anglo-Irish residence in decline, rather than as a place with any recognizable social, economic, or political resonances. Thus, Montefort's existence is more real to Jane when she experiences it through a dead man's descriptions in three-decade-old love letters than through her twenty years' acquaintance with her home. But Bowen's abandonment of social and political Big House tradition may be overstated, for she consistently exploits rather than rejects earlier conventions of the form. As her wisest critic notes, the scenes and passages that are most traditionally novelistic—embedded in the world of circumstantial realism—are the most successful (Lee, 1981, 195).

Significantly, Montefort is the classic—even stereotypical—Big House, with decaying roof and walls, overgrown gardens and avenues, and farmyard functions that intrude into the house. But whereas *The Last September* and *The Heat of the Day* are set during particular periods of social crisis for Ireland (the War of Independence or World War II), the action in *A World of Love* occurs simply in uneventful, postwar rural Ireland. Although the novel's young protagonist, Jane, believes that the passions and politics of her family too closely resemble those of the outside world (Bowen 1983, 34), the world's "passions" remain unspecified while those of her family lie at the center of the novel's action. Nevertheless, Jane's self-protective stand against the past—defeated for a time by her preoccupation with Guy's letters—resonates with such a resentment against a national as well as a family disability, that the bitterness of its specifically Irish context is unmistakable.

> Most of all she mistrusted the past's activities and its queeringness— she knew no one, apart from her own contemporaries, who did not speak of it either with falsifying piety or with bitterness; she sometimes had the misfortune to live through hours positively contaminated by its breath. Oh, there lay the root of all evil!—this continuous tedious business of received grievance, not-to-be-settled old scores. Yes, so far as she was against anything she was against the past. (35)

Bowen draws on powerful literary resonances when she evokes the Big House in *A World of Love;* she immediately sets her scene in familiar territory. In the novel's first three paragraphs, as we are introduced to a small mansion with "an air of having gone down," we enter a preexisting narrative—a literary convention of an irresposible and improvident Big House society. Montefort is the traditional decaying Anglo-Irish country house: isolated (the door no longer "knew hospitality"); impecunious (too many trees have been felled, the road is rutted, the fence "poor"); yet managing, nevertheless, to display style ("a stone archway . . . was still imposing") (9). The (briefly glimpsed) former landlord who married his cook and "went queer in the head from drinking and thinking about himself" (137) and the revelation that the Denbys have lost credit from a local shop-keeper belong to the world of Edgeworth's Rackrents or Somerville's Prendevilles. Thus Bowen fleetingly evokes the conventions of a traditional form that the action of the novel fails to develop.

Her inconclusiveness about the kind of fiction she was writing manifests itself in the strained quality of the novel's prose. Often, when two different novelistic impulses converge, the interior voice of psychological fiction is awkwardly yoked to imagery from the social and political realm. Such passages reveal both Bowen's ambition to develop her symbolic structures through the circumstantial realism of a traditional social novel and her failure to achieve a satisfactory blending of two forms. Attempting to write a novel of psychological transformation with traces of gothic spiritualism, Bowen used language rooted in an older, realistic social-political fiction. Thus, in dying, Guy neglects the physical well-being of his house, even though the decay in Montefort's walled garden frames and foregrounds more central psychic losses. By dying young and failing to settle the future, Guy is, of course, the quintessential absentee landlord, draining the emotional capital of the women at Montefort. But the language of an older, socially embedded plot and that of a new psychological romance plot coexist uneasily. "Hard was it not to tax him with, by having carelessly turned away, having somehow hastened the trend to ruin in such a life or lives as his own hand had touched. By striking when it did, before he had tried to see, even, whether he could consolidate, death made him seem a defaulter, a runner-out upon his unconsummated loves" (97). In Bowen's language, dead Guy is the "defaulter," the man who runs from his responsibilities to his land, who fails to "consolidate" his holding before he disappears. Thus, the irresponsible landlord and lover merge, and the social novel gives way to psychological romance. But Bowen's awkward syntax and seemingly willful obscurity is the cost of her turn inward.

On one occasion, when Bowen evokes Anglo-Irish history more specifically, political actions attenuate into mere gesture or routine. Closing up Montefort for the night, just after Guy has appeared to her as an apparition, Antonia is reminded of the history of such cautionary night rituals in the Big House.

> Not since Montefort stood had there ceased to be vigilant measure against the nightcomer; all being part of the hostile watch kept by now eyeless towers and time-stunted castles along the rivers. For as land knows, everywhere is a frontier; and the outposted few (and few are the living) must never be off guard. But tonight the ceremony became a mockery; when Antonia had done bolting and barring she remained, arms extended across like another crossbar, laughing at the door. For the harsh-grained oak had gone into dissolution; it shut out nothing. So was demolished all that had lately stood between him and her. . . (79)

In the last sentence of the passage, Bowen attempts to link the political and personal, implying an analogy between the decay of Montefort's door in time and the sudden dissolution of the barriers between Antonia and Guy. But the awkwardness of the analogy and the stilted language of the passage again suggest her difficulty in fusing the social and the psychological plots in *A World of Love.* How is the attrition of the barriers between the Big House and hostile native Ireland like the momentary, epiphanic renewal of Antonia's youthful bond with Guy?

Bowen creates a plot of psychic action that she imposes on a setting and language evoking a more political and social fiction; yet her insistent turning away from the conventions of the realistic novel highlights the discrepancy between the interior plot and the far less developed exterior one. Although one critic suggests that if we focus on the Big House as both a real presence and a "spatio-temporal symbol," the novel emerges as a unified work (Leray 1991, 165), Bowen's strained transitions between interior and exterior world deny her reader the experience of such unity. In fact, her awkward and mannered syntax frequently becomes the battleground for her conflicted views about the past and her subsequent irresolution about the kind of novel she was writing.

Although the past is a force that deadens and engulfs the present, the pervasive tone of *A World of Love* is comic, occasionally even parodically sentimental. Some illusions, like Jane's romantic dreams, survive; they are the impetus for liberating actions that propel her into the future. If the shabby Big House exists as a sign of the paralytic hold of a romanticized past on the present and on the future, it also becomes a memento of the fuller and richer life that existed at Montefort when Guy was alive.

Thus, Jane's final journey from decaying Montefort and the old love letters in its attic to the modernity of Shannon Airport to meet a new lover—who literally drops out of the sky—presumably signals her abandonment of the past. Yet when she meets the new arrival at Shannon—the setting of a spatially and temporally unbound future—the last line of the novel describes the event in the clichéd language of romantic fantasy: "They no sooner looked but they loved" (1983, 149). If Bowen intends, as one critic suggests, that "illusions are perpetuated because they are necessary to life" (Kenney 1975, 85), then Jane's shedding of fantasy (her obsession with a dead man and his letters) leads not to a rejection of nostalgia and romance, but to a wiser and more skeptical embracing of those illusions that are necessary to sustain life. If we manage to accept the ending, Bowen has had it both ways: her novel critiques the obsession with the past (the Big House, the old love letters, life based on fantasies about a dead man) but affirms Jane's youthful openness to new romances and new illusions. If we may reject Eden and picnic in it as well, then Bowen refuses the painful choices implicit in disloyalty.

The Persistence of Illusion in Molly Keane's Fiction

Molly Keane's great achievement as a novelist was to reject the nostalgia that is a major cultural production of a declining imperial state. In her denial of an idealized past, Keane differs from Elizabeth Bowen, who finally embraced the political conservatism that was so appealing to many other early twentieth-century writers. The Irish subplot of Bowen's *The Heat of the Day,* with its ambivalent yearning for the solidity and order represented by eccentric Uncle Francis's Big House, emerges from many of the same assumptions that lie behind the portrayal of a disappearing organic community in E. M. Forster's *Howards End* or D. H. Lawrence's *The Rainbow.* Central to the fiction of many modernists—Joseph Conrad and Ford Madox Ford, as well as Forster and Lawrence—is the sense of a lost coherent past, of the sacrifice of rural community values to the modern wasteland of urban capitalism, sexual confusion, and moral relativism. Thus, despite Elizabeth Bowen's identification of herself as an Irish writer, her work shares many of the social and political characteristics of British modernism—particularly when she evokes that sense of dislocation and abandonment so pervasive in the literature of a waning imperial power.

Molly's Keane last three novels, however, insistently reject the formulations of a lost organic cultural tradition and ruthlessly expose the fictitiousness of personal memory. These darkly comic explorations of individual delusion explode the nostalgia that her Big House settings promise readers accustomed to British country house literature. In Keane's best novels, nostalgia is, in fact, the disease of victims who are trapped by delusions about the past—characters who

174

resemble Thady Quirk in their inability to break out of fictive constructions of gentry life.

On occasion, Keane seems to replace one kind of nostalgia—for a coherently hierarchical society—with another, through her celebration of the sensuous texture of the gardens, architecture, and especially the food of the Big House. But her high-spirited evocations of the luxuriant surface of gentry life often parody the cultural style they appear to affirm and memorialize. In *Time After Time,* for example, the delicious meals served in the dining room are made from moldy bits of meat plucked from the dog's dishes; in *Good Behaviour,* the protagonist kills the mother she despises by feeding her carefully seasoned rabbit quenelles; at a dinner party in *Loving and Giving,* a magnificent dessert trifle is served at the very moment that the elderly hostess's similarly creamy bosom imprudently spills out of its bindings. Thus, in her late fiction, the sensuous good life of upper-class opulence that ordinarily accompanies or evokes nostalgia (the Molly Keane of *Architectural Digest*)[1] is itself undermined by such flamboyant depictions of style sliding into decadence.

Published under the pseudonym M. J. Farrell, Keane's ten early novels anticipate the critique of Anglo-Irish culture that emerges most powerfully in her three last works. Her ninth novel, *Two Days in Aragon* (1941), considers the intricate relationship between the Protestant Big House and Catholic Ireland. Like Edith Somerville's *The Big House of Inver,* Keane's one sustained attempt to set her narrative in a political context approaches Irish history as it is embodied in the lives of generations of an Anglo-Irish family. The Foxes occupy an eighteenth-century Georgian mansion that has managed to retain its surface integrity into the twentieth century. Keane presents Aragon on the eve of its destruction in 1920, as it hovers among its scented gardens in late spring, the season of its most exquisite but doomed beauty. Named as if to evoke an exotic Spanish city, surrounded by

---

1. In an *Architectural Digest* article describing her home after her husband's death, Keane's memories of Big House life in her marital "house of . . . dreams" evoke a nostalgic vision of Anglo-Ireland's aesthetic achievement unmediated by the irony of her late fiction. "The waste of building space was inspired and magnificent" (1986, 138). The article's subsequent description of how she converted a vulgar "villa" into an authentic "cottage" reflects a familiar Yeatsian grasp of the bond between Big House and peasant values. The real enemy for Keane is the middle-class world of villas. As a working journalist Keane knew the audience for *Architectural Digest,* an interior design magazine offering glimpses of the rich in their houses.

Spanish magnolias and Italian stone pines, the estate survives, not the defacement of past violence and arrogance, but with a melancholy, overripe perfection that precedes decay. The aesthetic merger of nature and architectural form is central to Aragon's meaning, for the house and gardens exist together as a magnificent and decadent cultural artifact. By eroticizing the sensuous texture of Big House life, Keane suggests its delights—and its corruption.

> There was too much beauty around Aragon, and too much beauty is dangerous. A complete thing is near its ending. The white brooms in the garden, even such slight mountainy things, had grown to a false fat stature, sleek as white, overfed cats in their ordered groupings. Behind the brooms rose the trimmed plumes of lilacs, grossly, unbearably sweet at night. A magnolia's horned and flowerless bones were crucified against a shallow alcove in a wall alcoved for no reason but to complete an alcove at the house's farther extreme. (Farrell 1985, 227)

Aragon's corruptions are darker and more covert than the Prendevilles' violent, sprawling, masculine disorder in *The Big House of Inver* or the willed ignorance and snobbery of the Naylors in Bowen's *The Last September.* In *Two Days in Aragon,* grand public rooms designed for expansive living are built directly over a cellar of labyrinthine quarters "where the hordes of servants had slept in dirt and confusion" (Farrell 1985b, 193). While such housing reflects costs implicit in any aristocratic society, Keane's examination becomes increasingly explicit. In a brief and somewhat obscure passage that attempts to account for a streak of cruelty in the Foxes, Keane suggests that sexual domination and sadism are integral to the Anglo-Irish colonial experience. In addition to the rabbit warren of servants' quarters, the Aragon cellar contains a long-unused and isolated chamber, papered in a peculiar old Chinese design and hung with mirrors. This room, "about which there remained an air of past luxuries," is equipped with devices of sexual perversion: "delicate ivory-headed cutting whips and other fine and very curious instruments." The contemporary Fox mistress who discovers the room imagines with horror that her husband's grandfather "had used such dreadful tools, . . . had built this far-off room for his pleasures" (193).

Keane gradually reveals how generations of Fox landlords exercised their *droit du seigneur* over Aragon's servant girls. The secret subterranean chamber in the Big House suggests that the idealized, hierarchical ascendancy community of peasant and aristocrat that Yeats celebrated was tinged with the sexual practices of De Sade. With a room of gothic horrors in the basement of Aragon, the architecture of the Big House entombs its own corruption. The spectacularly beautiful house and gardens overlook a river into which the illegitimate infants and aborted fetuses of servant girls were thrown and "where babies' bones were little and green scattered skeletons on the river bottom" (122).

Keane acknowledges the barbarity and lack of restraint underlying the aesthetic refinements of Anglo-Ireland. Her revelations are supported by David Thompson's memoir, *Woodbrook,* which describes how accounts of the seventeenth- and eighteenth-century Big House imposition of the *droit du seigneur* survived well into the twentieth century (1976, 117, 120). By transmitting the brutal narrative of sexual harassment he heard in the 1930s and 1940s in County Roscommon, Thompson confirms Keane's darkest fictional implications; he demonstrates how recollections of Anglo-Irish atrocities intrude upon and disturb the surface of Big House life.[2] In *Two Days in Aragon,* the sexual arrangements between gentry society and native Ireland center on Nan O'Neill, a bastard daughter of the Big House who is devoted to serving the Anglo-Irish culture of her patrimony. Like Shibby Pindy in Somerville's *The Big House in Inver,* Nan lives enthralled by the forces that will destroy her. Her aristocratic father's affection for her beautiful mother, "a stupid loquacious slattern" (1985b, 107) employed as a servant girl by the Foxes, saves Nan from the watery fate of other illegitimate infants born at Aragon. After

2. Even a brief exploration of Irish historical documents reveals anecdotal evidence for such sexual practices, although in the two cases presented in this note, English travellers surely brought significant biases with them to their writing. In describing eighteenth-century Ireland Arthur Young reports that "landlords of consequences have assured me that many of their cottiers would think themselves honored by having their wives and daughters sent to the bed of their master; a mark of slavery which proves the oppression under which people must live" (1892, 2:54). John Dunton's seventeenth-century letters about his tour of Ireland describe "an ancient custom for the landlord to have the first night's lodging with the maiden bride" (1939, 369). Lecky quotes sources who attest to the lawlessness of the early eighteenth-century Irish gentry and to the existence of private prisons in the houses of prominent landed proprietors for the "summary punishment of the lower orders" (1896, 1:285). These accounts, when combined with Thompson's assertions that twentieth-century Irish country people still recounted brutal stories about the *droit du seigneur,* suggest the narrative hold of such versions of Irish and Anglo-Irish relations on the imagination of rural society.

Nan's mother is safely married off to a keeper on the estate, she regales her daughter with stories of the dangers and the glamour of the Big House.

In Keane's genetic coding, which resembles Edith Somerville's preoccupation with bloodlines and breeding, Nan embodies the physical advantages of two worlds: her fine-boned, aristocratic body and features and her coarse, golden peasant hair "showed her father's quality and mother's beauty" (Farrell 1985, 111). As an adult, in spite of the vows of her putative father that she will never enter domestic service, Nan chooses to become a nursemaid at Aragon. She escapes her mother's fate by fleeing the sexual danger represented by her Fox employer—her own cousin—whom she loves. But although Nan marries a local mountain farmer and bears his son, when she is widowed she leaves her own child to be raised by her husband's family and returns to Aragon to care for the Fox children. There she lives out her life, a servant in her father's house.

Like Shibby, Nan becomes the powerful chatelaine of the Big House, her temple and shrine, over which she skillfully gains ascendancy. "Life was Nan's province, every aspect of life on which she could lay a finger, some octopus like quality in her seemed able to reach out its sensitive strength and grasp the essential . . . "(123). When Nan is captured by three IRA soldiers, they are eager to avenge her betrayal of her own people. Tied by her neck to a tree, with "her nails sunk into the very body of Aragon," she is forced to watch "her own soul burning" (254). Her horrified responses to the destruction of Aragon reveal how, in her conviction that she possesses and controls all the things of the Big House, she is, in fact, totally possessed by them. "Now she saw the smoke and the rosy flames from her linen-room window. My linen, my pillow cases, my sheets. Like all the furnishings of Aragon, they were hers, she had always experienced a sound satisfaction in so calling things 'mine'. My good brocade curtains, my fine new towels. Hers to keep from sun and moth and careless hands—most truly hers who could so cherish them, playing the careful steward of their excellence" (253–54).

The ironies of Nan's dispossession—and of her position as servant to her own patrimony—are clearest when she stands one night at the top of the wide double stairway of Aragon. Although she wishes to descend the staircase, pass the portraits of her Fox ancestors, and arrive at the great public hall of the Big House, she dutifully chooses to negotiate the cluttered backways of the house. There she passes a decorative motif banished to the servants' quarters: "a black plaster nigger in a blue starred petticoat that everyone thought so hideous . . . " (112). And, on the frantic last day of Aragon's existence, Nan learns that Grania Fox, the daughter of the Big House whom she has nursed from childhood, is sleeping with Foley O'Neill, Nan's dashing young son.

As Grania anticipates Nan's reaction to her affair with Foley, she reveals with painful exactitude how deeply her former nurse identifies with her Anglo-Irish masters and how the barriers between two social classes assume racial as well as economic and sectarian dimensions. "For a Fox, a daughter of Aragon, to carry on an affair with an O'Neill from the Mountain was as wrong, Grania knew, to Nan, as the love of black and white people seemed to her" (15). Erotic pleasure threatens imperial division and must, therefore, be suppressed.[3] Nan's plan to terminate Grania's pregnancy reverberates with the ironies of her own erotic temptations and her parentage. A misalliance between the Big House and Catholic Ireland, like that which produced Nan, must be aborted before it spawns her grandchild.

> A look of such desperation broke across Nan's face as was near madness. Was this the end of her sacrifice to the God of Aragon? Was the high giving of her life to be twisted to nothingness in an hour? A Fox

3. Such explicit suggestions of Anglo-Irish racist attitudes, comparable to those held by white slave owners toward their slaves, are not confined to Keane's novel. In writing about eighteenth-century Ireland, the nineteenth-century Anglo-Irish historian W. E. H. Lecky noted that "the upper classes were exposed to all the characteristic vices of slave holders, for they formed a dominant class, ruling over a population who were deprived of their civil rights and reduced to a condition of virtual slavery" (1896, 1:282). The sexual as well as the political anxiety of the Anglo-Irish ruling class about a people it attempted to subjugate is certainly expressed in acts like the attempt by the Irish Privy Council to mandate the castration of unrecognized priests in 1719 (Lecky 1896, 1:162), and in the long history of attempts to forbid marriages between Catholics and Protestants until the mid-eighteenth century. Lecky's discovery that the sectarian basis of stories of Catholic abductions and "exquisitely brutal" rapes of Protestant heiresses reported by Fronde was, in fact, totally unsubstantiated by historical evidence (1896, 1:375–80) further supports the notion of a sexual anxiety with powerful resemblances to post–Civil War fears in the American South. Molly Keane's fleeting twentieth-century reminders of the analogies between black and white race relations and those between the native Irish and Anglo-Ireland underscore the covert racial and sexual fears implicit in Irish history.

daughter in vulgar trouble with a servant's child. In just such trouble as the poor country girls who worked in the house had been in with the bad Fox's [*sic*] of all times, and they had been despised and aborted, their babies, dead or dying thrown to the river. (156)

Keane's exploration of the sexual relationship between the two Irelands foregrounds a persistent source of anxiety in the Big House novel. Although intermarriage between the Norman Catholic and Anglo-Irish Protestant aristocracies is a reconciling possibility in some nineteenth-century works (in, for example, Edgeworth's *The Absentee* and Le Fanu's early Jacobean fiction), the marital aspirations of a rising Catholic class were another matter for novelists who wrote from within gentry society. The possibility of marriage between Catholic and Protestant Ireland appears most often as a threat to the Big House. As the Catholic antagonist gazes longingly at the gentry estate, the defensive responses of most writers suggest the sexual dimensions of class and sectarian anxieties in Irish society. Lever's portrayal of the agent Scanlan's aspirations for Mary Martin's hand, when contrasted with Joe Nelligan's respectful and distant adoration of her, indicates the unwillingness of the nineteenth-century Anglo-Irish author to contemplate the breakdown of traditional class and sectarian barriers. Such discomfort appears in twentieth-century fiction as well; in *Mount Music,* Edith Somerville views a Catholic doctor's plans to marry his children into the Big House with sustained unease. In *The Big House of Inver,* a reverse pattern of downward mobility occurs when the daughters of the eighteenth-century Lady Isabella marry the grooms of the estate; such behavior, an enduring shame to the Prendeville family, marks the beginning of its rapid decline.

From the point of view of the ascendant class, the servicing of the Big House landlords by Catholic peasant women represents a less threatening sexual contact between the two Irelands. Somerville and Ross's *An Irish Cousin* and *The Big House of Inver* and Keane's *Two Days in Aragon* provide the obvious evidence that the *droit du seigneur* resulted not in the social assimilation of two classes, but in the victimization of one class by another. Figures like Shibby Pindy or Nan O'Neill, however, also reveal how sexual exploitation creates, not simply new victims, but new aggressors as well. The ruthlessness of Nan's devotion to Aragon makes her a darker and more ominous figure than Shibby.

Nan's final charge is Miss Pidgie, a frail and senile Fox maiden aunt who embarrasses the family drawing room and is therefore expelled to Nan's care in Aragon's dark and cold attic nurseries. There, Nan's sadism toward an infantalized old woman suggests unconscious rage directed toward the weakest link in the Anglo-Irish power structure. Thus both the cellar and attic of Aragon are sites of aggression against the weak. Terrorizing and starving helpless Miss Pidgie and locking her up in the attic, Nan expresses her absolute ascendancy over the one Big House representative who can never oppress her. In *The Big House of Inver,* Shibby directs her anger against Maggie Connor, the young Irish woman whose fate is all too similar to Shibby's own mother's and who threatens Shibby's ambitions for her half-brother, Kit. Maggie represents the Irish heritage that Shibby has denied rather than the Anglo-Irish one she has embraced. But Nan expresses her deepest contempt and sadism, not toward the frightened and brutal IRA soldiers who voice the political demands of her native Irish heritage, but toward the vulnerable Fox relation who has failed to live up to Nan's vision of Big House ascendancy. Thus for Molly Keane, as for Sheridan Le Fanu, the punishment for Anglo-Irish guilt is visited upon its own weakest descendants.

Good Behavior, Time After Time, and *Loving and Giving*

Reading Molly Keane's thirteen novels about life in the Anglo-Irish Big House in chronological order reinforces respect for the authority of age and the judgment of experience. *Good Behaviour* (1981), *Time After Time* (1983), and *Loving and Giving* (1988) were published when Keane was in her late seventies and early eighties.[4] Appearing almost three decades after the last of her ten earlier novels, they represent the most significant achievement of her long career.[5] All three echo

4. *Loving and Giving* was published as *Queen Lear* (1989) in the United States. Keane's first ten novels appeared under the pseudonym M. J. Farrell.

5. Although Seamus Deane's *Field Day Anthology of Irish Writing* excludes Keane from its pages, critics less hostile to the Big House novel praise the mastery of *Good Behaviour.* Although no book-length study of Keane exists as of the writing of this study, chapters about her novels by Imhof (1992) and Weekes (1990) acknowledge *Good Behaviour* as a masterpiece. Rachael Billington's often cited observation in the *New York Times Book Review* that *Good Behavior* "may well become a classic among English novels" (1981) unfortunately fails to emphasize the uniquely Irish and postcolonial qualities of the novel Keane wrote.

recurrent strands from her earlier fiction, but represent a new and fiercely corrosive dissection of the society she had previously evoked with occasional nostalgia. With age, Keane achieved a chilling distance from her Anglo-Irish heritage, a distance that allowed her to cast a cold eye on life and to view it with comic detachment. She insistently exposed what her nineteenth-century predecessors only implied: that the ever-receding ideal of the cultivated Big House at the center of an organic community is based on a fictive vision of the past. That nostalgic evocation of a harmonious and morally ascendant ruling class, suggests Keane, rests on carefully constructed patterns of delusion, on willful misinterpretation of the past in order to construct self-protecting illusions of stability.

Keane transforms the familiar Big House novel, attuned to the political pressures that undermine Anglo-Irish society, into domestic fiction, and, in the last three works especially, into unsparing parody of the very domestic form they seem to embrace. Much of her fiction exists at curious distance from any direct confrontations with politics or history. With the exception of *Mad Puppetstown* and *Two Days In Aragon,* in which the political troubles of the 1920s impinge directly on the lives of the characters, Keane's gentry world appears insulated from history. In the eleven other novels, country house settings are virtually untouched by Irish civil strife. On rare occasions the political troubles are referred to, almost as an afterthought: in *The Rising Tide* the Civil War is "an inconvenience" (Farrell 1984, 208) to social life; in *Time After Time,* the contemporary characters listen indifferently to the appalling radio news from Ulster as they await dinner. In *Good Behaviour,* history is present only insofar as the father of the protagonist is injured and a stablehand is killed fighting with the British in World War I. The period of the Free State Treaty, the subsequent Civil War, and the destruction of nearly two hundred Anglo-Irish homes is recalled by protagonist, Aroon St Charles, as if she is describing an illustration of social high life in a popular magazine: liberating clothing, new and intoxicating cocktails, luxurious parties, tennis, and hunting. Only once, when Aroon contemptuously dismisses of a young Irish fisherman as coming from a family of "drunks and Fenians" (Keane 1982, 102), does the novel suggest the political dimension of class difference that dominated Irish life for centuries. Although *Loving and Giving* chronicles the life of a gentry family from 1904 through World War II, it, too, minimizes the impact of

Irish political history. The loss of Anglo-Irish youth at Flanders merely curtails the guest list for the protagonist's first house party. Although a hunt ball is held in an empty Big House slated for demolition—a house whose "stubborn Protestantism held it aloof from usefulness to any new owner" (Keane, 1988, 80)—and Anglo-Irish landlords fight side by side with the British in World War II, the novel ignores the civil strife that endangered Anglo-Irish rural life in the early 1920s.

In much of her work Keane is redefining the Big House novel, seemingly recasting it into the form of traditional English domestic fiction which was more insulated from political and social issues than Irish literature. Yet for all the apparent historical insularity of Keane's novels, so domestically centered on the gentry family's life-sustaining attention to social decorum or "good behaviour," these works have little in common with the certainties of Jane Austen's fictional world or with the affirmation of a conservative and traditional social order that Bowen dramatized in *The Heat of the Day* or *Bowen's Court*. By emphasizing social decorum as a moral gauge of the individual, Jane Austen assures her readers of shared assumptions about behavior. Because of the narrative insistence on good manners and social decencies, Emma Woodhouse's rudeness to the helpless and vulnerable Miss Bates, for example, cannot go unreproved. In Keane's novels, however, good manners imply destructive self-delusion rather than moral decency. "Even then I knew how to ignore things, I knew how to behave" (Keane 1981, 13). In *Time After Time, Good Behaviour,* and *Loving and Giving,* children discreetly ignore their parents' sexual exploits and create a series of illusions, of layers of consciousness that deny the breakdown of family, class, and culture.

For the historically literate reader, the personal maladjustments in Keane's late fiction are linked to the political and economic impotence of twentieth-century Anglo-Ireland. Rather than imitate the triumphal marriage plot of the English domestic novel, Keane describes the downward social trajectory of a marginal gentry society facing extinction. Daughters remain spinsters, or if they marry—unhappily, to be sure—they fail to produce children. Gainful employment is unheard of for the proper Big House lady; for the weak and passive men, careers are manufactured out of leisure activities. They turn, on occasion, from their hunting, fishing, or financially draining stud farming to sexual liaisons with the servants (on one occasion to an incestuous relationship with a young niece), to homosexuality, or to suicide.

Anglo-Irish novelists writing about the Big House have registered the unmanning of the colonizer. In fact, the ways in which the death throes of empire affected gender roles in this fiction becomes an illuminating means of charting the collapse of colonial systems of domination. Until the nineteenth century, the landlord shaped himself within an imperial system that perceived a colonized people as feminine as well as infantile.[6] But Keane's fiction suggests that as Anglo-Irish power erodes, gender identities shift; the formerly submissive partner within the Big House marriage learns to mimic and undermine the dominant male role. Nineteenth-century Anglo-Irish fiction, beginning with Maria Edgeworth's *Castle Rackrent,* charts the progressive stages in the breakdown of the male Anglo-Irish colonizer's traditional identity.

The patriarchal world of the ascendancy is already dying on the Rackrent estate and continues to molder and decay throughout the novels of Charles Lever and Somerville and Ross. Landlords in these novels are strikingly incompetent men. Inhabiting the remains of vast territories that their ancestors conquered by the sword, they fail to uphold the military and aggressive values of their ancestral culture. As these men drink, gamble, and philander away their patrimony, a gradual shift in power occurs. In spite of their ability to resist patriarchal control, Maria Edgeworth's women characters occupy

6. The experience of colonizing . . . began to bring into prominence those parts of the British political culture which were least tender and humane . . . and justified a limited cultural role for women—and femininity—by holding that the softer side of human nature was irrelevant to the public sphere. It openly sanctified—in the name of such values as competition, achievement, control, and productivity—new forms of institutionalized violence and ruthless social Darwinism. (Nandy 1983, 32)

Both Ashis Nandy and Edward Said demonstrate how nineteenth-century British imperialists in India characterized their subject people as emotional, passionate, and thus implicitly feminine, in contrast to the inherently rational and thus masculine colonizers. Recent cultural analyses of Irish colonialism similarly focus on how nineteenth-century British imperial discourse about Ireland was influenced by Matthew Arnold's enumeration of the "feminine" virtues of the Celtic race: emotion, imagination, love of beauty, charm, spirituality, ineffectualness, and sensuality (see, for example, Cairns and Richards 1988, ch. 3). Even as the dominant Teutonic virtues of the British could be refined by the Celtic element present in their culture, the positional superiority of the more masculine race was reaffirmed.

relatively subordinate roles in her Irish novels. (Kit Rackrent's wife Jessica is imprisoned for seven years in her room because she refuses to hand over her jewels to her improvident husband.) But by the mid nineteenth century, Lever begins to create powerful and often dominant women. In *The Martins of Cro' Martin,* for example, the Big House is controlled by the proud English-born Lady Martin, whose manipulations of her indolent husband hasten the destruction of the estate that his family has occupied for centuries. In *The Big House of Inver,* which Somerville wrote early in the twentieth century, real authority is wielded neither by the drunken proprietor of the Big House nor by his improvident grandson, but by Shibby Pindy. Jas Prendeville's bastard daughter by a peasant mother, Shibby ruthlessly fights to save a patrimony that has already been lost through the very profligacy that led to her birth.

More recent twentieth-century Anglo-Irish fiction depicts a culture that is politically impotent and in the last stages of social and economic decline. Molly Keane and Jennifer Johnston's monstrous women, seen in the context of earlier Big House fiction, suggest the final collapse of a male-dominated ascendancy culture in the postcolonial era. Moving into the void created by politically and economically emasculated fathers and husbands, twentieth-century Big House women expend their voracious energies and appetites by decorating their homes, snubbing their social inferiors, or torturing their children. The maternal abuse of children in these novels is less pervasive in earlier Anglo-Irish fiction, where the horizons for the power-loving woman were wider. Lever's Lady Martin can wield her power by calling in the rents of the tenants who refuse to vote for the landlord's candidate. But in the early twentieth century, in Keane's insular Anglo-Irish society, Big House children are the most available and satisfactory victims for the power hungry. One reader comments on the level of female cruelty in novels by Elizabeth Bowen, Molly Keane, and Jennifer Johnston. She notes that "real power having collapsed, the vacuum is filled by a distorted expression of that power" (O'Toole 1985, 124–25). Male writers in England have occasionally turned with great virtuosity to mapping the twists and turns of adult ferocity toward children: Dickens' *David Copperfield* and Butler's *The Way of All Flesh* come immediately to mind. But such narratives can be and usually are read as reflections of authorial obsession with childhood trauma rather than as reactions to political change. In twentieth-century Anglo-Irish fiction, however, mothers who turn against their young respond to the ascendancy's waning authority. Underlying the streak of sadism that motivates these matriarchal monsters lies rage at male social and political impotence.

Fathers and husbands in Keane's fiction are ciphers, shadowy figures who have abdicated any role in governance of family, household, or country and whose neglect of their children works itself out as a passive tolerance of maternal brutalities. In *The Rising Tide* the first of the two abusive mothers in the novel, Lady Charlotte, is described as "a shocking despot, really swollen with family conceit and a terrifying pride of race. She had a strange sense of her own power, made real indeed by a life spent chiefly at Garonlea with her obedient husband, frightened children and many tenants and dependents" (Farrell 1984, 7). Lady Charlotte's husband, Ambrose, retreats from any exercise of authority, allowing his wife to rule the household and estate with complete tyranny. With gratitude, he turns instead to the mild pleasure of planting ash trees and rooting up elders and thistles. For Ambrose, his love of gardening and of tending to the land justifies the existence of his class; he conceives of himself as a "tenant," charged with maintaining his estate and handing it over to his son. But if such horticultural aspirations are a sign of admirable social responsibility, they are also a symptom of his retreat from any active role in family or social governance. Keane perceives that a weakening dominance in the personal and political worlds creates a gentle, deferential self; Ambrose, with his devotion to his trees and land, is a "dim, gloomy, kind man" (1984, 15) whom no one remembers save in the context of his wife's competence or his father's wit. Weakened, bullied, and unmanned, he is thus feminized; he is rendered ineffectual, but consequently far milder with his children and grandchildren than are their terrible mothers.

The fathers and landlords in Keane's late novels are gentler parents than the icy rejecting women they marry. But the final vision of the landlord in *Good Behaviour* depicts a paralyzed, one-legged old man, able to control neither his wife's cruelty toward their daughter nor his own philandering; finally, he lies in thrall to the sexual excitement provided by his nurse's hand massaging his "bad foot" under the bedclothes. Incontinent and drooling, he, like the inarticulate, cuckolded landlord in *Loving and Giving*, embodies the collapse of Big House patriarchy.[7]

7. Like Keane and Johnston, several twentieth-century novelists writing from a perspective outside the walls of the demesne also turn to the sexual dysfunction of landlords and agents as a metaphor for moral collapse and consequent powerless-

Like Elizabeth Bowen, Keane turned to the experiences of the exploited and defenseless child, but with less of Bowen's sympathetic identification with the child's victimization. Keane was far more interested in the dynamic of power, in the ways by which the exploitation and mistreatment of children (and servants) corrupts them—turning victims into manipulative adults whose good behavior masks the revenge-driven impulses of the abused. In several of her novels of the 1930s and 1940s, Keane began to emphasize the themes that control her late fiction. In some—*Full House* (1935), *The Rising Tide* (1937), and *Two Days in Aragon* (1941)—she reveals how fully the Big House dominates the lives of its inhabitants. As in Le Fanu's *Uncle Silas,* where in the name of loyalty to an "ancient and honourable" family name Austin Ruthyn makes terrifying demands of his daughter, Keane's Big House children are expected to sacrifice themselves to the altar of family reputation and genealogy.

In *The Rising Tide,* Keane anticipates the devastating critique of Anglo-Irish culture that later emerges in *Good Behaviour, Time After Time,* and *Loving and Giving.* The Big House is a claustrophobic prison presided over by a possessive mother, a matriarchal monster who does her best to destroy her daughters. Frightened of their horses, children are forced on grueling fox hunts; for the sake of propriety, an erring daughter is obligated to marry a man she loathes; spinsters in their late twenties and early thirties are terrorized by their tyrannical mother. The house is the setting of psychic battles between the generations, and Anglo-Irish life is reduced to oppressive social decorum. Sexuality appears as unpleasant physical couplings that women dread, as doomed passion, or as promiscuity. Fulfilled lives are struck down, and individual happiness is sacrificed to family reputation. Chastity, that most unnatural of all sexual predilections, is the fate of a disproportionate number of Big House children.

---

ness. In fiction written from outside the Big House, the landlord or his agent is occasionally portrayed as sexually incapacitated; see, for example, Padraic Colum's *Castle Conquer* (1923), Sean O'Faolain's "Midsummer Night's Madness" (1932), Liam O'Flaherty's *Famine* (1937) or *Land* (1946), or Julia O'Faolain's *No Country for Young Men* (1980). Several works emphasize the rage of an impotent old man living with the memory of a past sexual and political ascendancy but reduced to the position of ineffectual cuckold or dependent. Others depict agents and landlords as sexually perverse predators of peasant women—or as homosexuals. A demonized confusion of sexual identity or an impairment of sexual performance becomes a pervasive indicator of social and economic decline in postcolonial Ireland.

In her three last novels, Keane continued to present the domestic world of the Big House as the setting for power struggles in which the weak are maimed and seek to lash out against their oppressors— or against those still weaker than themselves. *Good Behaviour* begins with the well-bred murder of a sadistic, bed-ridden mother by the monstrous daughter she has created. In *Time After Time,* children maimed by "Darling Mummie's" love hide their private eccentricities behind locked doors. Their physical disabilities—deafness, blindness, deformed limbs, and dyslexia—suggest the psychic paralysis of their lives and their culture. In Keane's design the family deformities and disabilities reflect, certainly, the state of their Anglo-Irish cultural heritage. However, the symbolic resonances of blindness and deafness, and of crippled hands and retarded minds, are so delicately evoked, so concretely embodied in the personality of each character, that symbolic and literal levels are fused. Again, in *Loving and Giving,* the unloved child who is deserted by her mother matures into a permanently victimized adult. Abandoned by her fortune-hunting husband and unable to love those who cherish her, well-behaved Nicandra expresses her repressed anger in a deadly power struggle with a servant she had humiliated and abused when they were both children.

The country estates described in these novels suggest the familiar decay and decrepitude that has overtaken ascendancy society. *Good Behaviour*'s Temple Alice, the remnant of a once grand estate in the decades surrounding World War I, slowly bleeds away its resources. Designed to support the fox hunting and fishing of a leisure class, the Big House is depleted by waste. The narrator's grandfather, for example, has drawn away the meager water supply from the house by building a pond on which he could row about to escape his land agent and "other buzzing tormentors of a leisured life" (Keane 1982, 12). His son continues the familiar habit of improvidence.

> While, as though duty bound, Papa was hunting, fishing, and shooting in their proper seasons, at Temple Alice money poured quietly away. Our school fees were the guilty party most often accused. Then came rates and income tax and the absurd hesitations of bank managers. Coal merchants and butchers could be difficult, so days of farm labour were spent felling and cutting up trees—the wood burned up quickly and delightfully in the high fast-draughting Georgian grates.

As a corrective to the butcher's bills lambs were slaughtered on the place. Half the meat was eaten while the other half went bad, hanging in the musty ice house without any ice. (73)

In *Time After Time*, the family estate, Durraghglass, is the classic locus of the Big House novel: a twentieth-century Castle Rackrent described, on occasion, with a modernist nausea. The novel depicts the lives of four elderly Anglo-Irish siblings—April, Jasper, May, and June Swift, named, perhaps, in ironic reference to the past Anglo-Irish eminence and glory represented by the illustrious Dean Swift. The Swifts are trapped into living together in mutual dislike at Durraghglass by their poverty, their psychic disabilities, as well as by their controlling mother's posthumous wishes, which granted them all rights of residence.

Keane is unsparing in her minute depiction of the physical deterioration of the Swift homestead, a description that becomes an exuberantly hyperbolic vision of the decaying Big House. With a zest for the noxious details of decrepitude, she describes not just the potholed drive surrounded by a riot of briars and nettles, the weedy cobblestones in the stable yard, the tumbled down piggeries, and slateless cowsheds, but also the grosser manifestations of decay: the pollution of the mountain stream–fed river by untreated raw sewage (including bits of toilet tissue) from the house and stable, the appalling smells that rise from the kitchen, the filth amidst which Jasper concocts fabulous meals, the moldy meat he plucks from the dogs' dishes to supplement his pigeon pies, the white fly mites that emerge at night on the kitchen floor. In piling up such physical details to evoke the decline of the Big House, the septuagenarian writer is relentlessly unsentimental about the process of aging, willing to face the meaning of rot and decay with powerful literalness. Thus the neglected house, traditionally the symbol of a dying society, converges here with images of human decay and old age.

In *Loving and Giving*, the contraction of Anglo-Irish life is succinctly evoked in spatial terms, as the gentry mansion is abandoned for a mobile home. The last family occupant of the Big House purchases a secondhand caravan, which she parks next to the sunny dining room, in anticipation of selling the rotting edifice she and her brother-in-law can no longer afford to maintain. Happily settled in with her old parrot (later to be stuffed and mounted on a swing hanging from the caravan ceiling), with her whisky bottle easily within arm's reach in the cupboard, she resists leaving her leaking tin refuge for the luxuries of her former home after it is renovated by a new and welcoming owner. If Aunt Tossie's insistence on remaining in her caravan suggests her defiant choice of independence over gentility, it also underscores the downward social trajectory of the Anglo-Irish.[8]

With the detached, even chilling, vision of her own class that dominates her last three novels, Keane sloughs off the affectionately condescending tone toward the native Irish that controls her early works and recalls the class-bound vision of Catholic Ireland found in earlier Big House fiction. In *Mad Puppetstown* (1931), and *Conversation Pieces* (1932), for example, attractive young heroines are surrounded by sly, superstitious, and wayward servants, whose loyalty to their young masters and mistresses is equaled only by their good-humored unscrupulousness toward their adult employers. These grooms, butlers, mad cooks, and assorted other family retainers recall Somerville and Ross's comic vision of the native Irish in *Experiences of an Irish R. M.* The picturesque retainers remain types, perceived through the affectionately condescending categories of a rigid class system. In *Good Behaviour,* however, Keane's description of Rose, the St. Charles family maid, is presented with a humor and an admiration that transcend familiar stereotypes. Under the guise of warming the feet of her dying master under his bed sheets, Rose provides him with the sexual pleasures denied by his wife. On one level Rose is still the Irish peasant girl servicing the master with her favors, but the bizarre circum-

---

8. In a somewhat similar vein the journalist Frances Fitzgerald's account of her visit to her distant relative Desmond FitzGerald, the twenty-ninth Knight of Glin, records the ways in which contemporary, land-poor Big House dwellers accommodate themselves to their poverty: hiring patients from the local asylum to serve dinner to important guests, doing the housework and farm labor of their vast estates themselves, burning peat in the winter as the local farmers do. On occasion, Fitzgerald's unsentimental account of an isolated and dying aristocracy resembles Keane's depiction of the Swift family in *Time After Time* or of Aunt Tossie in *Loving and Giving.* While describing the extraordinary odds against its survival, Fitzgerald, like Keane, suggests the possible accommodation of the Big House to a new Ireland. She describes, for example, a young landlord who manages to support the ancestral home his family has owned for twenty-one generations by becoming a "traveling salesman" in his spare time, selling refrigerators and other kitchen appliances to his local "Irish Irish" friends (1979, 156).

stances of her clandestine sexual generosity to a paralyzed old man undercuts any traditional response to her. Finally, Rose's behavior, so offensive to a proper young nurse and incomprehensible to the resolutely deluded, virginal daughter-narrator, becomes a brilliant victory of the traditional victim of the *droit du seigneur.* Flouting her superiors, doling out the portions of whisky and pleasure that will both comfort and kill her dying master, Rose achieves real power and moral ascendancy over the Big House. More ominously in *Loving and Giving,* the physically stunted and retarded son of the lodge keeper, after a childhood of abuse at the hands of his Big House playmate, wreaks vengeance on her in his adulthood.

In *Time After Time,* as in *Good Behaviour,* the gentry house has become a psychic prison that traps four suspicious old people in the regressive patterns of childhood antagonisms. Even the supreme achievement of the Big House, the snobbery that so clearly separates "them" (the Catholic Irish) from "us" (the Anglo-Irish), collapses under the wear and tear of genetic decay. The youngest Swift sibling, Baby June, who speaks with the provincial accent she has learned in the village, "has the shape and weight of a retired flat race jockey—too heavy for her height" (Keane 1985, 10). She has become, virtually, the family's tenant farmer, attending their formal dinners in her clean jeans and blue Viyella shirt, isolated from the snobberies of her more verbal and mean-minded siblings. The fear of intermarriage between the Big House and Catholic Ireland that haunts earlier Anglo-Irish novels is irrelevant in *Time After Time;* a combination of genetic and economic collapse itself accomplishes June's social regression into the sartorial and speech habits of a stable hand.

Generally, though, Keane's later novels focus unrelentingly on the gentry world. In *Time After Time* and by the end of both *Good Behavior* and *Loving and Giving,* the money to sustain staffs of obliging native Irish servants has evaporated. In *Good Behaviour,* Keane's most accomplished and darkest domestic novel, Aroon St. Charles is the unloved and oversized daughter of the fading Big House. Her memories of childhood and youth at Temple Alice provide a mordantly comic vision of a mean-spirited gentry society trapped in its own rules of decorum. Her unreliable narrative voice, which is the stunning stylistic tour de force of *Good Behaviour,* allows Keane to expose her society with an ironic control comparable to that achieved by

Maria Edgeworth. Like Thady Quirk, Aroon reveals the horrors that she cannot allow herself to register, freeing Keane from the necessity of overt judgments, in this most judgmental of all Big House novels. With the new freedom offered by her unreliable first-person narrator, Keane turns with a cold, comic eye to the appalling ways in which Anglo-Irish society abuses its young. As the victimized child who turns monster, Aroon endures, for example, the hypocrisies of her brother, who arranges a romance between his fat, ungainly sister and his best friend in order to cover up a homosexual liaison; and those of her father, whose intimacy with his wife masks a lifetime of philandering. Keane's ironically named protagonist—in Gaelic, Aroon means "my love, my dear"—is despised by her elegant mother, who picks at her own food and is contemptuous of her daughter's huge appetite for food and for love. "The size of anything appalled her" (Keane 1982, 180).

In her endless capacity to delude herself, Aroon is a microcosm of a culture that avoids confronting the messiness of its emotional life and the extent of its social and political impotence. Grief, hatred, passion, even joy, cannot be expressed without violating decencies of good behavior. A brother's sudden death, a desolating event for his parents, is suffered wordlessly. "Our good behaviour went on and on, endless as the days. No one spoke of the pain we were sharing. Our discretion was almost complete. Although they feared to speak, Papa and Mummie spent more time together; but, far from comforting, they seemed to freeze each other deeper in misery" (Keane 1982, 114). Aroon's surroundings conspire to deny the truth of her own experience and thus encourage her in her delusions. One evening she watches her drunken father knock over an oil lamp, only to be rescued from danger by a coarse and playful Rose, who appears suddenly at his side without shoes or apron. The next morning, all is restored: her father brisk and clean shaven, his clothes cleaned, the glass swept up, the smell of spilled paraffin masked by the odor of furniture polish and roses. Even faced with overwhelming evidence of her father's sexual indulgences with both her former governess and with Rose, Aroon avoids acknowledging the sexual drives seething around her. "I was hypnotized. I was bemused. I was deprived of my certainty that Papa had been terribly drunk and that in Rose's approach to him, there had been something easy and practiced which I could not name" (134).

Good Behaviour, Keane's most pitiless work of domestic fiction, undoes virtually every assumption and sentiment about family life and moral intelligence advocated by the English domestic novel of Leavis's "great tradition." Decency and self-knowledge—the path to maturity for a heroine in a Jane Austen novel—leads Aroon's unhappy governess to suicide, while her hapless charge manages to survive only through self-delusion. Thus Aroon lives through her miserable youth by creating fictions about her brother's homosexual lover as a future husband. Growing up, she absorbs the patterns of avoidance and hypocrisy that endow her with the authority denied her as a child. Her adult voice, controlling and dominating those around her through the power of her self-delusion, suggests the awful fulfillment of her cultural training. After her mother's death, which she brings about by forcing abhorred food on a woman with a heart condition, Aroon refuses to hear Rose's accusations of murder. Rose's outburst can be ignored because she belongs to that servant class whose unpleasant habits must be tolerated but dismissed. In a chilling self-parody of attitudes toward the native Irish that control her own earlier novels, Keane has Aroon mouth the platitudes of Anglo-Irish racial condescension as she watches Rose. "She was opening the window as high as the sash would go—that's one of their superstitions, something to do with letting the spirit go freely. They do it. They don't speak of it . . . They revel in death . . . Keep the Last Rites going . . . She can't wait to get her hands on Mummie, to get me out of the way while she helps Mrs. Cleary in necessary and nasty ritual" (7).

Between her cultural indoctrination and her personal pathology—"I don't trust Rose. I don't trust anybody. Because I like things to be right" (3)—Aroon is well defended against the truth. The novel ends ominously, but with a certain rhadamanthine justice. Before her mother's death, Aroon learns that she, not her mother, is the beneficiary of her father's will. "I was claiming what was mine—his love, his absolute love. I wanted them to understand that he had loved me most" (243–44). Thus, the humiliated daughter, deprived by her elegant mother even of the food she needs to sustain her ungainly body, turns with all the resources of her self-delusion to the woman she hates most.

> I stood above her, shriveled back again in her chair, and I spoke to her in a voice I didn't know myself—a voice humid with kindness. "Drink this," I said, "and remember that I'll always look after you."

> She took the glass and looked up at me from under the absurd tilt of
> her hat; in an odd way her look reminded me of a child warding off a blow.
> "Yes. Always," I reassured her firmly. (145)

With such a chilling scene between mother and daughter, Keane
strips the domestic novel of its foundation in sentiment. Instead,
family life in the Big House is mediated by exercises in coercion and
power: power misused, abused, and corrupted. Surrounded by sexual forces that she cannot and will not comprehend, and denied love
and nurturance throughout her childhood, Aroon perpetuates the
abuse that has victimized her. Molly Keane's last three novels thus
reinscribe the family romance in a postcolonial setting; in doing so
they reinvent and repossess the familiar English domestic novel for
Anglo-Ireland. Although Keane did not write explicit political allegory, her novels about children, like Elizabeth Bowen's, suggest similar patterns in domestic and colonial exploitation. Those with
power—political, sexual, or economic—will abuse the weak, who
will, in time, turn on their oppressors or on themselves. Keane's
Good Behaviour represents the darkest satiric narrative of Anglo-Irish
domestic life since Edgeworth's *Castle Rackrent.*

Revisionism in Fiction

Jennifer Johnston and William Trevor

Elizabeth Bowen wrote *A World of Love*—her last and least politi-cally engaged work about an Anglo-Irish Big House—in 1955, when nationalist historiography still exerted a powerful influence over society in the Irish Republic. Since the late 1960s and early 1970s, after the eruption of hostilities in the north, the influence of historical revisionism has encouraged both reexamination of the re-lationship between England and Ireland and an undermining of the older nationalist narrative.[1] Revisionism has thus remapped the his-torical landscape that provides a context for Irish literature. In a modern state looking outward to England and all of Europe, this post-nationalist reading of Irish history seeks to rewrite and under-mine mythologies of the past. The revisionist historian, for example, reads the 1916 rising not as a triumphal moment of sacrificial na-tionalist assertion, but rather as a tragic eruption that led to a cen-tury of needless sectarian violence. Similarly, the nineteenth-century Famine is a natural disaster beyond the control of any political sys-tem, rather than an instance of England's genocidal neglect of a

1. Luke Gibbons provides a thoughtful discussion of the ongoing controversy about revisionism in his editorial introduction to the chapter "Challenging the Canon: Revisionism and Cultural Criticism" in *The Field Day Anthology of Irish Writing* (1991). Although Gibbons maintains that revisionism undertakes "the task of re-defining the relationship of a modernizing society to the legacy of the past" (1991, 561), in his introduction to Roy Foster's essay "We are all Revisionists Now" he sug-gests that the movement has become a "new orthodoxy" (1991, 583). Foster himself defends revisionism against those who would identify it as a "school hostile to Irish nationalism" (1991, 584). *Revising The Rising* (1991), edited by Mairin Ni Dhonn-chadha and Theo Dorgan, is Field Day's lively collection of essays, largely critical of revisionism, occasioned by the seventy-fifth anniversary of the 1916 Rising.

starving colony. Contemporary realistic fiction about the Big House inevitably responds to this revised interpretation of Irish society, an interpretation that seeks to undermine many traditional ideological divisions and seems to reach beyond the categories of class and sect that controlled earlier novels in the tradition.

The notion of revisionist fiction about the Big House implies a changing genre, a transformation of literary conventions to incorporate new versions of social organization and new possibilities of class and sectarian relationships. No longer viewed solely as the symbol of oppression and privilege or, alternatively, as the site of order and discipline in an uncivilized colony or disintegrating world, the Protestant Big House now represents part of a shared heritage in a nation that is recreating and rethinking its past. Concurrently, in Irish social policy, the ascendancy country house has become the concern of preservationists, increasingly recognized as a prime tourist site, and now exploited both as a nostalgic reminder of a disappearing world of privilege and as an architectural treasure.[2] Its inhabitants are viewed, more generously, as fellow sufferers in a tragic national history, not merely as the perpetrators of the suffering of others or the uneasy proprietors of dispossessed land.

Although the pluralist goals of modern Ireland are implicit in revisionism, the effects of the movement in recent fiction raise many questions. Is the increasingly sympathetic portrayal of the Big House by writers from both Anglo-Irish and native Irish backgrounds accompanied by a retreat from the narrow class and sectarian divisions of earlier novels in the genre—in recognition of a common Irishness that is the goal of President Mary Robinson's inclusive nation?[3] Or does the revised version of an older form merely represent a mode of forgetting and then rewriting the past, a way of implicitly perpetrat-

2. There are, of course, different kinds of preservation efforts. An illuminating contrast exists, for example, between the aims of the Irish Georgian Society—preservation as aesthetic rescue with a significant degree of historical nostalgia—and the historical retrieval of the Big House in the context of its native Irish setting at Strokestown Park House and Famine Museum in county Longford. By politically contextualizing a Big House (where a landlord was murdered by his tenants during the Famine), the Strokestown Park project avoids the ahistorical aestheticizing of so many Big House museums. See pp. 262–64.

3. In her inaugural address President Mary Robinson spoke of the new Ireland she would be representing as "open, tolerant, inclusive," and as part of "new common European home based on respect for human rights, pluralism, tolerance and openness to new ideas" (1990).

ing new kinds of elitisms and divisions, as a recent critic of both historical revisionism and the Big House literary tradition charges?[4] In
the shift from the realistic novel's wide-angled account of society to
psychological fiction's focus on the isolated self—an inheritance of
literary modernism as well as of political revisionism—the landlord
has become a psychic casualty rather than an economic or social
loser in postindependence Ireland. Just as revisionist economic historians emphasize, for example, the substantial losses and suffering of
the landowner (rather than just of his tenants) during and after the
Famine,[5] in fiction we meet a new version of the Big House landlord,
whose isolation from the larger nation is depicted with increasing sympathy. The revisionist Big House novel reinscribes and simultaneously
undermines the political, social, and economic divisions of the past
through its depiction of the sensitive protagonist as new victim. The
ability to suffer—to register the psychic pain that is the badge of a new
aristocracy of the spirit—replaces the bloodlines and political and economic power that defined an older elite. No matter how conscious it is
of the national past, revisionist fiction acts to neutralize history. When
all suffer equally in the present, does not the past become less urgent?

Reading Jennifer Johnston's and William Trevor's novels within a
long tradition of Big House literature reveals both the cultural continuities and the significant changes that their fiction embodies. By
understanding how their novels transform or retain conventions established by nineteenth-century writers, we can explore the social
implications of the revisionist aesthetic: its attempt, on the one hand,
to dissolve ideological conflict in the interests of a more humane society and its more problematic tendency, on the other, to reinscribe
the class differences that form the substrata for all ideologically
charged writing. Implicit in this discussion, more centrally perhaps
than in previous chapters, is a commitment to exploring the politics
of aesthetic production.

4. Seamus Deane, a leading critic of revisionism, attacks the modern Big House
novel for its dependence on a Yeatsian formulation of the ascendancy as an aristocracy of the spirit. Deane challenges Yeats's association of the ascendancy with the "fra-
grance" of intellectual elitism. "The Big House surrounded by an unruly tenantry,
Culture besieged by barbarity, a refined aristocracy beset by a vulgar middle class—all
of these are recurrent images in twentieth-century Irish fiction which draws heavily
on Yeats's poetry for them" (1985, 31).

5. See, especially, W. E. Vaughan's *Landlords and Tenants in Ireland, 1848–1904*
(1984) or Barbara Solow's *The Land Question and the Irish Economy, 1870–1903* (1971).

Neither novelist discussed in this chapter emerged from gentry society. Trevor, in fact, insistently distinguishes his own middle-class origins from the ascendancy world he depicts in several of his novels.
He reports that in post-1923 Ireland his family was part of a "sliver of
people caught between the past—Georgian Ireland with its great
houses and all the rest of it—and the new, bustling, Catholic state"
(1989, 131). With his ancestry of small-town, "lace curtain," unliter-
ary bank clerks descended from farming stock (Schiff 1992/1993,
161), Trevor presents himself as an outsider in Irish society who can
apprehend it from an enabling distance. Had he been the right age,
he notes, he would have observed the gentry world of Bowen's Court
from the perspective of the local Protestant boys of nearby Mitchels-
town, employed by the Bowen family to stand around the tennis
court collecting balls (Trevor 1989, 131). Johnston's background is only
marginally closer to the Big House culture she depicts in many of her
novels. As the daughter of the prominent Irish playwright Denis
Johnston and the actress and director Shelagh Richards, she belonged to a privileged literary world remote from Trevor's rural,
west-Cork childhood. But although she now lives in a Georgian Big
House in Derry built by an Anglo-Irish landlord,[6] she was born into
upper-middle-class urban Protestant Ireland rather than into the
landed gentry society that that figures so prominently in her fiction.

Because both Trevor and Johnston write without the same autobiographical pressure that impelled novelists like Somerville, Keane,
and Bowen, their choice of the country house as setting and central
trope is of special interest. Like Yeats, another middle-class writer
from a Protestant tradition, both Trevor and Johnston approach the
Big House as relative outsiders. They write with the outsider's perspective on both the society of the gentry estate and the Catholic
village. Not unexpectedly, then, they write without Molly Keane's im-
mediacy, without that immersion in the sensuous particularities of
twentieth-century country house settings that lies behind her dark
parody of a declining gentry society. But if their novels are less evocative of the surface of Anglo-Irish life than Keane's comic works,

6. Mark Mortimer suggests that "although Jennifer Johnston is not herself a
daughter of the Big House . . . she is closely linked to this world through family
connections, friends, and personal tastes. Her present home in Derry in Northern
Ireland, with its splendid gardens, spacious rooms and antique furniture, is clear in-
dication of her attraction to such a way of life" (1991, 209).

Johnston's and Trevor's fiction turns more explicitly to historical and political concerns.

Born in the decade following Irish independence, both novelists depict a gentry Anglo-Irish society that they have, as relative outsiders, witnessed only in its final stages of decline from ascendancy. For reasons of both social class and historical chronology, Johnston and Trevor escaped much of the earlier Protestant generation's anxious confrontation with its economic and social losses. Instead, they write, on occasion, with the intellectual's elegiac sense of a missing cultural unity, with a nausea toward modern Ireland that is closer to Bowen's wartime valorization of the Big House than to Keane's dark parodies of her own culture. But because Johnston and Trevor published their novels about Ireland after the resurgence of hostilities in the north and during a period of revision of the nationalist mythology in the south, their ambivalent nostalgia for aesthetic and emotional unity is undermined by their constant recognition of the costs of traditional schisms: between Catholic and Protestant, nationalist and unionist, Big House and village. Each has written about the contemporary crisis in the north: Johnston, for example, in *Shadows on Our Skin* (1977) and *The Railroad Station Man* (1984); Trevor in stories such as "The Distant Past" (1975), "Attracta" (1978), and "Beyond the Pale" (1981). Their fiction, particularly those works set in the early twentieth century, is influenced by their sense of the ongoing costs of Irish political and social divisions.

Together, Johnston and Trevor offer a more generous reading of the Anglo-Irish experience than previous Big House novelists. Many of their Protestant landlords have nationalist rather than explicitly unionist leanings, and in several works sympathetic Catholic Irish characters assume major roles. Their portrayals of landlords transform and complicate an existing convention and suggest, not that fierce cultural self-parody evident in the best works of Somerville or Keane, but instead a growing sympathy with a newly marginalized group. In choosing to write, on occasion, about the rare early twentieth-century landowner who supported revolutionary Ireland rather than England, Johnston and Trevor break not only with the conventions of previous Anglo-Irish fiction written from inside the demesne, but with the privileged older historical narrative as well. Since the publication of Maria Edgeworth's *Castle Rackrent,* major Big House novels have steadfastly portrayed the landlord as accelerating his own decline. Novels by Edith Somerville and Molly Keane, as well as Bowen's *Last September*, depict the self-imposed isolation of the late nineteenth- and early twentieth-century Big House from the insistent nationalism of the Catholic Irish community. This recurring portrayal of a reactionary Anglo-Irish proprietor who is increasingly alienated from the real politics of a vast majority of his fellow countrymen is supported by many historical analyses.[7] Thus, in depicting landlords with nationalist sympathies, Johnston and Trevor view Irish history through the lens of exceptional gentry families.

Critics celebrate both novelists for writing with an awareness of the pressures exerted by political and religious conflict and, simultaneously, for transcending narrow sectarian formulations. Several readers note the breakdown of traditional political lines among characters in their novels (Brian Donnelly 1975, 138–42; Kelly 1987, 232–33); Gregory Schirmer praises Trevor for his recognition of the antihumanistic potential of religious and political fanaticism, citing *Fools of Fortune* as Trevor's "most accomplished novel" (1990, 147) precisely because it is built on the tension between "personal values" (a positive and life-affirming love between a man and a woman) and "political ideology" (the burden of Ireland's past history, which destroys all that is good). Kristin Morrison argues that Trevor "writes about political and historical matters from what could be called a cosmological perspective" (1993, 9), thereby identifying and implicitly praising a transcendence of ideological divisions. Johnston, too, is celebrated for understanding the human costs of ongoing political conflict and for writing with a view of Irish society that transcends ideology. Jose Lanters, for example, praises her "awareness that the present divisions in (Northern) Ireland would not be so wide if people could liberate themselves from the past, and that the persistence of past experiences . . . is at the root of the present problem" (1989, 209).

To read Johnston and Trevor's Big House fiction in the light of earlier Anglo-Irish novels is, necessarily, to foreground their telling

7. A revisionist historian like R. F. Foster reports, for example, that southern Unionists were more vehement in their interpretation of the 1921 Treaty as "complete surrender" and as a sign of the doom of the British Empire than were intransigents from Ulster (1989, 508). Patrick Buckland describes the landed Protestant class as "essentially aristocratic" and as profoundly conservative and thus antagonistic to those democratic aspirations of modern nationalism which would remove the social as well as economic barriers between tenant and landlord class (1972, 282).

continuities with, as well as their departures from, an earlier tradi-tion. Johnston's subtle psychological novels suggest how a revisionist ideal of interpersonal connection does not inevitably embody a shed-ding of class divisions; such a perspective can, in fact, represent the reinscription of old divisions familiar to any reader of earlier fiction about the Big House. Trevor's *Fools of Fortune,* a novel set within a re-visionist rather than an older nationalist historical narrative, raises questions about the relationship between aesthetic success and polit-ical vision.

If, as Karl Marx so persuasively argues, "it is not the consciousness of men that determines their existence, but on the contrary, their so-cial existence [that] determines their consciousness" (1904, 11), we might examine the vision of class relations in Big House fiction as closely as we examine the psychic needs and aspirations of its charac-ters. The goal of transcending division and recovering from Irish his-tory is plausible only when genuinely new patterns of society accompany such ideals. Johnston's and Trevor's depictions of the in-dividual's search for autonomy from history—in spite of history—is on occasion accompanied by an unconscious narrative reinscription of class barriers between the Big House and the village.

Jennifer Johnston

The persistent if conflicting efforts of Johnston's critics to catego-rize her fiction suggest its elusiveness and her attempt, like Elizabeth Bowen, to synthesize the psychological with the social novel. Her works have been viewed alternately as interior explorations of the lives of artists, social-political studies of Ireland, or, more recently, as problematic depictions of women's experiences.[8] Entering into this

8. Sherri Benstock avoids "two common avenues of approach: to consider Jennifer Johnston as either a woman writer or as an Irish writer, although obviously she is both" and finally describes the first five novels as metafiction, as allegories of the alienated writer's life (1982, 192). Rudolf Imhof argues that the Irish Big House set-tings in Johnston's early novels are irrelevant, merely neutral sites for the interper-sonal plots that transcend any national or class parochialism (1985, 129–30). Heinz Kosok, however, focuses on Johnston's narratives as "chapters in the history of Ire-land over the past eighty years" (1986, 102), but then, in a puzzling retreat, describes her novels as "individual stories for which the Irish background provides no more than an accidental setting" (106). Christine St. Peter, although she credits Johnston with a "remarkable ability to use an individual life as an emblem of national catastro-

critical debate about the kind of fiction she writes, Johnston herself eschews the label of Big House novelist she has been given by many academic critics and upon which this chapter, merely by including her in the study, insists. She places her work in the less explicitly politicized English tradition of Jane Austen and E. M. Forster and sees herself creating new versions of the novel of manners on her own "very small canvas." Johnston's description of her fiction as by-passing the innovative modernism of Joyce and "working with fairly strict, rather old-fashioned terms" of the novel suggests her attraction to a traditional form (Johnston 1984a, 26), in spite of her significant stylistic experiments with interior monologue, flashback, and compression. Her return in *Fool's Sanctuary* and *The Invisible Worm* to conventions of the Big House genre underscores her continuing preoccupation with the class and sectarian barriers of a politicized Irish version of the country house novel. More successfully than Elizabeth Bowen in *A World of Love*, Johnston negotiates the fusion of the psychological with the political and social.

All of Johnston's novels set in Ireland exist as microcosms of a larger society. Her recurring use of Big House settings in five of them—in the three earliest, *The Gates, The Captains and the Kings*, and *How Many Miles to Babylon*, and two later works, *Fool's Sanctuary* and *The Invisible Worm*—suggests how the primary national fracture between English settlers and the native Irish provides her with skeletal psychic material, virtually the archetypal form, for her fiction. Although they focus on isolated characters, her novels explore the persistent social and political schisms that drive her protagonists to their lonely solitudes. Not only the occupants of gentry houses, like Alexander Moore (*How Many Miles to Babylon*) and Mr. Prendergast (*The Captains and the Kings*), but also middle-class Protestant Helen Cuffe (*The Railroad Station Man*) and young Catholic working-class Joe Logan (*Shadows on Our Skin*), suffer the consequences of class, sectarian, and political divisions in Ireland. The walled Big House settings of the three early works most concretely embody the separa-

---

phe," finds the fiction fraught with ideological contradiction in spite of Johnston's "political and cultural awareness" (1991, 113). St. Peter's reading of Johnston's Big House novels as displaying a "collision of ideologies" (126) is close to my own. Her discussion of *The Christmas Tree* and *The Railway Station Man* focuses on women's solitude as a source of their creative energy, and Ann Owens Weekes, in *Irish Women Writers*, turns to the same works, as well as to *The Jest*, as female bildungsroman (1990, 199–211).

tion between two societies. But the lonely occupants of those country estates are related to the Catholic adolescent in the Derry slum who reaches outside his caste, or even, in one of the least political of Johnston's novels, to a dying protagonist in urban Dublin whose class-ridden Protestant childhood has armored her against love. Emotional pain is implicitly tied to the divisions of class, sect, or creed in the postcolonial nation.

Not only in novels about the Big House but also in those set elsewhere, her sensitive protagonists attempt to escape their isolation through relationships across class and sectarian lines. Sixteen-year-old Minnie MacMahon, the orphaned protagonist in *The Gates,* returns to her family's shabby Big House in Donegal to find her alcoholic uncle hiding behind delusions of restocking his empty stable. Whereas young, Anglo-Irish Lois Naylor in Bowen's *The Last September* is merely stirred by her contacts with a forbidden native Ireland, Minnie reaches out to the son of her uncle's hired hand. Widowed Mr. Prendergast in *The Captains and the Kings* escapes from self-imposed isolation in his family home in Wicklow by opening it to an unhappy adolescent truant from the village. In *How Many Miles to Babylon,* the child of a luxurious Big House in pre–World War I Ireland, Alexander Moore, frees himself from the constricted world of his parent's unhappy marriage when he forms a clandestine friendship with a village boy, Jerry Crowe. The sublimated homoerotic relationships, between Jerry and Alex and between Mr. Prendergast and Diarmid in *The Captain and the Kings,* emphasize, moreover, that any loving bonds between Big House and village must remain covert, hidden, antisocial. The absence of viable socially sanctioned relationships in two of the early books suggests that love is ordinarily unavailable in a divided Ireland, that it must be sought transgressively, across lines not only of class and caste, but of gender as well.

The pattern of lonely protagonists venturing out of their group occurs in subsequent novels set in middle-class Protestant Ireland or in the slums of Derry. This recurring ur-plot of the Big House novel, in which an outsider invades the gentry sanctuary, is replicated in novels about other relationships forged across caste lines. Seeking her unknown father in *The Old Jest,* Nancy Gulliver periodically escapes her upper-middle-class home and shares a secret life with an IRA fugitive. Joe Logan, in *Shadows On Our Skin,* alienated by the hostile and violent slum world of Derry in the 1970s, finds solace in his friendship with a young schoolteacher who is engaged to a British soldier. In *The Christmas Tree,* Constance Keating flees her Dublin home and, after more than two decades of living alone in London, chooses a Polish Jew, a survivor of Auchswitz, to father her illegitimate child. Helen Cuffe, in *The Railroad Station Man,* abandons her middle-class life after her husband is shot by the IRA, enters into an affair with a eccentric British war veteran, and befriends a young man in the village who is rumored to be a Provo.

To examine technique in Johnston's novels is to confront her pre-occupation with the layered historicity of all experience. Her stylistic as well as thematic emphasis on the defining role of the past under-scores the familiar connections between individual and national history in Irish literature. For all the interiority of her plots, for all their emphasis on the brooding psychic narratives of their protagonists, Johnston's novels most often apprehend emotional pain within the larger context of social and political divisions. Many include memories of childhood trauma, often of brutal scenes of physic maiming by cold and class-ridden mothers in *The Captains and the Kings, How Many Miles to Babylon,* and *The Christmas Tree;* or the violent rape of an adolescent girl by her father in *The Invisible Worm.* A recurring stylistic device in Johnston's writing—one that distances her from the more traditional novelists she claims as her models—is to conflate the past with the present, to juxtapose a contemporary scene with insistent echoes of childhood trauma. Ghosts from the past intrude on the consciousness of her protagonists; several of the novels are themselves structured around the activity of memory, as retrospective narrative told from the perspective of approaching death or experienced disaster. Thus, *How Many Miles to Babylon* begins with the condemned protagonist remembering his unhappy youth on the eve of his wartime execution. In *The Captains and the Kings,* an uneasy conversation between two police officers preparing to call in Prender-gast for questioning initiates the story of his past history that becomes the substance of the novel. After Constance Keating's death in *The Christmas Tree,* her servant completes the story begun by her employer. In both *The Railroad Station Man* and *Fool's Sanctuary* we are plunged into retrospective narratives of women who have suffered traumatic loss as a result of political violence. Tellingly, an IRA officer in *The Old Jest,* hiding in a beach shack near his old home, reveals that "the past impinges on me. Nudges its way constantly into my life. Uninvited. . . . I find I can no longer act unimpeded by voices from the past" (1988c, 56).

Although conventions of the Big House genre shape Johnston's fiction and reveal her affinity for traditional Anglo-Irish values, she writes with attitudes formed as well by a competing perspective on Irish society. Thus, her first novel suggests the political irresolution present in all her work, which Christine St. Peter aptly describes as illustrating a "contradictory ideology" (1991, 120). With its decrepit country estate, its alcoholic and improvident landlord, and its young Catholic intruder from a brutal village world, *The Gates*—like the subsequent *The Captains and the Kings* and *How Many Miles to Babylon*—unmistakably revives familiar motifs from early ascendancy fiction and reinscribes persistent colonial anxieties that are evident in the genre. *The Gates* reveals both an unusually explicit critique of the land system that sustained the Big House and, simultaneously, a reluctance to move beyond the class assumptions of earlier ascendancy fiction. To some degree, in all of Johnston's early works, the sorry remnants of Big House society—ineffectual if well-meaning men and, in two of them, angry, even sadistic, women—are implicitly contrasted with the squalor of Catholic Ireland. In *The Gates,* purposeless village boys kill time "leaning over a seawall, throwing stones at a dead dog on the wrinkled sand below" (1983, 53). Kelly, the Big House's jack of all trades, has thick black hairs that "exploded out through the opening down the front of his shirt"; he appears to be "more like a monkey than a ram" to the young protagonist (47). His ever pregnant wife with her tinker's voice and his eight children live with him in a hovel, an abyss of poverty and disorder. "Stinging, smoky blackness. Potatoes boiled in their skins for a hundred and fifty years, in black metal pots over the smouldering turf on the hearth. Damp walls. Damp clothes. Sweat" (45). Here pregnant Mrs. Kelly— "a shadowy heap on the floor"—is beaten by her husband, who then turns on his son. The Kellys, and the Toorishes in *The Captains and the Kings,* are alternately violent, oversexed, dishonest, dirty, ignorant, and brutal. The world of the dungheap, of the pig, the goat, and the vulgarian—the colonizer's vision of the colonized "other"—looms large in Johnston's images of native Catholic Ireland.

In a historical digression, however, unique in its implications in Johnston's fiction and rare in earlier ascendancy novels, *The Gates* is unsparing in its depiction of the arrogance that drove tenants off Big

House land they had occupied for generations in order to satisfy, for example, a new mistress's desire for an unobstructed view from her windows (1983, 32). Far more explicitly than Somerville or Bowen, Johnston acknowledges a systemic injustice in ascendancy dominance. The aging landlord recalls sitting as a child in a pony cart with his governess, watching his father's men evict families of tenants, as he fought with his brother over sweets (89). Such a raw juxtaposition of bored and overfed Big House children with desperate tenant families is closer in its ideological thrust to William Carleton's brutal eviction scenes than to the work of most earlier Anglo-Irish writers. In the nineteenth century, among novelists from the ascendancy, only Lever offers a comparable description of injustice: in *The Martins of Cro' Martin,* another arrogant English-born landlady orders evictions in retaliation for the tenants' failure to vote for the family's candidate.

Like Lever, however, Johnston envisions the descendants of the dispossessed tenants with an uneasy repugnance that undermines and even subverts her own radical critique of Big House society. Her narrative skill in depicting the inner lives of Anglo-Irish protagonists in the first three novels—Minnie MacMahon, Alexander Moore, Mr. Prendergast—heightens our sense of her distance from the Catholic villagers. The weakest writing in *The Gates* surely emerges from an imaginative failure when Johnston depicts an Irish-American returning to his birthplace to buy the estate gates carved by an ancestor. Potentially a poignant confrontation between the present insolvent landlord and the descendant of a former tenant who is reclaiming lost family history, the scene rapidly descends into crude caricature dense with class-biased details: the visitor's boasts of his mansion in Peoria, his vulgar limousine, his shrill mink-draped wife who finds all European countries except Switzerland dirty—even his hairy body, which connects him, perhaps, with the ape-like Mr. Kelly (110–19).

Again like Charles Lever more than a century earlier, Johnston carefully differentiates between a brutal Catholic Irish tribe and the lonely individuals who flee from their origins. In *The Gates, How Many Miles to Babylon,* and *The Captains and the Kings,* village youths escape from their backgrounds through relationships they forge with occupants of the Big House. More resourceful, intelligent, or sensitive than their families, Kevin Kelly, Jerry Crowe, and Diarmid Toorish turn to the Anglo-Irish gentry for the emotional, economic, and, in the case of Diarmid, the aesthetic possibilities that village life denies them.[9] In *The Captains and the Kings,* a truant village boy chooses Mr. Prendergast's Big House as a refuge from the mean-minded and sordid life of his shopkeeping parents. Dirty and barely literate, Diarmid brings his overwhelming needs with him—for beauty, for education, and for love. He sees Prendergast's home as a grand shop or museum, filled with treasures he recognizes as part of a remote, inaccessible world. With a collection of lead soldiers—the captains and the kings—that have been stored in the Prendergast family nursery for more than fifty years, two alienated outcasts recreate the flamboyant battles of British history and begin to assuage their loneliness. Johnston's unsentimental vision of Prendergast and Diarmid—a selfish old man and a sullen, dirty adolescent—makes the transforming power of their brief encounter particularly moving. Huddled together in the decaying old house, eating the canned food Diarmid filches from his parents' shop or drinking the whisky and instant coffee supplied by Prendergast, they contrive a doomed but loving refuge from their pasts.

Although they are never as idealized as Lever's Joe Nelligan, the young intruders in Johnston's early novels are still the exceptional offshoots of a brutalized tribe. No matter how class-ridden or improvident gentry society has become, it still offers aesthetic refinement and at least the remnants of wealth—and thus provides an escape from the squalor of the Catholic village. In *The Captains and the Kings,* the Big House's association with good taste and high cul-

---

9. Johnston's depiction of the surviving appeal of Anglo-Ireland culture for the sensitive villager is evident in fiction from another tradition as well. John McGahern's short story "Old Fashioned" describes a retired Anglo-Irish couple's growing affection for the talented son of the local police officer. After employing him to work in their garden on weekends and becoming impressed by his promise, they attempt to help him better himself. The boy expresses his inchoate longings for a fuller life through his pleasure with the quiet decorum of their meals, with their imperturbable politeness and patience with him, with the order and luxury of their house. Raised by a philistine father who fears and resists his son's intellectual promise, the boy responds with interest to the old colonel's tentative offer to help him enter Sandhurst military academy and train for a career in the British army. The father's initial enthusiasm when his son is taken up by the rich gentry dissipates into rage—into wounded and wounding national pride: "You're going to no Sandhurst whether they'd have you or not, and I even doubt if the Empire is that hard up" (1985, 47). The similarities between the plot of "Old Fashioned" and *The Captains and the Kings* suggests that a revised reading of the relationship between two classes is not exclusively the product of writers from the Protestant Big House tradition.

ture (classical music, beautiful gardens, and great books) has considerable moral weight against Diarmid's brutish family. Similarly in *The Gates*, the reminders of literary culture associated with the Big House—even drunken and reactionary Uncle Frank has read Dostoyevsky—are in striking contrast to the chaos of the Kellys' lives and the vulgarity of the Irish-American Maguires. Although Johnston emphasizes how the intolerance of Alexander Moore's mother in *How Many Miles to Babylon* expresses itself in the perfection of her drawing room, gardens, and music, the novel nevertheless flirts with a Yeatsian view of the Big House, always with the concomitant rejection of the village culture.

Throughout Johnston's fiction, her acknowledgment of the snobbery, injustice, and self-destructive improvidence (represented primarily by many alcoholic landlords)[10] of gentry life is balanced by her idealization of ascendancy taste, an idealization that is strikingly absent from earlier (pre-Yeatsian) fiction about Anglo-Ireland. Alexander Moore's feelings for his home when he leaves for war suggest the moralization of aesthetics that Johnston brings to an Anglo-Irish world that she judges far more harshly in other passages. "I stopped and looked at the house and wondered if it would ever be able to love any person as I loved those blocks of granite, the sleeping windows, the uncompromising grayness, the stern perfection of the building in front of me" (1988b, 62). In *The Captains and the Kings* classical music, which is associated in several other novels with coldly arrogant mothers whose hostile mastery of the piano isolates them from their children, becomes the means by which Mr. Prendergast achieves his epiphanic moment. Death saves Prendergast from the disgrace of the legal action that Diarmid's parents have instigated against him for sequestering their son. His heart quietly gives out as the police prepare to bring him in for questioning, but only after he has finally played Chopin's Nocturnes as he has never before played them. The disciplined music of high culture, which in Johnston's novels is specifically associated with the Big House, thus becomes the means of spiritual fulfillment.

10. Drinking in the Anglo-Irish home, however, is now perceived as a stay against despair rather than as the violent squalor associated with the drunkenness of Catholic Mr. Kelly. Prendergast (*The Captains and the Kings*), Uncle Frank (*The Gates*), Mr. Moore (*How Many Miles to Babylon*), and Aunt Mary (*The Jest*) are all quiet and gallant drinkers, facing up to irretrievable personal or economic loss.

Johnston's deepest loyalties lie with a romantic ascendancy hero- ism, with dashing Anglo-Irish political radicals who turn against their own class without sacrificing the intrinsic personal advantages of their background. (They recall earlier heroes in the Protestant na- tionalist narrative of Anglo-Ireland—Wolfe Tone, Edward Fitzgerald, Robert Emmet, or Parnell—rather than the characters in most Big House fiction.) Minnie's dead father in *The Gates,* identified as a turncoat by his family, is accused of choosing a shop girl with a pretty face to father his daughter and of supporting the wrong political side. "A trouble-maker, a left-wing agitator, a writer of anti-capitalist, anti-colonialist, anti-British slogans on walls? Killed, not before his time, hurrying to some far-flung corner of the British Empire to fo- ment trouble. Biting the hand that had fed him and his for centuries. A traitor to his class" (1983, 38). But in supporting the War of Inde- pendence against his own Unionist father and brother and then, against the beliefs of his fellow Irish nationalists, in enlisting in the British army to fight fascism in World War II, Minnie's father is the most attractive member of her family. His romantic daughter yearns for this flamboyant lost family hero.

Even in its most violent manifestations, revolutionary ideology is far more acceptable when embraced by well-born Anglo-Irish men from the Big House rather than by working-class gunmen. In *The Old Jest,* young Nancy Gulliver, like Minnie, hears that her lost father was a radical turncoat: a Bolshevist "or an anarchist or a socialist" (1988c, 88); conveniently, he was also a "gentleman" from the west who trav- eled abroad (138). Nancy's secret friendship with a guerrilla leader who organizes the killing of twelve British soldiers during the War of Independence is driven by her fantasy that this middle-aged fugitive is her unknown father—mysterious, dangerous (he carries a gun), and romantic. She learns that the heroic stranger, gunned down at the end of the novel, is from her own class; he grew up with her mother's family attending the same balls and hunts. The violent imperatives of radical politics—which presumably lead Nancy's surrogate father to plan the cold-blooded murder of twelve men—are mitigated, not sim- ply by the heroic goal of national freedom, but also by the social and intellectual rectitude implied by his upper-class background.[11]

11. Johnston's partial appropriation of a historical narrative provides a revealing context for this episode in *The Old Jest:* On Nov. 9, 1920, Michael Collins's men de-

In two novels, Johnston depicts quietly heroic, if defeated, resident Big House landlords rather than romantic rebels from Unionist Anglo Ireland. In both works, however, the landlord's Irish identity and sympathy for nationalist aspirations involve even less sacrifice of class position. Mr. Moore in *How Many Miles to Babylon* and Mr. Martin in *Fool's Sanctuary*, both of whom passively support a free Ireland during the early twentieth century, are marginalized and, to different degrees, emotionally thwarted men. Both, however, are enlightened landlords in the tradition of the Edgeworthian ideal of high-minded commitment to the land and the country they occupy. For both, love of their property involves a sense of responsibility to their tenants, whom they recognize—as the Edgeworths never do—as the ancient owners of the land. These exemplary landlords reject imperial military service and instead devote their lives to improving the fields that they hold in trust for the "people." Embracing the ideology of unusual Anglo-Irish reformers, they retain the authority and economic benefits of class while preaching ecological husbandry. In *How Many Miles to Babylon*, Moore opposes his wife's attempts to send their son into World War I and instead proposes an alternative service for the future landowner. In *Fool's Sanctuary*, Mr. Martin, having rejected his family tradition of military service, devotes his life to reforesting the country that he feels his ancestors have violated.

But, even as both landlords declare themselves peasants at heart, devoted to the land they acknowledge as a trust rather than a possession, Big House sympathy for Irish nationalism does not include a breakdown of class lines or any immediate plans for handing over property to the "people." Moore's sense of responsibility to his tenants and his belief that he is merely a temporary custodian of the land that his class has expropriated fail to encompass a vision of social equality. In spite of his loyalty to the country of his birth, Alex Moore's father never questions the social gulf that separates his son

---

scended on safe houses of Castle undercover agents and killed fourteen British intelligence agents as well as two Royal Ulster Constabulary men (J. Boyer Bell 1971, 23). Although in *The Old Jest* the assassination of twelve British officers takes place at races in the Curragh, Johnston's plot reflects IRA campaigns during the War of Independence. But in the historical narrative, such acts of terror were masterminded by Michael Collins, a working-class leader—not, as in Johnston's fiction, by a disaffected Anglo-Irish aristocrat.

from his village friend. In *Fool's Sanctuary,* however, where Martin's socialism and Republicanism isolate him from his son, who serves with British intelligence during the War of Independence, the landlord's bond to his steward, Dillion, is a serious working relationship between men from different social worlds. But in spite of the narrator's denial of barriers between her father and Dillion, the friendship is mediated by their acceptance of enduring class differences. "Servant, some people would have said: master and servant. But it never seemed like that to me. . . . They never called each other by their Christian names, that is true; nor ate formally in each other's houses. But their lives were bound together, their dreams the same dreams, their tragedies the same tragedies, they spoke a language to each other that none of the rest of us really understood" (1988a, 35). The Yeatsian echoes of a loving bond between nobleman and peasant indicate how fully Johnston sanctions a neo-feudal view of the Big House; she envisions a deep and fruitful relationship between two men who retain the roles of master and servant.

In both *How Many Miles to Babylon* and *Fool's Sanctuary,* the injustice and snobbery of the Anglo-Irish are shifted to the piano-playing wives of the landlords, who are filled with contempt for their husbands' passivity and anti-imperial politics. This retrograde ascendancy world, represented by Alexander Moore's coldly arrogant mother, brutally maims not only servants and tenants but children of the Big House as well. Through Prendergast's fleeting memories of his unhappy childhood, *How Many Miles to Babylon* deepens the examination of parental inadequacy and rejection that Johnston alludes to in *The Captains and The Kings.* Alexander is dominated by his coldly elegant and frustrated mother, a woman who much resembles the appalling Big House matriarchs in Molly Keane's novels. Like Keane, Johnston recognizes the corruption latent in empty forms of power. Married without love and living without the real authority and responsibilities of the lady of the manor, this idle twentieth-century mistress of the Big House tends her garden, feeds her swans, and maims her child. In the tradition of Charles Lever's haughty Lady Dorothea, Mrs. Moore rejects contact with all intruders—her son's piano teacher, for example—who might drag intimations of poverty into her drawing room. In *How Many Miles to Babylon,* Johnston's portrayal of a devouring mother who sends her son to certain death in World War I suggests a brutal ascendancy version of the traditional

Irish figure of the *Shan Van Vocht,* a Mother Ireland demanding blood sacrifice. But those hostile and distant mothers (also in *The Christmas Tree* and *Fool's Sanctuary*) emerge not from a nationalist or patriotic agenda, but from Johnston's sustained observation of the politics of gender in Ireland.

By focusing her critique of Anglo-Ireland on its women, Johnston frees herself to indulge in her ambivalent nostalgia for ascendancy virtues. Rebels from the working class or tenantry are judged as much by their loyalty to the Big House or to the world of culture it represents as by their commitment to Republicanism. Like Edith Somerville, Johnston depicts many native Irish servants, tenants, and neighbors of the gentry estate who accept and embrace the class divisions of their society. In *The Gates,* a Republican hotel keeper's bloodthirsty memories of killing an informer during the War of Independence horrify Minnie. But his past brutality is mitigated by his nostalgic affection for her renegade upper-class father, a proud affection that expresses itself in his disapproval of her father's marrying out of his own class (1983, 59). In *The Old Jest,* bumbling IRA gunmen who attempt to ambush a car are chagrined and apologetic when they are recognized by the two Anglo-Irish women they have stopped on a dark road (1988c, 111). And, in the same novel, although the servant Bridie celebrates the IRA's success in killing the British—"that's twelve less English soldiers to torture our poor boys" (151)—she nevertheless fully supports the social divisions that make Nancy a "lady" and the newly rich family of Caseys "only fit to be sweeping the streets" (85).

Ruling-class memoirs frequently included similar accounts of native Irish devotion to, and subservience before, Anglo-Ireland.[12] Such

12. In "Divided Loyalties," an Anglo-Irish essayist from an old Big House family describes a confrontation between IRA men and the gentry that is reminiscent of a fictional episode in *The Old Jest.* Hubert Butler reports that two armed local men seeking guns or money for the IRA retreated sheepishly from the steps of his family's house when his mother identified them and scolded them for smoking in her presence (1990, 54). In her history of the Shelbourne Hotel, Elizabeth Bowen also reveals a familiar Anglo-Irish conviction that the working class exists in submissive admiration of ascendancy society—and fails to consider the possibility of any class hostility in the scene that she recalls. Describing the spectacle of elaborately dressed guests leaving the hotel for Castle balls—a spectacle performed before crowds of observers in the Dublin street—Bowen is certain that such display encouraged the onlookers to aspire for employment at the Shelbourne. "Ireland esteems pleasure and likes pomp; all she asks in return, from those who enjoy it, is that they should comport themselves in a worthy manner" (Bowen 1951b, 134).

accounts reflect the landowner's mistaken conviction that his tenants and servants accepted a system of rigid social, political, and economic barriers. But the actual working out of a national history that includes the burning down of two hundred Big Houses indicates a greater class animus than Johnston acknowledges in her depictions of rural Republicanism. Whereas Jerry, in *How Many Miles to Babylon,* joins the army in World War I to prepare himself for armed rebellion, the steward's son in *Fool's Sanctuary,* Cashel Dillon, is an intellectual version of the good country man, described from the perspective of the Big House. Cashel's work for his own people (he is a student at the National University and an IRA commandant) is finally overshadowed by his devotion to the landlord's family. His loyalty to his patron and his love for Mr. Martin's daughter compel him to reveal IRA plans to kill Martin's son. Thus, Cashel is virtually a twentieth-century version of Lever's Joe Nelligan: a talented Irish Catholic country man who raises himself above his class background by intellectual merits and who is saved from the coarseness of the new Catholic power structure (in his case, represented by the brutality of the IRA) by his devotion to a gentry family. But if Joe attains political and moral distinction in the mid-nineteenth-century *The Martins of Cro' Martin,* Cashel's decency, manifest in his refusal to be bound by narrow political hatreds, dooms him to death as an informer. Christine St. Peter notes the pessimism of Johnston's depictions of cross-caste relations in Ireland (1991, 118); nowhere is that pessimism more evident than in *Fool's Sanctuary,* Johnston's most nostalgic and idealized depiction of the Big House.

Political radicals from the urban working class, raised without any humanizing contact with the feudal traditions of rural Ireland, are always problematic figures in her fiction. Joe Mulhare, the young IRA intermediary in *The Old Jest* whom Nancy meets in Dublin, is more memorable for his devotion to literature and aspirations to become a writer (as well as for his resemblance to a friendly rabbit), than for the political ideals he learned from his socialist father.[13] Serious working-class radicals are frequently presented as ruthless, vulgar, brutal, or even cowardly exploiters of revolution. In *Fool's Sanctuary,* the polite but deadly gunmen who execute Cashel as an informer

13. In *The Dawning* (1988), the film version of *The Old Jest,* Joe is transformed into a serious terrorist and is shown participating in a violent IRA assassination plot. Unlike the film's director, Robert Knights, Johnston does not present a likeable, intelligent, and bookish working-class young man as a political killer.

are, predictably, from urban Dublin. In *Shadows on Our Skin* and *The Railroad Station Man,* two novels that deal with recent violence in the north, Johnston depicts contemporary Republicans or their supporters as exploitative, self-pitying cowards, as gunmen without decency—and without culture. In *The Railroad Station Man,* Manus, the urban terrorist, is condemned as much for his vulgarity as for his brutality. Republicanism becomes heroic when engaged in by gentry gunmen from the Big House, not by a Catholic lumpenproletariat from Dublin with weak eyes, allergies, a shrill voice, an addiction to Kit-Kat chocolate bars, and a hatred of poetry, democracy, and fresh air.

Johnston's later novels have deservedly elicited critical attention for their evocation of women's lives in Ireland[14] and thus for their explorations of the politics of gender rather than those of class and sectarian division that dominate her earlier fiction. *The Invisible Worm,* for example, supports contemporary feminist and postcolonial analyses of nationalist patriarchy as an extension of an earlier oppression.[15] Like *The Christmas Tree* and *The Railroad Station Man,* it explores an adult woman's struggles to free herself from her past and implies that the substitution of one political system for another has no ameliorating effect on her life. A Catholic, nationalist father is as inimical to the protagonist of *The Invisible Worm* as is the brutal Protestant Big House hierarchy to Alex Moore in *How Many Miles to Babylon.* Read in the context of current feminist concerns, *The Invisible Worm* depicts the vulnerability of women within seemingly protected family structures; but from a postcolonial perspective, the novel suggests that imperial values reinscribe themselves in the new nation. Johnston's transformations and reworkings of Big House conventions to reflect a new dispensation reveal as many continuities with the past as changes from it. The postindependence nation is tied to its history not simply by the desire of the newly ascendant

14. See St. Peter (1991, 123–25) and Weekes (1990, 204–11). As of the writing of this study I have discovered no significant critical analysis of *The Invisible Worm.*

15. Eavan Boland's *A Kind of Scar* (1989) argues that the dominance of female icons for the republican ideal of nation deprived Irish women writers of their most powerful poetic subjects. Edna Longley's *From Cathleen to Anorexia* (1990) denies the possibility of being both feminist and republican. In *Sex and Nation* (1991) Gerardine Meaney asserts that the suppression of individual rights for Irish women is a development of a misogynist nationalist agenda that simultaneously idealizes and dehumanizes women; she nevertheless maintains that feminism must "interrogate," not reject, Irish nationalism.

class to mimic the symbols and attitudes of a colonial order, but also by patterns of a class-bound rhetorical narrative. Although the novel depicts the democratized social arrangements of a postcolonial state, its narrative voice emerges from surviving Anglo-Irish anxieties about the "other" Ireland. In its revisionist depiction of a new democratic nation it reinscribes difference.

Like *Fool's Sanctuary, The Invisible Worm* returns to the Big House for setting. The house is now presided over by a Catholic statesman who represents the new postcolonial elite, rather than by a fading Anglo-Irish landlord. Laura Quinlin's husband, Maurice, is, like her father, a political leader in modern Ireland. Agoraphobic Laura, however, is imprisoned by the ancestral house of her Anglo-Irish mother, a house that has been passed through the matrilineal line for two generations. The novel appropriates the conventional symbol of the gentry house in the social and political novel for psychological fiction about a woman's life; this Big House thus exists as much as a phenomenological entity as an economic or social signifier. As the shell that encapsulates Laura's uneasy and unstable self, it is the external image of the interior prison she inhabits. The rooms and contents of Laura's home are never described, except for the display of exotic memorabilia collected by her traveling grandfather, who returned periodically to impregnate his wife and then resumed his travels. When compared to other fictional Big Houses, where the precisely evoked opulence or shabbiness of a property provides telling social and political resonances, Laura's home is disembodied, existing without concrete physical presence.[16] We know it only as a place from which she watches the sea, at the end of an avenue off the main road into town (1991, 60). Yet, to the thirty-seven year old woman, whose life is circumscribed by this building and its gardens, its existence is defining. "I suppose you could say that I guard this house, this mad museum. I am the curator of my ancestor's folly" (24). Laura admits that she married without love, largely to preserve

---

16. In *The Poetics of Space* Gaston Bachelard's analysis of the image of the house suggests how its meaning as psychological phenomenon is conveyed not through description but through thought and dream. His reading offers a theoretical explanation for Johnston's exclusion of almost all description of Laura's house in her psychological novel. "For the real houses of memory, the houses to which we return in dreams, the houses that are rich in unalterable oneirism, do not readily lend themselves to description. To describe them would be like showing them to visitors. We can perhaps tell everything about the present, but about the past!" (1969, 13)

her home. "I wanted a child. I wanted to secure my line. Keep this house in the family" (59). But despite her professed concern with inheritance and lineage, the pressures she feels are internal rather than explicitly material or social. The house, filled with echoes of a man's footsteps and unwanted caresses, is the frame of her terrified psyche and the sterile prison where she remains as an adult in a childless, unhappy marriage. It is, the novel finally reveals, the home where Laura lived with a father who assaulted her and with a mother who fled the house and drowned herself at sea upon learning of his violation of their child.

More present in the novel than the sketchily delineated main house is the summer house, a graceful little pavilion hidden in the fold of a small hill near a stream, an ancestral folly. This "doll house" has been abandoned to brambles, ferns, and shrubs since Laura's mother died. In that buried gazebo of leisure-class pleasure, Johnston creates a sustained metaphor of psychic trauma and recovery. Following her father's death, Laura retrieves the overgrown building, literally unburies it, and faces the foul odors that issue from the decaying structure. Her husband, who is insistently identified with her father in the novel, objects to her project, which she defends as "disinterring the past" (42). For Maurice, a successful Catholic politician who idolizes her father and routinely betrays his marriage, "the past's a waste of time. We should all forget about the bloody past" (43). Yet the buried past that Laura seeks as she hacks out the bamboo and brambles covering the summer house reveals itself as the unspeakable and unthinkable act of a parent: his rape of his fifteen-year-old daughter in that hidden retreat.

The Invisible Worm focuses on Laura's psychic narrative—the story of an armored woman who responds to her past first with retreat, repression, and solitude, and finally with an insistent drive to retrieve what she has suppressed. A culminating act in the novel, her burning of the resurrected summer house, a fiery purgation of the site of violent childhood betrayal, signals the beginning of a possible recovery. But this study of a victimized woman returns again and again to the familiar but transmuted patterns of earlier Anglo-Irish fiction: the story of religion and class that exists as inescapable context in all Big House novels. Like Johnston's first work, *The Invisible Worm* offers contradictory ideological positions; it depicts a nation where the apparent breakdown of traditional barriers, signaled by Laura's and her mother's marriages, is belied by an inexorable class narrative.

When the daughter of the Big House takes a groom to her bed in Yeats's *Purgatory*, she begets a history of murder, first of father by his son, and then of son by father. In *The Invisible Worm*, the Anglo-Irish mother's marriage to a member of the new Catholic ruling class, a Republican hero who reinvigorates the fading aristocratic line of his Protestant wife, again culminates in violence.

Patriarchal control has passed, but ominously so, to a new class of mimic men who ape the culture of the colonials. In a self-deprecatingly ironic passage that suggests the aristocrat's contempt for the pretensions of both the parvenu and her own class, Laura explains that her father sought in his Protestant wife the style and tradition of the ascendancy culture that he lacked. Speaking with a voice oblivious to the possibility of any native Irish heritage, she observes that he viewed tradition as a commodity to be acquired through marriage.

He liked . . . the air of history, of knowing where you came from . . . crests on the spoon, book plates, family portraits, all those museum-like objects collected down the years, centuries, by grandfathers and great-grandfathers. We use those artifacts every day, we live fairly comfortably with the ghosts of the past. It's quite seductive, that. You can't buy that. He became a part of it through me, not through my mother. I was part of that chain and I was also his. (121)

Her husband also views Laura as a treasure, linked with the ascendancy mementos she has brought him: "Like one of the objects that you love so much, crowding this house out, one of those things that you dust and polish and cosset. They and you are treasures" (146). Laura's mother contemptuously resisted her husband's hope that she would embrace his religion; thus, her adherence to a fading Protestantism (an empty church) in modern Ireland became her stay against a new oppression that she termed a "vulgarity."[17] Warding off

17. Johnston's emphasis on the marginalized ("embarrassed") position of Protestantism in the new Ireland includes an ongoing critique of the vulgarity of ("ornate" and "preening") Catholicism. "Just off the road leading to the Major's house, the Protestant church crouched like a little old lady, embarrassed at being found some place she had no right to be, behind a row of yew trees. The other end of the village, on a slight eminence, a semi-cathedral, topped by an ornate gold cross, preened itself triumphantly" (1983, 19). William Trevor, speaking of his sympathy for a now marginalized and dispossessed religion, describes his attraction for the Protestant Church of Ireland, a "shrunken, withered little church" (1989, 133). Both writers thus reposition a former symbol of imperial ascendancy as new victim.

his charm and appeal, she taunted the man who won her and who will violate their child. "Haven't you got my house and my land and my beautiful body? What makes you think you should have my soul as well?" (6) Thus, for Laura, the child of this mixed marriage, the Protestant church service remains embedded "like marrow in [her] bones" (148), as if to save her from the vulgarity of her father's world.

Although the formal barriers between the two Irelands have collapsed in this novel, Laura's and her mother's voices convey a familiar aversion toward the new nation. Protestant ambivalence about Catholic Ireland survives long after the disappearance of the economic or political basis for Anglo-Irish ascendancy. The newly marginalized Anglo-Ireland—represented by the narrative voice in the novel—envisions itself, not only as endangered, but also as dispossessed and victimized. Laura believes that she is hated by the Catholic community she has never joined. As a young girl she begs to escape from home and her father's sexual advances by telling her mother that she is mistreated as a "West Brit" or a "prod" by the girls in her convent school. As an adult she imagines that the neighborhood calls her "Protestant bitch above in her big house" (59).

From the perspective of the patterning of the novel, the emotional display, vulgarity, and, finally, the sexual violence of Laura's father are Catholic Irish traits; the withdrawal and distancing irony of her beautiful mother are Anglo-Irish failings. In this updated version of Arnold's distinction between the Celt and the Saxon, Johnston reinscribes difference. Although the elegance of Anglo-Irish ascendancy culture has been appropriated by new national leaders who now occupy the Big House, such appropriation brings only a surface gentility. Preparing a dinner so that her unfaithful husband can entertain his latest mistress, Laura loads her table with flowers, silver, glass, and candles, noting how both her father and husband are alike in "liking things to be done with style" (34). But, implicitly, the style inherited by the new Ireland is mere display, denoting a tradition purchased by a vulgarian to show off before his sexual conquest. Significantly, after this dinner party for her philandering husband and his mistress, Laura is overwhelmed by an intrusive memory of her father violently shaking her for cutting off her hair—her act of defiance precipitated by his rape. The conflation of the scenes, both depicting assaults on her by statesmen in the new Ireland, emphasizes the congruence between brutal father and husband.

In *The Invisible Worm,* the Big House is not only a prison for Laura, but also, as in *Fool's Sanctuary,* a violated retreat presented with a nostalgic sense of lost beauty and solidity, now replaced by a crude present. Progress toward a new nation is loss, not merely change; by yoking the environmental imperative to her argument (the non-biodegradable junk in the following passage) Johnston creates a moral framework for the novel's hostility toward modern Ireland, the world created and governed by Laura's father and husband.

> Men used to come with horses and cart when I was a child, and load [the seaweed] up and take it away to spread on the fields, and the beach would be clean again, and the air would be free of the heavy, repellent smell. Now the men come with tractors and they leave the scars of their wheels on the hill at the back of the beach, and they also leave behind them the detritus of the world that is today's sea wreck; plastic containers of all shapes and sizes, rusty tins, broken glass. (30)

Against her husband's wishes, Laura posts signs on her land near the beach requesting that picnickers take their litter home with them. "He said I had no right to bully people like that. 'Arrogant' was the word he used" (33). Anglo-Irish ecological foresight is opposed to native Irish slovenliness, just as inherited tradition is contrasted with purchased style. Laura also regrets the loss of language, of a vocabulary from the past that is no longer comprehensible. "I worry sometimes about all those lost words. It becomes more and more difficult to make yourself understood without them . . . and when you do use them people think you're batty. Its best to keep quiet. I keep quiet" (65). The "lost words" of course imply lost values; before the horror of modern vulgarity and crassness—and much worse—only retreat is possible.

In current feminist discourse, Laura's rape is evidence of the ongoing victimization of women in a postcolonial patriarchal state; thus, Johnston's novel inscribes the narrative of gender rather than the familiar themes of class and sectarian division that feminists charge have too long monopolized national literatures. But the novel's return to the Big House setting compels a corollary reading, one that foregrounds an older political narrative existing throughout Johnston's fiction. The usurper in previous novels—Edgeworth's Jason, Lever's Scanlan, Somerville's Dr. Magnan—no longer merely gazes longingly at the Big House; he now controls it. Coarser than the old gentry stock he replaces (witness his probable origins among a race of people like the Kellys or the Toorishes), the new aggressor—now explicitly a sexual marauder—comes from outside the walls of the demesne and begets his own victim. Moreover, in this Yeatsian view of postindependence Ireland, the father's violation of his daughter is part of larger social violation, an assault on the land, on culture, and on old pieties by a new nation. In Laura's past is a girlhood trauma that she must retrieve and master. By unburying and then burning the summer house, the Anglo-Irish incendiary mimics the conflagrations of countless gentry houses by the native Irish. But the invaded edifice is finally legitimately destroyed; such destruction by the inhabitant of the Big House now implies a healing purgation of violation, not mere depredation.

Johnston's inclusion of Dominic, the gentle ex-seminarian whom Laura learns to love, as well as her softening of her hostile portrayal of Maurice in the second half of the novel, significantly modulates the stark allegory of class and religion that I suggest as a disturbing context, as virtually an alternative narrative to that of gender in *Fool's Sanctuary*. But, himself traumatized and alienated from his past and destined to live as a rootless wanderer, Dominic is merely mediator and facilitator of Laura's recovery; he offers no future for her. Like Laura, he lives on the margins of society as an outcast from the new Catholic Ireland represented by his appalling family. If her discovery of a capacity to love this needful man theoretically liberates her, her liberation leads her back to solitude, to a loveless marriage with a kinder and gentler version of her father in the ancestral Big House.

William Trevor

That a novel includes an accurate report of an historical event is not necessarily a point in its favor. What would be a point in its favor is the presence of that quality we loosely call "true to life," more pertinently true to the moral complexities of political behavior. (Howe 1957, 99)

William Trevor's first novel about gentry society ignores the central conventions of earlier Big House fiction. In a revisionist formulation of early twentieth-century country house culture, he rejects the critical or parodic description of the Anglo-Irish in earlier novels. His landlord is more loyal to Ireland than to England, and *Fools of Fortune* describes a working family, the Quintons of Kilneagh in County Cork, who manage a prosperous lumber mill instead of parasitically and improvidently living off the rents of a decaying estate. The Quintons are neither incompetent, foolish, mean-spirited, nor alienated. Nor do they isolate themselves from the political rebellion that is occurring in Ireland in the early twentieth century. Willie Quinton's memories of his childhood in a beautiful Georgian home suggest an ideal of community—an ordered and ceremonious life in which Irish Catholic servants are treated with affection and respect. Mr. Quinton's insistence on this tranquil life at Kilneagh, moreover, distinguishes him from Somerville and Ross's blustering, fox-hunting landlords. In this idyll of sectarian tolerance, the Protestant Quintons welcome a defrocked priest, Father Kilgarriff, into their home as a tutor for their son, and everyone eats fish on Friday to accommodate the Catholics in the household. Father Kilgarriff teaches Willie to admire the nationalist leader Daniel O'Connell for his abhorrence of violence and to regret Ireland's failure to follow O'Connell's precepts.

The ties between nationalist Kilneagh and England are, nevertheless, strong. Like many other Anglo-Irish, Willie's uncle has died fighting for the British during the recent Great War, as have several Catholic workers at the Quinton mill.[18] Willie's mother and great-grandmother were both English brides from the grand manor house of Woodcombe Park in Dorset. Both of these English-born Quinton wives, however, become thoroughly Irish: the first of them dies of famine fever contracted while she distributes food to her starving tenants. Catholic and Protestant differences merge into a common hagiolatry when the Protestant Anna Quinton appears to her mourning husband eleven years after her death as "an apparition like the Virgin Mary" on a distant hill. Her devoted widower obeys her request that he give away the greater part of his estate "to those who had suffered loss and deprivation in the Famine" (1984, 13), an act

18. R. F. Foster's *Modern Ireland, 1600–1972* (1989) argues that in the postrevolutionary Irish Free State "the real nature of pre-1916 Irish society had to be glossed over, including, among much else, the hundreds of thousands of Irish who volunteered in the Great War" (535). Trevor's portrayal of the Kilneagh community reflects, like Foster's recent history, a revision of an exclusively nationalist narrative.

strikingly at odds with the post-Famine behavior of most Irish land-lords.[19] Willie's mother, the second English bride from Dorset, is similarly identified with her adopted nation; she marries an Irish man in spite of family disapproval and supports the revolutionary cause "more energetically" (38) than does her husband.

Trevor acknowledges the unusual role the Quintons play in Irish history, for to most Anglo-Irish they are traitors to their class. In 1797, they enraged their fellow landlords by refusing hospitality to a militia man who had shot down six local Irish men in the streets. They freely gave much of their land (but not all) to their tenants before the passage of the land acts and have long identified themselves with Home Rule rather than Unionism. From 1918 until his death, Mr. Quinton entertains and financially supports the Republican leader Michael Collins, upon whose head Dublin Castle has put a price—and whose politics have moved far beyond Home Rule for Ireland. Only because Quinton fears for the safety of his dependents does he refuse, against his wife's urgings, to allow Collins to drill his men at Kilneagh. To most southern Anglo-Irish, even to the many who were beginning to shed their traditional Unionism as a result of serving together with native Irishmen in the Great War, the Easter Rising of 1916 confirmed their worst fears about Sinn Fein and arrested the move toward conciliation with the nationalists (Buckland 1972, 51–52). Yet, when she speaks of the events of 1916 that occurred two years before, the English-born Mrs. Quinton tells her eight-year-old son that she wishes the rising had succeeded: "The whole thing would be over by now" (Trevor 1984, 23).

Fools of Fortune asserts, however, that the costs of history are ongoing and work themselves out irrationally; the "whole thing" is, in fact, never over. Tragedy strikes when a worker at the family mill, a returning Irish veteran of the war and informer for the British police reinforcements, the Black and Tans, is found hanged and mutilated on the estate grounds. In reprisal, Sergeant Rudkin of the Black and Tans burns down the Big House, killing Mr. Quinton and his two

19. Trevor's portrayal of Anna Quinton resembles Edith Somerville's depiction in *The Big House of Inver* of Jas Prendergast's self-sacrificing mother, who also dies of famine fever contracted while serving her tenants. Such portrayals suggest how the trauma of the Great Famine elicited strikingly self-protective responses from Anglo-Irish novelists—and, in the case of Somerville's 1925 novel, generations before a revisionist historiography rehabilitated the Famine landlord.

daughters and shooting the two gardeners who witness the attack. (Trevor makes a significant change in the novel from the earlier short story version that provides the ur-plot of *Fools of Fortune*. In the short story "Saints" the attackers on Kilneagh, because they remain unnamed, are presumably members of the IRA, who were ordinarily the perpetrators of violence against Big Houses in the revolutionary period.)[20] The rest of *Fools of Fortune* traces the endless repercussions of this act of political horror. Willie's beautiful and dignified mother becomes an alcoholic, obsessed with her husband's English killer. Her desire for vengeance is finally fulfilled ten years after the burning of Kilneagh by a hitherto gentle young man who completes the cycle of violence by brutally stabbing and virtually decapitating his father's murderer, who now owns a greengrocer's shop in Liverpool.

In *Fools of Fortune*, Trevor is not satisfied with merely depicting the ongoing and self-perpetuating effect of violence on the consciousness of the victims or observers of political outrage. Instead, he seeks for solutions, finding them in the notion of redemptive suffering, or more specifically, in a vision of healing sainthood that comes to those who endure and miraculously transcend the violence that has scarred them. Moreover, he evokes a community of victims in Ireland, for the agony of the country's history is shared by Catholic and Protestant alike. The Quintons' young Catholic maid, Josephine, who—with Willie, his mother, and Father Killgarriff—is a survivor of the massacre at the Big House, is transformed and redeemed by her vision of violence and suffering. She devotes her life to the broken and alcoholic Mrs. Quinton, and then becomes a maid in a home for

20. In *The Secret Army: The IRA, 1917–1970,* J. Bowyer Bell reports that "the Tans burnt creameries and Sinn Fein homes; the IRA burnt Unionist big house, two for one in Tom Barry's area" (1971, 25). *Fools of Fortune* is set in the turbulent West Cork area, which was controlled by Tom Barry's Flying Column of more than one hundred highly trained IRA men. Buckland argues that frequent murders of Protestants by the IRA in that area between 1919 and 1921 led many families to flee Ireland (1972, 213). Although Kilneagh is clearly not a Unionist Big House, neither is it presented as the kind of Sinn Fein safe house that was vulnerable to Black and Tan attacks in 1920. (In *Barry's Flying Column,* Ewan Butler reports that arson became more and more commonplace on both sides as the War of Independence reached its climax in the first six months of 1921 (1971, 107). But by envisioning an Anglo-Irish Big House with powerful connections both to England (Willie's grandparents work for the imperial system in India) and to nationalists (Michael Collins's visits), Trevor essentially depoliticizes the burning of the Big House in his novel.

old nuns after her mistress's suicide. In her old age, when Josephine knows she is dying, she sends for the aging Willie to bring him home from exile; as he walks into her room he hears her repetitive, murmuring prayers for the suffering: "Dear Mary, console them. . . . Console them everywhere." Her nurse tells Willie of Josephine's obsessive plea "that the survivors may be comforted in their mourning. She requests God's word in Ireland" (226–27). In "Saints" Josephine is even more pointedly sanctified and sanctifying: she becomes insane and is institutionalized in an asylum where the nuns believe she heals the ill and will one day be canonized as a saint.

In *Fools of Fortune* Trevor transfers this aura of sainthood to Willie's illegitimate daughter, Imelda, who is born as result of his brief encounter with his cousin Marianne, the third Quinton mother to come from the Woodcombe family in Dorset. Like Josephine, Imelda becomes insane when she discovers the violence of her family history, but ultimately her mad beatitude brings peace to those around her and she miraculously restores her parents to each other after fifty years of separation. Like her great-great-grandmother, Anna Quinton, who lost her life struggling to save the starving peasants and who appeared like the Virgin Mary to her mourning husband, Protestant Imelda, named after a Catholic saint over whose head the sacred host hovered as she knelt in prayer, exists as a symbol of healing and redemption in Ireland. She becomes a legend in the village: "Imelda is gifted, so the local people say, and bring the afflicted to her. A woman has been rid of dementia, a man cured of a cataract. Her happiness is like a shroud miraculously about her, its source mysterious except to her" (238).

Fools of Fortune, a romantic and melodramatic novel, attempts to address the injustices of Irish political history by transcending them. In "The News From Ireland," Trevor evokes a darker but more familiar vision of the Big House as he describes a well-meaning family that arrives from England during the Famine to take possession of its newly inherited estate. In this short story, Trevor emphasizes the absolute isolation between the Big House and the Catholic tenantry that condemns both classes to enduring violence and hostility. But the Quintons appear to defy every negative assumption about Anglo-Irish landlords. Nevertheless, they, as well as their devoted Catholic servants, are struck down by history as it manifests itself in the seemingly endless and irrational cycle of outrage and reprisal that surrounds the centuries of English occupation of Ireland.

Trevor's characterization of a rural gentry landowner as a supporter of Michael Collins suggests his idiosyncratic lens on Anglo-Irish history and his revisionist search for an ideal nationalist landlord. The memoir of an Irish economist, George O'Brien, describes that young Catholic intellectual's surprise when he found nationalists among the cultivated upper-class members of the Dublin Arts Club before the War of Independence. In speaking of Horace Plunkett, however, O'Brien suggests that even the most "enlightened" aristocrat remained totally alienated from his fellow countrymen. The memoir conveys the deep suspicion with which most Irish regarded such rare Anglo-Irish figures, whose loyalty to Ireland always remained tainted by their associations with imperial England.

> He was a very good example of the pathetic unrequited loyalty which the Irish aristocracy have—or perhaps I should say, had—for Ireland. They adored the country which hated them in return; they idolized the people who ridiculed them. They never could understand why they were unpopular. They were willing to give devoted service when it was not wanted. They simply could not understand that their neighbors despised the idols that they held sacred. Their own dual loyalty to England and Ireland was incomprehensible to the people by whom they were surrounded. They were nationalist in a fashion of their own. Their nationalism was set in a wider imperial loyalty. (quoted in Meenan 1980, 113)

In choosing to write about a decent and uncharacteristically radical Anglo-Irish family with ties to both imperial England and Michael Collins, Trevor recreates the Big House and virtually rewrites Anglo-Irish history. He carefully prepares his readers to accept a vision of Irish politics so horrific, so intractable and cruel, that political distinctions and political solutions are finally irrelevant. Mr. Quinton's decency in hiring Doyle, the local Irish veteran who served with the English Sergeant Rudkin in World War I and who is killed on Kilneagh grounds for informing to the Black and Tans, seals the Quintons' fate. Only by transcending politics through redemptive suffering can Trevor find meaning in the bleakness of the senseless violence he depicts. In *Fools of Fortune,* as in "Another Christmas," an earlier story about the role of politics in the lives of an Irish couple living abroad during the recent hostilities, political thinking is rejected in favor of a rudimentary human decency that transcends ideological brutalities.[21] In registering the ongoing horrors of Irish history in his stories about contemporary violence in Ireland—in, for example, "Beyond the Pale" or "Attracta"—Trevor depicts the transforming effect that violence has on the minds of his saintlike or spiritually awakened characters (1983, 691–711; 592–605). Similarly, Imelda's obsessive visions of the burning of Kilneagh and of her father's brutal vengeance on Rudkin become metaphors for Irish history itself, in which political heroism and political atrocity are perceived as inseparable. In the village convent school she attends, Imelda is obliquely told of her father's "heroic" act: "Your father will never be forgotten, Imelda, in Lough, or in Fermoy, in all County Cork, He is every day in our prayers" (1984, 197–98). But in her nightmares of her family's past Imelda conflates the two atrocities that she cannot erase from her consciousness. In her fantasies, her father's bloody revenge on the greengrocer in Liverpool merges with Rudkin's murder of her grandfather and his two daughters.

> She imagined the head, its weight tearing the flesh that still attached it to the body. (216)

> She closed her eyes and in the room above the vegetable shop blood spurted in a torrent, splashing on to the wallpaper that was torn and hung loosely down. The blood was sticky, running over the backs of her hands and splashing on to her hair . . .
> The screaming of the children began, and the torment of the flames on their flesh. The dogs were laid out dead in the yard and the body of the man in the teddy-bear dressing-gown lay smouldering on the stairs. The blood kept running on her hands, and was tacky in her hair. (218–19)

21. Thus, in "Another Christmas" middle-aged Norah realizes that she no longer loves her husband Dermot after he alienates an English friend. Rather than simply deplore the IRA outrages against human life, Dermot insists, albeit mildly, on the historical basis for the new atrocities taking place in England. By validating Norah's reaction to the position taken by her unpleasantly ascetic and priestly husband, the story insists on the betrayal of human values—Norah's and the old friend's horror at violence—by ideology. Hearing her husband speak with the voice of tribal Catholic-Irish loyalties, she feels shame for her nation, fear of her future in England, and antipathy for the man she has always believed she loved. Given the horrors of the present ideologically driven outrages, even his mild reminder of historical causes becomes a mark of his cruelty (Trevor 1983, 488–95).

As powerfully as these images of horror sustain Trevor's nausea with politics, they lead him first to seek comforting answers to the tragedy of Irish history, and then into sentimentality and over-simplification. His vision of the beatitude of a middle-aged madwoman who redeems the atrocities of history does not address the social and political issues of Irish life that are implicit in any novel about the Big House and the fate of its landlords. *Fools of Fortune* provides neither a convincing report of history nor does it achieve, in Irving Howe's terms, truth to "the moral complexities of political behavior" (1957, 99), which is the mark of a novel that successfully confronts history. By rejecting the conventions of earlier Big House fiction, which include some recognition of the landlord's responsibility for his losses, Trevor insists on the irrelevance of political choices in determining fate.

In "The Distant Past," an earlier short story about the Anglo-Irish Middletons, an aging brother and sister occupy their decaying mansion in modern Ireland. Like *Fools of Fortune* the story emphasizes the ways in which individuals are buffeted by political events they cannot control. Before the resumption of violence in the north, the unionism of the anachronistic Middletons is regarded as a harmless and picturesque eccentricity by the townspeople, former Republicans who are now earning money through tourism. In the years of the town's prosperity, the Middletons' loyalty to the past—for example, their display of the Union Jack on Queen Elizabeth II's coronation day—is received with affection and brings them attention and friendship. When the violence resumes in Ulster, however, tourists abandon the village, which is situated close to the border. Suddenly, the quaint unionism of the aging Big House occupants becomes alienating. Faced with economic loss, the townspeople turn against their former friends, depriving the Middletons of any sense of community and forcing them to face a friendless and lonesome old age. "Because of the distant past they would die friendless. It was worse than being murdered in their beds" (1983, 351). Although the old couple privately question their devotion to a decaying estate and a colonial past, they are presented as pitiful victims of history, pawns rather than as actors.

In *Fools of Fortune* individuals are even more powerfully depicted as helpless before fate, random victims of irrational waves of violence. In this novel about individuals trapped within political forces—a novel in which Michael Collins, a "great man" from Irish nationalist history, figures in the plot—Trevor depicts but curiously minimizes the implications of the economic and social realities of Big House life that exist beneath the surface kindness of the landlord with Republican sympathies. In spite of his efforts to suggest the closeness between Catholics and Protestants, class barriers are rigid at Kilneagh; the community that exists there is narrowly hierarchical. Although the Quintons identify themselves with nationalist causes, Mr. Quinton is described by his son as "very much the Irish seigneur" (1984, 16), and the family's ties to imperial England are significant. The Protestant accountant at the Quinton mill dares to admire Willie's Aunt Pansy, but his status as a middle-class clerk makes the Big House lady seem inaccessible to him as a future wife—in spite of Mr. Quinton's urgings that he propose. Josephine, the contented and devoted servant, works from morning to night while the Quintons live a far more leisurely and dignified life.

> Wash both night and morning, Mrs. Flynn commanded, rise at six-fifteen. Do not speak in the dining-room unless invited to, carry the vegetable dishes to the left of the person being served. . . ."Yes, Mrs. Flynn," Josephine endlessly repeated during her first few days of awkwardness and bewilderment. She blacked grates and shone brass, and seemed for ever to be sweeping floors. Her own small attic room, with its white enamel bowl and pitcher, was as strange as anywhere. (31–32)

In the short story "Saints" Trevor is more explicit about the distance between Josephine and Big House gentry.

> When Josephine came to clear away the dinner dishes no one stopped talking because Josephine was a shadow, even though we were fond of her. In Kilneagh her presence on the stairs or in the hall was always associated with work. She rose before the family did and lit the range, and then the fire in the drawing room and the one in the breakfast room. At breakfast time she looked as if she had never been to bed but had simply changed from her black into her morning blue. Not that she seemed tired, of course, because it wasn't her place to seem tired. (1981, 33)

The reality that does not particularly engage Trevor in *Fools of Fortune* is that even the most decent and enlightened people can, merely by their positions within structures of colonial governance, become the instruments of violence.[22] Trevor's descriptions of Josephine's position within Kilneagh suggest the precision with which an onlooker into the Big House world captured the nuances of class roles. One need not be a Marxist historian to understand, however, that the existence of families like the Quintons, whatever their politics, who owned more and controlled more than did their dispossessed Catholic tenants and employees, contributed to the presence and random violence of both the Black and Tans and the Republican forces. Political violence in early twentieth-century Ireland was no more inexplicable or irrational than it is in any colonial state where land and property are distributed to a colonial class and taken from a native people.

In *Mount Music, The Last September,* and *Two Days in Aragon* Anglo-Irish novelists also depict how Big House landlords become victims of historical forces that they are unable to comprehend or control. But in those novels Edith Somerville, Elizabeth Bowen, and Molly Keane insist, albeit to different degrees, on the responsibility of the ascendancy class for its own collapse. Big Houses are not just swept away by history; their owners actively participate in and contribute to the processes of class and sectarian division by which they are destroyed. In *The Captains and the Kings* and *How Many Miles to Babylon,* Johnston shows how Anglo-Ireland's failure to achieve any integration with the Catholic Irish community condemns her protagonists to lives of lonely isolation. And, in two of his later works, "The News from Ireland" and *The Silence in the Garden,* Trevor writes primal tales—virtual allegories of Irish history—in which the costs of dispossessing a colonized people are unflinchingly acknowledged. In *Fools of Fortune,* however, Trevor is simply interested in registering his responses to the terrible injustices of political history as it shapes individual lives.

The unfairness of history, which traps decent and enlightened people into patterns they have not chosen, is a legitimate subject for a serious novel. Thus, Trevor's re-creation of the Big House landlord as a heroic, nationalist victim is less a depiction of ordinary Anglo-Irish history than a meditation on the injustice of history, on the random-

22. Trevor acknowledges distrust of and lack of interest in political explanations for human behavior. "What seem to nudge me is something that exists between two people, or three, and if their particular happiness or distress exists for some political reason, then the political reason comes into it—but the relationship between the

ness of events and on fate's control of the individual. But the weaknesses of his novel, its final collapse into easy sentimental resolutions,
is surely related to its presentation of a historically anomalous Big
House. Whether or not *Fools of Fortune* reflects a real historical situation, the novel does not feel "true to life" to the reader with some
knowledge of the course of Irish history. Whereas most Big Houses
were burned by the IRA, Kilneagh falls victim to the Black and Tans,
an improbable historical event surely, but one that serves the novel's
moral intention to suggest the utter irrationality of political action.
The elegiac quality of the early chapters of *Fools of Fortune* evoke a
Yeatsian vision—a hierarchical Big House community of a peace-lov-
ing Protestant landlord and Catholic servants—that is difficult to reconcile with the Quintons' inclination to allow Republican forces to
drill at Kilneagh. Would the Gore-Booths' Lissadell, that "old Georgian mansion" that embodies Yeats's ideal of an aristocratic Big
House culture, have retained its symbolic meaning had Staff Lieu-
tenant Constance Markievicz brought her troops of the Citizen Army
home to drill there?

Unlike *Fools of Fortune, The Silence in the Garden* confronts Anglo-
Irish culpability; it searches to depict the power of past injustice
rather than to suggest resolution or solution. As an exploration of an
enduring historical guilt, Trevor's second Irish novel suggests that
the Big House is shadowed by its past, that its inhabitants act and
then reenact the original sins of colonialism, and thus find no peace.
The Silence in The Garden is, in fact, best read not as a realistic domestic novel, but as a moral fable in the tradition of American fiction by
Hawthorne, Melville, or Faulkner. Like those writers, Trevor creates
a densely symbolic work about his country's past. The aura of desolation and the memories of secret brutality surrounding Big House life
suggest the price a colonial heritage exacts from colonizers and colonized alike.

Whereas the Quintons in *Fools of Fortune* are presented as exemplary landlords with Republican sympathies, the Rollestons in *The Silence in the Garden* are more typical of their class. They read the *Irish
Times,* send their sons to English schools, and choose careers in the
British army. Carriglas, their ancestral home, sits defiantly on an is-

---

people come first. I'm always trying to get rid of a big reason—a political one, for instance. . . . Human reasons, for me, are more interesting than political ones" (1989,
130).

land off County Cork as an isolated lost Eden, the garden idyll of childhood memory, but also the site where Big House children once terrorized a tenant boy. Memories of this brutality—a symbolic reenactment of the primal sin of Irish history—haunt the children's grandmother and condemn all participants to lives of violence or desolation. "They terrified him. . . . Day after day, all summer, they hunted that child as an animal is hunted" (1988, 183). Corny Dowley, the victimized Catholic boy, grows up to become, in turn, a political terrorist in the War of Independence, celebrated in the village for his bloody ambush of nineteen Black and Tans. Dowley's attempt to avenge himself on his childhood torturers leads to the murder of an ill-fated Carriglas butler who walks on the mined avenue at the wrong time. The butler's death, in turn, leaves an illegitimate child with the Rollestons' kitchen maid and activates an incapacitating guilt among the intended victims. The three Rolleston children, as well as their cousin Sarah Pollexfen, who serves as a governess at Carriglas, are subsequently doomed to marginal and diminished lives: they remain celibate or enter loveless marriages or affairs; they bear no children; they find no fulfilling roles. As Sarah notes, they "cannot escape from the shadows of their abandoned lives" (132). Finally, at the insistence of their grandmother, who is obsessed by the violence occasioned by her family, Carriglas is bequeathed to Tom, the butler's son. Victimized in Catholic Ireland by his illegitimacy, that silent and innocent gate-lodge child grows up, like the Rolleston children, to become an emotionally crippled survivor of past atrocities.

Unlike Trevor's earlier Big House novel, *The Silence in the Garden* neither sentimentalizes nor obscures the burden of the past. In its exploration of the dense layers of Irish settlements on the island, the novel resonates with that insistence on inscribing present actions into the context of history that Faulkner, for example, brought to his fiction about the American South or that Aidan Higgins brings to *Langrishe, Go Down*. The slow revelation of plot through Sarah's awakening consciousness develops and intensifies the novel's thematic preoccupation with the power of the past to destroy the idyllic surface of Big House life. As she begs Mrs. Rolleston to forget her grandchildren's deeds, Sarah invokes the healing role of time. "No matter how it was, it belongs to the past now." Mrs. Rolleston's reply serves not only as a response to Sarah's wishful thinking, but as a gloomy epitaph for Ireland itself. "The past has no belongings. The past does not obligingly absorb what is not wanted" (Trevor 1988,

185). Unlike *Fools of Fortune, The Silence in the Garden* offers no routes to redemption.

The island setting that isolates Carriglas from the mainland becomes emblematic of Anglo-Irish history. An imposing symbol of ascendancy domination, the Big House welcomed viceroys for visits each summer. But the nineteenth- and early twentieth-century house represents only the most recent layer of the past. Although the Rollestons are remembered in the village for their compassion toward their starving tenants during the Famine, their original claim to the island is based solely on might. In the seventeenth century Cromwellian Rollestons savagely dispossessed the previous owners of the island and exiled them to the stony wilds of Mayo. And set against the remains of a still earlier history, the moral claims of the Anglo-Irish are fragile indeed. At the center of the island rest the ruins of an abbey and a holy well, evidence of the monastic settlements of medieval Catholic Ireland and still the object of an annual pilgrimage by village women. Even older are the mysterious standing stones and cemetery at the heart of the island, marking an ancient civilization that carried its corpses there for burial. As a prehistoric burial ground for the dead, the island's symbolic resonances are precisely evoked in this narrative of destroyed or diminished lives.

Like so many other Big House novels, *The Silence in the Garden* traces the decline of Anglo-Ireland through the physical neglect of the house and grounds. By the 1930s grass and weeds grow on the avenue; the lawns are roughly cut; the paint on the house is soiled and worn; water penetrates the drawing room and leaves brown stains on the walls (38). When a bridge is built to the island in 1931—an enterprise dedicated to Corny Dowley, the local hero who attempted to murder the Rolleston children—the project publicly marks the family's humiliation and diminished authority. Although it benefits both the villagers and Carriglas tenants, the bridge is significantly placed at an inconvenient distance from the Big House, far from the ferry slip that served generations of Rollestons.

Trevor's portrayal of the three Rolleston children living out their years in a decaying home echoes Molly Keane's more robustly comic vision of Anglo-Irish decline in *Time After Time*. Like the aging Swifts, the Rollestons turn to loveless marriages, secretive sexual liaisons, or downward social mobility. Their diminished aspirations for happiness are most tangibly illustrated when Villana, the youngest, accepts the propsal of an aging Protestant solicitor. She assuages her guilt by marrying a man who is committed to regaining the land that the family ceded to its tenants during the Famine and who adores the beautiful woman who sat on his knees when she was a child. His age and unattractiveness assure her of a marriage that will produce no children; her rejection of his dream to rebuild the estate suggests his future discontent. Lionel Rolleston most resembles Keane's June Swift, as he embraces the life of a tenant and relinquishes his social role by becoming the family farmer and groundsman. Only rarely, as on the day of Downey's funeral in 1921, does Lionel's mind register more than the diurnal concerns of the working farmer. Yet so powerful is his buried guilt that he wishes to join in the funeral procession of the man who tried, a year before, to murder him and who has finally been assassinated by the Black and Tans. Whereas Keane's Jasper Swift flirts with a homosexual liaison, James Rolleston, the first-born son at Carriglas, secretly and with self-disgust visits the bed of an aging widow in the village and dreams of his father's disapproval. But unlike Keane, whose comic eye and affection for the deplorable Swifts undermines the darker implications of *Time After Time*, Trevor finds only loss and diminishment in the guilt-ridden world he portrays. In *The Silence in the Garden*, all children of the Big House—Catholic and Protestant alike—are victims of history. Blame is narrowly apportioned to a brutal colonial system—encoded in the sin of the Rolleston children terrorizing a fleeing Catholic child.

Reinventing a Form

Aidan Higgins and John Banville

Among contemporary Irish novelists who write about the Big House, only Aidan Higgins and John Banville inherit the techniques and preoccupations of the experimental post-Joycean novel. Both dissolve the chronological sequences of realistic fiction, emphasizing traditional narrative far less than the exploration of individual consciousness. And both respond to and emerge from that breakdown of cultural certainties that accompanies all modernist writing. Higgins's and Banville's use of the conventions of the Big House genre as a catalyst for their innovations suggests the generative power of a traditional form. For each, the illusionary quality of Anglo-Irish life, its creation of fantasies of the past that fail to compensate for the decay of the present, becomes a source for setting, imagery, and theme. In turning to Big House conventions, Higgins and Banville reinvent, and in Banville's case, subvert, the form.

Higgins's *Langrishe, Go Down* internationalizes a parochial genre by juxtaposing the decline of Anglo-Ireland with the collapse of the Allies under the Axis aggressions that preceded World War II. Thus, a specifically local phenomenon becomes emblematic of a universal cultural debacle, implying the decline of Western civilization itself. In the tradition of Joycean naturalism, Higgins wrote *Langrishe, Go Down* as a supramimetic text, using the map of the village of Celbridge as assiduously as Joyce used local records in his recreation of Dublin. As in *Ulysses,* naturalistic details become symbolic, resonating within the novel with enormous force. Higgins's appropriation of the interior monologue—long subjective meditations by his protagonists—permits him to move beyond the mimetic realism of earlier

Big House novels. Although *Langrishe, Go Down* remains well within the boundaries of realistic fiction, Higgins's experiments with style and his vision of universal cultural decline establish him as a writer in the modernist tradition.

John Banville, a far more experimental novelist, subverts the traditional literary conventions that he adopts. Unlike *Langrishe, Go Down*, which retains a relatively stable sense of character and plot, Banville's two major works dealing with Anglo-Ireland—*Birchwood* and *The Newton Letter*—are parodies of earlier fiction. Both self-consciously play with the conventions of the realistic novel in order to dissolve them. In *Birchwood* Banville fragments the traditional fictional elements of plot, setting, and chronology. In the *Newton Letter* the narrator's delusions and misperceptions destabilize the realistic conventions of Big House fiction. These epistemological and metaliterary enterprises explore the limitations of remembering and knowing in order to undermine the mimetic premises of the form they exploit. They serve, moreover, as commentaries on the individual and the nation. In both, the possibility of accurate "historical" recollection is undermined by the activity of a deluding imagination: history is fiction.

Langrishe, Go Down

Although Seamus Deane argues that the persistence of the Big House novel reveals the "comparative poverty of the Irish novelistic tradition" (1985, 32), Higgins's *Langrishe, Go Down* suggests the richness, not the impoverishment, of Irish fiction. Higgins approaches his subject both as an Irishman and as a cosmopolitan; he writes not only in response to Yeats, but even more powerfully in the shadow of Joyce's, Eliot's, and Beckett's vision of a dying modern culture. Using the conventions of an earlier form, Higgins creates a work that moves beyond parochialism into the world of international fiction. Like most innovative novels, *Langrishe, Go Down* cannot be contained by the descriptive terminology of a single tradition. Based on his earlier story "Killachter Meadow," Higgins's novel reveals the creative force of a writer who works within an established form and, in so doing, redefines and reinvents it. If Higgins is writing yet another account of the death of Anglo-Irish culture, he is also presenting the death in life of the Catholic culture that has inherited Anglo-Irish power and, finally, the collapse of European culture itself (Harmon 1973, 6; Imhof and Kamm 1984, 156). In the last section of the novel newspaper headlines announce the 1938 *Anschluss,* the annexation of Austria by Nazi forces.

Higgins releases his innovations through the formal characteristics of a tradition. The neglected house, stripped of its furnishings and grandeur, conveys the loss of power and prestige of Anglo-Ireland. The alienated proprietor of the Big House fails to take responsibility for his property; he thus undermines his relationship with the Irish community, a relationship that purportedly sustained and masked a brutal system of land tenure. In earlier novels, land owners are brought down by outsiders, usually rising Catholics whose intelligence, unscrupulousness, or sheer energy defeats the isolated Anglo-Irish gentry world. Higgins's protagonist is, however, undone by a true outsider, a German intellectual who exposes the moribund condition of the contemporary Big House.

Langrishe, Go Down focuses on two Anglo-Irish sisters, Helen and Imogen Langrishe, whose purposeless lives reflect the decay of their class; the Langrishe sisters neither work, nor form enduring relationships, nor bear children. The novel begins in 1937 as Helen confronts the failures of her life. In a flashback to 1932, the second section depicts Imogen's ill-fated affair with a thirty-five-year-old German intellectual who occupies one of the lodges on the Langrishe estate. The final section describes Helen's death and burial in 1938 and traces Imogen's growing isolation and despair as she contemplates her own death.

Springfield House, the Langrishe family home, is the archetypal decaying Big House. Its architectural mass, with imposing "high rooms lit up" (Higgins 1966, 93), impresses the outsider as being "well pleased with itself, set apart" (99). Its rooms, however, are dilapidated, stripped of most furniture, or decayed. Only the drawing room, filled with "suffocating screens and cushions," second-rate paintings or copies of paintings of self-reflecting historical events (*The Sacking of Rome* and *Scotland Forever*), can be used for entertaining. The staff has been reduced to one maid, and the Langrishe sisters wallow in their own disorder. The drive is filled with rotting leaves; the tennis court is overgrown; the summer house has collapsed.

Behind all this decay lies the characteristic sloth of the Big House proprietor. Major Langrishe, the "absentee landlord permanently in residence" (17), is the father of four daughters whom he leaves with little inheritance other than his vision of a perfectly idle and passive life.[1] Although Langrishe is a man with a "great dread of mould and decay" (51) who wears suits with mothballs in their pockets, he leads a wasteful and erratic life. Early in his career as a landowner he gives up managing his own estate. In the tradition of the Rackrent landlords, he hands over all control to his land steward and devotes himself to a life of contemplation and study while his property disintegrates. His wife's dour warning that the estate will not last into the third generation is fulfilled. "The inheritance had not come. Offers of marriage had not come. The money they had, it had dwindled away. Where had all the fine life gone to, and what would they do now?" (49). In 1937, when the novel begins, his three living daughters, all middle-aged spinsters, face a life of privation. Helen Langrishe resolves to force her two sisters to confront the social and economic realities before them. "The old impossible world was ending. They would have to sell the house, that was all there was to it. Solicitors, land-agents, undertakers—as they came tramping in, the Langrishe world was falling down" (18).

Writing in the shadow of Joyce, Higgins creates a carefully particularized Anglo-Irish world set, not simply somewhere in the Irish countryside, but in his own birthplace: Celbridge, County Kildare, part of the eighteenth-century Anglo-Irish pale. *Langrishe, Go Down* provides a detailed fictional map of Celbridge; as, for in the course of the novel, Helen and Imogen Langrishe wander through the town, passing its grand architectural monuments, reminders of ascendancy opulence and power. Mentioned again and again are the houses of Celbridge, each with its specific historical associations. Dominating the town, at the end of the main street, is Castletown Conolly, the largest and most influential eighteenth-century house in Ireland, designed by the Florentine architect Galilei in 1719 for Speaker William Conolly. Nearby are Oakley Park and a Gothic abbey, the

---

1. In the autobiographical sketch "Imaginary Meadows" (1983) Higgins's description of his own Catholic childhood at Springfield House in Celbridge evokes many of the characteristics of the Langrishe family. In an unpublished interview on May 2, 1989, he notes that "everything is autobiographical. I don't believe in invented stories," and he reveals that in writing "Killachter Meadow," he changed his brothers into sisters. The appropriation of a fatally incapacitating Anglo-Irish set of behaviors—sloth, improvidence, and passivity, for example—by the Catholic purchasers of the Big House suggests a central irony of *Langrishe, Go Down*, and, of course, of a postcolonial set of aspirations.

home of Esther Vanhomrigh, Swift's Vanessa. A half-mile outside of the town stands Celbridge College, erected by the Conolly family in 1730 and later turned into a girls' school (Craig and the Knight of Glin 1970, 29).

Writing with a Joycean particularity about place and time, Higgins creates a dense pattern of social contexts for his novel. The effect of the piling up of place-names, each with major historical or social resonances, achieves a complex, even kaleidoscopic layering of meaning in the novel, which comes finally to deal with the effect of history itself, as it passes over and destroys individual lives. Far from idealizing the eighteenth-century ascendancy, which left its most golden droppings in Celbridge, *Langrishe, Go Down* entombs that society in its own mausoleums of architectural splendor. Although the novel exists in the shadow of Yeats's myth of Anglo-Irish culture, Higgins never for an instant succumbs to the poet's class aggrandizement; instead, he writes to undermine the myth. "Kildare is a place of follies. Satan himself is reputed to have dined there" (Higgins 1983, 116).

For Helen Langrishe, arriving home from Dublin in a claustrophobic bus filled with the "smells of sweat and stout, of long lain in clothes"—the smells of ordinary working-class men and women—Celbridge's history merges into her personal vision of death. Watching the swiftly passing ascendancy landmarks from the moving bus, she registers her sense of loss.

> Presently they were crossing the bridge at Celbridge. . . . Traveling out between Oakley Park and the abbey. A high pebbledashed wall surmounted by battlements, crowned with ivy, broken glass, overhung by yew boughs. Behind the wall the lawns sloped down to the river, toward a plantation of old trees, gravelled walks by the rivers, shrubberies of rhododendron, laurel, a giant cedar from Japan, Vanessa's bower.
>
> The bus went into low gear at the foot of the hill. A change before death. The wind moaned through the yews beyond the wall. No sign of a living soul. Brief life, she thought, brief life, breathed on for a while, allowed to live, then blotted out. Paisley's corner now. . . . (15–16)

In its most powerful moments *Langrishe, Go Down* describes the loss of historical memory and, even more painfully, depicts a world in which history itself has been transmuted into the debris of civilization. For Stephen Dedalus, history is a nightmare; for Helen Langrishe, history consists of the dead monuments of a dead culture. Like the flow of consciousness that characterizes the protagonists in *Ulysses,* Helen's seemingly random memories and associations are coherent and whole.

In her meditations, particularly in her responses to Anglo-Irish decline, Higgins simultaneously achieves a particularity of reference and a general historical sweep. Standing in the roofless church of Donycomper churchyard, searching aimlessly for the graves of her dead relatives, Helen sees the shards of a distant and more recent history: the partially obliterated inscriptions on family memorials, a font for holy water filled with discolored liquid, a rusting lawnmower once used to maintain the grass, headstones sinking into the lawn. Moving beyond her perception of the particular object to her vaguely recalled sense of the past, she remembers her former ambitions:

> To write a history of the whole area, tracing back the names, the grand estates: Swift and later Grattan at the Abbey, Speaker Conolly at Castletown, Charles Napier at Oakley Park. But nothing had come of this. It all lay in bits and pieces in three big green notebooks. Her grasp of history was poor; she could not assemble the material she had collected, no, not in any coherent way. In the course of years the evidence itself was disappearing back into the ground. (39)

In the cemetery, Helen meets an old gardener, the first in a series of characters who provide inadequate sources of knowledge about the nation's past. She asks him about the age of the church but finds that his personal memories about the gentry living in the abbey and his vague recollections of stories about "a Dutchman . . . Venessy's da . . ." (41) do not fulfill her desire to know history in some systematic way. Although he can reminisce endlessly, "his tongue wagging effortlessly over the history of Ireland," he stares "hopelessly" at her when she asks about the age of the church. He talks with certainty about his personal and local memories—the loss of his son in the Great War, the accidental discovery of the Guinness recipe by a local gardener, the shooting of Michael Collins in the Civil War. On the etymology of Irish names he is helpless; like the old woman in "Telemachus" who delivers milk to Stephen Dedalus and Buck Mulligan, he speaks no Irish. "I was never a hand at the language myself, although the dear Lord knows we had it baiten into us often enough" (Higgins 1966, 40). Although the old man's personal reminiscences cannot provide the information Helen seeks, his garrulous memories remind her of her deracination, of her own inability to grasp the self-conscious wholeness of vision he does not have and need not seek.

> I am under the trees she thought, under the old Donycomper trees. I hear water flowing. It's the Shinkeen flowing by. He called it the Shinkeen. The old man is speaking to me, telling me all over again the history of my home that I never bothered to know; or, if I did by chance know it once, did not bother to remember. He will never stop talking. I hear it all. No doubt irrefutable facts about dead people and places which still exist. I hear it. In my head I hear it. Do I? No, I hear nothing, remember nothing, am nothing. (41)

In Helen's last monologue in the novel, as she lies in bed in 1937, anticipating her death, she moves from her personal vision of mortality to the death of ascendancy culture. She envisions Anglo-Irish history, not as a source of common experience or community, but as a series of disconnected events and buried documents: parliamentary statutes, land deeds, ordnance survey records, land commission files, wills. The history of Anglo-Ireland is a history of disputed land: "Forfeited over and over again since the Anglo Normans. And 74 acres of it mine today—a forgotten battlefield that means nothing to me. Nothing. The grand names and the grand estates. Castletown. Allenscourt. Donycomper where Madame Popoff lives, married to the White Russian. Killadoon where Miss Kitty Clement lives with her mother. The empty Abbey. Oakley Park." (77) Her litany of names and place names leads, not to a recognition of community, but to bewilderment, loss, and despair. In her final epiphany, in which the anguish of her personal history and the nightmare of her nation's history merge, Helen Langrishe perceives her own empty life as the end of Anglo-Ireland. "As it was in the beginning, is now, ever shall be, world without end. Nothing. Invasion after invasion; occupation after occupation. Silent mills, bear testimony. Over-grown ruins, bear silent testimony. Round towers beloved of King John, bear testimony. Disused graveyards, bear testimony. Broken monuments of the

Geraldines, bear testimony. . . . History ends in me. Now. Today."
(77)

The deracination of the Langrishe family has many causes. By
choosing to write within the conventions of a literary form, Higgins
emphasizes the fatedness of his characters' lives as they succumb to a
decline common to Big House landowners. But the Langrishes are
not, in fact, members of an old Anglo-Irish family trapped on an ancestral estate they can no longer maintain. Although the sisters occupy Springfield as if it were an ancestral holding, it is a recently
attained property, purchased by their father: "The moment he saw
Springfield, he wanted it." (54) Thus, the family's occupancy is based
on the unsentimental power of cash, not, as in most Big House novels, on an inherited sense of possession. Although Helen Langrishe
seeks to know something about the history of her home, her information is incomplete—inadequate (Beja 1973, 166). Genealogical
surveys, an obsession of Anglo-Ireland, fail her.

> The house was all about her; there the Warrens had lived, and before
> them the Goughs, and before them Timothy Daly, at the beginning of
> the previous century, according to the Genealogical Office in Dublin
> Castle. And before Timothy Daly, others no doubt, whom she had
> never heard of, for she had not been able to trace the house back to its
> foundations, searching in the Registry Deeds Office in Dublin, in the
> Death Record Office in the Custom House, all to no purpose. (Hig-
> gins 1966, 19)

In their recently purchased estate the Langrishe family replicates
the patterns of life of the traditional landowning class. In spite of her
father's improvidence, Helen remembers that they were "admired
and respected" (19) by their tenants. Imogen recalls how her
mother, a "hard, cold woman" who advised her husband to deal
harshly with his tenants, was eulogized in her obituary as a Big House
lady, "a survival of the dead and gone generation" filled with benevolence and generosity toward the poor (47). Yet, toward the end of
her life their mother converted to Catholicism, as if to acknowledge
the isolation of Anglo-Ireland. Whereas in the seminal Big House
novel, *Castle Rackrent,* the Catholic Irish landowner presumably has
abandoned his faith to retain his land, the twentieth-century Big

House family joins the church of its tenants in search of a community that is denied them.

Helen Langrishe's only moments of peace occur in her fleeting responses to Catholicism when she listens to the Keenans, tenants in the gate lodge, reciting their prayers. "Paternoster by Paternoster, Ave Maria by Ave Maria, Gloria Patri by Gloria Patri, a decade at a time, an oratorio for the voices of the humble, the good in heart. She stood listening. It moved her deeply; it always had. What she was listening to, said in secret, had held the people together, the faith of poor and oppressed Catholic Ireland in the penal times" (17). Yet if the Keenans momentarily represent emotional wholeness, they exist for Helen as an easy, even sentimental, escape from her isolation. Her actual encounters with country people are far less satisfying, and Higgins presents these meetings between the Big House lady and the native Irish with significant irony.

As Helen leaves the cemetery she resents the "ostensibly pious attitude" of the old gardener who cannot speak his native language and who assumes she is a Protestant. "He stared ahead into the gloom, moving his lips, in a rapt pose that spoke for the properness of his faith, the rightness of the scene, the edification of his example" (59). Leaving him, she is further troubled by her meeting with another Irishman, an encounter that mercilessly exposes the mutual deceptions of the landlord–tenant relationship. Greeted by her family's former gardener, Joseph Feeney, she is embarrassed by her own failure to recognize him and by his sentimental recollections of the past. "Sure everything is changed now. . . . Aye, and not altered for the better" (61). Feeney, for example, remembers her beautiful singing voice—"Aye, like a bird"—while she insists that she never sang, but played recordings on her gramophone. "Galli-Curci. John McCormack. What does it matter now? Let him think what he pleases" (62). Between Feeney's need to idealize the Big House and Helen's guilt-ridden fury at his respect emerges a sense of the burden of falsehood represented by their mutual cultural myth making. "Will you let me go? Will you let me be? We are paupers like the rest of you, except we live in a big house, and enjoy credit. But we can't pay our bills anymore. There's nothing to eat in the place except a few maggoty snipe hanging up in the larder. For all the eating we do, we might just as well not eat at all. Porridge and tea, tea and porridge. Heavy old stirabout that lies heavy on the stomach all day. Will you let me go?" (61)

Higgins's version of the Big House antagonist is a complex figure whose background thrusts *Langrishe, Go Down* into modern European history and whose attacks on the Langrishe world reveal how the gentry house becomes emblematic of a dying European culture. Imogen Langrishe's lover is neither Irish nor Catholic; he is, rather, a self-exiled German scholar, a Weimar intellectual who, as Morris Beja suggests (1973, 169), exhibits his fascist leanings in the Big House lodge. Unlike the traditional antagonist, Otto Beck seeks, not to usurp the Langrishe estate, but to exploit it and its owner for his own pleasures. In using Imogen he violates her. Higgins places Otto in the intellectual world of post–World War I Germany with the same exactitude with which he creates the Irish setting of the novel. Otto's cultural attributes—his reading list of existential philosophers, contemporary German fiction, nineteenth-century German writers revived by Weimar culture (Hölderlin and Kleist); the philological thesis topic he is interminably working on; his pictures by Munch; his hostility to his father; his fascination with the animal nature of man—all place him as a postwar German intellectual with ambiguous political leanings (Gay 1970, passim). But his professed "indifference" to (superiority to?) politics, his belief in "culturally superior nations" and "culturally insignificant" individuals (Higgins 1966, 166), his admiration of German higher education and of the teachings of Heidegger all finally suggest those conservative attitudes that lead to extreme right-wing alignments.

Higgins uses dates for telling purposes. Otto enters Imogen's life in 1932, the year of Hitler's overwhelming parliamentary victory in the Reichstag. He speaks with admiration of Heidegger, the philosopher who gave academic respectability to the Teutonic fascination with unreason and death. In 1932 Otto yearns to return to Germany to study with Heidegger, one year before the philosopher gave his notorious address of May 27, 1933, in which, as the first Nationalist Socialist rector of the University of Freiburg, he celebrated the glorious "Role of the University in the New Reich" (Grene 1967, 459). Otto's stated distaste for the Nazis suggests the intellectual's disdain for their boorish violence and anti-Semitism. His lack of homesickness—"Germany is changing. I am well out of it" (Higgins 1966,

209)—suggests, perhaps, his personal fastidiousnes rather than a moral decision.

Otto attacks the Langrishe world not through schemes to possess the family land, but through his sexual and intellectual domination of Imogen. By mastering her, humiliating her, and casting off her aging body when new sexual opportunities arise, he exercises his personal version of Fascist aggression. Higgins surrounds the narrative of the Langrishe decline with newspaper headlines that chronicle stages of Fascist expansion: the arming of Italy, the bombing of Madrid, Franco's speeches on "the destined march of free Spain" (Higgins 1966, 10), the suicide of prominent Austrian anti-Nazi figures at the *Anschluss*. Thus, Otto's depredations against the Langrishe family are set against a larger cultural debacle.

Langrishe, Go Down, like T. S. Eliot's *The Wasteland* or Shaw's *Heartbreak House*, evokes a moribund, flaccid civilization that yearns for violation. Helen Langrishe responds to the newspaper reports of Fascist encroachments with *schadenfreude* rather than with dismay. "Let it be, she thought, let it be. Let it happen, and as violently as possible—with the utmost ferocity. . . . She would not live to see another war" (Higgins 1966, 10). Her sister Imogen yearns to be abused by Otto Beck, her "cruel lover." "I wouldn't mind being his trollop. Him to be cruel to me, as such men are reputed; he could do anything he likes with me. What else is my soft white useless woman's flesh good for? What else?" (91) The dominant imagery in Otto's relationship with Imogen is that of predator of willing prey. "He could see poultry and game only as potential dinners, his eyes on the white breastmeat. And on mine too, she thought" (179). "How he stared at me with famished eyes! He treats me as if I were meat" (208).

In a successful sexual act Otto humiliates his partner: "Once again he had run his quarry to earth" (163). When he fishes for trout, he splits open the stomach of the fish to show Imogen the helpless larvae "twitching in the palm of his hand" (208)—a foreshadowing of her stillborn child. In view of future German policies, Otto's distaste for certain forms of life is ominous. Cutting a wasp in half with a nail scissors he observes, "The human eye cannot allow certain shapes. . . . Very hard to resist the temptation not to stamp on certain shapes, put an end to them" (200). His contempt for Imogen expresses itself in images of sadism, just as her sexual enthrallment to him is revealed through her masochism. "You're so soft, Otto said, staring before him with a vindictive face. Some soft spineless insect that's been trodden on. I can feel you beginning to curl up at the sides" (227).

Otto's social position in the novel suggests the snobbery of the Big House, its fear of gossip, and the imprisoning nature of its class structure. As a slovenly dressed, aging bohemian student, he strikes Imogen as an "upstart" when he talks in a "too familiar manner" with her in a Celbridge store. She creeps into his lodge under cover of night and insists, on their trip to Dublin, that he enter the bus at a different stop. She refuses to take him on a holiday with her: "There would be talk. Had he no idea how small Ireland was?" (205) The social framework for their relationship is that of the Big House lady taking a peasant lover, admitting a poacher into the house of the Irish ascendancy. But Otto first appears to Imogen not just as an upstart who occupies the back lodge rent-free; she imagines him as a satyr-like figure, with a fox's face—a Lawrentian hero, an outsider. "His small-boned body and animal nature suit that first image of him I carried away as a silly girl; a still face staring from among the leaves. Not stepping on a twig, alert and ready to pounce; the fire of life is burning in him" (91).

Otto's dominance asserts itself not in their social relations but in the sexual politics of their affair. He is neither the Lawrentian game-keeper who sexually liberates the Big House lady (although he does do that) nor the scheming agent or gombeen man of earlier Big House novels. He is, rather, the upper-middle-class son of a prosperous German chemical manufacturer and a cultivated Viennese woman with a task for classical music. Growing up in prosperity in Bavaria, Otto was sent to an English boarding school. The misleading social position imposed on him by his bohemian existence and by Imogen's snobbery is reversed, however, by his intellectual subjugation of her. He dominates her, not simply by the force of his sexual presence, but by his mental ascendancy.

> He established his intellectual superiority. Namely that she accept the role that had been given her: that of being unable to contribute anything. He indicated pretty plainly enough that her accomplishments were inadequate. He put questions to her that he knew she could not answer. Then his intolerable sharp pedagoguing. What? *What?*, as though she were a hopelessly backward student. In that rea-

soning she began to feel no better than a whore; all that she was good
for was to be made love to. (231)

Using his intellect to brutalize Imogen Otto achieves an absolute reversal of the social roles she has imposed on their relationship. The Big
House lady is subjugated by the sadistic poacher who bewilders her
with his facts and exposes her ignorance of her own Anglo-Irish history.

—The Pale, Otto said. The English Pale. The Plantagenets. We're
lying in the middle of their bloody fields. This is Pale ground . . .
—Dublin, Meath, Kildare, where else? four counties. Offaly isn't it? he
said, wiping his eyes.
Yes, it would be Offaly.
—No, not Offaly—Louth. Dublin, Kildare, Meath, Louth. You are an
ignoramus, dear.
—It's true, she admitted. I am an ignoramus. (175)

Otto's information about Ireland provides, on one level, the lost
history of their country that Helen Langrishe seeks and that Imogen
is shamed into acknowledging she lacks. But finally, his facts, his
anecdotes about historical events, his etymologies of Irish words, his
knowledge of Celtic mythology and folklore are merely recondite
data—the mechanical overflow of his scholarship. It is during her
moments of self-assertion, when Imogen reacts with fury to his intellectual domination, that she responds most accurately to him. Otto
uses knowledge to obscure or to dominate, not to illuminate. "His
fondness for explaining the unknown by the still less known, *ignotum
per ignotius,* he says, what's that but a cloud of words, self-indulgence
and nothing more?" (230) History as a living tradition does not exist
in *Langrishe, Go Down.* In Higgins's bleak vision of modern Ireland,
Joseph Feeney's limited personal reminiscences, Helen Langrishe's
poorly recalled images of Anglo-Irish documents and monuments,
and Otto Beck's pedantic scholarship all represent modes of isolation from the past.

What consolation does Otto leave the Big House lady freed from
her sterile virginity? Although one reader argues that, if Imogen is
dominated, "she is also awoken from an inertia which is more destructive" (Baneham 1983, 174), Imogen's "awakening" is achieved
at great cost. Her final attempt to regain her self-respect as Otto bicy-

cles off to his next mistress is neither "liberating" rage nor effective self-assertion. Shooting at her lover with her father's gun, which Otto appropriated for his poaching on the Langrishe demesne, she not only misses him, but is struck by terror and guilt. Soon afterward, she begins to drink heavily. The product of their affair is a stillborn child who exists in her consciousness as a prehistoric monster, a deformed thing with the head and shoulders of a man, resembling a cement mold dug up out of the ground by Otto's spade—"its blank eye sockets, heavy presence, dismembered body." Her flaccid muscle "didn't hold" its burden: "The stitches undone . . . whole thing came away . . . flood of dead matter" (248). The Big House is truly undone.

John Banville

Although Aidan Higgins is strongly influenced by the techniques and themes of literary modernism, *Langrishe, Go Down* retains many of the conventions of traditional mimetic fiction. Like earlier Anglo-Irish novelists, Higgins exposes the shabby realities behind illusions about ascendancy life in the Irish countryside. But exploiting the conventions of a traditional form only to subvert them, John Banville examines the process by which such historical mythologies and illusions are themselves created and sustained. In both *Birchwood,* a gothic parody of the Big House novel, and in *The Newton Letter,* an epistolary exploration of fantasies about Anglo-Irish culture, Banville plays with the central archetype of the Big House. In these works, fixed patterns of response engendered by conventions signal human misperception and distortion of a reality, which can, in fact, never be known. An insistent memory, "beady-eyed and voracious" (1984b, 52), invents versions of truth that the novels relentlessly deconstruct. In *Birchwood* and *The Newton Letter* a self-professed international writer revives a parochial Irish form to insist, as he does in all of his works, that "truth in fact does not exist, that there are only workable versions of the truth we contract to believe in" (Banville 1981a, 8).

Birchwood

Banville notes that Americans bought 10,000 copies of *Birchwood* because Irish Americans "mistook it for a novel about the Big House" (1982, 414). Even without his ironic warning, the sophisticated reader of modernist and postmodernist literature recognizes that *Birchwood* is not really about a Big House at all; it is, rather, a novel about subjectivity and despair, about ways of knowing and remembering, about form rather than content, and thus about the writing of fiction. This postmodernist text is presented by a self-reflecting narrator whose remarks about his memories of the events he recounts turn our attention from the content of the book to the process of creating it. Readers have interpreted it as an internationalist, antimimetic, experimental piece of metafiction—and as a parody of the Big House novel (Deane 1975–76; Imhof 1989, 53; Molloy 1981, 41).

Banville repudiates the concepts of personal, national, or realistic fiction. He tests the trusting relationship between author and reader established by the realistic nineteenth-century novel and challenges his audience to accept the fictionality of plot and the primacy of form over content. "Content, I would maintain, is an aspect of form, no more" (Banville 1981a, 5). Just as he rejects a literature of self-expression—"Forgive me—but when I hear the term *self expression* applied to art, I reach for my revolver" (1981b, 15)—Banville subverts the premises of traditional realistic fiction, which assume that a subjective narration can reveal the world, the thing in itself. "To me, this kind of art is truly subversive, truly destructive" (1981b, 16). Finally, he rejects a national literature in favor of an international one. "I never really thought about Irish literature as such. I don't really think that specifically 'national' literatures are of terribly great significance" (1982, 408).

Repudiating so many premises of nineteenth- and early twentieth-century Big House fiction (realism, national literature, literature emerging from personal historical situations), Banville nevertheless reconfigures them through parody. In *Birchwood* he plays with familiar tropes—the decaying house, the disputed inheritance, the irresponsible and improvident landlord, and the threatening intruders—but tosses in, he tells us, stock characters and literary strands from other traditions as well—"the quest, the lost child, the doppelganger" (1981a, 11)—as though to emphasize the inclusiveness of his metaliterary enterprise. But if, in writing *Birchwood*, Banville turns to conventional literary forms in order to dissolve and then reinvent them, he is strikingly aware of the implications of the forms he recalls and exploits. His version of the Big House novel is, in a significant way, a fulfillment of the tradition as well as a parody and subversion of it.

Most novels of ascendancy life revolve around a paradox that Banville's reinvention of the form faces more directly than does the earlier fiction. His preoccupation with the ways in which memory fails to recreate reality and instead reinvents subjective versions of the past suggests how *Birchwood* comes closer than any other work in the tradition to exposing the illusions of Big House culture. "We imagine that we remember things as they were, while in fact all we carry into the future are fragments which reconstruct a wholly ilusionary past" (1984a, 12). In *Birchwood* the Big House is an object of contemplation, the focus for the act of memory, the possession at once prized and perpetually threatened—to some extent by family intrigue and by political turmoil, but primarily by memory itself. Banville's radical reworking of the Big House form transforms a literary symbol of political and economic loss into a haunting image of the failure of memory and the inaccessibility of the past. *Birchwood* charts the incapacity of the mind to grasp anything more tangible than the relentlessly subjective response to an elusive reality. "Often now, late at night, or working in the house on rainy days, I feel something soft and persistent pressing in on me, and with sadness and joy I welcome back this scene, or others like it suffused with summer and silence, another world. Forgetting all I know, I try to describe these things, and only then do I realize, yet again, that the past is incommunicable" (29).

The ultimate inaccessibility of the past, its haunting control of the present, and the subjectivity (and distortion) with which its images are transmitted by an inaccurate memory are central concerns in *Birchwood*. Epistemological issues about the possibility of knowing and remembering, which reveal Banville's preoccupations with the major philosophical questions of modernist fiction, are fully developed in his subsequent novels, *Doctor Copernicus* and *Kepler*. But these topics are not just international modernist themes; they are also central preoccupations of Irish culture. For all Banville's repudiations of a national literature in favor of an international one, *Birchwood* is a strikingly Irish novel, not just because it is set amidst the gothic mythologies of the nation's history, but also because it describes—even takes as its thematic center—the process by which personal and historical mythologies are themselves created.

Every society generates and acts upon particular national myths, but the controlling power of such images to transmit the past into the present is especially compelling in Irish culture. The symbol of Mother Ireland and the myth of sacrificial martyrdom (evoked during the 1981 hunger strikes at Long Kesh Prison) represent traditional images of nationalist Ireland. Similarly, for Anglo-Ireland, the vision of a Big House aristocracy and of a feudal bond between landlord and tenant embodies the tropes of a cultural mythology rather than, necessarily, historical actualities. To demythologize cultural history is to subject the pieties of particular groups to scrutiny—as Sean O'Casey does to nationalist ideologies of blood sacrifice in *The Plough and the Star* and as countless Big House novelists do to pretensions of aristocratic life in the Irish countryside. Although other novelists, such as Edgeworth, Lever, Le Fanu, and Somerville, expose the content of Anglo-Irish mythology, Banville considers the very process by which such perceptions of history are created.

In *Birchwood* the physical solidarity of the symbolic, decaying Big House, which is so carefully presented in the previous novels of the tradition, dissolves into a pattern of personal evocation. The house is seldom described, but it is obsessively recalled and lamented—with the focus always on the self-consciously literary angle of vision in the act of recollection, rather than on the object that is lost. The "second silent world" that exists outside subjectivity is unattainable; if seeing occurs through a prism, then there is, finally, no difference between seeing and imagining, between history and subjectivity.

> Such scenes as this I see, or imagine I see, no difference, through a glass sharply. The light is lucid, steady, and does not glance in spikes or stars from bright things, but shines in cool cubes, planes and violent lines and lines within planes, as light trapped in polished crystal will shine. Indeed, now that I think of it, I feel it is not a glass through which I see, but rather a gathering of perfect prisms. There is hardly any sound, except for now and then a faint ringing chime, or a distant twittering, strange, unsettling. Outside my memories this silence and harmony, this brilliance I find again in that second silent world which exists, independent, ordered by unknown laws, in the depths of mirrors. This is how I remember such scenes. If I provide something otherwise than this, be assured that I am inventing. (21)

The narrator obsessively searches for a certainty about the past that eludes him; reconstructing the past is a necessary task, "since all thinking is in a sense remembering" (11). Again and again, Banville reminds us of his narrator's reactions to his discoveries; the subjectivity of the book intrudes so powerfully that it floods and finally dominates the things remembered. "I had dreamed of the house so often on my travels that now it refused to be real, even while I stood among its ruins. It was not Birchwood of which I had dreamed, but a dream of Birchwood, woven out of bits and scraps" (12).

This retrospective novel about a self-consciously Proustian search for identity through memory takes as its structure a quest theme; the narrator, Gabriel Godkin, is convinced throughout much of the book of the existence of a lost twin sister; his search becomes an image of his incompleteness. Instead of discovering his longed-for sister, Gabriel learns that he is the incestuous child of his father and his aunt, and that his twin is no distant forsaken sister—an elusive dream child—but his sly, brutal "cousin," Michael, who seeks to dispossess him of the family estate. Again and again, the fantasies of love, of beauty, or of fulfillment dissolve into the horror of dispossession and violence.

Birchwood begins, appropriately, with a section entitled "The Book of the Dead"; in this first section of the novel Gabriel recalls his childhood among the mad or eccentric members of his family and reconstructs the "new mythologies" that his childhood perceptions have created. The past is dominated by the specters of relatives who have met death violently—through fire, explosion, madness, or murder. The image of a dignified, patriarchal gentry family life evoked by the Georgian architecture of ascendancy culture dissolves into a vision that alternates between gothic horror and comic excess. "Ruin and slaughter and blood, brickdust, a million blades of shattered glass, the rooftree splintering—the poppies! Suddenly I see them, like a field of blood!" (24) Although the narrator once refers to the "magnificent" house amidst its "quiet grandeur" (70), Birchwood is no object of longing for his family; the house is a "baroque madhouse" to his father and a "kind of desert, bleak, magnificent, alien" (15) to his gentle mother, who is finally driven to caged madness by her life there.

The stylistic elegance of Banville's prose, his frequent allusions to other literary texts in the course of the novel (to Descartes, Dante, and Proust for example, in the first few pages), his creation of scenes that reverberate as set pieces in the novel all remind us of the primacy of imagination in the act of recollection. In *Birchwood*, to remember is to generate fictions. Through a kaleidoscope of gothic scenes, Gabriel recalls (creates) characters from his childhood who are, for the most part, larger-than-life grotesque monsters: his sneering, tiger-eyed, drunken father; his grandmother, whose jealousy and rage kill her in a Dickensian scene of spontaneous combustion—". . . the ashes on the wall, that rendered purplish mass on the chair, Granny Godkin's two feet, all that was left of her, in their scorched button boots" (77). The equally surreal death of the wizened and demented Granda Godkin is precipitated by his collision with a fleeing peasant carrying the dead fowl he has poached. Granda's "mind was forever frozen in that moment of collision and clatter, feathers and blood, when that furious winged great creature had flung itself upon him in the dawning garden" (55). "Aunt" Martha, Gabriel's secret mother, who schemes to disinherit him in favor of his twin, her acknowledged son, dies in an unforgettable moment of stylized gesture as she attempts to save Michael from a fire. "Her dress burst into flames, and she trotted on through the door. Her wild, ululating cry was the perfect counterpart of her rippling figure as it drifted, so it seemed, slowly, dreamily, wrapped in an aureole of light, into the furnace" (97). In such scenes memory and imagination coalesce.

Banville plays with many conventions of the Big House form, always, as Francis Molloy notes, with careful attention to the verifiability of the historical details of Irish life (1981, 42). The struggle to retain possession of the land, the major conflict of the nineteenth- and early twentieth-century Anglo-Irish novel, runs as a leitmotif through *Birchwood*. The history of the estate includes the dispossession of the improvident Lawless family during the nineteenth-century Famine and the seizure of the house through marriage by a brutal but efficient Godkin landlord. In Gabriel's youth during the twentieth-century Civil War new intruders threaten the Godkins, who have evolved into eccentric gentry landlords, involuntarily selling off property to their old enemies, the Lawlesses. (The names of the landlords—Lawless and Godkin—again insist on the self-conscious artifice of this fiction.)

In his evocation of the decaying estate Banville often echoes descriptions from earlier novels in the genre. The Godkins' "genteel slide toward penury" is evident everywhere: ". . . in the cracked paint and the missing tiles, the dry rot that ate its way unchecked across the floors and up the stairs" (Banville 1984a, 49). But through carefully presented descriptions that undercut any possibility of an elegiac response to the demise of a house and of a civilization, Banville turns his novel into macabre parody rather than into another mimetic notation of decline. When the schoolroom ceiling collapses, Gabriel and Michael discover ". . . up in the rotten cavity, a decayed hanging forest of rank green growths stirring like seaweed in the swell of the cross draughts. We locked away that horrible aquarium, and in the morning Papa's headache would allow no mention of catastrophe. Two boards in the lavatory floor crumbled to dust under him on a silent Sunday morning, leaving him perched on the bowl, instantly constipated, his feet and crumpled trousers dangling above an abyss" (69).

As in earlier novels, the world of Catholic Ireland hovers at the borders of the demesne, covetously eyeing the fading spoils of a decaying culture. Gabriel's dispassionate assessment of relations between the Big House and the tenantry undercuts any sentimental evocation of feudal bonds. The carefully controlled tone of the passage warns against any elegizing of ascendancy decline.

> The final proof, the clincher, as they say, that the Godkins were going the way of all the gentry, that is down, was the newfound boldness of the peasants. As my people knew, and lucky they did, there is nothing that will keep the Irish in their place like a well-appointed mansion. They may despise and hate you, only put a fine big house with plenty of windows in it up on a hill and bejapers you have them be the balls, stunned into a cringing, cap-touching coma. But beware. It is a fragile thraldom. The first unmended fence will mean the first snigger behind your back outside the chapel yard, an overrun garden will bring them grinning to the gate, and roof left in visible disrepair will see them poaching your land in daylight. (49–50)

With neither the snobbish condescension nor the guilt with which his Anglo-Irish predecessors conceived of Catholic Ireland, Banville presents the intruders at Birchwood as remote, ominous forces. Representing threats too fearful to be acknowledged by the Big House, these mysterious and purposeful men and women maintain their aloofness as they invade the demesne. In this fiction the forces of dispossession are not moneygrubbing parvenus, like Edgeworth's Jason Rackrent or Somerville's Dr. Mangan, but are instead nameless hordes. Like Elizabeth Bowen's young man in a trenchcoat who strides through the Danielstown demesne, Banville's intruders are indifferent, impersonal in their hostility, and thus relentless, fearless, and implacable.

> Poachers were one thing, but more sinister by far were those other intruders who began to appear, mysterious wanton creatures glimpsed across the lake, or trailing down the fields toward the beach, a crowd of them, five or six, moving through the woods at dusk. The curious thing is that no one spoke of them, although we all must have seen them unless we were subject to visions. It was as if their presence were an embarrassment. . . . They were like people at the far end of a room bent in unheard laughter whose private joke invests them with an impenetrable self-possession. It seemed impossible that they feared god or man, and perhaps it was their lack of fear which frightened us, for indeed we were afraid of them. (52)

Despite Banville's attention to the authenticity of historical detail in his allusions to the past, political Ireland exists here less as social reality, more as another metaphor of violence, instability, and loss. As one critic insists, the anachronistic universe of *Birchwood* is "a timeless one which does not coincide with any one historical period" (Imhof 1989, 70). Banville telescopes time and space in the second section of the novel, as if to remind his reader once more of the imagination's freedom to invent its own mythologies and to choose, from among the brutal images of Irish history, those moments that best suit a fictional purpose. In search of his lost sister, Gabriel joins a mysterious magic circus and moves from the early twentieth-century civil war period at Birchwood to the horrors of the nineteenth-century Famine in the Irish countryside. Finally, as if unconscious of secret purpose or direction, he returns to the ravaged family estate. There, in a wildly melodramatic convergence of a multitude of plot strands, the invading Lawless family is slaughtered by the members of the circus, in collusion with Gabriel's brother and the early nineteenth-century Irish revolutionary group the Molly Maguires. Banville's commentary on the ending of the novel is instructive, revealing, as it does, it his subversion of the notion of a well-made plot. "I like the end of *Birchwood,* where everything is wrapped up and nothing is wrapped up" (1981a, 1).

Violence in one world parallels that in another; the decaying Big House and the sinister circus are oddly similar, one presided over by Gabriel's charming, duplicitous father, the other by the manipulative ringmaster, Silas, who genially rules his "collapsible kingdom." Life offers Gabriel no sanctuary, as disappointments and betrayals pursue him. The magnificent Big House crumbles with internal rot and is infiltrated by the schemes of his secret brother; the circus's well-publicized wild animals consist of a "melancholy tubercular grey monkey in a birdcage" and a glassy-eyed stuffed tiger. Victimized and savage women exist in both worlds: Gabriel's gentle mother and his scheming "Aunt" Martha at Birchwood, the brutally raped and murdered Ida and the vicious Sybil at the circus. The grotesque death of Granny Godkin by spontaneous combustion at Birchwood is echoed by the death of the old circus woman Angel, whose wounded body balloons up and "pour[s] itself into every nook in the caravan" (1984a, 163–64).

The picaresque quality of Gabriel's travels conveys a love of place and land, recalling his earlier evocation of a lost childhood. In *Birchwood* the dream world is particularized and localized, always transformed into the landscape of Ireland that is longingly invoked by the dispossessed. As he travels, Gabriel creates new images of possibility, new "mythical horizon[s]" that hover before his eyes: "the land, revolving in great slow circles around our slowly moving center, the sad land, the lovely land" (125).

Concluding his circular journey of self-discovery at Birchwood, Gabriel is left stripped of old illusions. Alone on the battlefield—an empty "white landscape"—and surrounded by slaughtered bodies, he realizes that although his fantasies of a lost sister and a god-like Prospero are destroyed, his future is clear. Clinging to Birchwood, because "outside is destruction and decay," the author of new mythologies and new fictions is born. *Birchwood* itself is his creation: "and so I became my own Prospero, and yours" (1984a, 172).

The return to Birchwood suggests the failure of purposeful action in the external world and a recognition that only through art, through the creation of new fictions and new mythologies, can Gabriel survive. *Birchwood* subverts the notion that political progress or action will free the individual from the burden of the past. Journeys go nowhere, history is circular; only the land and the places of Ireland remain, scarred by recurring brutalities. Seamus Deane complains about the persistence in modern Ireland of false imagery of the ascendancy class (1985, 31–32). *Birchwood* suggests, however, that only by debunking, and then reinventing the imagery of the past, do new forms emerge.

The Newton Letter

In *Birchwood,* Banville invokes the gradual dispossession of the landlords, putting his narrator within the Anglo-Irish culture as the heir apparent of the Big House in both its nineteenth and twentieth-century permutations. In *The Newton Letter,* however, the unnamed contemporary narrator speaks from outside that culture, articulating, with great self-consciousness, the outsider's fantasies about a remote and glamorous survival of ascendancy life. This perspective on the Big House allows Banville to engage in yet another sort of parody of the literary convention.

The narrator-protagonist of the *The Newton Letter* impulsively rents a lodge on the demesne of Ferns, seemingly an Anglo-Irish Big House, occupied by Edward and Charlotte Lawless, their niece Ottilie, and a child, Michael.

> I had them spotted for patricians from the start. The big house, Edward's tweeds. Charlotte's fine-boned slender grace that the dowdiest of clothes could not mask, even Ottilie's awkwardness, all this seemed the unmistakable stamp of their class. Protestants, of course, landed, the land gone now to gombeen men and compulsory purchase, the family fortune wasted by tax, death duties, inflation. But how bravely, how beautifully they bore their losses! Observing them, I understood that breeding such as theirs is a preparation not for squiredom itself, but for that distant day, which for the Lawlesses had arrived, when the trappings of glory are gone and only style remains. . . . Shorn of the dull encumbrances of wealth and power, they were free to be purely what they were. (1984b, 20–21)

Ferns and its occupants become the fulcrum, as it were, for a virtual array of fantasies, an endlessly generated series of visions of a totally unstable reality that exists solely for the purpose of generating yet new fantasies, new versions of its shifting center. The narrator's misperceptions of the human scenery at Ferns provide a steady stream of inventions in the novel. The lodge becomes a sentry box, allowing him to gaze at the Big House with "remote prurience" as members of the household trudge to work or to school, all metamorphosed in his eyes into a literary genre piece. "It all had the air of a pastoral mime, with the shepherd's wife and the shepherd, and Cupid and the maid, and scribbling within a crystal cave, myself, a haggard-eyed Damon" (20).

Like *Birchwood, The Newton Letter* is written retrospectively, not as another memoir, but as the narrator's letter to Clio, his "teacher," "friend," and "inspiration" (10). With growing disinclination, this obsessively literary narrator recounts his struggles to write a historical study of Isaac Newton. Clio's name, as well as her role in his life, suggests her relationship to the muse of history—a discipline whose legitimacy is subverted by his fictional treatment of Newton's life. Writing her from somewhere in the frigid tundra where he has retreated in disgrace to a new academic post, the unnamed narrator-protagonist appropriately tells Clio the restrospective story of his failure of love and sympathy. He reveals that while at Ferns, he turned in his writing to a period of breakdown and despair in his subject's life. With his major discoveries behind him, the great Newton had found himself more and more obsessed with the meaninglessness of his life's work and with his desire, not to write scientific treatises, but to discover some new way of knowing the ordinariness of life. "The language in which I might be able not only to write but to think is neither Latin nor English, but a language none of whose words is known to me; a language in which commonplace things speak to me" (59). (Characteristically, Banville tells us in a note that Newton's obsession, which is supposedly taken from a letter he wrote in 1693, is in fact fictitious, based on yet another literary text, *The Letter of Lord Chandos* by the early twentieth-century romantic symbolist poet and dramatist Hugo von Hofmannsthal.) The narrator's incapacity to continue with his own study of Newton coincides with a personal crisis resembling that of his subject. He begins to question the celebration of Newton as heroic deliverer of reason and science to a medieval world, and turns instead to "another kind of truth" (30).

The purported "truth" the narrator embraces, involved with the ordinary happenings of the world about him, leads him into a loveless affair with the passionate and awkward Ottilie, an unconsummated infatuation with her aunt Charlotte, and a series of misperceptions of reality. Abandoning the landscape of scientific and historical knowledge, he enters the territory of emotional need; burdened by his own literary delusions, he fails miserably to negotiate its terrain. He constructs a complex fantasy about the inhabitants of Ferns, who are in actuality stained with ordinary human troubles—cancer, depression, and unrequited love—rather than with the special and, for him, more interesting traits of alcoholism, aristocratic reserve, and incest. "I dreamed up a horrid drama, and failed to see the commonplace tragedy that was playing itself out in real life" (90).

Edward Lawless is misperceived alternately as a drunken lout, a social-climbing parvenu, and an incestuous violator of his wife's niece (and, thus the father of the child, Michael). In fact, he is merely a desperate man dying of stomach cancer, drinking to assuage his fears, whose attempts to communicate with the narrator are scornfully rejected. Charlotte, the object of a "passion of the mind" (53), appears as the remote, unrequited love, *die ferne Geliebte* (51), who is so ethereal that "her physical presence itself seemed overdone, a clumsy representation of the essential she" (52). Obsessively, the narrator perceives her as a cultural artifact, as a Cranach painting or as Yeats's vision of the Gore-Booth sisters in "In Memory of Eva Gore-Booth and Con Markiewicz"—a poem about an archetypal twentieth-century Big House, Lissadell. "I stopped to watch her, the dark glossy head, the pale neck, and those hands that now, instead of Ottilie's, seemed to be in mine. Light of evening, the tall windows—Oh, a gazelle!" (48) Charlotte's patrician manner seems so extreme, her face so "empty of all save a sense of something withheld" (22–23), that he imagines her as remotely existing behind a glass barrier. The anticlimactic revelation, that Charlotte's aristocratic reserve is the product of a steady dose of tranquilizers, brings a cold taste of ashes to the narrator's mouth. "Something had ended, with a vast soft crash" (85).

Banville's allusions in his novel to Goethe's *Elective Affinities* (the characters in the novel, for example, have the same names as Goethe's) suggest how *The Newton Letter,* like *Birchwood,* calls attention to itself as a literary artifact, as a self-conscious creation rather than as a mimetic representation. In Goethe's novel about early nineteenth-century German gentry life, Charlotte's husband Eduard

is fatally attracted to his wife's niece Ottilie. Only the deaths of Eduard and Ottilie resolve the pain of renounced passion that ravages
the socially sanctioned loyalties of marriage. On virtually every level
of plot and theme, Banville creates similarities between the two
works to emphasize their differences. Goethe's protagonist inhabits a
world of patrician leisure and somewhat decadent refinement that
The Newton Letter's narrator mistakenly perceives at Ferns. Goethe's
upper-class characters spend vast sums of money to move mountains
and reconstruct lakes to improve their views; the occupants of Ferns
are, in reality, native Irish Catholics who run a garden nursery business in the greenhouses behind the Big House. Their meals run to
cold cuts and limp lettuce served on a plastic tablecloth in the
kitchen, rather than in the "gaunt dining-room, [with] linen napkins
with a faded initial, a bit of old silver . . . " (25) that the narrator's literary imagination postulates.

When Goethe's Eduard sleeps with his wife Charlotte, "imagination at once asserted its rights over reality," and he holds Otillie in his
arms (Goethe 1971, 106). Banville's narrator, on the other hand,
makes vigorous love with his Otillie, but conjures up his beloved
Charlotte as a substitution. In one of the most effectively derivative
scenes in the novel, Banville transforms Goethe's gentle vision of the
imagination's capacity, at least temporarily, to satisfy unrequited
physical longings into a great comic portrayal of an overliteral working out of such fantasy.

> At first I had conjured Charlotte's presence to be only witness to
> the gymnastics in my narrow bed, to lean over us, Ottilie and me, with
> the puzzled attention of a pure spirit of the night, immune herself to
> the itch of the flesh yet full of tenderness for these sad mortals strug-
> gling among the sheets, but as time went on this ceased to be enough,
> the sprite had to fold her delicate wings, throw off her silken wisps,
> and, with a sigh of amused resignation, join us. Then in the moon-
> light, my human girl's blonde hair would turn black, her fingers pale,
> and she would become something new, neither herself nor the other,
> but a third—Charlottilie! (Banville 1984b, 57)

Negotiating *The Newton Letter* becomes an act of literary detective
work; in making such demands it is, of course, a quintessentially
modernist production. On its surface the novel appears to be a
straightforward narrative, but once its sources are integrated it be-

comes a many-layered puzzle. Each major allusion emphasizes the deluded narrator's quandary, for each undercuts and parodies his attempt to know and respond to what he hopelessly assumes is a stable reality. His biographical research on Newton unveils the great scientist's rejection of the physical laws by which he had given form to reality in favor of a visionary spiritual world. Goethe's *Elective Affinities,* a novel about tragic passion and infatuation in a landed gentry class, underscores the triviality of the narrator's philandering. The traditional Big House fiction that lies behind his own experiences misinforms and deludes him. Misreading the Anglo-Irish experience, he misperceives his world and substitutes a spurious and delusionary glamour for the painful tragedies of ordinary life. Even the false source in the novel, Newton's fictionalized second letter, conveys the twentieth century's radical skepticism about interpretation and suggests the inadequacy of language to convey experiences. Finally, the narrator of *The Newton Letter* faces the same Wittgensteinian despair about the possibility of arriving at any understanding of the world that Gabriel Godkin experiences at the end of *Birchwood,* a novel that concludes with a passage from *Tractatus logico-philosophicus:* ". . . and whereof I cannot speak, thereof I must be silent" (Banville 1884a, 175). Questioning the very possibility of meaningful recollection and interpretation, Banville offers a radical critique of a literary tradition that straddles the worlds of history and of imaginative literature.

Conclusion

Like the Celtic cross and the round tower, the Irish country house has become an iconographic staple of tourist board promotional campaigns rather than an imperial interloper in the countryside. As tourism is increasingly accepted as the nation's major industry, a growing recognition of the commercial value of Ireland's architectural heritage has encouraged efforts to stay further destruction of ascendancy estates, despite any lingering remnants of political hostility to them.[1] The demands of a growing tourist economy should continue to preserve many Big Houses as luxury hotels or heritage centers for the whole nation—notwithstanding the costs of preservation.

The avid commodification of country house imagery in recent years,[2] however, reflects and elaborates a misleadingly ahistorical presentation of gentry residences by preservationists. Whereas the ar-

---

1. In his preface to *Vanishing Country Houses of Ireland,* a photographic catalog of country house ruins, Noel Grove Annesley suggests that "Ireland can ill afford to neglect its tourist attractions" (Knight of Glin, Griffin, and Robinson 1989, 1). In a subsequent introductory essay readers are again reminded of the key role of country houses in the tourist industry. In "Wasting Assets" Nicholas K. Robinson informs us that 30 percent of tourists in Ireland "visited historic country houses and gardens, while a mere 15 percent engaged in fishing and 8 percent in golf" (6).

2. Ralph Lauren has become, according to the *New York Times*'s architectural critic, the "ultimate life-style purveyor, the ultimate producer of a completely packaged perfect life" (Goldberger 1992, 1). Paul Goldberger describes the interior of Lauren's corporate headquarters in a sleek glass skyscraper on Madison Avenue as resembling the library of a great country house more perfectly wrought "than anything that exists in the real world"; Lauren's conservative reinvention of the past is a "fantasy of escape into a past, rendered more perfect than the real past ever was" (34). The designer/decorator's motifs have a pervasive colonial cast: Scottish manor houses, African safaris, Caribbean beach houses (32).

chitecture, furnishings, paintings, and gardens of Anglo-Irish Big Houses represent significant achievements of the ascendancy culture, the display of these estates solely as collections of aesthetic artifacts isolates a social and economic phenomenon from its own history. Because the strongest voices for preservation emerge from financially besieged proprietors of these houses, an element of self-interest in a rapidly expanding heritage industry is perhaps inevitable.[3] But to separate the gentry estate as agent of imperial domination of the countryside from its status as aesthetic object worth preserving is to dehistoricize and misread it. The quality of most country house tourism in Ireland, nevertheless, follows the model of the British National Trust. Big Houses in Ireland are valued and interpreted as aesthetic masterworks, as showcases of the art collections, plaster work, furnishings, and architecture of the gentry. Their economic and social roles in the colonial system are left unexplored.[4]

Country house tourism in Ireland was transformed in May 1994 with the opening of a famine museum at an Anglo-Irish Big House in Strokestown, County Roscommon. By juxtaposing an imposing Palladian mansion with the narrative of the mid-nineteenth-century Great Famine on its estate, Luke Dodd, the museum's founder and curator, situated the ascendancy house squarely in the colonial his-

3. David Cannadine's observations about conservative preservationist impulses in Britain serve as a useful reminder of the dangers facing any heritage industry. "The committees of the great preservationist societies were—and still are—groaning beneath the weight of great grandees. The idea of a 'national' heritage which is somehow 'threatened' and must be 'saved' is sometimes little more than a means of preserving an essentially elite culture by claiming—quite implausibly—that it is really everybody's. The claim is usually accompanied by a highly value-laden version of the past, not so much history as myth" (1985, 17).

4. A 1994 pocket guide for tourists—*Irish Country Houses*—describes Big Houses in Ireland as "splendid surviving testimony to the confidence and rich culture of generations of Ireland's ruling families" (5). In its short background paragraph it also highlights the "remarkable quality and distinctive character of eighteenth- and nineteenth-century Irish craft" and regrets the "tragic loss of so many country houses over the past seventy years" (Reeves-Smyth 1994, 5). Although a report of the Irish American Partnership briefly acknowledges the political and social history of the Big House, it foregrounds its aesthetic importance as cultural shrine. "The great house is a *tour de force* display of the highest creative skills of the architect, builder, stucco worker, stone mason and wood carver. Together with its contents and setting it encompasses almost the entire skill range of higher human achievement. They are living cultural shrines often intertwined with a rich tapestry of political and social history" (quoted in McDowell 1992, 291).

tory of Ireland. A visit to the two Strokestown Park House sites—the domestic mansion and the Famine Museum in its stables—rapidly dispels the mythologies of Yeats's aristocratic ascendancy culture and substitutes a disturbing narrative of undercapitalized and exploitative Anglo-Irish land policy and local governance. In 1847, while evicting more tenants than in all of County Cork that year, the Strokestown landlord devised and implemented a more "humane" plan to rid himself of eight hundred starving famine victims on his estate. He paid for their passage to Canada on ill-equipped ships, on which about one-half of the passengers died (Campbell 1994, 41–42). The landlord's subsequent murder late in the year, reportedly celebrated with bonfires by his Strokestown tenants (49), shocked Britain and was the subject there of a parliamentary debate.[5]

The exhibits at Strokestown Park House and Famine Museum scrutinize the domestic economy of the gentry landlord as he interacted with his tenants during the nineteenth century. But that political agenda is not accompanied by a denial of Strokestown's significance for art historians. The preservation of the Big House highlights its monumental Palladian architecture and affirms the lasting value of ascendancy domestic ambition even as it exposes its

5. The version of the role of the Famine-era landlord offered at Strokestown's museum differs strikingly from that narrative offered by several Big House novelists. Bowen, Somerville, and Trevor describe the self-sacrifice, sometimes to death, that was the gentry's response to the Famine. In *Bowen's Court* the mistress of the estate presides over a soup kitchen in the basement of the Big House where "her work was exhausting, relentless, impersonal" (Bowen 1979, 308). In *The Big House of Inver* Jas Prendeville's mother dies of famine fever after setting up a soup kitchen and arranging for a shipment of American maize to feed her starving tenants. Somerville refers to "the martyrdoms, and the heroisms, and the devotion" of such landlord families (1978, 18–19). (As I point out on page 133, Somerville's clearest source for the Prendeville family in this novel is the St. George family in Galway. The St. Georges, in fact, were forced to defend themselves against charges of "relentless severity" toward their tenantry during the Great Famine.) In Trevor's *Fools of Fortune* Anna Quinton begs her English relatives to persuade "this most monstrous of governments" (Trevor 1984, 75) to save the starving Irish and also dies of famine fever after distributing grain and flour to her dying tenants. Her devoted husband obeys her wish that he "must give away the greater part of his estate to those who had suffered loss and deprivation in the Famine" (1984, 13). Only in Jennifer Johnston's *The Gates* do we fleetingly hear of landlords, like the historical Mahons of Strokestown, who used the Famine as an opportunity to rid themselves of unwanted tenants. "Nature, on the side of England's statesmen, solved their problems caused by Irish overpopulation" (Johnston 1983, 33).

human costs. Through the reconstructed five-acre walled garden, the sweeping grounds, imposing façade, and grand estate entrance, as well as through the careful preservation of the interior of the mansion, Strokestown Park House memorializes the imposition of an imperial domestic aesthetic on rural Roscommon.

Strokestown conveys the complex and often dark history of the Big House that most Irish country house museums ignore in their presentations of its art and architecture. Visiting there for the first time helped me sort out the ambivalences I felt as I considered ascendancy fiction: my discomfort with narrative assumptions about the superiority of the imperial culture and "race"; my fascination with the novels' persistent, often self-lacerating circling around the sources of Anglo-Ireland's failures. Ambivalence was also central to the work of Strokestown's curator, who carefully preserved and restored the opulent setting of an imperial estate and simultaneously exposed its brutal exploitation of the countryside. Strokestown has it both ways: instead of offering one totalizing narrative it forces the viewer to experience two versions of history. Through its juxtapositions of imagery and text—the actual Big House revealing the landlord's lifestyle and the Famine Museum describing the tenants' deaths—it presents the dissonances of Irish history that have created a social landscape with constantly shifting meanings. Prominent in this landscape is the splendid architecture of the eighteenth-century official government edifices of Dublin and the hundreds of gentry homes in the Irish countryside. Such buildings can be viewed as the useless relics of a dead society, the irrelevant residue of an oppressive colonial state. Alternately, they are the great achievement of an impoverished country, reminders of a period in Irish history when the Protestant nation created an aristocratic culture. This second reading of the architectural landscape of Anglo-Ireland, of Lissadell and Coole Park, for example, has created a Yeatsian vision—virtually a history of Anglo-Ireland—that is not in fact the reading the Big House novelists give to their society.

What do they offer instead?

As the preceding chapters indicate, novelists from within the Big House writing after Maria Edgeworth's creation of Thady Quirk failed to evoke the experience of the other Ireland: the Catholic tenants whose labor supported the country estates. Although Big House novels invariably include tenants and servant characters, such portrayals usually reveal the fear or condescension of a beleaguered colonial class facing a people it cannot envision as fully human. Even the most successful novels do not offer the double narrative that is attempted at Strokestown: the Big House and the cabin, Protestants and Catholics, ascendancy and peasant culture, the conquerors and the dispossessed. In the face of O'Connell's campaign for Catholic emancipation, Maria Edgeworth wrote in 1832 that reality in Ireland was too threatening for her to encompass in fiction; subsequent novelists also struggled to come to terms with an increasingly recalcitrant Irish reality.

If we are to compare Big House fiction with the wide-ranging and more inclusive masterworks of nineteenth-century realism by Balzac or George Eliot, for example, the efforts of the Anglo-Irish novelists must be judged deficient. In Ireland, only a postmodern mode of abrupt juxtapositions of very different "realities"—a form we see in Strokestown's double vision—could encompass the often brutal discordances of a colonial culture. Arguing that "Ireland is a remarkably difficult society to totalize in fiction," Eagleton suggests that "if there is a novel of the gentry and the Big House, there is also one of the cabin, small farmer and gombeen; but the two rarely interact in some synoptic viewpoint" (1995, 151). Although Eagleton over-dichotomizes Irish fiction (Carleton's Big House novel *The Squanders of Castle Squander* shares many of the conventions of those written by ascendancy novelists), he identifies key sources for the breakdown of classical representational realism in Anglo-Irish fiction. If a politically turbulent and insecure society cannot be represented through the forms of the realistic novel, another mode of fiction will emerge.

Big House fiction in Ireland reflects cultural ambivalence and self-irony; it defines the Anglo-Irish experience as doomed from the start. As this study has indicated, the novels fail to evoke any certainty of a stable and continuous culture, of belonging to a social narrative that, like Jane Austen's or George Eliot's, is assumed to be permanent. Virtually all the fiction I have discussed exists in an increasingly uneasy and insecure relationship to those cultural values of English Protestant colonialism that the Anglo-Irish landed gentry class unsuccessfully struggled to represent and sustain throughout the nineteenth and early twentieth centuries. Edgeworth, Lever, and Somerville, although occasionally invoking the nostalgic ideal of a semifeudal relationship between tenant and landlord, created their most powerful fiction when they turned, on occasion with savage irony, to the inevitable decline of the Big House and to the instability of their own society. Through their depictions of corrupt gentry proprietors, the gothic writers Maturin and Le Fanu expressed the guilt-ridden Protestant unconscious of their culture. The persistence of the motif in contemporary fiction indicates the enduring attraction of this tradition for Irish novelists as different as Molly Keane, Jennifer Johnston, William Trevor, Aidan Higgins, and John Banville. Revising, reclaiming, reinventing, internationalizing, or subverting the form, they return to the same decaying house and declining culture that Maria Edgeworth evoked in *Castle Rackrent*.

Although nineteenth- and early twentieth-century novelists undoubtedly wrote with a sense of alienation from and superiority to the world of Catholic Ireland, their fiction acknowledges that the collapse of their own culture is closely involved with its failure to overcome its isolation from the larger Irish community. In *Castle Rackrent*, in which Thady Quirk is presented as the quintessential "house nigger," Edgeworth suggested how the retainer's loyalty to the Rackrent family undermines his ties to his own family and class. By showing that Thady is doomed, whether he allies himself with the improvident Rackrents or with his conniving son Jason, Edgeworth demonstrated the intolerable choices posed by a colonial system that pits one set of loyalties against another. Through the figures of Shibby Pindy in *The Big House of Inver* and Nan O'Neill in *Two Days in Aragon*, women who devote their lives to a patrimony that victimizes them, Edith Somerville and Molly Keane also explored the false consciousness that is an enduring colonial legacy. In Elizabeth Bowen's *The Last September* and in the novels by Jennifer Johnston and Aidan Higgins, the snobbery of the dying Big House reveals larger issues of individual isolation or social malaise. Communication between those inside the Big House and the Catholic outsider fails, aborted by social pressures in Johnston's novels or by the psychological dysfunction of three entombed sisters in Higgins's *Langrishe, Go Down*.

Surprisingly, few of the novelists succumb to the power of Yeats's vision of the Protestant nation as the spiritual inheritor of an ancient aristocratic society threatened by a crass Catholic philistinism. Jennifer Johnston occasionally flirts with such a version of cultural history, and, in the chaos of London during the Nazi offensive, Elizabeth Bowen turned to her ancestral home as an image of stability and permanence. But most Big House novels relentlessly undermine Yeats's deification of the Anglo-Irish tradition. Molly Keane's savage exposure of her society in *Good Behaviour* is far closer in spirit to the subversive gaze on the gentry estate of *Castle Rackrent* or the modernist parody of fictional conventions in Banville's *Birchwood,* for example, than to Bowen's vision of her ancestral property as a stay against disorder. And when Johnston and Trevor revise an older nationalist narrative and envision Anglo-Irish landlords with Republican sympathies, they abruptly break with the conventions of both earlier and contemporary novels that depict the landlord as improvident and irresponsible rather than heroic.

The economic and social constraints that discourage literary production by Irish women need to be weighed against the enabling power of class and wealth as we consider the number of women who wrote novels from within the gentry house. In establishing the outline of a plausible Big House tradition, I have considered the widest possible contexts of class, politics, and gender. But the special attraction of a domestic setting for women novelists is evident as early as 1800, when Maria Edgeworth focused on the poor housekeeping of the Rackrents as evidence of their decline. The preceding chapters on individual women novelists explore recurring perceptions about gender roles in the Big House by Bowen, Somerville, Keane, and Johnston. Somerville and Keane each structure a novel around the sexual victimization of Irish Catholic women by Big House landlords; with the eugenic preoccupations of an insecure "aristocracy," they trace the lasting costs of this ascendancy version of miscegenation. In contrast to the feudal image of the bountiful lady of the manor—an image abandoned or reduced to a few references to self-sacrifice by Big House mistresses in their Famine soup kitchens (see footnote 5)—all four of the women novelists offer new and disturbing images of gender roles in Anglo-Ireland. They create chatelaines who respond to social decline by moving into the positions of dominance abandoned by their emasculated husbands. These women turn their frustrated energy and rage at their husbands' losses on the children of the household. In many novels, lonely, terrorized, or guilt-ridden children of the Big House are the powerless victims of postcolonial society.

Irish novelists employ the circumstantial realism that since the eighteenth century has been the great innovative contribution of the genre, but with an increasingly symbolic, rather than naturalistic, emphasis. Aidan Higgins's *Langrishe, Go Down,* merging naturalism and symbolism, is thus indebted to a whole tradition of Big House fiction rather than simply to the influence of Joyce. The Big House as presented by Edgeworth, Lever, Somerville, and Keane, for example, is grounded in the minutiae of daily life; decay or decline is inherent in the small cracks of the plaster, the leaking roof, and the endless stratagems by which a society wards off unpleasant truths. The hypocrisy, self-delusion, or drunken improvidence of Edgeworth's Rackrents, Lever's Martins, Somerville's Prendevilles, and Keane's Swifts are presented to the reader in detailed account books, as it were, of physical decay and social irresponsibility. The novelists accumulate evidence against their own culture. By examining the discrepancy between the ideals of a society and the shabby realities of actual Big House life, they create those images of self-delusion that are the sources of much great irony. Collectively, the novels are complex structures of ironic plotting and characterization. Thady Quirk praises his drunken sot of a master whose death will strip him of his very identity; Shibby Pindy is enthralled to the family that denies her legitimacy; Aroon St. Charles deludes herself about a girlhood of physical and emotional hunger.

Out of such irony emerges the doubleness that is so characteristic of the novelists in this tradition. Seeing Anglo-Ireland's failures with a lacerating clarity, they invoke a vision of a lost ideal and a failed cultural purpose—of social responsibility, enlightened landlordism, or personal dignity—that their historical role as conquerors and exploiters of a native population has denied them. The potential tragedy of Anglo-Ireland thus shifts easily to bitter comedy: the contrast between personal illusion and historical circumstances is the lasting impression of this fiction.

Works Cited

Index

Works Cited

Altieri, Joanne. 1987. "Transparent Thady Quirk." In *Family Chronicles: Maria Edgeworth's Castle Rackrent,* edited by Cóilín Owens, 97–102. Dublin: Wolfhound.

Arnold, Matthew. 1976. *On the Study of Celtic Literature and Other Essays.* 1867. Reprint. London: Dent.

Austen, Jane. 1952. *Jane Austen's Letters to her Sister Cassandra and Others,* edited by R. W. Chapman. 2nd ed. London: Oxford Univ. Press.

Austin, Allan. 1989. *Elizabeth Bowen.* Rev. ed. Boston: Twayne.

Axton, William. 1961. Introduction to *Melmoth the Wanderer,* by Charles Maturin. Lincoln, Neb.: Univ. of Nebraska Press.

Bachelard, Gaston. 1969. *The Poetics of Space.* Translated by Maria Jolas. Boston: Beacon.

Baneham, Sam. 1983. "Aidan Higgins: A Political Dimension." *Review of Contemporary Fiction* 3, no.1: 168–74.

Banville, John. 1981a. " 'My Readers, that Small Band, Deserve a Rest.' An Interview with John Banville," by Rudiger Imhof. *Irish University Review* 11, no.1: 5–12.

———. 1981b. "A Talk." *Irish University Review* 11, no.1: 13–17.

———. 1982. "Novelists on the Novel. Ronan Sheehan Talks to John Banville and Francis Stuart." In *The Crane Bag Book of Irish Studies: 1977–82,* edited by Mark Patrick Hederman and Richard Kearney, 408–16. Dublin: Blackwater.

———. 1984a. *Birchwood.* 1973. Reprint. London: Granada.

———. 1984b. *The Newton Letter.* 1982. London: Granada.

Barrington, Sir Jonah. 1967. *The Ireland of Sir Jonah Barrington: Selections from His Personal Sketches.* Edited by Hugh B. Staples. Seattle: Univ. of Washington Press.

Beja, Morris. 1973. "Felons of Ourselves: The Fiction of Aidan Higgins." *Irish University Review* 3, no. 2: 163–78.

Bell, J. Bowyer. 1971. *The Secret Army: A History of the IRA, 1916–1970.* New York: John Day.

Bell, Mrs. Martin [Mary Letitia Martin]. 1850. *Julia Howard: A Romance.* New York: Harper and Brothers.

Bence-Jones, Mark. 1978. *Burke's Guide to Country Houses: Volume 1—Ireland.* London: Burke's Peerage.

Benstock, Shari. 1982. "The Masculine World of Jennifer Johnston." In *Twentieth-Century Women Novelists,* edited by Thomas F. Staley, 191–217. Totowa, N.J.: Barnes and Noble.

Billington, Rachel. 1981. "Fictions of Class." Review of *Good Behavior* by Molly Keane. *New York Times Book Review,* 9 Aug., 13.

Blodgett, Harriet. 1975. *Patterns of Reality: Elizabeth Bowen's Novels.* The Hague: Mouton.

Bloom, Harold, ed. 1987. *Elizabeth Bowen.* New York: Chelsea House.

Boland, Eavan. 1989. *A Kind of Scar: The Woman Poet in a National Tradition.* Dublin: Attic.

Bowen, Elizabeth. 1942a. *The Last September.* 1929. Reprint. New York: Penguin.

———. 1942b. *Seven Winters.* Dublin: Cuala.

———. 1951a. "The Cult of Nostalgia." *Listener* 45 (Aug.): 225.

———. 1951b. *The Shelbourne Hotel.* London: Knopf.

———. 1962. *The Heat of the Day.* 1949. Reprint. New York: Penguin.

———. 1975. *Pictures and Conversations.* New York: Knopf.

———. 1979. *Bowen's Court.* 1942. Reprint. New York: Ecco.

———. 1983. *A World of Love.* 1955. Reprint. New York: Penguin.

———. 1986. *The Mulberry Tree: Writings of Elizabeth Bowen.* Edited by Hermione Lee. New York: Harcourt Brace Jovanovich.

Boyd, E. A. 1922. *Ireland's Literary Renaissance.* New York: Knopf.

Brown, Terence. 1981. *Ireland: A Social and Cultural History, 1922–79.* Glasgow: Fontana.

Browne, Nelson. 1951. *Sheridan Le Fanu.* London: Barker.

Buckland, Patrick. 1972. *The Anglo-Irish and the New Ireland: 1885–1922.* Dublin: Gill and Macmillan.

Burke, Edmund. 1968. *Reflections on the Revolution in France.* New York: Penguin.

Butler, Ewan. 1971. *Barry's Flying Column.* London: Leo Cooper.

Butler, Hubert. 1990. *The Sub-Prefect Should Have Held His Tongue.* London: Penguin.

Butler, Marilyn. 1972. *Maria Edgeworth: A Literary Biography.* Oxford: Oxford Univ. Press.

Cairns, David and Shaun Richards. 1988. *Writing Ireland: Colonialism, Nationalism, and Culture.* Manchester: Manchester Univ. Press.

Cahalan, James M. 1983. *Great Hatred, Little Room: The Irish Historical Novel.* Syracuse: Syracuse Univ. Press.

Campbell, Stephen. 1994. *The Great Irish Famine: Words and Images From the*

Famine Museum, Strokestown Park, County Roscommon. Strokestown, Ireland: The Famine Museum.

Cannadine, David. 1985. "Brideshead Revisited." *The New York Review of Books,* 19 Dec., 17–23.

[Carleton, William.] 1843. "National Literature, 'The Dublin University Magazine' and Mr. Lever." *The Nation,* 7 Oct., 826–27.

————. 1852. *The Squanders of Castle Squander.* 2 vols. London: Illustrated London Library.

————. 1970. *Valentine M'Clutchy: The Irish Agent.* 1845. Reprint. New York: Garland.

Chekhov, Anton. 1956. *Best Plays by Chekhov.* New York: Random House.

Chessman, Harriet. 1987. "Women and Language in the Fiction of Elizabeth Bowen." *Twentieth-Century Literature* 29, no. 1: 69–85. Reprinted in *Elizabeth Bowen,* edited by Harold Bloom, 123–38. New York: Chelsea House.

Colgan, Maurice. 1982. "After Rackrent: Ascendancy Nationalism in Maria Edgeworth's Later Irish Novels." In *Studies in Anglo-Irish Literature,* edited by Heinz Kosok, 37–42. Bonn: Verlag Herbert Grundmann.

————. 1979. "The Significant Silences of Thady Quirk." In *Social Roles For The Artist,* edited by Ann Thompson and Anthony Beck, 41–45. Liverpool: Univ. of Liverpool Press. Reprinted in *Family Chronicles: Maria Edgeworth's Castle Rackrent,* edited by Cóilín Owens, 57–62. Dublin: Wolfhound.

Colum, Padraic. 1923. *Castle Conquer.* New York: Macmillan.

Corkery, Daniel. 1966. *Synge and Anglo-Irish Literature.* 1931. Reprint. Cork: Mercier.

Craig, Maurice. 1976. *Classic Irish Houses of the Middle Size.* London: Architectural Press.

Craig, Maurice and the Knight of Glin. 1970. *Ireland Observed: A Guide to the Buildings and Antiquities.* Cork: Mercier.

Cronin, John. 1972. *Somerville and Ross.* Lewisburg, Penn.: Bucknell Univ. Press.

————. 1980. The Anglo-Irish Novel: *The Nineteenth Century.* Vol. 1. Totowa, N.J.: Barnes and Noble.

————. 1985. " 'An Ideal of Art': The Assertion of Realities in the Fiction of Somerville and Ross." *The Canadian Journal of Irish Studies* 11, no.1: 54–78.

Cullen, L. M. 1987. *An Economic History of Ireland Since 1660.* 2nd ed. London: Batsford.

Daly, Mary. 1981. *Social and Economic History of Ireland Since 1800.* Dublin: Educational Co.

Deane, Seamus. 1975–76. " 'Be Assured I Am Inventing': The Fiction of John Banville." In *The Irish Novel In Our Time,* edited by Patrick Rafroidi and Maurice Harmon, 329–38. Villeneuve-d'Ascq: Publications De L'Universite De Lille III.

————. 1985. *Celtic Revivals.* Boston: Farber and Farber.

————, ed. 1991. *Field Day Anthology of Irish Writing.* 3 vols. Derry: Field Day.

de Breffny, Brian and Rosemary Ffolliott. 1984. *The Houses of Ireland.* London: Thames and Hudson.

Dictionary of National Biography. 1967–68. S.V. Martin, Richard. London: Oxford Univ. Press.

Donnelly, Brian. 1975. "The Big House in the Recent Novel." *Studies* 64: 133–42.

Donnelly, James S. Jr. 1995. "Mass Eviction and the Great Famine: The Clearances Revisited." In *The Great Irish Famine,* edited by Cathal Póirtéir, 155–73. Dublin: Mercier.

Duffy, Charles Gavan. 1843. "Mr. Lever's 'Irish' Novels." *The Nation,* 10 June, 554.

Dunne, Tom. 1987. "A Polemical Introduction: Literature, Literary Theory and the Historian." In *The Writer as Witness: Literature as Historical Evidence,* edited by Tom Dunne, 1–9. Historical studies series, no. 16. Cork: Cork Univ. Press.

Dunton, John. 1939. "John Dunton's Letters." Appendix B of *Irish Life in the Seventeenth Century,* by Edward MacLysaght. London: Longmans, Green.

Eagleton, Terry. 1976. *Marxism and Literary Criticism.* Berkeley and Los Angeles: Univ. of California Press.

————. 1978. *Criticism and Ideology.* London: Verso.

————. 1995. *Heathcliff and the Great Hunger.* New York: Verso.

Edgeworth, Maria. 1821. *Memoirs of Richard Lovell Edgeworth Esq. Begun by Himself and Concluded by His Daughter, Maria Edgeworth.* 2 vols. Boston: Wells and Lilly.

————. 1895. *Life and Letters.* Edited by Augustus J. C. Hare. Boston: Houghton Mifflin.

————. 1950. *Tour in Connemara and The Martins of Ballinahinch.* Edited by Harold Edgeworth Butler. 1867. London: Constable.

————. 1972. *Ormond.* 1817. Reprint. Shannon: Irish Univ. Press.

————. 1980. *Castle Rackrent.* 1800. Reprint. New York: Oxford Univ. Press.

————. 1988. *The Absentee.* 1812. Reprint. New York: Oxford Univ. Press.

————. 1992. *Castle Rackrent and Ennui.* 1800 and 1809. Reprint. Harmondsworth, England: Penguin.

Fabricant, Carole. 1982. *Swift's Landscape.* Baltimore: Johns Hopkins Univ. Press.

Farrell, M. J. [Molly Keane]. 1984. *The Rising Tide.* 1937. Reprint. London: Virago.

————. 1985a *Mad Puppetstown.* 1931. Reprint. London: Virago.

————. 1985b. *Two Days in Aragon.* 1941. Reprint. London: Virago.

————. 1986. *Full House.* 1935. Reprint. London: Virago.

————. 1991. *Conversation Pieces.* 1932. Reprint. London: Collins.

Fehlmann, Guy. 1991. "An Historical Survey." In *The Big House in Ireland: Re-*

ality and Representation, edited by Jacqueline Genet, 15–18. Dingle, Ireland: Brandon Book Publ.

Fitzgerald, Barbara. 1946. *We Are Besieged.* London: Peter Davies.

———. 1983. *Footprints on Water.* Galway, Ireland: Blackstaff.

Fitzgerald, Frances. 1979. "The Anglo-Irish Gentry: Guardians of a Vanished Empire." *GEO* 1, no. 1: 138–56.

Flanagan, Thomas. 1959. *The Irish Novelists, 1800–1850.* New York: Columbia Univ. Press.

———. 1966. "The Big House of Ross-Drishane." *The Kenyon Review* 28, no.1: 54–78.

———. 1989. "Literature in English, 1901–91." In *Ireland Under the Union,* edited by W. E. Vaughn, 482–522. Vol. 5 of *A New History of Ireland.* Oxford: Clarendon.

Fleishman, Avrom. 1971. *The English Historical Novel: Walter Scott to Virginia Woolf.* Baltimore: Johns Hopkins Univ. Press.

Foster, R. F. 1989. *Modern Ireland: 1600–1972.* New York: Penguin.

———. 1991. "We Are All Revisionists Now." In *The Field Day Anthology of Irish Writing,* edited by Seamus Deane, 3: 583–86. Reprinted from *The Irish Review* 1, no.1:1–5.

———. "Nations, Yet Again." 1992. Review of *The Field Day Anthology of Irish Writing,* edited by Seamus Deane. *Times Literary Supplement,* 27 Mar., 5–7.

———. 1993. *Paddy and Mr. Punch.* London: Penguin.

Gay, Peter. 1970. *Weimar Culture: The Outsider as Insider.* New York: Harper and Row.

Genet, Jacqueline, ed. 1991. *The Big House in Ireland: Reality and Representation.* Dingle, Ireland: Brandon Book Publ.

Gibbons, Luke. 1991. "Challenging the Canon: Revisionism and Cultural Criticism." In *The Field Day Antholology of Irish Writing,* edited by Seamus Deane, 3:561–68. 3 vol. Derry: Field Day.

Gill, Richard. 1972. *Happy Rural Seat: The English Country House and the Literary Imagination.* New Haven, Conn.: Yale Univ. Press.

Glendinning, Victoria. 1993. *Elizabeth Bowen: Portrait of a Writer.* London: Phoenix.

Goethe, Johann Wolfgang. 1971. *Elective Affinities.* 1809. Reprint. Harmondsmith, England: Penguin.

Goldberger, Paul. 1992. "The Art of Artifice: Ralph Lauren, Etc." *The New York Times,* 2 Feb., sec. 2: 1f.

Grene, Marjorie. 1967. "Martin Heidegger." In *The Encylopedia of Philosophy,* edited by Paul Edwards, 3:459–65. 8 vol. New York: Macmillan.

Gwynn, Stephen. 1936. *Irish Literature and Drama in the English Language: A Short History.* London: Nelson.

Harden, O. Elizabeth McWhorter. 1971. *Maria Edgeworth's Art of Prose Fiction.* The Hague: Mouton.

Hardwick, Elizabeth. 1949. "Elizabeth Bowen's Fiction." *Partisan Review* 16: 1114–21.

Harmon, Maurice. 1973. "By Memory Inspired: Themes and Forces in Recent Irish Writing." *Eire-Ireland* 8, no. 2: 3–19.

Heaney, Seamus. 1989. *The Place of Writing*. Atlanta: Scholars.

Heath, William. 1961. *Elizabeth Bowen: An Introduction to Her Novels*. Madison, Wisc.: Univ. of Wisconsin Press.

Hellman, Lillian. 1942. *Four Plays by Lillian Hellman*. New York: Random House.

Henderson, Peter Mills. 1980. *A Nut Between Two Blades: The Novels of Charles Robert Maturin*. New York: Arno.

Henn, Thomas. 1976. "The Big House." In *Last Essays: Mainly on Anglo-Irish Literature*, 207–220. New York: Harper and Row.

Hibbard, G. R. 1956. "The Country House Poem of the Seventeenth Century." *Journal of the Warburg and Courtauld Institutes* 19, no. 1–2: 159–74.

Higgins, Aidan. 1966. *Langrishe, Go Down*. London: Calder and Boyars.

———. 1978. "Killachter Meadow." In *Asylum and Other Stories*, 9–32. London: J. Calder.

———. 1983. "Imaginary Meadows." *Review of Contemporary Fiction* 3, no.1: 114–23.

Higgins, Aidan. 1989. Interview by Ursula Mayrhuber. In "Aidan Higgins: An Analysis of His Work." Ph.D. diss., Univ. of Vienna, 1990. 303–15.

Howe, Irving. 1957. *Politics and the Novel*. Cleveland, Ohio: World.

Imhof, Rüdiger. 1985. " 'A Little Bit of Ivory, Two Inches Wide': The Small World of Jennifer Johnston's Fiction." *Etudes Irlandaises* 10 (Dec.): 129–44.

———. 1989. *John Banville: A Critical Introduction*. Dublin: Wolfhound.

———. 1992. "Molly Keane, *Good Behaviour, Time After Time*, and *Loving and Giving*." In *Ancestral Voices: The Big House in Anglo-Irish Fiction*, edited by Otto Rauchbauer, 195–202. Dublin: Lilliput.

Imhof, Rüdiger and Jürgen Kamm. 1984. "Coming to Grips with Aidan Higgins. 'Killachter Meadow': An Analysis." *Etudes Irlandaises* 9: 145–60.

Jameson, Fredric. 1981. *The Political Unconscious*. Ithaca, N.Y.: Cornell Univ. Press.

———. 1988. *Nationalism, Colonialism and Literature: Modernism and Imperialism*. No. 14. Derry: Field Day.

Jeffares, A. Norman. 1975a. "Lever's 'Lord Kilgobbin.' " In *Essays and Studies*, edited by Robert Ellrodt, 47–57. London: Cox and Wyman.

———. 1975b. "Place, Space, Personality, and the Irish Writer." In *Place, Personality and the Irish Writer*, edited by Andrew Carpenter, 11–40. New York: Barnes and Noble.

Johnston, Jennifer. 1972. *The Captains and the Kings*. London: Hamish Hamilton.

————. 1982. *The Christmas Tree.* 1981. Reprint. Glasgow: Fontana.

————. 1983. *The Gates.* 1973. Reprint. Glasgow: Fontana.

————. 1984a. "Q and A with Jennifer Johnston." Interview by Michael Kenneally. *The Irish Literary Supplement* 3:25–27.

————. 1984b. *The Railroad Station Man.* 1974. Reprint. London: Fontana.

————. 1988a. *Fool's Sanctuary.* 1987. Reprint. London: Penguin.

————. 1988b. *How Many Miles to Babylon.* 1974. Reprint. London: Penguin.

————. 1988c. *The Old Jest.* 1979. Reprint. London: Penguin.

————. 1991a. *The Invisible Worm.* London: Sinclair-Stevenson.

————. 1991b. *Shadows on our Skin.* 1977. Reprint. London: Penguin.

Jordan, Heather Bryant. 1992. *How Will the Heart Endure: Elizabeth Bowen and the Landscape of War.* Ann Arbor, Mich.: Univ. of Michigan Press.

Keane, Molly. 1982. *Good Behaviour.* London: Abacus.

————. 1985. *Time After Time.* New York: Dutton.

————. 1986. "Molly Keane's Irish Cottage." *Architectural Digest,* Jan., 136f.

————. 1988. *Loving and Giving.* London: Deutsch.

Kelly, Patricia. 1987. "The Big House in Contemporary Anglo-Irish Literature." *Literary Interrelations: Ireland, England and the World,* edited by Wolfgang Zach and Heinz Kosok, 3:229–34. Tubingen, Germany: Gunter Narr Verlag.

Kennedy, Dorothy. 1989. "The Big House in Irish Literature." *Bulletin of the Irish Georgian Society* 32: 6–30.

Kenney, Edwin, Jr. 1975. *Elizabeth Bowen.* Lewisburg, Penn.: Bucknell Univ. Press.

Kenny, Virginia C. 1984. *The Country House Ethos in English Literature, 1688–1750: Themes of Personal Retreat and National Expansion.* New York: St. Martin's.

Kiberd, Declan. 1982. "The Perils of Nostalgia: A Critique of the Revival." In *Literature and the Changing Ireland,* edited by Peter Connolly, 1–24. Totowa, N.J.: Barnes and Noble.

————. 1988. "The War Against the Past." In *The Uses of the Past: Essays on Irish Culture,* edited by Audrey S. Eyler and Robert Garrnatt, 24–53. Newark, N.J.: Univ. of Delaware.

————. 1996. *Inventing Ireland.* Cambridge, Mass.: Harvard Univ. Press.

Kickham, Charles. 1988. *Knocknagow, or The Homes of Tipperary.* 1870. Reprint. Dublin: Anna Livia.

Kiernan, V. G. 1969. *The Lords of Human Kind: Black Man, Yellow Man, and White Man in an Age of Empire.* Boston: Little, Brown.

Kipling, Rudyard. 1987. *Kim.* 1901. Reprint. New York: Oxford Univ. Press.

Knight of Glin, David J. Griffin, and Nicholas K. Robinson, eds. 1989. *Vanishing Country Houses of Ireland.* [Leixlip, Ireland]: Irish Architectural Archive and The Georgian Society.

Kosok, Heinz. 1986. "The Novels of Jennifer Johnston." In *Studien Zur En-*

glischen und Amerikanischen Prosa Nach Dem Ersten Weltkrieg, edited by Maria Diedrich and Christoph Schoneich, 98–111. Darmstadt, Germany: Wissenschaftliche Buchgellschaft.

Kowaleski-Wallace, Beth. 1991. *Their Fathers' Daughters.* Oxford: Oxford Univ. Press.

Lally, Des. N. d. "History of Ballynahinch Castle." N. p.

Lanters, Jose. 1989. "Jennifer Johnston's Divided Ireland." In *The Clash of Ireland: Literary Contrasts and Connections,* edited by C. C. Barfoot and Theo D'haen, 209–22. Amsterdam: Rodopi.

Lassner, Phyllis. 1990. *Elizabeth Bowen.* Savage, Md.: Barnes and Noble.

Leavis, F. R. 1964. *The Great Tradition.* New York: New York Univ. Press.

Lecky, W. E. H. 1896. *A History of Ireland in the Eighteenth Century.* 5 vols. London: Longmans, Green.

Lee, Hermione. 1981. *Elizabeth Bowen: An Estimation.* Totowa, N.J.: Barnes and Noble.

———, ed. 1986. *The Mulberry Tree: Writings of Elizabeth Bowen.* New York: Harcourt Brace Jovanovich.

Le Fanu, Sheridan. 1979. "Passage in the Secret History of an Irish Countess." In *The Purcell Papers,* 1–102. 1880. Reprint. New York: Garland.

———. 1981. *Uncle Silas.* 1864. Reprint. New York: Oxford Univ. Press.

Leray, Josette. 1991. "Elizabeth Bowen's *A World of Love.*" In *The Big House in Ireland: Reality and Representation,* edited by Jacqueline Genet, 163–77. Dingle, Ireland: Brandon Book Publ.

Lever, Charles. 1839. *The Confessions of Harry Lorrequer.* Dublin: W. Curry.

———. 1841. *Charles O'Malley, The Irish Dragoon.* Dublin: W. Curry.

———. 1943. *Jack Hinton, the Guardsman.* Philadelphia: Carey and Hart.

———. 1895. *The Martins of Cro' Martin.* 1854. Reprint. 2 Vols. Boston: Little, Brown.

———. 1897. *The O'Donoghue.* 1845. Reprint. London: Downey.

———. 1899. *Lord Kilgobbin.* 1872. Reprint. Boston: Little Brown.

Lewis, Gifford. 1985. *Somerville and Ross: The World of the Irish R. M.* New York: Viking.

Lloyd, David. 1993. *Anomalous States.* Durham, N.C.: Duke Univ. Press.

Longley, Edna. 1990. *From Cathleen to Anorexia: The Breakdown of Irelands.* Dublin: Attic.

Lougy, Robert E. 1975. *Charles Robert Maturin.* Lewisburg, Penn.: Bucknell Univ. Press.

Lukacs, Georg. 1963. *The Historical Novel.* Translated by Hannah Michell and Stanley Michell. Boston: Beacon.

Lyons, F. S. L. 1973. *Ireland Since the Famine.* Rev. ed. Bungay, England: Fontana.

MacDonagh, Oliver. 1970. *The Nineteenth Century Novel and Irish Social History: Some Aspects.* O'Donnell lecture series no. 14. Cork: Univ. College.

Madden-Simpson, Janet. 1987. "Haunted Houses: The Image of the Anglo-Irish in Anglo-Irish Literature." In *Literary Interrelationships: Studies in Irish and Comparative Literature,* edited by Wolfgang Zach and Heinz Kosok, 3:41–46. Tubingen: Gunter Narr Verlag.

Mark, Gordon St. George. 1976. "Tyrone House, Co. Galway." *Quarterly Bulletin of the Irish Georgian Society* 19, nos.3–4: 22–69.

Martin, David. 1982. "The 'Castle Rackrent' of Somerville and Ross: A Tragic 'Colonial Tale?' " *Etudes Irlandaises* 7: 43–53.

Marx, Karl. 1904. Preface to *A Contribution to the Critique of Political Economy,* translated by N. I. Stone, 9–15. Chicago: Charles H. Kerr.

Maturin, Charles. 1977. *Melmoth The Wanderer.* 1820. Reprint. Harmondsworth, England: Penguin.

McCormack, W. J. 1980. *Sheridan Le Fanu and Victorian Ireland.* Oxford: Clarendon.

———. 1981. Introduction to *Uncle Silas,* by Sheridan Le Fanu, vii–xxii. New York: Oxford Univ. Press.

——— 1985. *Ascendancy and Tradition in Anglo-Irish Literary History from 1789 to 1939.* Oxford: Clarendon.

———. 1988. Introduction to *The Absentee,* by Maria Edgeworth, ix–xliv. New York: Oxford Univ. Press.

———. 1991. "Irish Gothic and After." In *The Field Day Antholgy of Irish Writing,* edited by Seamus Deane, 2:832–54. Derry: Field Day.

———. 1992. "Setting and Ideology: With Reference to the Fiction of Maria Edgeworth." In *Ancestral Voices: The Big House in Anglo-Irish Literature,* edited by Otto Rauchbaurer, 33–60. Dublin: Lilliput.

———. 1993. *Dissolute Characters.* Manchester: Manchester Univ. Press.

McDowell. "The Big House: A Genealogist's Perspective and a Personal Point of View." *Ancestral Voices: The Big House in Anglo-Irish Literature,* edited by Otto Rauchbauer, 279–93. Dublin: Lilliput.

McGahern, John. 1985. *High Ground.* London: Faber and Faber.

Meaney, Gerardine. 1991. *Sex and Nation: Women in Irish Culture and Politics.* Dublin: Attic.

Meenan, James Francis. 1980. *George O' Brien: A Biographical Memoir.* Dublin: Gill and Macmillan.

Mercier, Vivian. 1969. *The Irish Comic Tradition.* New York: Oxford Univ. Press.

Meredith, Robert. 1977. "Lever's *St. Patrick's Eve* in Proper Perspective." *Eire* 19, no. 1: 74–80.

Mitchell, Hilary. 1968. "Somerville and Ross: Amateur to Professional." In *Somerville and Ross: A Symposium,* 20–37. Belfast: Queen's Univ.

Molloy, Francis. 1981. "The Search for Truth: The Fiction of John Banville." *Irish University Review* 11, no. 1: 29–51.

Montrose, Louis. 1986. "Renaissance Literary Studies and the Subject of History." *English Literary Renaissance* 16, no. 1: 5–12.

Morash, Christopher. 1992. "Reflecting Absent Interiors: The Big House Novels of Charles Lever." In *Ancestral Voices: The Big House in Anglo-Irish Literature,* edited by Otto Rauchbauer, 61–74. Dublin: Lilliput.

Morgan, Lady [Sydney Owenson]. 1986. *The Wild Irish Girl.* 1806. Reprint. London: Pandora.

Morrison, Kristin. 1993. *William Trevor.* New York: Twayne.

Mortimer, Mark. 1991. "Jennifer Johnston and the Big House." In *The Big House in Ireland: Reality and Representation,* edited by Jacqueline Genet, 209–14. Dingle, Ireland: Brandon Book Publ.

Moss, Howard. 1986. *Minor Monuments: Selected Essays.* New York: Ecco.

Moynahan, Julian. 1982. "The Politics of Anglo-Irish Gothic: 'The Return of the Repressed.' " In *Studies in Anglo-Irish Literature,* edited by Heinz Kosok, 43–53. Bonn: Bouvier Verlag Herbert Grundman.

———. 1995. *Anglo-Irish: Literary Imagination in a Hyphenated Culture.* Princeton: Princeton Univ. Press.

Nandy, Ashis. 1983. *The Intimate Enemy: Loss and Recovery of Self Under Colonialism.* Delhi: Oxford.

Newcomer, James. 1967. *Maria Edgeworth the Novelist.* Ft. Worth: Texas Christian Univ. Press.

Ni Dhonnchadha, Mairin and Theo Dorgan, eds. 1991. *Revising the Rising.* Derry: Field Day.

O'Brien, George. 1989. *The Village of Longing and Dancehall Days.* New York: Viking.

O'Faolain, Julia. 1980. *No Country For Young Men.* Harmondsworth, England: Penguin.

O'Faolain, Sean. 1983. "Midsummer Night Madness." 1932. In *Collected Stories,* 1–43. Reprint. Boston: Little, Brown.

O'Flaherty, Liam. 1946. *Land.* New York: Random House.

———. 1984. *Famine.* 1937. Reprint. Dublin: Wolfhound.

O'Grady, Standish. 1886. *Toryism and the Tory Democracy.* London: Chapman and Hall.

O'Keefe, Thomas. 1977. "Maria Edgeworth and Charles Lever: The Big House and the Garrison." *Eire 19,* no. 1: 81–92.

O'Toole, Bridget. 1985. "Three Writers of the Big House." In *Across A Roaring Field: The Protestant Imagination in Modern Ireland,* edited by Gerarld Dawe and Edna Longley. Belfast: Blackstaff.

Owens, Cóilín. 1987a. "Irish Bulls in *Castle Rackrent.*" In *Family Chronicles: Maria Edgeworth's "Castle Rackrent."* edited by Cóilín Owens, 70–78. Dublin: Wolfhound.

———, ed. 1987b. *Family Chronicles: Maria Edgeworth's "Castle Rackrent."* Dublin: Wolfhound.

Partridge, Eric. 1973. *A Dictionary of Slang and Unconventional English*. 8th ed. London: Routledge and Kegan Paul.

Power, Ann. 1964. "The Big House of Somerville and Ross." *The Dubliner* (spring): 43–53.

Rafroidi, Patrick. 1975. "A Question of Inheritance: The Anglo-Irish Tradition." In *The Irish Novel in Our Time,* edited by Patrick Rafroidi and Maurice Harmon, 11–29. Villeneuve-'Ascq: Publications de L'Universite De Lille.

Rauchbauer, Otto, ed. 1992. *Ancestral Voices: The Big House in Anglo-Irish Literature*. Dublin: Lilliput.

Reeves-Smyth, Terence. 1994. *Irish Country Houses*. Belfast: Appletree.

Rix, Walter. 1982. "Charles James Lever: The Irish Dimension of a Cosmopolitan." In *Studies in Anglo-Irish Literature,* edited by Heinz Kosok, 54–64. Bonn: Bouvier Verlag Herbert Grundmann.

Robinson, Hilary. 1980. *Somerville and Ross: A Critical Appreciation*. New York: St Martin's.

Robinson, Mary. 1990. "Address by Mary Robinson on The Occasion of Her Inauguration as President of Ireland." 3 Dec.

Sabin, Marjorie. 1991. "The Suttee Romance." *Raritan* 11, no. 2: 1–24.

Said, Edward. 1979. *Orientalism*. New York: Random House.

———. 1983. *The World, The Text and The Critic*. Cambridge, Mass.: Harvard Univ. Press.

Scanlan, Elizabeth. 1985. "Rumors of War: Elizabeth Bowen's *The Last September* and J. G. Farrell's *Troubles*." *Eire-Ireland* 20, no. 2: 70–89.

Schiff, Stephen. 1992/1993. "The Shadows of William Trevor." *The New Yorker,* 28 Dec./4 Jan., 158–63.

Schirmer, Gregory. 1990. *William Trevor: A Study of His Fiction*. London: Routledge.

Shaw, Bernard. 1931. *Heartbreak House*. London: Constable.

Solow, Barbara Lewis. 1971. *The Land Question and the Irish Economy, 1870–1903*. Cambridge, Mass.: Harvard Univ. Press.

Somerville, E. Œ., and Ross Martin. 1903. *An Irish Cousin*. 1889. Reprint. London: Longmans, Green.

———. 1918. *Irish Memories*. New York: Longmans, Green.

———. 1920. *Mount Music*. 1919. Reprint. New York: Longmans, Green.

———. 1923. *Wheel-Tracks*. New York: Longman, Green.

———. 1944. *Experiences of an Irish R. M.* 1899. Reprint. London: Everyman.

———. 1977. *The Real Charlotte*. 1894. Reprint. London: Quartet.

———. 1978. *The Big House of Inver.* 1925. Reprint. London: Quartet.

Stallybrass, Peter and Allon White. 1986. *The Politics and Poetics of Transgression*. Ithaca, N.Y.: Cornell Univ. Press.

St. Peter, Christine. 1991. "Jennifer Johnston's Irish Troubles: A Materialist-Feminist Reading." In *Gender in Irish Writing,* edited by Toni O'Brien Johnson and David Cairns, 112–27. Buckingham: Milton Keynes.

Swift, Jonathan. 1967. *Poetical Works*. Edited by Herbert Davis. London: Oxford Univ. Press.

Thompson, David. 1976. *Woodbrook*. Harmondsworth, England: Penguin.

Tracy, Robert. 1986. " 'The Burning Roof And Tower': Literary and Sexual Politics in Elizabeth Bowen's *The Last September.*" Paper read at Conference of American Committee of Irish Studies, 10 May, at Boston College.

Trevor, William. 1981. "Saints." *Atlantic Monthly,* Jan., 29–36.

———. 1983. *Stories*. Harmondsworth, England: Penguin.

———. 1984. *Fools of Fortune*. 1983. Harmondsworth, England: Penguin.

———. 1986. *The News from England and Other Stories*. New York: Viking Penguin.

———. 1988. *The Silence in the Garden*. New York: Viking Penguin.

———. 1989. "The Art of Fiction cviii," *Paris Review* 10: 119–51.

Vaughan, W. E. 1984. *Landlords and Tenants in Ireland 1848–1904*. Dublin: Dundalgan.

Vendler, Helen. 1990. "Feminism and Literature." *The New York Review of Books* 37, no. 9: 19–25.

Watson, George. 1980. Introduction to and commentary on *Castle Rackrent*, by Maria Edgeworth. London: Oxford Univ. Press.

Weekes, Anne Owens. 1990. *Irish Women Writers: An Uncharted Tradition*. Lexington, Ky.: Univ. of Kentucky Press.

Whelan, Kevin. 1995. "Pre- and Post-Famine Landscape Change." *The Great Irish Famine,* edited by Cathal Póirtéir, 19–33. Dublin: Mercier.

———. 1996a. "Immoral Economy: Interpreting Erskine Nicol's 'The Tenant.' " In *America's Eye: Irish Painting from the Collection of Brian P. Burns,* edited by Adele Dalsimer and Vera Kreilkamp, 57–67. Boston: Boston College Museum of Art.

———. 1996b."Interpreting the Famine." Manuscript.

White, Hayden. 1978. *Tropics of Discourse: Essays in Cultural Criticism*. Baltimore: Johns Hopkins Univ. Press.

Williams, Raymond. 1973. *The Country and the City*. New York: Oxford Univ. Press.

Woolf, Virginia. 1984. *The Diary of Virginia Woolf,* edited by Anne Oliver Bell, vol. 4. 1982. Reprint. New York: Harcourt Brace Javanovich.

Wurgaft, Lewis D. 1983. *The Imperial Imaginations: Magic and Myth in Kipling's India*. Middletown, Conn.: Wesleyan Univ. Press.

Yeats, William Butler. 1952. *The Collected Plays*. New York: Macmillan.

———. 1956. *The Collected Poems*. New York: Macmillan.

———. 1979. Introduction to *Representative Irish Tales*. 1891. Reprint. Atlantic Highlands, N.J.: Humanities Press.

Young, Arthur. 1892. *Arthur Young's Tour in Ireland (1776–1779)*, edited by Arthur Wollaston Hutton. 2 vol. London: George Bell and Sons.

Index

Act of Union, 4, 26n. 1, 96, 100
Altieri, Joanne, 40
Annesly, Noel Grove, 261n. 1
Arnold, Matthew, 77, 184n. 6
Ascendancy, Protestant, 19
Austen, Jane, 2n. 2, 4–5, 24, 125–26,
  131, 183, 202, 265
Axton, William, 97

Bachelard, Gaston, 215n. 16
Ballinahinch Castle, 7, 79, 80–81n. 5,
  81–82
Balzac, Honoré de, 265
Banville, John: on Catholic Ireland,
  253–54; on cultural mythologies,
  250; decaying house in, 252–53;
  Goethe in, 258–59; Hugo von Hof-
  mannsthal in, 257, 260; and mem-
  ory, 249–52; and modernist and
  postmodernist fiction, 248–49, 259;
  parody in, 248, 267; Wittgenstein
  in, 260; women in, 255. Works:
  Birchwood, 51, 169, 247–56; *Doctor
  Copernicus*, 249; *Kepler*, 249; *Newton
  Letter*, 169, 256–60
Barrington, Jonah, 147
Bell, J. Bowyer, 223n. 20
Bence-Jones, Mark, 7n. 8
Benstock, Sherri, 201n. 8
Big Houses in Ireland: architecture of,
  7–8, 34–35, 38; destruction of, 6,
  21, 65, 140; preservation efforts,

196n. 2, 261–62; as term, 7, 8n. 9;
  tourism of, 261–64
Big House novel: children's roles in,
  23, 141–42, 185, 187, 267; conventions of, 20–25, 264–65, 268; critical attitudes toward, 1–3, 9–12,
  18–19 (*see also* Corkery, Daniel;
  Deane, Seamus; Eagleton, Terry;
  McCormack, W. J.); definition, 6–7;
  domestic disorder in, 35–38,
  118–19, 129; and English domestic
  novel, 4–5, 24, 125–26, 183, 194,
  265; eugenic preoccupations in,
  125, 135, 178–88, 191; family decline in, 22–23; and the Famine, 9,
  10, 222n. 19, 263n. 5; feudal
  mythologies in, 12, 17, 25, 111;
  gothic elements in, 59, 62, 96–98,
  118–20; as historical novel, 15; and
  history, 3–4, 24–25; holocausts in,
  150–52; and ideology, 12–13,
  15–16; landlord in, 23, 184, 197,
  199–200; and Literary Revival, 11;
  marriage plot in, 183; misalliance
  in, 87, 125, 135–37, 180; and modernist fiction, 174, 197, 234–35; as
  moral fable, 230; and neo-feudal
  mythology, 17–19, 25, 89–90, 147
  (*see also* country house poetry); and
  nostalgia, 2, 174–75, 182; and the
  primitive, 157; Protestantism in,
  44, 76, 183, 217; and revisionism,
  10, 195–97; sense of place in, 19;